TR's
Summer White House

Oyster Bay

***

SHERWIN GLUCK

Acknowledgements

Thanks to my brother, Jerritt, for encouraging me to begin,
To my Mom and Dad for encouraging me to continue,
And to my wife, Hanit, for encouraging me to finish.

Thanks also to Dr. John Gable of the Theodore Roosevelt Association for his assistance, guidance, and advice. To Bill Blier of Newsday for his suggestions and guidance. To Amy Verone and Susan Sarna of Sagamore Hill, Wallace Dailey of the Houghton Library at Harvard University, Stuart Chase, formerly of Raynham Hall, and Thomas Kuehhas of the Oyster Bay Historical Society for their assistance in locating many of the photographs used in this book. To Mrs. Dorothy Moore of the Oyster Bay-East Norwich Public Library for her invaluable assistance in locating and obtaining the many rolls of microfilm of the Theodore Roosevelt Papers from Columbia University. To Ms. Dorothy McGee, Town of Oyster Bay Historian for sharing her love of Oyster Bay's rich history with me and to John Hammond for piquing my interest in the history of Moore's Building and Theodore Roosevelt. Thanks also to the reference librarians at the New York Public Library and Columbia University for their kind assistance. Finally, thanks to Joe McNicholl of the Roger Printing Company for his time, advice, and help.

Comment on Source Material

The material used in this book was compiled from articles from various newspapers, predominantly *The New York Times*. Citations from *The New York Times* are noted by the phrase *NY Times*. Other newspaper sources include the *East Norwich Enterprise* and the *Oyster Bay Guardian*. These papers are all readily available on microfilm. Three periods ("...") indicate areas where portions of text were removed from an article.

The copies of internal, executive office letters and documents are from the "Theodore Roosevelt Papers." This collection of 485 reels of microfilm contains images of almost 250,000 items pertaining to Theodore Roosevelt stored in the Library of Congress's Manuscript Division. It is an archive of every document, official and private, sent or received by the President, his staff, or other members of the government as well as documents (newspaper clippings, pictures, etc.) collected and compiled by his staff. The letters and documents used in this book are almost exclusively from Series 1 of this collection. Series 1 is a collection of the documents received by the Executive Office, including inter-office documents sent between members of the Executive Office staff. Although Series 1 includes letters that were addressed to President Roosevelt himself, they were for the most part, not included in this book because they have already been printed in "*The Letters of Theodore Roosevelt*." (Elting E. Morison, Harvard University Press, 1951.) Citations from "Theodore Roosevelt Papers" are noted by the phrase *TR Papers*.

The photographs were provided courtesy of The Houghton Library of Harvard University, Sagamore Hill National Park, The Friends of Raynham Hall, and the Oyster Bay Historical Society, as indicated.

Contents

TR's
Summer White House

Oyster Bay

Foreword

In the first decade of the twentieth century, the eyes of the world looked in the summertime to Oyster Bay, on the North Shore of Long Island, the residence of President Theodore Roosevelt. Theodore Roosevelt (1858-1919) became the twenty-sixth President of the United States on September 14, 1901, after the assassination of President William McKinley. TR was elected to a second term in 1904, and concluded his administration in March of 1909. The President and his family in the years 1902-1908 left the White House in Washington during the summers and took up residence at Sagamore Hill, their home about two miles from the village of Oyster Bay. Oyster Bay was the "summer White House" for seven summers. As Sherwin Gluck shows in this detailed and interesting book, the "summer White House" was an institution larger than the Roosevelt family and Sagamore Hill.

President Roosevelt expanded the White House in Washington by adding the west wing, where the executive offices were located, separated from the formal reception areas and the family living quarters of the White House. Likewise, in Oyster Bay, the Sagamore Hill home could not accommodate all the business functions of the Presidency. Space was rented in the village at the Moore's Building over a grocery store from 1903 on. Here the President's secretary, William Loeb, Jr. and his staff, including assistants and typists, had their offices, with direct communications links to the White House in Washington and Sagamore Hill.

The President of the United States could no longer take a vacation without continuing the functions of government and keeping in touch with the rest of the world. TR's communication hook-up from William Loeb's office over the grocery store in the Moore's Building was global in scope. On July 4, 1903, after completion of the trans-Pacific cable, the first trans-global message was sent and received at the Moore's Building. It took twelve minutes for the message to circle the earth. Papers were brought back and forth from Sagamore Hill, and messages were phoned in to the President at his home, from the offices in the Moore's Building. Although the offices in the village were essential to the functioning of the summer Presidency, the President did not personally use them.

Theodore Roosevelt is often called the first "modern President," and this book documents how the modern Presidency functioned when the President was in summer residence at Oyster Bay. *TR's Summer White House, Oyster Bay* by Sherwin Gluck is an important contribution to the history of Oyster Bay, the record of T.R.'s administration, and the history of the office and institution of the Presidency. Consisting for the most part of passages from *The New York Times* and letters and other materials from the Theodore Roosevelt Papers in the Library of Congress with commentary by Sherwin Gluck, *TR's Summer White House, Oyster Bay* will be of great use to historians and writers as well as anyone seeking to understand what life was like in Oyster Bay during the historic summers at the beginning of the twentieth century.

Oyster Bay, because of Theodore Roosevelt, became one of the most famous small towns in the United States, and people from all over the world still come to Oyster Bay and visit Sagamore Hill and the President's grave in Youngs' Memorial Cemetery. They find the village much like it was in TR's lifetime, and Moore's Building is still here. Daria and David lamb, who opened the Book Mark Café on the first floor of the Moore's Building in 1995, and Sherwin and Jerritt Gluck, are to be commended for their restoration and enhancement of the historic structure on the corner of South Street and East Main Street. The Moore's Building is in the center of the village and contributes to the charming Victorian atmosphere of Oyster Bay.

John Allen Gable
Executive Director,
Theodore Roosevelt Association

Oyster Bay, New York
July 12, 1998

TR's
Summer White House

Oyster Bay

***

SHERWIN GLUCK

Introduction

Some called it the "Bay," others the "Hill," but they weren't referring to San Francisco Bay or Capitol Hill. In the summers, at the beginning of the twentieth century, they were referring instead to Oyster Bay and Sagamore Hill. To the world, these words meant one thing only, Theodore Roosevelt's Summer White House in Oyster Bay. Although many people are familiar with Sagamore Hill, President Theodore Roosevelt's home at Oyster Bay, very few understand the significance of the name, "The Summer White House." After all, most people associate the name "The White House" with the President's official residence in Washington where the President and the President's Executive Staff have their offices. Indeed, The White House in Washington has been recognized as the location of the Executive Branch of the United States Government since President John Adams. However, during the summers of the years 1902-1908 Oyster Bay replaced Washington as the site of the Executive Branch.

This was unprecedented in the history of the United States. Although it was common for Presidents to go on vacation accompanied by a secretary and a stenographer, leaving the remainder of their staff in Washington, the Roosevelt Presidency marked the first time in the peacetime history of the United States that the Executive Branch of government was physically moved to suit the needs of a vacationing President. The move to Oyster Bay was so complete that at times The White House in Washington was, more or less, closed for the summer.

In Washington and in Oyster Bay President Roosevelt made every effort to separate his important family life from his day-to-day presidential responsibilities. Therefore, he demanded separate working quarters for his Executive Staff. In Washington, Roosevelt relocated the ever-expanding Executive Offices from within the residential quarters of the White House to the new West Wing. Construction of the West Wing was completed specifically for this purpose in 1902. In Oyster Bay, however, it was impossible to establish the Executive Offices within Sagamore Hill. Instead, the Executive Staff rented office space in downtown Oyster Bay. During the Summer of 1902, the first summer of Roosevelt's Presidency, the Executive Offices were located in the Oyster Bay Bank Building across from the unfinished building of James Moore. President Roosevelt had rented space in the Bank Building earlier when he was Governor of New York State. It was not until May 1903 that the Executive Staff rented rooms in the new, state-of-the-art building owned by James Moore. From the summer of 1903 through the summer of 1908, Roosevelt's last summer in Oyster Bay as President, the Executive Offices were located in Moore's Building. In short, Moore's Building, in conjunction with Sagamore Hill, constituted The Summer White House at Oyster Bay.

1

At Sagamore Hill, the President handled matters claiming his personal attention and met with visiting dignitaries and guests. Most guests visited to discuss both political and personal matters during luncheon or dinner, with some staying overnight. Either the Executive Secretary or another member of the Executive Staff would meet daily with the President at Sagamore Hill to attend to the day's executive business. At these meetings the President received the bundles of important military and civilian letters and telegrams that were received at the Executive Offices. The President would review these documents and then either dictate his replies to the attending staff member or write them himself. As necessary, these replies were cabled to The White House in Washington where they would be directed to the appropriate party. At Sagamore Hill, the Executive Secretary would also work with the President to formulate various press announcements, upcoming speeches, daily schedules, and travel itineraries.

During the Summer of 1902, while the Executive Offices were located in the Bank Building, the Executive Staff consisted of Executive Secretary George B. Cortelyou, Assistant Secretaries William Loeb, Jr. and B.F. Barnes, as well as other members of the Executive Staff brought up from Washington. However, much of the Executive Staff remained in Washington and the routine that would be established in Oyster Bay in later years was not clearly discernable.

The following Summers, with the Executive Offices located at Moore's Building, most of the Executive Staff was brought to Oyster Bay from Washington. The Executive Staff consisted of Executive Secretary William Loeb, Jr., Assistant Secretaries B.F. Barnes, and Rudolph Forster, stenographers John L. McGrew and Maurice C. Latta, telegraphers Benjamin F. Montgomery and N.P. Webster, as well as other typists, telegraphers, and messengers. Messrs. Forster, Montgomery, and Webster remained at work in the White House in Washington. Here they directed all communications sent to the White House to the Executive Offices in Oyster Bay. In Oyster Bay, Mr. Barnes, and occasionally Mr. Latta assumed Mr. Loeb's duties while the latter vacationed. During these times they were referred to as the Acting Secretary to the President.

The Executive Secretary often acted as the President's spokesman. Information that the President wished released to the public was released by the Executive Secretary. The Executive Secretary also withheld information from the press, usually for security or political reasons. Since the Executive Secretary usually briefed the press from Moore's Building reporters were always waiting nearby. At the briefings, announcements were made on almost every subject. The President's positions were officially stated, Presidential documents were released for the public, Presidential appointees were announced, the President's itinerary was announced, the President's list of visitors was distributed, and the topics discussed at Presidential meetings were often outlined. Although the journalists sometimes reported from Oyster Bay that "it was formally announced to-day" without specifying who made the announcement, such announcements were made by the Executive Secretary, unless otherwise noted.

The Executive Staff's other clerical duties included sorting the mail, the newspapers, and the departmental and State documents. Most of these items were then submitted to the President for him to review and respond to. Some letters, however, were answered by the Executive Secretary after consulting the President. The staff also arranged for the executive carriages, and later automobiles, to meet visiting dignitaries and to bring them to and from Sagamore Hill. Any uninvited person who wished an audience with the President first had to request one from the Executive Secretary at Moore's Building.

Inasmuch as the Secret Service men guarding the President worked in tandem with the Executive Offices at Moore's Building, each day the Secret Service men at Sagamore Hill were given a list of the day's scheduled visitors. The list would be prepared in advance by the Executive Secretary and delivered to the Secret Service men. If a visitor's name did not appear on this list, they were denied entry to the road leading to Sagamore Hill and were sent back to the Executive Office at Moore's Building.

Members of the Executive Staff, especially Secretary Loeb, accompanied the President to numerous government and social activities as well.

A special telephone and telegraph wire connected the offices at Moore's Building to the White House in Washington. Another direct telephone line connected Moore's Building to the President's library at Sagamore Hill. Therefore, the Executive Offices at Moore's Building functioned as a switchboard for Sagamore Hill. Since the Executive Staff was able to maintain telephone contact with the President without ever leaving the Executive Offices, the President could receive important civilian and military communications from around the world twenty-four hours a day. Urgent news that was telephoned to Moore's Building was instantly relayed to the President at Sagamore Hill. All the incoming mail and telegrams were received at Moore's Building and were then hand-delivered to the President at Sagamore Hill. The President's replies were collected from Sagamore Hill and then mailed or transmitted from the Executive Offices. Consequently, the Executive Staff was vitally important in maintaining the lines of communication between the President and the members of his Cabinet, the other branches of government, the public, the press, and to other countries as well.

With their numerous and varied duties, the Executive Staff was always quite busy. As Albert Loren Cheney, former editor of the *Oyster Bay Pilot*, noted in his memoirs, *Home Life of the Late Theodore Roosevelt*, "It was the rule, rather than the exception, to burn 'midnight-oil' in the Summer White House offices over Moore's grocery store." (Cheney *Memoirs*, page 76)

This book, with its newspaper excerpts and the letters directed to the Executive Offices, relates the many significant state, national, and international events that kept the Executive Staff busy during the summers that President Roosevelt stayed in Oyster Bay. Furthermore, it gives a clear understanding of the role that Sagamore Hill and Moore's Building played in the Presidency of Theodore Roosevelt and how the two buildings together became known the world over as TR's "Summer White House" at Oyster Bay.

A Brief History of Oyster Bay

The unincorporated village of Oyster Bay has a long history dating back to the region's settlement period in the late 17th century. In 1653, three Englishmen bought the tract of land that now includes Oyster Bay from the Matinecock Indians. In addition to acquiring title from the Indians, a patent was issued in September 1677 creating the Town of Oyster Bay. For much of its early history the village remained a small, regional agricultural center and a busy maritime port.

During the American Revolution, Oyster Bay was home to Robert Townsend. Code named Culper Jr., he was the head of General Washington's spy system within the city of New York. During the war, Townsend's colonial saltbox house, known as Raynham Hall, also served as housing for the Queens Rangers, a loyalist regiment commanded by Lt. Col. John Graves Simcoe. Information gathered by Robert Townsend and his family in Raynham Hall led to the capture of Major John André, thus thwarting Benedict Arnold's plot to surrender West Point to the British. Raynham Hall is still located in Oyster Bay on West Main Street. After President Washington was inaugurated, he returned to Oyster Bay to express his gratitude. The President slept in Oyster Bay at "Young's House", which is still located on Cove Road.

By the late 19th century, especially after extension of the Long Island Rail Road to Oyster Bay in 1889, adjoining areas on the North Shore of Long Island began to be developed as grand estates for wealthy New Yorkers. Consequently, the area became known regionally as the "Gold Coast." Theodore Roosevelt's Queen Anne-style "Sagamore Hill," which was built during 1884-85, is an example of this development. Oyster Bay village enjoyed increased growth along with the development of these grand estates and their demand for services and housing.

Much of the village's fame, however, is due to the Roosevelt presidency. As a 1922 Long Island guide noted, Oyster Bay was "...known throughout the entire world during the regime of the late President Theodore Roosevelt as the "summer capital..." (*Suburban Long Island*, New York, c.1922, p.46.) This renown continued on for many years, at least locally, as a 1939 guidebook of Long Island noted:

> To the present-day American, however, the immediate association with the name Oyster Bay is Theodore Roosevelt. He is still the tutelary spirit of the village...turn right on South Street at the stop light...the brown brick business structure with a turret which stands on this corner was the "Summer White House" in the years when T.R. was President. (Stevens, *Discovering Long Island*, New York, 1939, page 24.)

*FIGURE 1: East Main Street, Oyster Bay, L.I. at the turn of the century.
Courtesy of Sagamore Hill*

*FIGURE 2: The Shore Road, Oyster Bay, L.I. at the turn of the century.
Courtesy of Sagamore Hill*

FIGURE 3: *On the road to Sagamore Hill, at the turn of the century.*
Courtesy of Sagamore Hill

Sagamore Hill

FIGURE 4: Sagamore Hill, President Roosevelt's Home, Oyster Bay, L.I.
Courtesy of Sagamore Hill

When Theodore Roosevelt was 15, his father established the family's summer residence at Oyster Bay. Three years after graduating from Harvard, Theodore Roosevelt purchased the hill on Cove Neck where his home, Sagamore Hill, now stands. Sagamore Hill was built by Theodore Roosevelt during 1884 and 1885 and remained his home during the remainder of his life. The architectural plans for Sagamore Hill were drawn up by the firm of Lamb and Rich and the house was built by John A. Wood & Son of Long Island. The house was named after the Indian Chief, Sagamore Mohannis, who signed away his rights to the land two hundred years earlier.

Sagamore Hill is a 23-room Victorian frame and brick building. On the first floor are a large center hall, the library that served as Mr. Roosevelt's private office, the dining room, the kitchen, and the spacious north room, added in 1905. The second floor contains the family bedrooms, the nursery, and the guest rooms. The top floor, contains the Gun Room, which was the President's study. Here also are the cook and maid's quarters, a sewing room, and a school room. For more information about Sagamore Hill seethe pamphlet, "Sagamore Hill, An Historical Guide" by Hermann Hagedorn and Gary G. Roth (Theodore Roosevelt Association, 1977.)

The History of Moore's Building

Built in 1902, Moore's Building is a two and one-half story late Queen Anne-style commercial building located in Oyster Bay. Moore's Building is historically significant as the building that housed the Executive Offices of President Theodore Roosevelt. His staff, most notably the President's private secretary, William Loeb, Jr., worked here during the summers of the years 1903-1908.

Moore's Building was built in the context of estate driven growth in the late 19th and early 20th century. Prior to the construction of the existing building, James Moore operated his grocery store, Moore's Fruits and Vegetables, out of a one-story wood frame commercial building with a brick facade on the same site at the northeast corner of East Main Street and South Street.

Figure 5: Moore's Grocery Store before 1901.
Courtesy of The Friends of Raynham Hall

By the turn-of-the century, business was apparently good, and Moore contracted to have the existing building constructed as a replacement for his original wood frame building. The contractors were William S. Moore, George Powers, Louis R. Gitto and Thomas Ellison. The original brick facade was incorporated into the new design. On

February 1, 1901, the *Oyster Bay Guardian* noted that construction had just begun. On February 22, 1901 the *Oyster Bay Guardian* reported that:

> Contractor Wm S. Moore commenced the work of brick-laying on Jas. Moore's new building on South Street, on Tuesday. This job will be pushed forward as rapidly as possible...

On May 3, the *Oyster Bay Guardian* reported that the adjoining 77-81 South Street building was still unfinished. It was however, completed by May 10, 1901. Emil Hill's Bakery opened in this part of Moore's Block on May 13, 1901. James Moore did not close his grocery while 77-81 South Street was being constructed. Instead, he continued doing business from his wood frame building until January 1902.

> James Moore on Monday next will begin moving his stock of goods into the store formally occupied by J.H. Randall where he will conduct his business until his new building is completed. As soon as the old store is empty, it will be torn down. The contract for the new building has not as yet been let. The new building is to be an imposing structure, two stories in height, built with pressed brick front and will cover the entire lot on South Street. This will be one of the most notable improvements ever made in this village. With a few more such buildings to replace the old rookeries that abound, we will have what nature provided for—one of the most attractive villages on the Island (*Oyster Bay Guardian*, January 27, 1902).

FIGURE 6: Inside Moore's Grocery Store after 1902.
Courtesy of The Friends of Raynham Hall

On May 2, 1902, the new edifice was praised:

> James Moore has moved into his new store. His is one of the finest country stores on Long Island. It gives him an opportunity to display his goods to good advantage. Mr. Moore has been very successful as a business man and has made an enviable reputation for himself, not alone as a fair and honest dealer but as an enterprising citizen. His property has recently been covered with new and modern buildings and he takes pride in the appearance of the village (*Oyster Bay Guardian*, May 2, 1902).

Before the Executive Staff rented rooms in Moore's Building in May 1903, the upper floors were used as speculative offices and meeting space. The first floor housed the Moore's Family Fruit and Vegetable Store. This store continued operating during the years that the Executive Staff were located in Moore's Building. Since the President returned to Oyster Bay during each summer of his Presidency, the Executive Staff returned with him, too. Consequently, the Executive Offices above Moore's Grocery reopened each summer through 1908, the last summer in Roosevelt's term.

FIGURE 7: Moore's Building after it was rented by the President's staff. Courtesy of The Friends of Raynham Hall

Upon removal of the executive staff, Moore's Building returned to a more typical commercial existence. Until the early 1920s, Moore's Fruit and Vegetables continued the grocery business begun by James Moore. During the twenties, the upstairs rooms once occupied by the President's staff became the headquarters for the Nassau County Police Department. Later, they were subdivided to form several private apartments. The main commercial store once occupied by Moore's Grocery was replaced by several other grocery stores (Modern Market, Dan Reeve's & Son) a dress store (WinWards, owned by Winny Ward), and many restaurants (JJ's, Charlie's Inferno, La Casa Bianca, La Seranata, Rancho Ribs, Teddy's Den, Theodore's.) It is presently occupied by the

Book Mark Cafe, a bookstore and café.

While Moore's Building never attained the widespread national fame that Sagamore Hill did, it was vital to the operation of Sagamore Hill during Roosevelt's terms in office, and remains a well-recognized local landmark. Moore's Building, despite some interior changes, continues to convey its historic significance not only as a local example of the Queen Anne style of architecture, but also as the location of President Theodore Roosevelt's executive staff: the vital companion to Sagamore Hill that made possible the nation's "Summer White House."

Moore's Building was designated a Town of Oyster Bay landmark on November 26, 1985 and was placed on the New York State Register of Historic Places June 7, 1996 and on the National Register of Historic Places September 30, 1996.

The Architecture of Moore's Building

Architecturally, this mansard roofed building is a late example of the Queen Anne style, which had peaked in the 1880's and had almost disappeared by the turn of the century. While the Queen Anne style first appeared in the United States in the 1870s and had its heyday during the 1880s and early 1890s, it lingered on as a popular style into the first decade of the 20th century. In the United States, the style is characterized by irregular massing, varied materials and colors, classical and medieval ornament, and often modern innovations such as large, single-light sash windows. Moore's Building is clearly representative of the later (especially commercial) phases of the style, when decoration was kept to a minimum. The hallmarks of the Queen Anne style found at Moore's Building include, the tower, the varied massing of the roof with its mansard slope and multiple dormers, the different colored wall surfaces, the denticulated cornice, and the Palladian windows. The most prominent feature of the building is the three-storey tower located at the front corner. This tower has curved sash windows and the same brick, lintel, and cornice treatment found on the rest of the facade.

Structurally, Moore's Building is a four course deep, brick building with wood joists, stone lintels, and masonry load bearing walls. The commercial first storey features rose-colored brick walls and an entrance flanked by indented brick piers and large plate-glass windows set in sash with rounded corners and paneled skirts. These window sash and frames are reproductions of the originals. The main entrances on both East Main Street and South Street are reproductions of the originals, as is the archway on South Street.

The upper stories of the building are separated from the first by a denticulated belt-course cornice with a narrow flush board concave soffit. This soffit is a reproduction of an earlier soffit, but not a reproduction of the original one. The second storey and tower are faced in sand-colored pressed brick, with rose-colored brick in the splayed window lintels. The windows on the second storey contain large one-over-one double hung sash of varying widths. The eaves above the second storey are similar in design to the cornice above the first, with dentils and a concave flush-board soffit. This soffit is a reproduction of the original. Boxed gutters located within these eaves drain through exterior downspouts. This eaves treatment is carried around the entire building.

The third storey of Moore's Building is composed of a mansard roof sheathed in fish-scale-patterned blue-gray slate on the lower slope. This storey has one dormer on the short (East Main Street) facade, three dormers on the South Street side, and two dormers on the east (rear) side. The East Main Street dormer and the middle South Street dormers are larger than the others and feature gambrel roofs, vertical match-board siding, and Palladian windows with keystone moldings. Thus, the influence of the derigour Colonial Revival style can be seen in the gambrel roofed dormers with their

15

Palladian windows. The other dormers on the west and east sides have gable fronts, paired windows, and applied raised ornament in the gables. The building's original lightening rods can still be seen above the dormers. Furthermore, since Moore's Building had electric service from the beginning, the original exterior connections for electric service are also visible.

At 77-81 South Street, adjacent to the north side of the Moore's Building, is a two storey two part commercial building. This structure, which housed Emil Hill's bakery and a bicycle shop during the Roosevelt presidency, was completed in April 1901, several months before the completion of Moore's Building. Although it resembles Moore's Building, it has a distinct square mass, a lower height, and minor distinct details, including corner quoins, recessed storefronts, and a paired window. It has always been physically and functionally distinct from Moore's Building and was completed immediately after construction on Moore's Building began.

Over the years, Moore's Building has suffered from changes in use and multiple rehabilitations, yet its overall form and details have remained remarkably intact. Following the summer of 1908, after the executive staff vacated their offices, several minor changes occurred on the exterior of the building. According to the Sanborn Fire Insurance maps, the fire escape on the South Street side was added and the wooden archway, also on the South Street side, was bricked closed sometime between 1909 and 1922. The wooden archway was enclosed in order to install a cork lined cooling box for the grocery store. The East Main Street front originally had an open canopy that was supported by wooden posts and extended to the curb. It provided shade from the summer sun and gave Moore's Grocery a place to display groceries and other items. The sidewalk canopy was removed sometime between 1928 and 1943. In 1976, a wooden porch was built in the area where the sidewalk canopy had been. Having already been whitewashed in a mistaken effort to show the building's details to best advantage, not unlike many other Victorian buildings, the entire building was also painted white.

FIGURE 8: Moore's Building in 1976 after being painted white.
Author's Collection

In 1985, the wood porch was replaced by an enclosed brick porch. On November 2, 1986 *The New York Times* described the condition of Moore's Building as follows:

> The building, built in 1905 of beige brick with red accents, is covered with peeling white paint. Except for the modern brick and glass facade of Teddy's Den, the restaurant that occupies the first floor, little has been done to maintain the exterior. "This is one of the worst examples of what happens to landmarks," Mr. Kahofer said. "This building is interesting stylistically and important historically. It has good possibilities, but it's a pile of junk right now."

In 1987, Stuart Chase, the then director of Raynham Hall, attempted to pick the appropriate Victorian colors to cover the white paint and Moore's Building was painted a brick red.

FIGURE 9: Moore's Building in 1987 after being painted red.
Author's Collection

Recently however, the entire building has been restored to its original appearance. A storm in the winter of 1991 wrought severe damage to the building's wooden cornice and yankee gutters. In an effort to preserve this historic landmark, the Town of Oyster Bay Landmark Commission eagerly gave its approval in June 1992 to rebuild the cornice and gutters using late 19th century materials and construction techniques. Under the supervision of the Site Engineer, Jerritt Gluck, work steadily progressed on the cornice until it was completed in mid-September. At the same time a facelift was also approved. This removed the already peeling red paint and exposed the magnificent, multicolored brickwork that lay hidden below.

In 1995, with the arrival of a new tenant on the first floor, the Book Mark Café, the Town of Oyster Bay Landmark Commission eagerly gave its approval to restore the windows to their full, majestic height and to restore the detailed wood panels below them. The archway and entrance door on South Street were also reconstructed. For structural reasons the archway was made from brick and does not resemble the wooden original. Furthermore, the 1985 brick porch addition, the "box," that was attached to the Main Street Facade prior to the building's designation as a Town of Oyster Bay Landmark was also removed. With the addition's removal, the original Main Street facade was restored. This phase of the restoration was completed in November 1995 again under the supervision of Jerritt Gluck with architectural drawings for the restoration provided by his brother, Sherwin Gluck, EIT. In July 1998, the restoration was completed when new fishscale-patterned roofing shingles and a weathervane were put on the Queen Anne dome. Currently, the building looks much as it did when President Roosevelt called Oyster Bay home, with the exception of the missing front canopy.

FIGURE 10: Moore's Building in 1995 after extensive renovations.
Author's Collection

The Secret Service in Oyster Bay

Following President McKinley's assassination, Congress established the Secret Service to guard the President. Consequently, President Roosevelt was the first President to be guarded by the newly created Secret Service. While the President was in Oyster Bay, no visitor could gain access to the President without first passing under the watchful eye of the Secret Service. Consequently, the Secret Service men guarding the President worked in tandem with the Executive Secretary at Moore's Building.

It was the assassination of William McKinley that prompted Congress to pass a law providing for the President a carefully chosen guard of Secret Service men. Eight of these attend President Roosevelt at his Summer home. Day and night they guard him on Sagamore Hill and when he goes on a journey or appears in a crowd there are always two or three of them within a few feet of him, on the alert for the emergency that may arise at any instant.

They watch all trains that arrive at Oyster Bay. The stranger that comes to town is under their espionage, quite unknown to himself, until they are certain of his business and his status.

...The guard, of whom there are usually two sharing the eight-hour watch, sit under a big maple by the house...

...The vehicles of visitors by appointment often appear around the turn in the road which leads up the hill through the woods, but these require no other action on the part of the Secret Service men than an inquiry as to the name of the visitor and a signal to the driver to pass on up to the house if the name given corresponds to one on a slip of paper supplied by the President's Secretary when the morning guard goes on duty. If the name of the caller is not on the list he is politely but firmly informed that he must make an appointment through the Secretary at the Executive offices in the village before he can see the President.

"Very few cranks have come up the hill this season, and all that have put in an appearance have been harmless. One elderly gentleman in the seedy clothes of a broken-down school teacher came ambling up the road one afternoon, bowed politely when he got here to the tree, and remarked in the manner of a millionaire in disguise that he had heard that the President's house was for sale, and would like to see the latter for the purpose of talking over the terms. I *(a Secret Service man)* replied, in polite tone to match his own, that I had not heard of the President's desire to sell and that he conducted all negotiations of this kind through the Executive offices in the village, where it would be necessary to go to learn the details. The old gentleman said he hoped he could buy it because the beautiful views made a strong appeal to him. With this he thanked us and started back on his way, I suppose, to interview the

Secretary...We always deal gently with individuals such as this ambitious purchaser of real estate, and usually do nothing but tell them that they must return to the village and call at the Executive office.*(NY Times*, August 20, 1905)

Occasionally however, some of these visitors had to be restrained. Desiring to meet with Mrs. Roosevelt and the President during the Summers of 1905 and 1906, the mysterious Mrs. Asi L. Esac was one of the most persistent.

OYSTER BAY, N.Y., July 13 — ...The persistent woman, last year in blue, who calls herself Mrs. Asi L. Esac, but whose name, read backward, is Lisa Case, was still hovering about the executive offices to-day, in a vain effort to see Mrs. Roosevelt and, if possible, the President. She is a slim and dark woman, and seems to be depressed by some secret grief. To-day she took lodgings next door to Secretary Loeb's house, and when the secretary was going to luncheon accosted him in the street.

"What do you want?" he asked her.

"I must see the President and Mrs. Roosevelt," she said imploringly.

"That will be impossible," Mr. Loeb assured her, and walked away.

She spent the rest of the day in attempts to induce leading business men here to use their influence to let her see the President. *(NY Times*, July 14, 1906)

On August 12, "Mrs. Esac" tried to halt the President while he attended Christ Episcopal Church.

OYSTER BAY, Aug. 12 — Mrs. Asi L. Esac, as she calls herself, or Mrs. Lisa Case, who has for weeks been hanging about Oyster Bay making vain efforts to see the President, and caused some excitement in the President's church on July 15, took the bull by the horns to-day and addressed both the President and his son-in-law, Congressman Nicholas Longworth, in church. Her effort was futile, for neither the President nor Mr. Longworth would speak to her, but, nevertheless, she succeeded in causing a great excitement, and all worshippers at Christ Church are telling the story breathlessly...

...Mrs. Esac entered the church unobtrusively and softly tiptoed over to the pew behind the Longworths. She had no sooner sorted herself than John Duffy, one of the ushers of the church, to whom her face has by now become familiar, bent over her and asked her to leave the pew. She declined and he insisted. According to Mrs. Esac the usher laid hands upon her and tore her blouse and broke her watch chain. This Duffy denies. He says he merely gave her his arm. At any rate Mrs. Esac was led to the other side of the church.

In a few moments, however, she again attempted to sit down behind the Longworths. Then Secret Service Agent Connell spoke to her and induced her to leave the pew. She did not sit down again, but stood in the aisle with Agent Connell on one side and Agent John Henry on the other.

Once during the service she made a move as if to approach the Roosevelt pew, Connell gently but firmly laid his hand upon hers. The troubled expression vanished from her face, the woman smiled up at the athletic secret service man and remarked ingenuously: "I regret this sin, but I cannot help but liking the sinner."

Connell stole a sidelong glance at her and grinned. Then she laid her hand on his and thus they stood in the aisle through the service.

The service over, President Roosevelt started to leave his pew. That was Mrs. Esac's opportunity. She literally bounded forward and cried:

"Mr. President, President Roosevelt, let me speak to you."

The President glanced at her sharply and continued on his way. The two secret service men held her fast. Behind the President came Mrs. Roosevelt, followed by Mrs. Longworth and Mr. Longworth. Again Mrs. Esac leaped forward.

"Mrs. Longworth," she called; "Congressman Longworth — Mr. Longworth, they won't listen to me. Let me speak to you."

Congressman Longworth paused for a moment. Mrs. Longworth, in front of him, also wavered, shot a glance at her husband, and turned somewhat pale. But again the Secret Service men were to the fore, and caged the woman in the small space in which she stood.

The Roosevelt procession passed and the Secret Servicemen followed the family out of the church, with Mrs. Esac close upon their heels. She emerged from the throng outside the church just as the Roosevelt family had entered their carriage. Mrs. Esac made one more dash in the President's direction, calling on him to hear her, but Secret Service Agent Henry was in front of her in an instant, and "Pop" Washer, another of the guards, brought up the rear. In the mix-up Mrs. Esac's watchchain snapped and her watch fell to the ground. Tousled and dishevelled she stood, facing her captors wretchedly. From time to time she cast sad looks at the disappearing carriage of the President.

The Secret Service men followed the woman two or three blocks, and then left her...

...Secretary Loeb said that he was perplexed as to what to do with the woman. She had been in Oyster Bay ever since the President arrived, and has given the authorities considerable trouble. While she apparently intends no harm, Mr. Loeb thinks it would be an act of charity to have her looked after.

Mrs. Esac has resorted to various devices calculated to win Mr. Loeb's cooperation. She is constantly sending flowers to his house, and tries to induce his servants to take her messages to him and Mrs. Loeb. She assures the Secret Service men that she has no quarrel with them, and always smiles upon them benignly. *(NY Times*, August 13, 1906)

The story was summarized briefly in the local papers as well.

The mysterious woman who has been stopping here for the past two months, to the great discomfort of the secret service men, has finally left town. She appeared to have but one aim and that to get an interview with Mrs. Roosevelt. She came here and gave the name of Miss Esac. She took up residence at a boarding house, and opened an account with the Oyster Bay Bank. She haunted the home of the President, hoping to be able to accomplish her object. Failing in this she sought influence to get a pass through Secretary Loeb, but this also failed. The trouble culminated on Sunday, when she attempted to accomplish her purpose while the President and family were at worship in Christ Church. She was foiled in her design, but not until considerable force was used. (*Oyster Bay Guardian*, Fri. Aug. 17, 1906.)

The Summer of 1902

The Summer of 1902, Roosevelt's first summer in Oyster Bay as President, set the tone for the years to follow. Although the President was on vacation, many of the nation's most pressing problems would be discussed during the many luncheons and dinners given by the President at Sagamore Hill. However, the Executive Staff's offices in Oyster Bay were still in the very early stages of development. Secretary Bruce G. Cortelyou was the President's Secretary while Mr. Loeb was still only the Assistant Secretary. Of national concern was the Anthracite Coal Strike. The strike continued throughout the summer without any public comment from the President.

On July 4, 1902, President Roosevelt visited Pittsburgh, Pennsylvania for the first time as President. After addressing an audience of half a million people at Shady Side Stadium, the President boarded a train to return to Oyster Bay.

> PITTSBURGH, Penn., July 4 — Half a million persons greeted President Theodore Roosevelt in Pittsburgh to-day. They came not only from Pittsburgh and Allegheny, but from scores of industrial towns within 100 miles of the city. It was the distinguished guest's first visit to Pittsburgh as President, and his welcome was most enthusiastic...
>
> ...When the President concluded his address the banqueters adjourned to their parlors, where a reception was held, and shortly before midnight the Presidential party were driven to their train, standing on a siding at Shady Side Station, where they retired, their car being attached to the Eastern train on the Pennsylvania Railroad at about 3 o'clock in the morning, en route to Oyster Bay...(*NY Times*, July 5, 1902)

The President arrived to Oyster Bay on July 5, 1902. The Secret Service men were immediately put on guard at Sagamore Hill to keep intruders off the grounds.

> OYSTER BAY, L.I., July 5 — President Roosevelt's special train arrived here this evening during one of the worst thunder storms of the season. The President, in spite of the downpour, drove to his home, two miles away, in a station wagon. He was accompanied by his children, and all were thoroughly wet when Sagamore Hill was reached.
>
> The train arrived at 5:14 o'clock. There were between 300 and 400 men, women, and children standing in the rain to welcome the President. The engineer of the special opened the whistle when nearing the station to announce the President's arrival.

When the cars came to a standstill there was a rush to get aboard, but before this was accomplished Mr. Roosevelt ran down the steps and into the crowd, who cheered him heartily. The President made his way slowly to the side of the station, bowing and shaking hands left and right. He was followed by Secretary Cortelyou, Dr. Ury, and two stenographers...

...Secretary Cortelyou, Dr. Ury, the stenographers, two Secret Service men, two New York detectives, and two Post Office Inspectors followed the President later. The detectives will remain with the President for some time. They are on guard to-night with orders to keep everybody off the grounds.

Secretary Cortelyou found time to say that the President intends to remain at Oyster Bay about three weeks, though he says the programme is not entirely settled, and he may return to Washington earlier.

The question of the location of the executive offices at Oyster Bay still remains unsettled. All the White House paraphernalia is in the meantime carefully stored in the station here. The matter will be decided probably on Monday...*(NY Times*, July 6, 1902)

FIGURE 11: R.R. Station, Oyster Bay, L.I.
Courtesy of Sagamore Hill

On the same day it was also reported from Oyster Bay that the President was eager for legislation to control the trusts.

OYSTER BAY, L.I., July 5 — It has been ascertained that the President's speech at Pittsburgh yesterday in reference to the trust question was merely a forerunner of determined efforts by him to have Congress take up that subject and enact definite legislation for the control and supervision of trusts at its next session...

...In addition to this proposed action the President is going to talk upon the trust question a good deal on the several trips to be made by him in the Fall. The President has announced to friends that the question is a vital one, and that he proposes to push it vigorously until there is some action by Congress. (*NY Times*, July 6, 1902)

The President's first Sunday in Oyster Bay was spent playing with his children and attending Christ Episcopal Church. Secretary Cortelyou announced the nature of the President's stay in Oyster Bay.

OYSTER BAY, L.I., July 6 — President Roosevelt, rested and refreshed after his hot trip to Pittsburgh, was up bright and early this morning, and wandered about with his children...

...It was getting time for church, and so he ordered horses harnessed to two light wagons...

...The President, with Miss Carow (*his sister-in-law*) and Archie, were first to arrive at Christ Episcopal Church...

...Secretary Cortelyou said to-day that there seems to be considerable mis-apprehension in regard to the President's stay here.

"There will be no elaborate office established," he said, "and the only cleri-cal force maintained will consist of two stenographers. The President has planned to make his holiday as brief as possible and get all the rest he can and freedom from the burden of public affairs.

"To that end he will transact in Oyster Bay only the most immediately press-ing business. Everything else will be transmitted to Washington for attention there, either by the regular White House force, or, in cases where other action is required, by the various departments.

"This is in accordance with the practice which has been followed success-fully during previous Summers. The President will not receive delegations, and hopes to have all matters intended for him, not of the most pressing impor-tance, submitted by correspondence."

It is not all fun for the President on his vacation, however, as he is dealing with a serious political problem. On the lines of his Pittsburgh speech he is considering the question of curbing the trusts. There will be several consulta-tions here on the subject, but as Mr. Cortelyou says, there will be no delega-tion to discuss the subject. Senators, however, may come one at a time to see the President. Mr. Roosevelt refuses to talk about the trust legislation, and refers questioners to his Pittsburgh speech.

It has been decided that he is to leave here on Aug. 20 for a tour of New England, where he will appear at county fairs and other places to be selected. He will return here on Sept. 19, and will go to Detroit Sept. 22. He will go to Washington Oct 8. for the Grand Army of the Republic encampment. Then there will be a tour of the Southwest with some hunting. This trip has not yet been mapped out. He expects to be in Washington by Nov. 1. (*NY Times*, July 7, 1902)

On July 8, it was reported that Father John H. Cushing, the first of many uninvited vis-itors, had tried to see the President. The priest, a missionary in Colorado, claimed that he and many other priests had been ordered to leave their work in Colorado by Bishop Matz of Denver. Although he sought redress at the Vatican in Rome he claimed that another Bishop there ordered him beaten. The priest said he had appealed to the President before and had followed the President's advice to try all legal methods in Italy. Having failed, he again sought the President's assistance. He was, of course, turned away. Meanwhile, it was reported that the new executive offices had been opened in the Bank Building.

> OYSTER BAY, N.Y., July 7 — ...The Executive offices of the President were opened to-day in the Oyster Bay Bank Building, on Audrey Street. There are two small rooms on the second floor, and Secretary Cortelyou hopes to secure a third one. This branch of the White House is a red brick three-story building. In addition to the bank's offices there are two dentists, of whom the President might make a choice if his teeth should need attention. In the basement there is a poolroom, where Mr. Roosevelt could play, if he chose, at the rate of 2 1/2 cents a cue. Next door there is a saloon.
>
> Secretary Cortelyou said yesterday that it was improbable that the President would be down to the new offices this week, though he might be. Desks for the two stenographers, the secretary, and Assistant Secretary Loeb were placed in the rooms yesterday, and telegraph instruments were put in place.
>
> There was a large mail yesterday, including many proposed delegations. They were all wired that they must not come, as there was absolutely no accommodation for them...
>
> ...President and Mrs. Roosevelt gave a delayed Forth of July party to-night at their home...(*NY Times*, July 8, 1902)

On July 9, 1902 the activities of the Executive Staff in Oyster Bay were described.

> OYSTER BAY, L.I., July 8 — President Roosevelt again missed his long-anticipated horseback ride this morning, and a stableman had to exercise his anxious hunter...
>
> ...After breakfast there was the mail to be attended to, and it was of amazing proportions. The President worked like a Trojan with his secretaries. There were a number of army commissions to be signed and appointments of Postmasters. There was also a great amount of necessary correspondence. The President was busy all morning and did not leave the house, though the rain had ceased immediately after breakfast.
>
> Secretary Cortelyou and Assistant Secretary Loeb reached the Executive Branch of the Oyster Bay "White House" about 11:30, where they worked over the correspondence that did not require the President's personal supervision for some hours.
>
> Harry C. Pearse, chief operator, worked with them, being busy in superintending the telegraphic connections with the office and the outside world, Washington in particular. There are to be five wires and a quadruplex.
>
> The executive quarters were increased by one room, so that the chief bureau of the United States Government is now quartered in rooms about 10 by 12 feet, and another without a window, which measures perhaps 8 by 6 feet. There is still hope of getting another small room. A trunk and box, presum-

ably filled with official documents and papers, was delivered to-day.

While the Secretaries were busy with their work in their rooms at the Oyster Bay Bank Building, in the basement below them, where pool, billiards, and ping-pong can be played sat two citizens of Oyster Bay...

...The President and Mrs. Roosevelt had as their guest at luncheon Montague White, who has been as personal friend of Mr. Roosevelt's since he was Governor of New York. Mr. White was formerly agent in the United States for the South African Republics, and at one time represented them in London. At the outbreak of the war with Great Britain he espoused the cause of the Boers and their allies.

Mr. White arrived shortly after noon and was driven at once to Sagamore House. As he was going up the steep hill he was stopped by one of the Secret Service men and asked politely what his business might be and who he might be.

He attempted to explain that he had been invited to dine with the President, but the Secret Service officer could not understand his decided English accent for some time. Then he permitted Mr. White to go on to the house...

...It was semi-officially announced to-day that whatever action may be taken by Congressman Littlefield to frame a bill to curb or control the trusts will not be the action of the President. There are no arrangements for a consultation by the President, Attorney General Knox, and Littlefield. It was stated that the trust question would undoubtedly be most prominent in the Winter's legislation and that the President's attitude was best shown in his Pittsburgh speech...(*NY Times*, July 9, 1902)

On July 9, 1902 it was announced that the President had invited members of his cabinet to visit him individually at Sagamore Hill. His first guests were to be Secretary of War Root and Attorney General Knox. In the village, the Stars and Stripes was finally raised over the Executive Offices.

OYSTER BAY, L.I., July 9, 1902 — All the members of the Cabinet have been invited to visit the President at Sagamore Hill. Their invitations call for their coming at separate times. Secretary Root and Attorney General Knox are to be the first guests. It now appears that the others will be unable to accept the President's invitation.

President Roosevelt's holiday to-day began with work. Immediately after the family breakfast the President sat at his desk to sign a great pile of official documents, many of them army commissions and appointments of Postmasters. The President was busy until late in the morning, when he called for his horse...

...There were no callers on the President, and he had the whole day with the exception of his early morning to devote to his family.

There was a flag raising in Oyster Bay to-day. When the executive offices of the Oyster Bay branch of the "White House" in the bank building were opened, it appeared that there was no flag to float above the building, though there was a pole ready for the Stars and Stripes. A beautiful banner arrived from Washington this morning. New halyards were purchased, and the flag was raised over the "little White House." There was no ceremony, though several of the townsmen and the reporters took off their hats while one of the patriotic boys of Oyster Bay set off a package of firecrackers as a salute to the flag. *(NY Times, July 10, 1902)*

In another story on the same day, it was reported that the President had decided that the announcement of new appointments would be given out from Washington rather than Oyster Bay.

OYSTER BAY, L.I., July 9 — It has been decided by the President that no information in respect to appointments will be made public from Oyster Bay. All appointments, as heretofore, will be announced from Washington, the announcement being made from the temporary White House here. From the various departments in Washington information concerning appointments made will be given to the public.

The day here is bright and clear and very hot. The assurance is given from Sagamore Hill that nothing of particular importance demanding the President's attention has developed. *(NY Times, July 10, 1902)*

Also on July 9, the President received a telegram in Oyster Bay from King Edward of England.

RECEIVED at   *July 9*

Dated *London*
To *The President*
            Oyster Bay, NY

I have the great pleasure in entertaining Admiral Cotton and the captains of his squadron and have just proposed your health with every feeling of cordiality and friendship.

                              Edward R

(TR Papers, Series 1, Reel 28)

On July 10, the itinerary for the President's trip to New England was announced in Oyster Bay. The article also relates a comical anecdote about the Executive Office's lack of space.

OYSTER BAY, L.I., July 10 — It was announced to-day that President Roosevelt on his trip through New England, which begins on Aug. 20, will visit a number of the Senators of those States. He will visit Secretary Hay, Senator Lodge of Massachusetts, and Senator Proctor of Vermont. He may also, if possible, accept the hospitality of other Senators in New England...

...Among the arrivals to-day were Judge Spencer B. Adams of Greensboro, N.C...

...Judge Adams was recently appointed Chief Judge of the Chicksaw Citizenship Court of the Indian Territory. It has been stated that the United States Court has admitted Indians to citizenship and three Judges have been appointed to settle the matter. Judge Adams said that he had been summoned by the President for a conference, as the question involves the citizenship of many thousand Indians in the Territory...

...There is a difference of opinion between the little "White House" officials and Dr. W.C. Root, a dentist, occupying three fourths of the floor of the Oyster Bay bank building, where the Government has its vacation headquarters. Dr. Root uses his office here on Wednesdays only. He said the Government might have them on other days, but must move out "its traps" on Wednesdays, that he might fill or extract the teeth of the natives on one day in the week. This would be awkward for the Government, and there was the danger that laughing gas leaking might muddle minds busy with important affairs of State, to the detriment of the peace and prosperity of the Nation.

Secretary Cortelyou said this morning that he thought the matter would be amicably arranged, but Dr. Root is positive that if the Government wishes to use his offices there should be a willingness to let him have them for the one day, when the Government might move back with its "duds." In the meantime the Government of the United States of America must be content with the cramped quarters on the floor where the dentist has abundant room. *(NY Times*, July 11, 1902)

On July 11, 1902, the President met with Senator McLaurin of South Carolina, a candidate for Judgeship in the United States Court of Claims, Father Thomas Malone of Denver, Collector Stranahan of the Port of New York, and William Barclay Parsons, chief engineer of the Rapid Transit Commission. Secretary Cortelyou arranged to have them come to Oyster Bay at the same time. The Secretary also announced that Secretary of War Root was expected to arrive the following day. It was also reported that the President was considering the ongoing negotiations with the Vatican regarding the withdrawal and replacement of the Spanish friars in the Philippines with friars of another nationality. *(NY Times*, July 12, 1902)

On July 12, Secretary of War Root arrived in Oyster Bay for two days of consultations with the President.

OYSTER BAY, L.I., July 12 — Secretary Root, who has been expected here for some days, arrived to-night, being the first member of the Cabinet to respond to the invitation of the President...During the visit the President and Mr. Root will go over matters of importance. Among them are the Smith and Waller court-martial cases and the Philippine friars question. The negotiations respecting the friars are in an acute stage and demand delicate handling...

...It was announced to-day through the Secret Service men that the President is weary of photographers. No man with a camera is to be allowed near Christ's Episcopal Church to-morrow if the President attends services...The Secret Service are under orders to see that the curious do not gather outside of the edifice...*(NY Times*, July 13, 1902)

The following day, the President and Mr. Root considered the situation in the Philippines in detail.

OYSTER BAY, L.I., July 13 — President Roosevelt and Secretary Root were so busily engaged to-day in the consideration of important subjects that they did not attend church services. One of the subjects discussed was that of Gov. Taft's negotiations with the Vatican respecting the Philippine friars.

The President and the Secretary of War deem it unwise that the friars should remain in the archipelago with the prestige they now possess. The attitude that the friars assume is regarded as a menace to the peace of the Islands and as an obstruction to the government and to the civilization of the inhabitants.

No statement of the conclusion reached by President Roosevelt and Secretary Root could be obtained at Sagamore Hill, but, unofficially, it is understood that a note is being drafted in response to that transmitted by the Pope through Gov. Taft to the Administration. As Gov. Taft initiated the negotiations, it is likely that the reply of this Government will be sent to the Vatican authorities through him. Assurance is ample that the United States will take strong ground in support of its contention that the friars must be eliminated from the Philippine equation.

It is positively said that no official statement of any phase of the situation will be made public until the negotiations with the Vatican have been concluded, and that then the announcement will come from Washington...

...The President and Secretary Root practically completed their arduous work to-night. To-morrow is to be devoted by them to recreation...

...Secretary of the Navy Moody is expected to arrive here some time during the present week, the day not having been determined definitely. Secretary Cortelyou will go to Washington this week to make final arrangements for the President's New England trip, which is to be begun on Aug. 22. The trip will occupy ten days, and in that time the President will visit six States. *(NY Times,* July 14, 1902)

On July 14, 1902, President Roosevelt met with Senator Spooner of Wisconsin. Their discussion included the proposed purchase of the Panama Canal Company's property. It was also announced that Gen. Leonard Wood would visit Sagamore Hill. The President extended the invitation in order "to appoint Gen. Wood to direct and supervise the construction of the Panama Canal." *(NY Times,* July 15, 1902)

On the same day, a brief description of the interaction between the President at Sagamore Hill, the Executive Offices, and the Secret Service was reported.

OYSTER BAY, L.I., July 14 — ...President Roosevelt's vacation is of the sort that some men, who think that they are overworked, would regard as a succession of days where one labors. It has been, and still is, his effort to make a real vacation during his stay at his home in Oyster Bay, but there is a great deal of official business that must be attended to.

The positive rule that no one is to see the President without having made an appointment previously through Secretary Cortelyou and the fact that the accommodations of Oyster Bay are limited have made it possible for the

President to have a reasonable amount of sleep, to eat his meals in peace, and to have a romp, a ride, a swim, or a row with his children...

...The Secret Service men perform the important duty of seeing that undesirable persons do not enter the grounds and that no one who is not warranted in doing so rings the doorbell. The President does as he pleases and takes long, strenuous walks, without being shadowed by the men of the Secret Service. He has more freedom to do as he will than the Secret Service men, whose chief occupation is to watch the trains and the grounds of the President's home.

There are many yachts off Centre Island and on board are many persons who would like to see the President. They have not received cordial responses to their requests for appointments to meet Mr. Roosevelt. *(NY Times,* July 15, 1902)

On July 15, Secretary Cortelyou received a letter from U.S. District Attorney William Michael Byrne. Mr. Byrne corresponded regularly with Secretary Cortelyou, and later Secretary Loeb. In his correspondence with the Executive Secretary, Mr. Byrne regularly gave his advice and opinion on the political situation at hand.

Department of Justice
OFFICE OF
United States Attorney
DISTRICT OF DELAWARE

July 15, 1902

Hon. George B. Cortelyou
    Secretary to the President
        Oyster Bay, L.I., N.Y.

My dear Mr. Cortelyou,
                    Dispatches of this morning con-
firm the confidence I have a long time felt that the vexed questions
in the Philippines would receive a solution satisfactory to us as pa-
triots and Catholics; but they further enforce my impression that the
friends of the President should not undertake to discuss the public
aspect of these questions until the President speaks on these important matters. If he speaks on them the last vantage ground of the Democrats will be captured. A dispatch from Atlantic City advises me
that their speakers will come from Massachusetts, Maine, Pennsylvania,
and Michigan, and the gathering will be widely representative. If I
were able to make a strong presentation of the Republican attitude on
these questions it might do some good, owing to the character of the
assemblage; and my ability to make such an address would be increased
by a short discussion with you.

    But if you agree with me that it is as well for the friends of
the President to abstain from present discussion, or if you think
it is not necessary for me to discuss the matter with you, then you can
dismiss my intimation of a desire for a conference as contained in
my former letter.
                       Very truly yours,
                       Wm Michael Byrne

(TR Papers, Series 1, Reel 28)

On July 15, Secretary Cortelyou returned to Washington to finish preparing the itineraries for the President's upcoming trips to New England in August and to the Northwest in September. Assistant Secretary Loeb was left in charge of the Executive Offices in Oyster Bay.

> OYSTER BAY, July 15 — ...Secretary Cortelyou left here to-day on his way to Washington, where he is to arrange the itinerary of the President's contemplated trips. He is also to plan for the proper disbursement of $45,000 appropriated by Congress to cover the expenses incurred at the time of the wounding and the funeral of President McKinley. These bills will be paid by the Treasury on warrants drawn by Mr. Cortelyou. The President's secretary does not believe that his business will detain him long in Washington, and he will on its completion go with his family to Hempstead, L.I., for the first vacation he has had in twelve years. Assistant Secretary Loeb will act as the secretary in the absence of Mr. Cortelyou...*(NY Times,* July 16, 1902)

On July 16, 1902, President Roosevelt, on the urging of Secretary of War Root, reprimanded and retired Gen. Jacob H. Smith, after he was court-martialed and found guilty of having used language in giving oral orders to one of his subordinates that exceeded his own written orders. *(NY Times,* July 17, 1902)

On July 17, John Hay, Secretary of State wrote to President Roosevelt at Oyster Bay regarding the visit to Oyster Bay of Prince Ching (Chen) of China.

DEPARTMENT OF STATE
WASHINGTON
July 17, 1902.

Dear Mr. President:

The Chinese Minister informs me that Prince Ching, with a large suite, will sail on the steamer "Philadelphia" from England, to arrive on the 1st or 2d of August. Mr. Wu Ting-fang will be in New York to meet him, and I have begged the Treasury Department to issue the necessary orders, that His Highness be not treated as a coolie. As you are not in Washington, and the Prince would like, of course, to pay his respects to you, I would suggest that all that would be necessary for you to do would be to ask him to luncheon, so that he may arrive at Oyster Bay and depart at a reasonable hour. If Mr. Wu has any more formal communication to make, it will be sent to you in due time. Mr. Cortelyou can give him what information he needs in regard to trains.

The Prince is, as you know, a great personage in his own country, was a special ambassador for the Coronation in London, is a son of the Prime Minister and a cousin of the Emperor. It is his misfortune, and not his fault, that he arrives here when Washington is in its summer torpor. Mr. Hill will do what he can, with our limitations. We shall try to get a special car for him from New York to

Washington. I am not quite sure yet but I will be required
to come down from Newbury, but I will arrange that later.

The Crown Prince of Siam will probably be here
the first week of September. I will try to be in Washington when he arrives. I hardly know whether you will be at
Oyster Bay at that time or not. In any case, he must take
his chance.

The Grand Duke Boris of Russia impends upon us
also, but Cassini has not as yet made any demands.

The trouble is, they will all compare themselves
with Prince Henry, and feel very much left in consequence,
but this we cannot help.

Yours faithfully

John Hay

(TR Papers, Series 1, Reel 28)

On July 18, Assistant Secretary Loeb denied knowledge of the Mayflower's destination
after the Presidential yacht left Oyster Bay. He also denied that the President's daughter, Alice, was engaged to marry Robert Clark. *(NY Times*, July 19, 1902)

On July 19, Mayor Low of New York City visited the President at Sagamore Hill.
(NY Times, July 20, 1902)

Also on July 19, the shirtmaker "Kaskel and Kaskel" wrote to Assistant Secretary Loeb
regarding the President's specially ordered shirts.

KASKEL & KASKEL
SHIRT MAKERS
FIFTH AVE. COR.32D STREET

New York
77 JACKSON BOULEVARD
CHICAGO

New York, July 19th, 1902

Mr. Wm. Loeb Jr.
Secry. to Prest. Roosevelt,
Oyster Bay, L.I.

Dear Sir:

We are in receipt of your kind favor of the 18th in reference to the sample shirts which we made for the President.

We shall proceed with the balance of the order and make the
white linen false collars somewhat larger for the neckbands.

We expect to send the shirts in about ten days and trust
that they will come out to the President's full approval.

At all times glad to serve you, we are,

Yours respectfully,

Kaskel & Kaskel

(TR Papers, Series 1, Reel 28)

On July 21, 1902, Senator McLaurin, a recent visitor to Sagamore Hill, announced his decision that he would decline the Judgeship in the U.S. Court of Claims offered to him by President Roosevelt. He declined the judgeship because newspapers had declared it to be a reward to a Democratic Senator that supported the President's Philippine policy. The President expressed great regret at the Senator's decision. *(NY Times,* July 22, 1902)

Also on July 21, Nicholas Murray Butler, President of Columbia University, wrote to President Roosevelt to accept the latter's invitation to visit Sagamore Hill. Mr. Butler frequently visited Sagamore Hill and informally advised the President on many issues throughout Mr. Roosevelt's term.

COLUMBIA UNIVERSITY
IN THE CITY OF NEW YORK

PRESIDENT'S ROOM

July 21, 1902.

Dear Mr. President:

I have Mr. Loeb's kind note of the 19th, and shall come down on Wednesday at 12.50, which I find is a train running only Wednesday and Saturday. This will bring me to Oyster Bay at 2.23, and I hold myself in readiness to play tennis, or anything else, immediately thereafter.

Sincerely yours,

Nicholas Murray Butler

To the President,
       Oyster Bay,
              L.I.

(TR Papers, Series 1, Reel 28)

On July 22, the President met with Frederick S. Gibbs, a member of the Republican National Committee from New York. *(NY Times,* July 23, 1902)

On July 23, the President met with Nicholas Murray Butler, Jacob Schurman, President of Cornell University, Capt. F. Norton Goddard, leader of the Twentieth Assembly District, and George Edward Graham, an author. Among other things they discussed the Philippines, the tariff, and the trusts. *(NY Times,* July 24, 1902)

On July 24, the President, in Sea Girt, New Jersey, addressed the National Guardsmen of that State. He spoke of their duties as soldiers and as citizens. He sailed on the Presidential yacht Mayflower from Oyster Bay to New Jersey. *(NY Times,* July 25, 1902)

FIGURE 12: U.S.S. Mayflower, the Presidential yacht.
Courtesy of Theodore Roosevelt Collection, Harvard College Library

On July 25, friars from the Augustinian Order visited the President to present him with resolutions passed by that order protesting the concerted effort to have them removed from the Philippines.

OYSTER BAY, N.Y., July 25 — The Rev. P. O'Reilly of Lawrence, Mass., and the Rev. W.A. Jones, President of St. Augustine's College, in Havana, were callers upon the President to-day.

The two clergymen, who are friars of the Augustinian Order, one of those in the Philippines, the presence of which is opposed by the natives, handed to the President a copy of the resolutions which were adopted by the quadrennial chapter of the Augustinian Order at Villanova, Penn., on July 16.

The resolutions protest "the concerted effort which is being made to defame and vilify the friars of the Philippine Islands, and to alienate from them the love and reverence of a people whom they have ransomed from ignorance and barbarism." They also deplore "the seeming disposition of our Government to discredit the services of the friars," and, "regard any hindrance to the legitimate exercise of their labors as a serious menace to the civil and moral well-being of the people of the islands, an unwarranted precedent fraught with peril to the Catholic Church, and a grave violation of the treaty of Paris."

The same measure of justice and protection is demanded for the friars as is accorded to all other persons under the jurisdiction of the United States.

Secretary Moody did not come to-day, although he had been expected. He is to arrive here to-morrow afternoon. Secretary Shaw who arrived on the Gresham, was saluted with seventeen guns from the Mayflower. He landed at the dock of Emlen Roosevelt, and was met by the President...

...W.B. Sleeper of Wyoming arrived to-night to present to the President res-olutions of the stock-raisers of Big Horn County, Wyo., concerning the exclu-sion of cattle and sheep from the additional Yellowstone Park timber reserve...*(NY Times,* July 26, 1902)

On July 25, 1902, Philip B. Stewart wrote to Secretary Cortelyou, urging that his letters remain confidential, especially since a confidential letter to the President appeared in the newspapers.

WILLIAM A. OTIS & CO.
BANKERS AND BROKERS.
COLORADO SPRINGS.
COLORADO.

July 25th, 1902

Mr. Geo. B. Cortelyou,
        SECRETARY, Oyster Bay, N.Y.

My Dear Sir:-

I enclose herewith a copy of the Denver news in which is the copy of a letter written by me to the President. I suppose this letter went to the Senate with the nomination of Bailey as Marshall. It was not intended by me to be used in that way, for reasons which are apparent in the letter.

I have written other communications, especially in reference to the controversy over the re-appointment of Gordon in the Pueblo land office. It would be a serious mistake from all points of view if these letters should be made use of as the one has been by the Denver News.

I am aware that in the rush and quantity of communi-cations received, it is easy for accidents to happen, and yet I sincerely hope that these private communications can be destroyed or so filed that they are not available for political uses. It would be disastrous to harmony in this section.

I remain,

Very sincerely,

Philip B. Stewart

(TR Papers, Series 1, Reel 28)

On July 26, the President met separately with Secretary of the Treasury Leslie Shaw, Secretary William Moody, and Attorney General Knox. He also discussed the Panama Canal with Senator Spooner. The President had many other visitors during the day and evening as well. *(NY Times,* July 27, 1902)

On July 28, "President Roosevelt and his family, with the exception of Miss Alice, paid a farewell visit...to the officers and men of the Mayflower, which then started for Newport under orders from Washington, to join the Atlantic Squadron for target practice. The President took occasion to compliment Lieut. Edward McCauley, who early in the morning had saved one of two deserting members of the crew from drowning..."*(NY Times*, July 29, 1902)

On July 29, it was announced that the President would travel by train to Greenport to meet the Mayflower and sail on her to witness the Atlantic Squadron's target practice. He preferred to travel by train because he would be able to witness the shooting and return in one day rather than the two it would take aboard the Mayflower. *(NY Times*, July 30, 1902)

On July 30, the President met with Senator Thomas Platt and Col. George Dunn, Chairman of the Republican State Committee of New York.

> OYSTER BAY, N.Y., July 30 — "President Roosevelt will have a solid delegation from New York State to the next Republican National Convention."
>
> This was what Senator Thomas C. Platt said this afternoon after he had a conference with the President at Sagamore Hill. The Senator was accompanied to Mr. Roosevelt's country home by Col. George W. Dunn of Binghamton, Chairman of the Republican State Committee of New York. The visit was by appointment.
>
> Baring serious contingencies, said the Senator, Mr. Roosevelt would be nominated to succeed himself...
>
> ...During the two hours' conference, which took place after luncheon, both National and State politics were discussed, but the discussion was chiefly about State affairs.
>
> The President found it necessary to-day to send word to the gun crews of the Mayflower that it would be impossible for him to witness their target practice to-morrow, and later he was informed that this event would be postponed until his coming next Wednesday. If he finds he cannot be with the men on that day, he will notify them and ask them to go to work at the guns and smash the targets in his absence...*(NY Times*, August 1, 1902)

Also on July 30, Executive Clerk Rudolph Forster in Washington wrote a memorandum to Assistant Secretary Loeb in Oyster Bay regarding the unauthorized release of Philip Stewart's letter to the President.

WHITE HOUSE,
WASHINGTON.

July 30, 1902.

Memorandum for Assistant Secretary Loeb:

Your memorandum of the 24th instant, enclosing your letter to the Attorney General and accompanying communication and newspaper clipping from Mr. Philip B. Stewart, of Colorado Springs, Colo., is just received.

After looking up this case as much as is possible here, I can only report that it seems only to have passed through my hands in returning the papers with the Secretary's letter of May 15th, requesting

the reappointment of Mr. Bailey. This letter has the
Secretary's personal signature. Originally the case
did not pass through my hands. As you know, letters
which the President personally dictated very rarely
came to me. The President's personal letter book
was taken to Oyster Bay and an examination of the
copy of his letter to the Attorney General of May
12th will probably enable the gentleman who handled
the case to recall upon what authority he enclosed
with it Mr. Stewart's letter.

      I send you the memorandum card showing the
reference to the Attorney General under the same date
as the President's personal note - May 12th. Also
the card showing the return to the Attorney General
May 15th.

      I have enclosed the papers with your letter to
the Attorney General.

Rudolph Forster

Executive Clerk.

(TR Papers, Series 1, Reel 28)

Mr. Loeb replied to Mr. Forster's memorandum on the same day.

**WHITE HOUSE,
WASHINGTON.**

Oyster Bay, N.Y.,
July 30, 1902.

Memorandum for Mr. Forster:

      Perhaps Mr. Stewart has hit on the way
the letter was made public; that is through
the Senate Committee sending for the papers.

      I suggest that steps be taken to have
the files of the different Departments looked
over, so that confidential letters from Mr.
Stewart to the President should not appear
in them, particularly the papers in the Department of the Interior, concerning the
Pueblo Land Office.

Wm. Loeb, Jr.

(TR Papers, Series 1, Reel 28)

On July 31 "President Roosevelt...spent his usual busy morning getting rid of a mass of official business. Among his callers...was William H. Hunt, Governor of Porto Rico..." The President and Mr. Hunt discussed the general affairs of Porto Rico and conferred in detail as to the working of the government there and how it might be used as a model for the government of the Philippines. *(NY Times,* August 1, 1902)

On August 4, the President met with Archbishop Ryan. The Archbishop told the President "that the excitement in the Catholic Church in regard to the Philippines would die out rapidly, just as soon as it was realized that the United States Government was, as it is, dealing fairly with his church in the substitution of American priests for those of the old orders that grew to be hated by the people under the Spanish régime." The President also met with Gifford Pinchot, Chief of the Forestry Division of the Department of Agriculture. They talked of Mr. Pinchot's upcoming mission to study forests of the Philippine Islands. *(NY Times,* August 5, 1902)

On August 5, the President, having changed his original plan to travel by train to Gardiner's Bay, sailed on the Sylph from Oyster Bay to watch the navy's target practice.

OYSTER BAY, N.Y., Aug. 5 — President Roosevelt was up early this morning, and spent the greater part of the day at his desk.

At 4:11 o'clock in the afternoon Mr. and Mrs. Roosevelt were taken from the dock of J. West Roosevelt's place in the launch of the Sylph. The Sylph carries no guns that could possibly give a Presidential salute, but the commanding officer of the Sylph, Capt. W.H. Buck, believes in the proprieties, and so he gave the President and his wife when they came alongside a good, old-fashioned, recognized-all-over-the-world salute of three long blasts of the whistle.

...The sailors and marines stood at attention. After greeting the officers the President bowed to the men...The anchor was weighed and the Sylph pointed her sharp nose for the Sound, bound for Gardiner's Bay, where to-morrow the men behind the guns of the Mayflower are to show the Commander in Chief of the Navy what they can do in the way of shooting...*(NY Times,* August 6, 1902)

The President returned to Oyster Bay on August 7.

On August 8, the President and Attorney General Knox held an important conference on the new conditions negotiated between the U.S. Government and the Pacific Cable Company for the laying and operation of the Pacific Cable to the Philippines.

OYSTER BAY, L.I., Aug. 8 — Attorney General Knox and H.L. McCollough of Chicago visited the President to-day. The Attorney General was there on important business, and he conferred with the President for several hours...At the railroad station he announced that the important matter in his conference with the President was the proposed cable across the Pacific to our new possessions in the Orient. The Attorney General submitted to the President a number of conditions to be added to those offered by the Pacific Commercial Cable Company. They are to be offered to Congress at its next session, and they will give to the Government additional rights in the control and management of the company. The President's decision as to the conditions for the cable, if ratified by Congress, means that there will be direct communication with the Philippines in twelve or fourteen months.

Under a bill offered in Congress a specific rate of 50 cents a word was fixed. The present rate is $1.50 a word. The defeat of a measure empowering the Government to build its own cable made it necessary to grant the privilege to the Pacific Commercial Cable Company to lay a cable to Honolulu, Guam, and the Philippines.

The conditions of the company and its concessions to the Government were given to the Attorney General, who learned that the President is in agreement with him that the rights of the United States must be safeguarded by additional stipulations with the company.

There had been a disagreement between the Government and the company in regard to the demand of the latter that the charts, the result of the work of the navy, in its soundings along the line of the proposed cable route, should be turned over to the company. It was urged that this would make it possible to have the cable in operation within a year, and that it would take two years to complete the undertaking, if the company should be forced at its own expense to chart the route. It was pointed out to the Administration that at the present rate it would cost the Government in cable charges an amount in excess of the cost incurred by the work of the navy, and that there would be a year without direct cable communication.

The Attorney General said after the conference that in the mutual agreement, with its concessions and conditions, the company would have the right to the Government charts. Among the conditions is the very necessary one that the Government shall have absolute control of the line of the Pacific Commercial Cable Company in time of war. Mr. Knox said:

"There is the advantageous condition that the Government is to fix the rate for its cablegrams...that Government cablegrams must have priority over all other messages at all times...that at any time it may acquire the property of the cable company, the price to be determined by a board of arbitration...that the company must lay a line and maintain a cable from the Philippines to some point in China, connecting with telegraphic lines...there shall be a prescribed rate of transmission..."*(NY Times*, August 9, 1902)

On August 9, the General Superintendent of the Long Island Railroad wrote to Assistant Secretary Loeb regarding a special car attached to a train to Oyster Bay for Governor Odell of New York.

THE LONG ISLAND RAILROAD COMPANY

OFFICE OF THE GENERAL SUPERINTENDENT

W.F. POTTER,
     GENERAL SUPERINTENDENT

LONG ISLAND CITY, N.Y., Aug. 9, 1902.

Mr. Wm. Loeb, Jr.,
     Act'g Sec'y to the President,
         Oyster Bay, L.I.

Dear Sir:-

     I beg to acknowledge your letter of Aug. 7th in reference to providing a special car for Governor Odell, L.I. City to Oyster Bay, 11 o'clock A.M. train, Tuesday Aug, 12th, and to say that the same will receive prompt and proper attention.

     You make no mention of a return trip, and if you desire a car to move from Oyster Bay to Long Island City on any afternoon train, kindly advise me and we will make arrangements accordingly.

Yours truly,

WF Potter
General Sup't.

(TR Papers, Series 1, Reel 28)

Also on August 9, A.M. Young, President of the Army War College Board replied to a letter from Assistant Secretary Loeb inviting Mr. Young to Oyster Bay.

ARMY WAR COLLEGE BOARD,
OFFICE OF THE PRESIDENT,
Washington.

Aug. 9, 1902.

My dear Mr. Loeb:-

     Referring to your note of July 19th, in which you say, "the President directs me to say he would be glad to have you come here and take lunch with him just before you sail. Please advise me in advance of your coming", I have the honor to state that I expect to leave here and arrive at the Waldorf-Astoria, New York, on Wed-

nesday, the 13th instant, and will be able to go
to Oyster Bay on Thursday the 14th, or Friday
the 15th, whichever one of these two days may be
more convenient for the President to have me.
    Please advise me either here or at the Wal-
dorf of the President's pleasure in the matter.

Yours cordially,

AM Young

Wm. Loeb, Jr., Esq.,
    Act'g Secretary to
        The President, Oyster Bay,
            New York.

(TR Papers, Series 1, Reel 28)

On August 10, the President received a telegram from Herbert H.D. Peirce, Third
Secretary of State, informing him that Prince Chen of China had arrived in New York.

TELEGRAM

New York, Aug. 10th, 1902.

To   President
        Sagamore Hill,
            Oyster Bay, N.Y.

Prince Chen arrived at Quarantine this morning at ten thirty.
I met him there with revenue cutter accompanied by the representative of the Mayor and brought him to the city. Prince Chen
desires me to present his compliments to you and to say that he
deeply appreciates your courtesy in sending a representative
to meet him, as well as the kindness of your invitation to lunch
with you on Monday sending the Sylph to New York to take him to
Oyster Bay. He has very much pleasure in accepting this invitation.

Herbert H.D. Peirce.

(TR Papers, Series 1, Reel 28)

On August 11, the President announced that Oliver Wendell Holmes was his choice to
succeed Horace Gray as a Justice of the Supreme Court of the United States.

OYSTER BAY, N.Y., Aug. 11 — The President to-day appointed Oliver
Wendell Holmes, Jr., Chief Justice of the Supreme Court of Massachusetts, to

be an Associate Justice of the United States Supreme Court, because of the vacancy caused by the retirement of Justice Horace Gray on account of ill-health...

...It is said that the resignation of another United States Supreme Court Justice is likely, and that in this event Judge Taft, Governor of the Philippines, will get the place. In the meantime the President is pleased with the satisfaction of Justice Holmes's appointment expressed in telegrams and messages from New England. *(NY Times,* August 12, 1902)

Also on August 11, the President received a message from the Emperor of China from Prince Chen. The Prince and his entourage visited the President at Sagamore Hill.

OYSTER BAY, N.Y., Aug. 11 — The President's day was enlivened by the coming of his distinguished visitors, Prince Chen, Minister Wu, Sir Liang Chen, and the personal attendants of the Prince, making a party of six celestials. They were arrayed in the finest silks, and when the Sylph cast anchor off the dock of Mr. J. West Roosevelt, they were loaded into the little launch of one of the Government boats.

Prince Chen took occasion, soon after the party arrived, to express to the President, on behalf of the Emperor of China, the deep sense of gratitude the Chinese people feel toward the United States, because the army of this country protected and really prevented the destruction of many of the handsome palaces in the City of Peking during the trouble there two years ago. He also expressed the hope that the bonds of amity and commerce between the United States and China might become closer and closer as time went on.

To this the President responded that it would be his effort by all means at his command to promote the good feeling at present existing between the two countries, as well as to increase the commercial relations.

Oyster Bay, usually pacific, was a bit boisterous, and the distinguished party with an Ensign, three sailors, Third Assistant Secretary of State Peirce, loaded down the launch, so that the Prince and his party were drenched every now and then with spray. A large launch filled with the camera men kept close. Prince Chen said that the devil machines were not as objectionable as usual, for, if the little launch were to sink, there was help at hand in the big boat, where the shutters clicked as their owners made desperate efforts to use up all their films to get at least one good picture of a Prince of China in a very wet yellow jacket.

The Prince brought to the President of the United States the good will of his people for the United States.

He was met on the steps of Sagamore House by the President, Minister Wu making the formal presentation. The Prince shook hands with the President and then the party was ushered into the drawing room...*(NY Times,* August 12, 1902)

On August 12, it was reported that the President intended to call for an extra session of Congress after the November elections to take up the Cuban Reciprocity Treaty. This treaty was negotiated to set favorable tariff rates between the two countries and thus prevent Cubans from starving and Cuba from lapsing into ruin and revolution.

OYSTER BAY, N.Y., Aug. 12 — From information gathered here there appears to be little doubt that an extra session of Congress will be called immediately after the elections in November. Apart from the fact that the term of Congress is short, and that there is a vast amount of business to be disposed of, the President, it is understood, feels that something must be done in the matter of the relations of the United States to Cuba, and done without delay...*(NY Times*, August 13, 1902)

Also on August 12, Secretary Loeb received a reply to his letter from the Vice President of the Western Union Telegraph Company, Thomas F. Clark.

Executive Office
Western Union Telegraph Company
New York, August 12/'02.

William Loeb, Jr. esq.,
        Acting Secretary to the President,
              Oyster Bay, L.I.

Dear Sir:-

        I have to acknowledge receipt of
your esteemed favor of the 8th instant, with
which you send me, by the President's direction, a communication from the Attorney
General on the question of the Pacific cable.
        Please express to the President
my thanks for his courtesy, and say that the
conditions prescribed therein seem to me to
be a fair protection to the interests of both
the United States Government and the American public.

                Yours truly,

                Thos. F. Clark,
                Vice-President.

(TR Papers, Series 1, Reel 29)

On August 14, a denial was issued from Oyster Bay that the President would interfere in the Delaware Senatorial deadlock. Earlier in the year the President attempted to enforce party unity in Delaware but to no avail. On the same day, Governor Odell of New York met with the President at Sagamore Hill. *(NY Times*, August 15, 1902)

On August 15, a day in which thirteen people dined at Sagamore Hill, the President announced that in the future, the death of any soldier serving in the Philippines would be cabled to the War Department, and not just the death of an officer.

> OYSTER BAY, N.Y., Aug. 15 — ...The President announced to the visiting military men and others that in the future all deaths of privates in the Philippine service were to be cabled to the War Department, as was done when the volunteer regiments were fighting in the islands. Since the return of the volunteers only the names of officers have been cabled, they coming by code, so that a single word designated the man, his rank, and regiment. This curtailment was due to the enormous expense the Government had to incur in cabling the names of the killed and wounded. The President, however, has received many requests to let those at home know the fate of the soldiers in the regular army. He announced that he believed this was the right thing to do, and that at Gen. Young's suggestion the War Department had been instructed to issue an order in regard to the cabling...(*NY Times*, August 16, 1902)

On August 16, the President received a letter from Pope Leo confirming that the question of the removal of the friars from the Philippines had been settled.

> OYSTER BAY, N.Y., Aug. 16 — Bishop O'Gorman of Sioux Falls, S.D., presented to President Roosevelt to-day a letter from the Pope, which would indicate that the question of the removal of the friars from the Philippines as outlined during the conference of Gov. Taft and the representatives of the Roman Catholic Church at the Vatican had been settled, and in accordance with the propositions of the Administration...(*NY Times*, August 17, 1902)

On August 20, the President, in a meeting at Sagamore Hill with Cecil Lyon, Chairman of the Republican State Committee of Texas, denounced factional fighting within the ranks of the Republican Party.

> OYSTER BAY, N.Y., Aug. 20 — President Roosevelt to-day, in no uncertain terms, expressed his disapproval of factional differences in the Republican Party. Cecil A. Lyon, Chairman of the Republican State Committee of Texas, called on him and presented his side of the controversy which has arisen among the Republicans of the Lone Star State.
>
> The President told him, with the utmost emphasis, that no man had any authority to speak for the President as regards Texan matters, that the President was taking no side for or against any man or any faction among the Texan Republicans, and that as a matter of fact the President was exceedingly impatient with those Republicans who went into factional divisions.
>
> He added that in any such States as Texas and Virginia, or in any other State in which the Republican Party is in a minority, but yet had a chance to do something, the President felt the credit would fall on those Republican leaders who were able to make a good showing at the polls, especially for Congressional candidates, and not to those who spent their time plotting how they could get delegates or receive offices. He told Mr. Lyon that he could explain these sentiments to all Texas Republicans of every faction.

The President also told him that if ever, in any such Southern State, a Republican Congressman was elected, it would amount to far more in the President's mind than anything which could be done in the way of offices, and that he felt there was little need of recognition for an organization which existed only for offices and delegates.

It was learned that the President told Chairman Babcock of the Republican Congressional Committee when the latter visited him a few days ago that he was profoundly discontented with the Virginia Republican organization for not making a resolute effort to elect Republican Congressmen from the western districts of Virginia, and that he felt that an organization which did not try to develop the fullest party strength at the polls had no claim upon him...*(NY Times*, August 20, 1902)

Also on August 20, the President's itinerary for his upcoming trip through New England was released by Secretary Cortelyou from Washington. Surprisingly, Representative Littlefield's home was not included, especially since it was announced earlier "from Oyster Bay that the President, Mr. Littlefield and Attorney General Knox were going to form a great anti-trust triumverate, and devise legislation which should strangle every octopus left alive by the Sherman *(Anti-Trust)* law. The President would be accompanied on this trip by Secretary Cortelyou and other members of his personal staff, including Assistant Secretary Barnes, two stenographers, and two messengers. *(NY Times,* August 21, 1902)

On August 21, the President met with representatives of the Brotherhood of Locomotive Firemen. They invited the President to attend their annual meeting in Chattanooga. The President expressed hope that Secretary Cortelyou would be able to rearrange his schedule to enable him to attend. *(NY Times,* August 22, 1902)

On August 22, the President left Oyster Bay for New Haven, Connecticut for the start of his New England trip.

> OYSTER BAY, Aug. 22 — The President of the United States left here this morning on the Sylph for his New England trip...
> ...The President is a very prompt person. Secretary Cortelyou had arranged that he should leave on the Sylph at exactly 9:30 in the morning. The President was on the dock off J. West Roosevelt's home at exactly thirteen minutes before the appointed time...
> ...The Sylph was under way exactly on schedule time. With the President were Mrs. Roosevelt and little Ethel. In addition there was Secretary Cortelyou, Dr. Lung, Stenographers Latta and Weaver and two men of the Secret Service...*(NY Times*, August 23, 1902)

On August 30, Assistant Secretary Loeb sent the following telegram to Col. Benjamin F. Montgomery at the White House in Washington.

TELEGRAM.

𝔚𝔥𝔦𝔱𝔢 𝔥𝔬𝔲𝔰𝔢, 𝔚𝔞𝔰𝔥𝔦𝔫𝔤𝔱𝔬𝔫.

Oyster Bay, N.Y., August 30, 1902.

Memo for Col. Montgomery:

Please wire Secretary Cortelyou following telegram in cipher: Mrs. Roosevelt feels that vulgarities indulged in by Grand Duke Boris in New York City and elsewhere *as reported in newspapers,* make it impossible for him to meet her and thinks reception here by President of him should be of the briefest official character, and hopes it can be arranged that she be not present and that private car on Long Island railroad and not Sylph will bring him here. Please advise me for her information what program has been agreed upon.

William Loeb, Jr.

(TR Papers, Series 1, Reel 29)

The following day, Secretary Cortelyou sent a telegram via Western Union to his Assistant.

RECEIVED at
2 NY DY PC   133 paid govt   Sept 1/1902

Bellows Falls Vt   1

Hon Wm Loeb Jr   Asst to the President Oyster Bay NY
                (Personal) See telegram to the President to Mrs
Roosevelt referring to your cipher message arrange with Long
Island Railroad company for private car to be attached to the
ten fifty AM train from Long Island City September fourth car
to be held in Oyster-Bay and attached to train out of there two
twenty three pm after luncheon for Long Island City.
Have explained fully to Mr. Adee that Sylph will not be available
on that day and that these arrangements have been made have also
told Adee if representative of State Dept cannot accompany Grand
Duke to Oyster-Bay to ask war Dept to detail an officer for that
duty. Advise commander of Sylph of this change of arrangements.

Geo B Cortelyou.
Secr.

(TR Papers, Series 1, Reel 29)

Upon the conclusion of the President's tour of New England, his carriage was struck by an electric trolley car in Pittsfield, Massachusetts. Although the President suffered minor injuries, a Secret Service Agent was fatally wounded and died at the scene. The President returned to Oyster Bay the same day.

PITTSFIELD, Mass., Sept. 3 — The carriage in which President Roosevelt, accompanied by Gov. Crane, Secretary Cortelyou, and others, was being driven from this place to Lenox this morning was struck by a trolley car at the foot of Howard's Hill, and instantly demolished.

The occupants of the landau were thrown into the air, and Secret Service Agent William Craig, who fell on the tracks directly in front of the rapidly moving car, was instantly killed. The President, who fell by the roadside, sustained no injuries other than a bruise on the cheek and a severe shaking. Gov. Crane also escaped unhurt and Secretary Cortelyou's hurts were minor. D.J. Pratt of Dalten, the owner of the carriage, who was driving the four horses attached to it at the time of the accident, sustained a dislocation of the left shoulder, a sprained ankle, and was otherwise seriously bruised and cut...

...All four of the occupants of the carriage were thrown out. Gov. Crane seems to have escaped entirely, and the injuries to the President and his secretary are not regarded as being serious. President Roosevelt and Gov. Crane, who occupied the rear seat of the carriage, were both flung violently forward into the highway, but they saved themselves by clinging to one another...*(NY Times*, September 4, 1902)

OYSTER BAY, N.Y., Sept. 3 — President Roosevelt returned to Oyster Bay at 8:20 o'clock to-night but little worse for his thrilling experience of this morning. His right cheek was swollen, there is a black bruise under his right eye, and his mouth is slightly swollen. Otherwise he shows no effects of the accident. He will go South the latter part of the week according to the original schedule, and will be accompanied by Secretary Cortelyou, who, while he was considerably shaken up, expects that his injuries will not incapacitate him from duty. Mr. Cortelyou's nose is badly bruised, there is a lump on the back of his head, and bruises behind his left ear and on his body.

The President says he may have to make his first public appearance with a black eye and a swelled face, but the accident has not interrupted his work for ten minutes, and it will not interrupt his Southern trip. The President is pledged to attend the annual convention of the Brotherhood of Locomotive Firemen at Chattanooga on Monday, and he would not on any account disappoint them...

...The President was busily engaged to-night signing commissions and disposing of work that had accumulated during his absence...*(NY Times*, September 4, 1902)

In Washington, Assistant Secretary Barnes, who was with the President's party when the accident occurred, spoke at length about the accident.

WASHINGTON, Sept. 4 — B.F. Barnes, Assistant Secretary to the President, arrived in Washington to-day. Mr. Barnes was with the Presidential party at Pittsfield, Mass., yesterday, being in the second carriage behind that occupied by the President, Mr. Cortelyou, and Gov. Crane at the time of the accident.

Although Mr. Barnes disclaims having any special knowledge as to all the circumstances of the accident not shared by many others, yet from what he saw and heard on the spot he thinks the responsibility for the accident lies between the driver of the President's carriage and the motorman, with the greater burden upon the latter.

The trolley road at this point, Mr. Barnes says, is straight for some distance, and the motorman must have seen and recognized the President's carriage with its four white horses some time before the crossing was reached, but instead of stopping or materially reducing his speed he came on at a rate that made it impossible for him to stop when he saw that a collision was imminent...*(NY Times*, September 5, 1902)

FIGURE 13: The wrecked carriage that carried President Roosevelt and Governor Crane, showing the rear wheel smashed by the trolley car. Secret Service Agent William Craig was also thrown from the carriage and was struck and killed. Courtesy of Theodore Roosevelt Collection, Harvard College Library

The following day, the President again left Oyster Bay on his Southern tour, with Chattanooga, Tennessee his objective, with stops in Wheeling, West Virginia, Knoxville, Tennessee, and Asheville, N.C.. The itinerary having been released by Secretary Cortelyou from Washington. He was accompanied by both Secretary Cortelyou and Assistant Secretary Barnes. The President's trip was comparatively short, and he returned to Oyster Bay on September 10, accompanied by Secretary Cortelyou, Assistant Secretary Loeb, Mrs. Roosevelt, and their daughter Ethel.

On September 10, the first announcements were made that the President would hold a reception at Sagamore Hill for the people of Nassau County. It was expected that at least 15,000 visitors would attend.

> Oyster Bay, L.I., Sept. 10 — The days that now intervene before the Presidential reception to the people of Nassau County on the 15th will be devoted to preparation. On that day Oyster Bay expects to entertain fully 15,000 visitors. Chairman A.L. Cheeney of the Reception Committee says that the notification from the various villages as to the number of visitors to expect exceed the first estimates. Freeport, alone, has spoken for ten cars on the railroad where five were expected to suffice. Cold Spring and Huntington are engaging stages from the city to handle their delegations. Hicksville, besides coming over in a body, is to bring a battery along, and two salutes of twenty-one guns each will be fired, one as the reception begins and the other as it closes.
>
> The President will be assisted in receiving by his wife, Secretary and Mrs. Cortelyou, and Assistant Secretary and Mrs. Loeb. The plan now is to have the line approach Sagamore Hill by one road and leave by another. All wagons are to be hitched in a meadow near by. The bicycles will be checked near the same spot. *(NY Times,* September 11, 1902)

It was also authoritatively denied on September 10 "that the United States Government has sounded the German Government as to the appointment of Bellamy Storer...Minister to Spain, as the successor to Andrew D. White, American Ambassador to Germany." It was also stated that no successor had yet been selected. *(NY Times,* September 11, 1902) By September 12, the number of expected visitors to the Presidential reception at Oyster Bay had climbed to over thirty thousand.

> OYSTER BAY, N.Y., Sept. 12 — Everything is progressing favorably for the great Presidential reception on Monday. The decorations are rapidly being put up in all parts of Oyster Bay, and preparations are being made to handle a big crowd. The local committees have been figuring on ten or fifteen thousand, but the Long Island Railroad expects to handle thirty thousand people.
>
> The New York and New Jersey Telephone Company and the Oyster Bay Electric Light Company have united in something that is considered unusual. They will decorate each pole on the road from the village to the entrance of Sagamore Hill. Each pole will be ornamented by a shield, three flags, and a streamer.
>
> At the station, which by President Baldwin's orders, will be most elaborately decorated, there will be a big "Welcome" shield. At the entrance to Sagamore Hill there will be another. Many of the visitors will be transferred to Sagamore Hill by water, launches having been loaned for the purpose...*(NY Times,* September 13, 1902)

On Sunday, September 14, President Roosevelt attended church services as usual at Christ Episcopal Church. Some time earlier, Mr. Roosevelt had asked the rector of the church to make a memorial service to the life of President William McKinley and Mr. Roosevelt thought that this was the rector's intention. Instead, the rector glorified Mr. Roosevelt, comparing him to the biblical David.

OYSTER BAY, N.Y., Sept. 14 — President Roosevelt attended Christ Episcopal Church to-day, and at the conclusion of the services left with angry eyes blazing through his spectacles. Few persons have ever seen the President quite as enraged and at the same time self-controlled. He was filled with rage like man abused by a woman, who is too much of a man to hurt or harm her, and has to be content with compressing and controlling his anger between his set teeth.

Some time ago the President intimated to the Rev. Henry Homer Washburn, rector of Christ's Church, that he would highly appreciate a sermon that would deal with the life of President McKinley, and later he conveyed to the rector a second suggestion that the memorial service should be strictly confined to the late President.

To his utter amazement and chagrin the rector, after some general remarks, referred incidentally to William McKinley and then devoted the greater part of his remarks to a eulogy of President Roosevelt, a denunciation of the trusts, and even went so far as to ask whether the killing of McKinley was an accident or a work of God in the fullness of time, bringing another David to the head of the Nation...*(NY Times*, September 15, 1902)

It was also reported on September 15, that the changes to the White House in Washington, begun by President Roosevelt, were nearing completion. Orders were received in Washington that the part devoted to the President's family must be completed by October 1. Mrs. Roosevelt was kept abreast of the many changes, and the color schemes and decorations were submitted to her in Oyster Bay for her approval. *(NY Times*, September 15, 1902)

On September 15, the President summoned to Oyster Bay six influential Senators to a conference in Oyster Bay for a discussion about tariff revision. Those in favor of tariff revision felt that any article whose cost of production is less in this country than it is abroad should be put upon the free list.

President Roosevelt has summoned to Oyster Bay to confer with him to-day Senators Hanna of Ohio, Spooner of Wisconsin, Lodge of Massachusetts, Aldrich of Rhode Island, Allison of Iowa, and O.H. Platt of Connecticut...

...If information received from reliable sources is correct, the conference will be one of great significance to the Republican Party. President Roosevelt is said to be contemplating a further step forward on the trust question. He is also said to be seriously considering the advisability of coming out for tariff revision. Before definitely making up his mind as to the propriety of such a step, he desires to confer upon the subject with the leading men of the party. It was for this purpose he has summoned the six men whose united influence would command the Senate, as at present constituted, on any proposition...

...President Roosevelt, it is said, while realizing that he is undertaking a delicate task in advocating tariff revision, is nevertheless optimistic about the outcome...*(NY Times*, September 16, 1902)

Also on September 15, the President's reception for the people of Nassau County brought some 8,000 people to Sagamore Hill to greet the President.

OYSTER BAY, N.Y., Sept. 15 — The President's reception to the people of Nassau County to-day was a huge success, democratic in its simplicity, charming in the wholesome, hearty welcome the Chief Executive gave to his visitors, and the evident delight of the thousands who shook hands with him, drank of his lemonade, ate of his ginger snaps, and carried away as souvenirs the cups from which they had drunk. Mr. and Mrs. Roosevelt entertained over 8,000 persons, and even those who went away without the souvenir cup left the grounds of Sagamore Hill in a happy frame of mind.

Every one was closely scrutinized by the men of the Secret Service, aided by a large staff of detectives from Police Headquarters. Theodore Roosevelt, Jr., constituted himself guardian of his father and, standing next to one of the cleverest men of the Secret Service, watched every hand before it was extended to the President.

Oyster Bay was founded in 1640, but never before in all its history had it harbored within its borders so many people as flocked into the little village to-day. Never had it heard such a crash of drums and blowing trumpets. Six big bands came with the multitude of visitors. Even the most modest house was gay with the American flag and red, white, and blue bunting. From Oyster Bay, at intervals of every fifty yards along the three miles of road leading to Sagamore Hill, there hung from wires stretching from one tall locust tree to another flags measuring seven by nine feet. Every telegraph and telephone pole was decorated with the Stars and Stripes, two flags crossed. The same idea was carried out along the private road to the President's house. The big banners waved their red, white, and blue among the brilliant foliage of a steep road that is abundantly shaded, because the trees are so many and so old that their branches almost interlock, forming an arch over the driveway, where the people came in every imaginable conveyance...

...The long excursion trains of seven and eight cars commenced to come shortly after noon, pouring out their thousands. Everything that could be converted into a stage was used, and the Cove Road never saw so much dust and so many funny looking wagons and queer-looking horses. At the docks everything from a rowboat to a good-sized steamer was there to carry the visitors of the President to a dock, or, rather, series of floats that had been anchored just below the landing of J. West Roosevelt's house, and manned by sailors from the Sylph. Even the old oyster boats were used as passenger-carrying craft. They were highly decorated with flags and bunting.

The reception was scheduled to begin at 3 o'clock and to end at 6 o'clock. This was not adhered to. By 2 o'clock the entrance to the grounds was blocked with vehicles, people on foot, and many with bicycles. The President learned that his guests were early and were being detained by the police. He sent word to let them in at once...*(NY Times*, September 16, 1902)

On September 16, the President met with five of the six Senators whom he invited to Sagamore Hill.

OYSTER BAY, Sept. 16 — There came here to-day one of the most remarkable expeditions to see a President that have occurred in the history of the country, with the exception of such as have been made to a Chief Executive in war time. Five Senators and the Postmaster General called on Mr. Roosevelt. They arrived at 12:20, the party including Senators Hanna, Spooner, Allison, Aldrich, and Lodge, and Postmaster General Payne.

At the conclusion of their long visit it was rumored — no one being willing to stand for the statement — that Mr. Roosevelt had decided not to call a special session of Congress to revise the tariff; that he would maintain his stand in regard to the trusts, and he would still insist that reciprocity be granted to Cuba. He is to give his views and intentions in regard to this subject on his Western trip.

It was quite evident on the return from the President's home that there had been trouble, and it looked as if the President had declared his intentions very plainly and had held to his ideas in a way distressing to his advisors. It was rumored that he had practically told them that he was the chosen Chief Executive of the people and would do as he thought best. It was denied that the coal strike was discussed...(*NY Times*, September 17, 1902)

On September 16, Speaker of the House of Representatives D.B. Henderson announced his intention to decline renomination to Congress. The President sent a telegram to him from Oyster Bay on September 17 asking him to reconsider his decision not to run. (*NY Times*, September 18, 1902)

On September 17, Secretary of State Hay, under the direction of the President in Oyster Bay, sent a diplomatic note to several European powers, asking them use their influence to stop the Government of Roumania from oppressing the Jews of that country.

WASHINGTON, Sept. 17 — With the double purpose of protecting the long-suffering Jews of the Balkan States and of averting the danger of an immigration into the United States of a horde of poor people, Secretary of State Hay has adopted the unusual course of appealing to the powers of Europe to force one of their protégé to observe the obligations of humanity in the case of the Jews.

The appeal takes the form of a state paper, remarkable in several respects, which has been dispatched in identical form to every Ambassador and Minister of the United States residing in one of the countries of Europe which were parties to the treaty of Berlin of 1876 — namely, Great Britain, France, Germany, Russia, Italy, Austria, and Turkey, marking the termination of the Turko-Russian war, and the creation by the direct act of the powers of the independent Balkan States.

Because the powers are thus responsible for the existence of Roumania, the culprit in this case, the Secretary of State has directed the note to them in the hope that they will bring that Government to a sense of its duties toward civilization at large as well as to cause it to ameliorate the condition of the Roumanian Jews.

In a measure this action by the Department of State may be traced to numerous petitions from Jewish societies and humanitarians generally, as well as to the warnings of publicists respecting the growing dangers of immigration of degenerates...(*NY Times*, September 18, 1902)

On September 18, Secretary Cortelyou made public the President's Western trip itinerary. The main cities visited by the President would be Cincinnati, Milwaukee, Minneapolis, Kansas City, St. Louis, Chicago, and Cleveland, with many other stops as well. The President was accompanied by both Secretary Cortelyou and Assistant Secretaries Loeb and Barnes, as well as three stenographers, a messenger, and a number of Secret Service officers. He left Oyster Bay on the Sylph for Jersey City on September 19, 1902 and returned to Washington after completing his tour.

The Summer of 1903

One of the first announcements that the President's staff would occupy new quarters during this summer was made in the *Brooklyn Standard Union* of May 1903.

> Preparations are now going actively forward for the transfer of the Presidential offices from Washington to the "summer capital," at Oyster Bay, L.I. This movement bodily of the working equipment of the executive office of the Nation to the retreat chosen by the Chief Magistrate as the scene of his vacation is an innovation introduced by President Roosevelt. Other Presidents, notably McKinley, were wont, in their day, to indulge in long vacation absences from the seat of government, but for the most part they contented themselves under such circumstances with a single secretary and stenographer, leaving the remainder of the executive office force at the White House, through which indeed most of the public business was transacted.
>
> However, the increase in the scope of governmental affairs, now that Uncle Sam has become a world power, renders impossible a continuance of this simple plan. It has remained for the resourceful Mr. Roosevelt to meet the exigencies of the new conditions by virtually removing the White House offices to the little village on the north shore of Long Island during the summer months. According to present plans, the White House staff will be doing business at the new stand by July 1, and it is unlikely that the Presidential business office will move back to the city on the Potomic earlier than Oct. 1.
>
> The President has just leased for the use of his secretaries, clerks and stenographers a suite of rooms in the brick block owned by James Moore...the Presidential offices were located in the bank building, and plans were originally made to again establish them there this season, but upon further consideration it was decided that the bank building could not well accommodate the larger staff of workers which will be necessary this year, and accordingly larger quarters were secured.
>
> The transfer of the Presidential offices is by no means a removal in name only. Not only are typewriters, letter files and all the other paraphernalia of modern business administration shipped from the White House to the temporary seat of government on Long Island, but even the horses and carriages of the secretaries and the messengers are taken to Oyster Bay. The National Government maintains seven horses and several carriages exclusively for the use of the White House secretaries and messengers, and four of these horses and two carriages will be placed in service at the summer capital.
>
> There have been secretaries and executive clerks at the White House in days

gone by who would have been sadly perturbed and thrown out of the routine of their duties had they been compelled to pack up at such short notice and suddenly transfer their operations, but fortunately for his purposes President Roosevelt now has as his assistants a force of up-to-date young men who are readily adaptable to unusual conditions and who last season proved that they could continue on the even tenor of their way quite as well at Oyster Bay as at the capital.

The summer White House at Oyster Bay will this year be under the direction of William Loeb, Jr., secretary to the President. Mr. Loeb was in reality in command last summer. To be sure Mr. Cortelyou was at that time secretary to the President, but during the summer he spent much time at his own house on Long Island, leaving the active direction of things to Secretary Loeb, who has been associated with the President ever since he was Governor of New York, and is more familiar with his tastes and business methods than any other man. Mr. Loeb will be assisted by the regular White House staff, including the Assistant Secretaries, B.F. Barnes and Rudolph Forster, both young men who have risen from the ranks so to speak — that is, have advanced to their present positions from clerkships in the Presidential offices.

Of course, it is highly essential that the Presidential office at Oyster Bay have at all times perfect facilities for prompt communication with Washington and a special telegraph wire and special telephone wire (reserved exclusively for the transaction of Presidential business) will connect the Oyster Bay offices and the White House. Not only will members of the Cabinet and other prominent officials call at the Telegraph and Cipher Bureau at the White House from time to time to have telephonic conferences with the President, but if the plan of last year is followed, "long-distance Cabinet meetings" may be conducted in this same manner. Reports from army and navy officers, advises from our diplomatic representatives abroad, and other important communications which come direct to the various departments, but of the contents of which the President should be advised, will also be transmitted over the White House wires to Oyster Bay...the telephone office is never closed night or day and by means of the direct wires to Oyster Bay it will be possible to promptly inform the Chief Executive of any new event which might threaten to disturb the peace of the world...

(*Brooklyn Standard Union*, May 1903 reprinted in *East Norwich Enterprise*, June 13, 1903.)

Secretary Loeb, and occasionally Assistant Secretary Barnes, accompanied the President on his trips to and from Washington at the beginning and end of his summers in Oyster Bay. Sometimes Secretary Loeb even gave the orders for the train to Oyster Bay to depart the station. On June 27, 1903, the President returned to Oyster Bay from Washington.

President Roosevelt arrived in Jersey City...yesterday afternoon, accompanied by Secretary Loeb, Assistant Secretary Barnes, Dr. and Mrs. Lung, and several Secret Service men. Gen. Greene, Detective Sergeants Powell, Carey, Vallelly, and Fogherty of the Central Office met the President at Pennsylvania

Station and accompanied him on the trip across the rivers and Manhattan to Long Island City, where a special train was waiting to take him to Oyster Bay...Preceding the carriage was a quartet of mounted policemen with one on either side and two behind. A Secret Service officer sat on the box with the driver, while Gen. Greene and Secretary Loeb rode in the carriage with the President and the Secretary of War...Mr. Loeb gave the order for the run to Oyster Bay to begin. *(NY Times,* June 28, 1903)

FIGURE 14: Moore's Building, the new home of the Executive Offices. Courtesy of Sagamore Hill

One of the first announcements made from Oyster Bay during the summer of 1903 was by Mr. Loeb stating that all visitors to the President must first make an appointment through the Executive offices.

OYSTER BAY, June 28 — ...It is announced by Secretary Loeb that the President will receive few callers at Sagamore Hill this Summer, and those who hope to see him will be obliged to make engagements through Mr. Loeb in advance of their arrival at Oyster Bay...The President will devote his mornings to the transaction of executive business and his afternoons to recreation and rest. During the afternoons, too, he will receive such callers as may have engagements with him or those whom he may invite to Sagamore Hill...

...The executive offices selected for Secretaries Loeb and Barnes and the clerical force this year are much more commodious and convenient than those occupied last year.

President Roosevelt will spend no time in the offices, as his work will be done in the library...*(NY Times,* June 29, 1903)

On June 30, 1903, Gov. Hunt of Porto Rico, Senator Long of Kansas, and ex-Postmaster General William S. Bissell of Buffalo were the President's guests.

> OYSTER BAY, June, 30 — ...After a conference with Gov. Hunt, the President signed a formal order making reservations of lands in the Island of Porto Rico for the purpose of this Government. The action was taken under the provisions of a law passed at the first session of the Fifty-seventh Congress, which authorized the President to make the reservations before July 1, 1903. All lands not reserved will accrue to-morrow to the Island of Porto Rico...
>
> ...Things have now settled down to the regular routine of Summer work by the Executive and his force here. The office force to-day got down to hard work and caught up with the matters which had accumulated while it was getting settled in its new quarters. *(NY Times, July 1, 1903)*

On July 1, 1903, the President's position regarding the B'nei B'rith petition to the Russian Government was announced from Oyster Bay. The B'nei B'rith petition was in response to the Kishineff Pogrom that occurred in Russia earlier in 1903. This and other acts of anti-semitism were occurring in Russia during the years 1902-03. Many influential Americans were appalled to learn that the Czar and the local Russian rulers were either turning a blind eye to the massacres or were assisting those who were carrying them out. Therefore, they felt that the President, as leader of the United States, should deliver a petition from American citizens of all religions, pleading for religious liberty and tolerance in Russia.

> OYSTER BAY, N.Y., July 1, 1903 — Action by the United States Government in transmitting the petition of citizens of this country of the Jewish and of other religious faiths will not be affected by the inspired pronouncement of the Russian Government given to the public to-day. It evidently is the intention of the Administration to forward the petition to the Russian Government as soon as it is in readiness.
>
> This is rendered certain by a statement made here to-night by authority, which says that "the action of the Administration in reference to the outrages on the Russian Jews would be wholly unaffected by any newspaper publication purporting to emanate from the Russian Government or by any communication not properly forwarded to the State Department."
>
> President Roosevelt declined to discuss for publication the statement authorized by the Russian Government. He said that any presentation of the position of this Government properly ought to come from the State Department. *(NY Times, July 2, 1903)*

On July 2, Secretary Loeb received a telegram from Francis Loomis, Acting Secretary of State, regarding the petition to the Russian Government.

RECEIVED at July 2/03

2 w wn pc 85 paid govt

Washington DC 2

Wm Loeb Jr
Secty to the President, OYSTER BAY N.Y.

Simon Wolf says that if petition is to be signed by
leading men in the principal cities of the country irrespective of faith
as was arranged it cannot reach Washington before July tenth, he
can, however, furnish the petition signed by the executive
Committee who called on the President in their representative
capacity if it is so desired and it could be forwarded and additional
names added by cable if necessary.

Francis B Loomis,
Acting Secretary.

11;15 a

(TR Papers, Series 1, Reel 34)

In the evening of the same day Secretary Loeb received another telegram from Mr.
Loomis regarding a statement reportedly made by the Russian Ambassador to the
United States, Count Cassini.

RECEIVED at July 2/03

Dated *White House Washington DC 2*
To *Hon Wm Loeb. Secy to the Prest*
OyBay. NY

*Count Cassini called today to present his secretary who is to act
as charge when he sails for Europe next Tuesday. Cassini said
that his statement of yesterday was called forth by a newspaper
report in St. Petersburg to the effect that he had made abject
official apologies or explanations to the President respecting the
Kishineff massacre. He did not explain the last part of his
statement respecting Russia's categorical refusal to receive any
representation from any power.*

Francis B Loomis

(TR Papers, Series 1, Reel 34)

On July 2, 1903, it was announced that President Roosevelt, Gov. Taft, King Edward of England and Emperor William of Germany would be the chief actors on the Fourth of July, in the opening of the Commercial Pacific Cable between the United States and the Philippines. This was the first telegraphic message sent around the world.

> ...The message of President Roosevelt, which will be the first sent, will be put on the wire at his Oyster Bay home by George H. Usher, General Manager of the Commercial Cable Company. From Oyster Bay it will go direct to San Francisco; thence to Hawaii, to the Midway Islands, to Guam, and to Manila.
>
> Copied there from its fifth relay, the message will be given to Gov. Taft, whose congratulatory reply will be ready on the moment. The sixth relay will bring the message to Hong Kong, the seventh to Bombay, the eight to St. Petersburg, the ninth to Moscow, the tenth to Berlin, the eleventh to London, and the twelfth and last, back direct to Oyster Bay, where General Manager Usher will copy it.
>
> Following the sending of this message Emperor William and King Edward will exchange greetings, and then each will send to President Roosevelt congratulations on the completion of the cable and best wishes for the Nation's holiday. Simple ceremonies will attend the transmission of the message at Oyster Bay. There will be a gathering of distinguished men, representatives of the National Government and officials of the cable company, and short addresses will be made...(*NY Times*, July 2, 1903)

On July 3, the laying of the Pacific cable was completed and the final connections were being made for the transmission of the first global telegraph message, transmitted from Oyster Bay.

> HONOLULU, July 3 — The cable ship Anglia arrived here this morning bearing the Honolulu end of the transpacific cable, now extending from Manila via Guam and Midway Islands to this port. The cable will be landed at once and connected with the section of the line from Honolulu to San Francisco, already in operation.
>
> Unless some untoward event should occur, the complete line will be in operation by to-morrow morning, in accordance with the announcement made long since by Clarence Mackay, President of the Pacific Commercial Cable Company. No hitch in the arrangements is anticipated, and the first message over the new line will almost certainly be transmitted by President Roosevelt to Gov. Taft promptly at noon to-morrow... (*NY Times*, July 4, 1903)

On July 3, 1903, it was also made clear from the State Department that many officials there believed that the President's decision to forward the B'nei B'rith Petition to the Russian Government would be a serious mistake, having repercussions both for the Jews of Russia and for the relationship between the United States and Russia.

> WASHINGTON, July 3 — The relations between the United States and Russia are likely to become somewhat strained by recent publications in regard to the Kishineff matter. Experienced diplomats here are inclined to the belief that the utterances on both sides are likely to produce bitterness of feeling, but

at the same time believe that the incident will finally terminate with the offer of the petition of the B'nei B'rith and its respectful declination on the part of Russia to receive it.

The semi-official utterance from the State Department on Wednesday, in which it was said in effect that the President would send the petition to St. Petersburg notwithstanding the positive declaration on the part of the Russian Foreign Office that it would be refused, is regarded by many conservative persons as unfortunate and impolitic, and as calculated to interfere with the effort to insure the Jewish people in Russia against further persecution. It is the understanding that the utterance given out by Assistant Secretary Loomis was authorized by Oyster Bay...*(NY Times*, July 4, 1903)

Also on July 3, Assistant Secretary Forster arranged for a picture of the President to be sent to the Sultan of Morocco.

WHITE HOUSE,
WASHINGTON.

July 3,1903

Personal.

MEMORANDUM FOR SECRETARY LOEB:

This morning I received through Mr. Smithers, a telephone message from Mr. Sydney Y. Smith, Chief of the Diplomatic Bureau, Department of State, who said he was speaking from Acting Secretary Loomis, to the effect that Mr. Langerman, who was to carry a letter from the President to the Sultan of Morocco, was at the Department with a note from the President asking him to get from the office a photograph to take back to Oyster Bay for inscription to the Sultan, and that Mr. Langerman would come over to see me. On this instruction I, of course, gave to Mr. Langerman the best photograph I could find, a very large Pach picture, and also sent to Clinedinst for a horseback picture, the best he had ready. I then, at the request of Mr. Langerman telegraphed you asking if the letter from the President to the Sultan could be signed early enough in the morning to enable Mr. Langerman's messenger to leave Oyster Bay on the 8:50 A.M. train. On the receipt of your answer I told Mr. Langerman not to wait, that the letter would go through the regular diplomatic channels, but he said he would wait anyhow, that there were no regular diplomatic channels to the interior. I immediately telephoned to the State Department, trying to get Mr. Loomis, but was informed that he was engaged, and that Mr. Smith of the Diplomatic Bureau was out. Finally I talked with Chief Clerk Michael and asked that he immediately explain the situation to Mr. Loomis. Mr. Michael was evidently not very clear in his explanation as Mr. Loomis came over to see me a few moments afterwards and I told him personally.

I regret very much that the best photograph in the office is
gone, but after receipt of the message from the State Department that
the President desired Mr. Langerman to bring him a photograph for
the Sultan, I felt that I was justified in treating him as the chosen
messenger of the President and in giving him every attention and
assistance in my power.

This memorandum is sent so that you may be fully advised
of all that has been done in the office in the matter.

Rudolph Forster.
Assistant Secretary

(TR Papers, Series 1, Reel 34)

Assistant Secretary Forster also sent a telegram to Secretary Loeb with the correct
spelling of the Sultan's name.

RECEIVED at   Oyster Bay NY   July 3/03

MEMO.

Secty Loeb

The State Dept advises that the following is official title of
the Sultan of Morocco "His Sheriffian Majesty Moulai Abd-El-Aziz
Sultan of Fez, tafibalt, Marakech And Sus, Emir - Al - Moumenin,
Etcetc.
Rudolph Forster.

Asst. Secty

446 p

(TR Papers, Series 1, Reel 34)

The following day, Secretary Loeb received a letter from Acting Secretary Loomis
regarding the same letter and the matter of the petition to the Russian Government
regarding the Kishinoff massacre.

DEPARTMENT OF STATE
WASHINGTON

July 4, 1903.

Honorable William Loeb, Jr.,
    Secretary to the President,
        Oyster Bay, Long Island.

My dear Mr. Loeb:

      My cipher cable to you in reference to Langerman
was sent an hour or more before your cable in reference to the same
gentleman, directing that the letter to the Sultan be forwarded
through the regular channels, reached me. I was glad to hear from
you on the subject, but of course did not know until your message
came that you had been warned concerning him.

      I enclose an article on the Chairmanship in this morning's
"Post" which you may find interesting.

      I judge from the tone of the foreign press despatches that the
President's statement addressed to Russia hit the mark just as
effectively as did his telegram from Walla Walla. You will see that
the Russian press has branched off on the question of the refusal of
the Russian Government to honor American passports when
presented by Jewish citizens. This is a very important point and I
enclose a clipping which the President may like to see, if he has not
already done so. We are in position morally, and diplomatically to
make a strong fight for recognition of our passports, no matter what
may be the religious faith of the citizen who bears them and I think it
would be very wise after the other points are cleared up to make an
issue of this matter for our contention is right and proper and just
and would enlist the active sympathy and support of the public.

      Very truly yours,

Francis B Loomis

Enclosures:
    Newspaper clippings.

(TR Papers, Series 1, Reel 34)

On July Fourth, 1903, prior to sending the first trans-global telegraph message,
President Roosevelt attended the village of Huntington's 250th anniversary celebration.

    HUNTINGTON, L.I., July 4 — The old town of Huntington, rich in memories
of a historic past, rich in a heroic tradition, voiced many times during the
anniversary exercises to-day, is richer to-night by the knowledge that in the

celebration that marked the town's two hundred and fiftieth birthday as well as the one hundred and twenty-seventh of the Union, the Nation's President was the central figure.

President Roosevelt talked for almost an hour, addressing himself directly to the veterans of the Grand Army of the Republic, and shaping the message of his words about the lesson which their service taught the men of their own and all coming times. From this point of departure the President voiced his thought on the duties of citizenship, the need of honesty in public life as in private, the need of robust virtues, and, in a word on international affairs, the continuing need of a navy able to cope with the best that might be sent against the country...*(NY Times*, July 5, 1903)

*FIGURE 15: The President, speaking in Huntington, L.I. at the town's
250th anniversary celebration.
Courtesy of Sagamore Hill*

The President was joined by Secretary Loeb at the Huntington celebration.

Mrs. Roosevelt and Secretary William Loeb, Jr., accompanied the President who was attended by representatives of the reception committee...The President and Mrs. Roosevelt, Mayor Low and Secretary Loeb chatted a few moments upon the platform...*(East Norwich Enterprise*, July 11, 1903)

Although it was reported that the President never visited Moore's Building (*East Norwich Enterprise*, July 22, 1905), July 4, 1903 was one of the few times President Roosevelt is said to have been inside. However, there is no documentation to support this. On this historic occasion, Roosevelt sent a message to Governor William Taft in Manila, the Philippines, greeting him and the Philippine people at the completion of the trans-Pacific cable, the last link in the trans-global telegraph system.

The first official message over the new cable was sent at 10:50 P.M. by President Roosevelt at Oyster Bay to Gov. Taft at Manila. The message read as follows:

Oyster Bay, July 4

Gov. Taft, Manila: I open the American Pacific cable with greeting to you and the people of the Philippines.

THEODORE ROOSEVELT

...President Roosevelt then sent a message around the world westward to Clarence H. Mackay, who was with Mr. Roosevelt at Oyster Bay, the message being given to the operator at 11:23 P.M. and received by Mr. Mackay at 11:35 P.M. making the time around the world twelve minutes. The message was as follows:

Oyster Bay, N.Y., July 4, 1903

Clarence H. Mackay, President Pacific Cable Company Oyster Bay, N.Y.:
Congratulations and success to the Pacific cable which the genius of your lamented father and your own enterprise made possible.

THEODORE ROOSEVELT

(NY Times, July 5, 1903)

Mr. Taft sent his reply to Washington and Mr. Mackay sent his to the President at Oyster Bay. The replies were received at 11:20 P.M. and 12:02:45 A.M. respectively.

Manila July 4th 1903.
President,
       Washington.
The Filipino people and the American residents in the Islands are glad to present their respectful greetings and congratulations to the President of United States conveyed over the Cable with which American enterprise has girded the Pacific thereby rendering greatly easier and more frequent communication between the two countries It will certainly lead to a closer union and a better mutual understanding of each others aim and sympathies and their common interest in the prosperity of the Philippines and the education and development of the Filipinos. It is not inappropriate to incorporate in this the first message across the Pacific from the Philippines to America an earnest plea for the reduction of the tariff on Filipino products in accordance with the broad and liberal spirit which the American people desire to manifest toward the Filipinos and of which you have been an earnest exponent.

Taft. Manila.

(TR Papers, Series 1, Reel 34)

Oyster Bay July 4th 1903.

The President
          Oyster Bay.
I thank you deeply for your message and I earnestly hope that the
Pacific Cable by opening the wide horizon of the great East may
prove a useful factor to the commerce of the United-States.

Clarence H. Mackay.

(TR Papers, Series 1, Reel 34)

The Executive Offices and the Executive Staff's duties were described in the first local
paper to be printed since the President returned to Oyster Bay.

The new executive offices in Moore's building were opened for business
early Monday morning. Secretary Loeb and his assistants, without any formalities, began their work of sorting the large mail pouch of letters, official
and personal, the newspapers and departmental documents. Such as could be
attended to on the spot were handed to Assistant Secretary Barnes, who proceeded to go through them with the same dispatch that characterizes the routine at the White House. Those communications that required the personal
attention of President Roosevelt were bundled up and taken to Sagamore Hill
by Secretary Loeb. The President had finished his breakfast and was waiting
for the secretary in the big library, so no time was lost in getting to work. The
President paced about the room or lounged in one of the easy chairs while dictating his correspondence, and the secretary was at the flat top desk upon
which the long distance telephone receiver stands. (*East Norwich Enterprise*,
July 4, 1903.)

On July 6, the commander of the U.S.S. Sylph, the President's yacht, wrote to Mr. Loeb
regarding the President's travel arrangements.

U.S.S. SYLPH,
Oyster Bay, N.Y.,
July 6, 1903

My dear Mr. Loeb:-

I was mistaken when I told the President the SYLPH could run to West Park in four hours. I took it to be opposite Hyde Park, a little above Yonkers. It is (as you told me) a few miles above Poughkeepsie and I would say nine instead of four hours from here.

The pilot on board has taken the DOLPHIN and the Olympia up the Hudson at night and I would suggest that the Presidential party leave here about four or five in the afternoon and run up the river at night; we will have a moon and it ought to be a pleasant trip. hoping you are very well,

Yours truly,

C. F. Preston

Wm. Loeb, Esq.,
Secretary to the President
Oyster Bay, N.Y.

P.S. I did not have charts (which should be here tomorrow) as far up as West Park + the Pilot misunderstood me as to the location of West Park.

C. F. P.

(TR Papers, Series 1, Reel 34)

On July 7, Acting Secretary of State Loomis wrote to Secretary Loeb regarding final preparations for the President's letter to the Sultan of Morocco.

DEPARTMENT OF STATE,
WASHINGTON

July 7, 1903

Dear Mr. Loeb:

The letter for the Sultan of Morocco will have to be signed by the President, and I enclose it herewith for that purpose. It is usual for the President to sign before the head of the Department of State, but in order to save the time necessary for sending it to him and returning it for my signature I have signed it to-day.

Respectfully yours,

Francis B. Loomis

Hon. William Loeb Jr.,
Secretary to the President
Oyster Bay, N.Y.

(TR Papers, Series 1, Reel 34)

Also on July 7, 1903 Secretary of State, John Hay, conferred with the President at Sagamore Hill.

> OYSTER BAY, N.Y., July 7 — Secretary of State John Hay is a guest of President Roosevelt to-night at Sagamore Hill. Matters of grave importance to this country, in its international relations, were under consideration during the afternoon and evening.
>
> The conclusions reached at the conference are not disclosed...Most of their attention was given to two subjects of serious concern. They considered in all its phases the Russian situation, particularly with respect to the B'nei B'rith petition, which it has been determined will be forwarded to the Russian Government, and the Alaskan boundary question, which next month is to be taken up for what is hoped may be a final adjustment by the American and British Commission in London...Secretary Hay arrived here from Newport, R.I., where he has been visiting his daughter...He was accompanied by Senator Fairbanks of Indiana. Senator Thomas Kearns of Utah arrived on the same train, although he did not meet the other two until they alighted at the Oyster Bay station. The party was met by one of the executive carriages and driven direct to Sagamore Hill.
>
> Prior to their arrival at the President's home Senator Hanna of Ohio, accompanied by Mrs. Hanna...had reached Sagamore Hill... *(NY Times*, July 8, 1903)

The following day, July 8, some of the conclusions of the conference were made public from the Executive Office. It was announced from the Executive Office that the following week a conference would be held between the President and Oscar S. Straus (who would in 1906 become the first Jew to hold a cabinet position,) Simon Wolf, and Leo N. Levi regarding the B'nei B'rith petition.

> OYSTER BAY, N.Y., July 8 — President Roosevelt and Secretary Hay concluded their conference at a late hour last night. The Secretary left Sagamore Hill shortly after 8 o'clock this morning...
>
> ...It is understood that the exact method of procedure relative to the B'nei B'rith petition to the Russian Government has not been determined. The petition itself has not been completed, and it can be said that the President deeply regrets the delay in placing the document in his hands.
>
> Next week, probably on Tuesday, the President expects to have a conference at Sagamore Hill with three of the Jewish citizens who have promoted the idea of forwarding a petition to the Russian Government. Simon Wolf of Washington and Oscar S. Straus and Leon N. Levy of New York will take luncheon with the President. It is expected that the petition, which has been revised by its authors, will be handed to the President at that time. In any event the subject will be considered extensively...*(NY Times*, July 9, 1903)

Secretary Loeb made the necessary arrangements for the conference by telegraph.

RECEIVED at   Oyster Bay NY July 8/03
       3 ny yf pc   46 Paid

New York   NY   8

Wm Loeb Jr,
              Secretary to the President
                          Oyster Bay NY

The request contained in your telegram to Simon Wolf asking me to
call on the President only reached me last evening. I shall be glad to
call whenever convenient for the President. My office address is
forty two Warren Street telephone number 450 Cortlandt.

                          Oscar S Straus.

       11:20 a

(TR Papers, Series 1, Reel 34)

The Secretary also received a letter from the commander of the Sylph, C.F. Preston
finalizing arrangements for the President's voyage to West Park.

                                    U.S.S. SYLPH,
                                    Oyster Bay, N.Y.,
                                    July 8, 1903
My dear Mr. Loeb:-

       The SYLPH will be ready as the President wishes after
dinner Thursday evening to leave for West Park. I simply
suggested 5.00 p.m. as an extra precaution in case it was cloudy.
Will you please let me know when and where to have the launch to
bring off the President and Mrs. Roosevelt ?

                          Sincerely yours,

                              C.F. Preston

                              Lieutenant, U.S.N.,
                                Commanding.

Wm. Loeb, Esq.,
       Secretary to the President,
       Oyster Bay, N.Y.

(TR Papers, Series 1, Reel 34)

From Washington, it was announced that the Manchurian question between China and Russia, wherein China asked President Roosevelt to mediate, would be put off until after the B'nei B'rith petition had been sent.

> WASHINGTON, July 9 — The President has decided that the matter of the Jewish petition must be finally disposed of before any further effort is made here to compose the issues arising out of the Manchurian situation. Therefore it is now said that nothing is likely to be done in regard to Manchuria until next September, by which time, according to the last Russian agreement, the evacuation of Manchuria by Russian troops, save railroad guards, should be complete...
>
> ...The President is being deluged with singly signed petitions in behalf of the Russian Jews, and these are being forwarded from Oyster Bay to the State Department by every mail. The petitions are identical and declare that the action of the United States Government in the case of the Roumanian Jews warrants even more vigorous action in the case of the Russian Jews, wherefore the President is petitioned "to employ the good offices of our Government with the Imperial Government of Russia, with the aim of securing more safety to Jews in Russia, and making their existence there less wretched."
>
> As the petitions are directed to the President alone, no question of transmission to Russia is involved, and they are being filed at the State Department. *(NY Times,* July 10, 1903)

Assistant Secretary Barnes often took over Mr. Loeb's duties when the latter vacationed. The announcement that the Executive Secretary was leaving was made from the Executive Offices.

> OYSTER BAY, N.Y., July 10 — ...Secretary Loeb will leave to-morrow for Albany, N.Y., and Lake George, where he will spend a month's vacation. Assistant Secretary B.F. Barnes will be in charge of the executive offices in the absence of Mr. Loeb. *(NY Times,* July 11, 1903)

On July 13, Secretary of War, Elihu Root was a guest of the President at Sagamore Hill. They discussed the pending investigation of army contracts, the Alaskan boundary question, and some problems relating to the Philippines, as well as some departmental matters requiring the President's attention. They also announced that Robert Shaw Oliver would be appointed to be Assistant Secretary of War, to succeed William Cary Anger, resigned. *(NY Times,* July 13 & 14, 1903)

On July 14, 1903, the conference between the President and the Jewish committee on the Kishineff petition took place, as planned the prior week.

> OYSTER BAY, L.I., July 14 — Oscar S. Straus and Leo N. Levi of New York and Simon S. Wolf of Washington had a conference with the President at Sagamore Hill to-day regarding the petition to the Russian Government on the Kishinoff outrages.
>
> The Administration has been embarrassed by the delay of the representatives of the B'nei B'rith Society in presenting the petition. The draft of the docu-

ment was handed to the President several weeks ago by Mr. Wolf. But it was decided after some consideration to modify the text of the petition before presenting it formally to this Government for transmittal to Russia. Time was desired, too, to obtain to the petition the signatures of representative citizens of the United States of all religious faiths. As a result the document was not placed in the hands of the President until to-day.

Inasmuch as the Russian Government has indicated by the adoption of severe measures a genuine disposition to punish adequately the perpetrators of the Kishinoff murders and, in addition, those who instigated them, it is a problem for the President and Secretary Hay to solve whether representations concerning the incident now are either desirable or necessary.

It is suggested that the whole matter may be resolved into a brief statement through diplomatic channels to the Russian Foreign Office that such a petition is in the hands of the United States, thus leaving it to Russia to say whether it would or would not receive the document if it were presented. It would close the incident without subjecting the United States relations with Russia to a strain, and, it is regarded, would be quite as effective as the actual presentation of the petition...*(NY Times,* July 15, 1903)

In the late afternoon on the 14th Acting Secretary of State Francis Loomis sent a telegram to the President regarding a statement made by Count Cassini regarding the Russian Government's opinion of the proposed Kishineff petition.

T ny yf pc 84 Collect Govt   July 14/03

Springfield Ohio 14

The President,   Oyster Bay NY

Secretary Hay wires me you have been informed that Cassini told me officially the Russian Government would not receive Petition.

This is a misunderstanding, Cassini said he hoped it would not be sent and intimated in an academic sense his government was opposed to the idea *of the* petition but he did not say officially to me that Russian government would not receive it. He said the statement he gave to the Papers was official however.

Francis B Loomis.

4:35 p

(TR Papers, Series 1, Reel 35)

The members of the committee made a statement regarding the conference the following day.

OYSTER BAY, L.I., July 15 — ...In accordance with the understanding at Oyster Bay on Tuesday, Leo N. Levi gave out the following statement yesterday regarding the conference between the President and the Jewish committee on the Kishineff petition:

"The conference was entirely satisfactory to us. Our views and those of the President are in perfect accord. It has been decided that it would not be well at the present to make public any details of the conference. An official statement will be made by the State Department at Washington. In the meantime it is desired and expected that the petitions now being circulated for signatures should be signed and mailed so as to reach me in ten days. The returns thus far received indicate that uniformly throughout the country, the petition is being signed by the most prominent and representative men."

In addition Mr. Levi said:

"Some very erroneous impressions have been formed, which it is important to correct immediately. This is not easy within the limitations imposed by State considerations. I venture, however, to say that the petition has not been modified in any particular: that no reason exists for discontinuing the signing of the petitions: that it is desired that they should be signed for a week longer, and then sent to me, and that the most perfect accord exists between us and the President.

"Our course has his full approval, and his is in every respect just as we desire it to be. There are no differences of any kind whatsoever, and there has been no receding. I have wired the Executive Committee of the B'nei B'rith throughout the country that the situation is entirely satisfactory and to go ahead with the lists, but to send them in, so as to reach me in ten days.

"It should be distinctly understood that the petition is neither a protest nor a remonstrance. It does not seek to interfere in Russian affairs. Finally, it is not a petition by Jews, but in behalf of them. It is a petition by Americans regardless of religious affiliations." *(NY Times, July 16, 1903)*

Oscar Straus sent a telegram to the President at Oyster Bay at noon on July 15 regarding the petition.

5 ny yf pc 11 Paid   July 15/03

Washington D.C., 15

President Roosevelt,
                    OYSTER BAY N.Y.

Have executed your commission delivered papers to Hay all as directed.

                    Oscar S. Straus.

12 NOON

Secretary of State John Hay confirmed this in a separate telegram to the President.

8 NY YF PC 12 DH   July 15/03

Washington D.C., 15

President,
   OYSTER BAY N.Y.

Mr. S has been here, your instructions will go to Riddle today.

John Hay

12:55 p

(TR Papers, Series 1, Reel 35)

On July 16, 1903, President Roosevelt expressed to Senator Lodge of Massachusetts his desire that early action should be taken by Congress regarding financial legislation that would provide for a more elastic currency and for the general relief of the country in a financial way. Consequently, he announced he would call for an early session of Congress on November 9, 1903 to consider such legislation and to approve the treaty ratified by the Senate in the Spring. The President also received a letter from the Sultan of Morocco on the 16th *(NY Times*, July 17, 1903)

It was also reported that China would open several ports that had been closed to foreign trade. This was one of the great foreign policy successes of Mr. Roosevelt's first term.

WASHINGTON, July 16 — The Manchuria question has been settled, the open door is assured, and the State Department, under Mr. Hay's direction, has met with another success. China has agreed to open as treaty ports several ports now closed to the world's trade, and Russia assents...

While the ports to be opened are not yet specified, it is gathered from the communications received that they are Moukden, the principal inland port of Manchuria, and Ta Tung Kao, at the mouth of the Yalu River. The State Department is highly gratified at this outcome, feeling that it has secured, not only for American commerce, but for the commerce of the world at large, a very substantial gain...

It now remains for Minister Conger to define in the trade treaty which he is negotiating with China the terms and conditions under which the new ports are to be opened... *(NY Times*, July 17, 1903)

On July 16 the President received a long telegram sent by Secretary Hay to the Executive Offices in Oyster Bay. It contained the news of Russia's refusal to accept the Kishinoff petition.

T.R.'s Summer White House, Oyster Bay

WESTERN UNION TELEGRAPH CO.

——— INCORPORATED ———

message NEWSPAPER SPECIAL REPORT. *message*

SEND BY WESTERN UNION LINES

Page.........
Letter........

2wh Gi Wn 313 Pd Gvt
    White House Washington DC July 16 - 1903
The President
            OyBay Ny
Following just recd from Petersburg: Secy of State.
Washington. Minister for Foreign affairs after returning
yesterday afternoon from Seeing the Emperor, summer palace of
Peterhoff, sent for me and said that he wished to speak
confidentially and in a friendly way on subject which has lately
filled the newspapers. He said he had seen that a Jewish petition
addressed to the Emperor of Russia was about to be forwarded to
the Embassy under the auspices of the govt of the U.S. As he
wishes to avoid all friction and did not wish to be under the
necessity of offering the least discourtesy to me personally, he
thought it would be better to notify me informally that such a
petition would not be recd. If I delivered it to him in person he
would at once hand it back without looking at it. If I sent it
accompanied by an official note he would at once place it in
another envelope and return it to me unopened, unread; that the
Emperor whose will is the sole law of the land has no need of
information from outside sources as to what is taking place within
his dominions, and that even a respectful petition or prayer
relating to international matters could not be rec'd from
foreigners. The Emperor's kindly feeling toward America and the
minister's own esteem for the Embassy, made them desirous of
avoiding the smallest diplomatic incident. This prompted his
present conversation, but the Russian Govt did not think that any
sovereign state whether big and powerful, or little and weak,
could permit observations on the management of its internal
affairs to reach it officially from outside.
        Your cipher telegram just received this morning. In view of
the foregoing statement of Minister for Foreign Affairs for
Russia I shall consider your instructions as already carried out
by the present report unless I am ordered to take further steps.
                Riddle

        John Hay

Early in the morning on July 17, 1903, Secretary of State John Hay, in consultation with the President, released the story to the press. Mr. Hay briefed the President in a telegram to Oyster Bay.

1w f pc 32 DH   July 17/03
SD Washington D.C.17

The President,   Oyster-Bay NY

                    Could not execute your instructions
last night. It arrived at midnight and documents were inaccessible.
I have given the story to Press this morning and written letters to
Straus, Levi and Wolf.

                    John Hay

    10 A.M.

(TR Papers, Series 1, Reel 35)

Following Mr. Hay's telegram, Leo N. Levi sent a telegram to the President as well. In it he concurred with the President that all the documents relating to the petition should be released to the press.

3 NY YF PC   82 paid   July 17/03

New York NY 17

The President,   Oyster-Bay NY

        Unless for some reason satisfactory to your-self you have
    changed your mind, might I suggest that your original plan be
    carried out, namely, that the State Dept give out in full to the press
    the note to Riddle and from him to the Russian Government. It
    would seem to us desirable for the purpose of removing false
    impressions and of closing the incident on all sides, both here and
    abroad, in the most satisfactory way. Cannot consult Wolf, Straus
    concurs in this.

                    Leo N Levi.
    11:50 A

(TR Papers, Series 1, Reel 35)

On July 17, 1903 the State Department made public the text of the petition sent on July 15 to Mr. Riddle, the American Chargé d'Affaires in St. Petersburg and his orders to present the same to the Russian Foreign Office. These letters and the story behind them were printed the following day.

OYSTER BAY, L.I., July 17 — The action of the Russian Government in declining to receive the B'nei B'rith petition or any other representation regarding the Kishinoff massacres was not unexpected by President Roosevelt, as it had been forecasted unofficially. The information of Russia's declination was received here late last night in a long telegram from Secretary Hay. The telegram was sent immediately by special messenger to the President at Sagamore Hill. Toward midnight the President sent Secretary Hay an extended reply. It is known that the President requested the Secretary to make public the action of the Government respecting the incident...*(NY Times,* July 18, 1903)

WASHINGTON, July 17 — The State Department to-day made public the correspondence that has taken place in connection with the Kishinoff petition, which Russia has refused to receive. At the same time it was announced by Secretary Hay that the incident created by the presentation of the petition is closed...

...The official statement of the facts is as follows:

The Russian Government has declined to receive or consider the petition in relation to the condition of the Jews in Russia signed by several thousand citizens, and cabled to St. Petersburg by direction of the President.

At the conference Tuesday, the 14th of July, at Oyster Bay, the President conferred with Messrs. Leo N. Levi, Simon Wolf, and Oscar S. Straus in regard to the presentation of the petition, and decided to send the following dispatch to Mr. Riddle, the American Chargé d'Affaires in St. Petersburg:

Department of State
Washington, July 15, 1903

Riddle, St. Petersburg:

You are instructed to ask an audience of the Minister of Foreign Affairs and to make to him the following communication:

"Excellency: The Secretary of State instructs me to inform you that the President has received from a large number of citizens of the United States of all religious affiliations and occupying the highest positions in both public and private life, a respectful petition addressed to his Majesty the Emperor, relating to the condition of Jews in Russia, and running as follows:

" ' To His Imperial Majesty the Emperor of Russia:

" ' The cruel outrages perpetrated at Kishineff during Easter of 1903 have excited horror and reprobation throughout the world.

Until your Majesty gave special and personal directions the local authorities failed to maintain order or suppress the rioting.

" ' The victims were Jews, and the assault was the result of race and religious prejudice.

" ' The rioters violated the laws of Russia.

" ' The local officials were derelict in the performance of their duty.

" ' The Jews were the victims of indefensible lawlessness. These facts are made plain by the official reports of and by the official acts following the riot.

" ' Under ordinary conditions the awful calamity would be deplored without undue fear of a recurrence. But such is not the case in the present instance. Your petitioners are advised that millions of Jews - Russian subjects - dwelling in Southwestern Russia, are in constant dread of fresh outbreaks. They feel that ignorance, superstition, and bigotry, as exemplified by the rioters, are ever ready to persecute them; that the local officials, unless thereunto specially admonished, cannot be relied on as strenuous protectors of their peace and security; that a public sentiment of hostility has been engendered against them, and hangs over them as a continuing menace.

" ' Even if it be conceded that these fears are to some extent exaggerated, it is unquestionably true that they exist, that they are not groundless, and that they produce effects of great importance.

" ' The westward migration of Russian Jews, which has proceeded for over twenty years, is being stimulated by these fears, and already that movement has become so great as to overshadow in magnitude the expulsion of the Jews from Spain and to rank with the exodus from Egypt.

" ' No estimate is possible of the misery suffered by the hapless Jews who feel driven to forsake their native land, to sever the most sacred ties, and to wander forth to strange countries. Neither is it possible to estimate the misery suffered by those who are unwilling or unable to leave the land of their birth, who must part from friends and relatives who emigrate, who remain in never ending terror.

" ' Religious persecution is more sinful and more fatuous even than war. War is sometimes necessary, honorable, and just; religious persecution is never defensible.

" ' The sinfulness and folly which give impulse to unnecessary war received their greatest check when your Majesty's initiative resulted in an international court of peace.

" ' With such an example before it the civilized world cherishes the hope that upon the same initiative there shall be fixed in the early days of the twentieth century the enduring principle of religious liberty; that by a gracious and convincing expression your Majesty will proclaim, not only for the government of your own subjects, but also for the guidance of all civilized men, that none shall suffer in person, property, liberty, honor, or life because of his religious belief; that the humblest subject or citizen may worship according to the dictates of his own conscience, and that government, whatever its form or agencies, must safeguard these rights and immunities by the exercise of all its powers.

" ' Far removed from your Majesty's dominions, living under different conditions, and owing allegiance to another government, your petitioners yet venture, in the name of civilization, to plead for religious liberty and tolerance; to plead that he who led his own people and all others to the shrine of peace will add new lustre to his reign and fame by leading a new movement that shall commit the whole world in opposition to religious persecutions.'

" I am instructed to ask whether the petition will be received by your Excellency to be submitted to the gracious consideration of his Majesty. In that case the petition will be at once forwarded to St. Petersburg.

"I avail myself, &c."

You will report at the earliest possible your execution of this instruction. HAY. *(NY Times,* July 18, 1903)

On July 18th, as Pope Leo lay on his deathbed, Acting Secretary of State Loomis sent a telegraph to Acting Secretary B.F. Barnes requesting Mr. Barnes to get the President's approval of the text of a message that he would send to the Pope's representative.

1 wh jm pc 67 Paid Govt   July 18/03

Washington DC   18

Hon B F Barnes,   Acting Secretary to the President,
                             Oyster-Bay NY.

     Please ask the President if the following message to Cardinal Rampolla will be satisfactory: the President directs me to convey through you appropriate expression of his sincere sympathy with His Holiness in this hour of supreme suspense, and to request that he be advised of the condition of the venerable sufferer"

                    F B Loomis,   Acting Secty

1045 a

(TR Papers, Series 1, Reel 35)

Cardinal Gibbons replied to Mr. Loomis's telegraph on July 19th. The telegraph was sent from Rome to Mr. Loomis in Washington and from there to Mr. Barnes in Oyster Bay.

RECEIVED at   *7 /19* 1903

Dated *White House. Washington DC 19*
To *Memo for the Secretary to the*
               President. OBay NY

The following message received Rome to Mr. Francis B. Loomis Acting Secretary of State Washington. I beg of you to present in his holiness name to his excellency the President the warmest and most sincere thanks for his sympathy towards his holiness in this hour of dreadful suspense and I am very sorry to advise you that unfortunately the condition of the august sufferer is becoming very dangerous. Cardinal Gibbons. Secretary Loomis inquires of the President if he shall give these to the Press.

(TR Papers, Series 1, Reel 35)

The President's statement of condolence was prepared in advance of the Pope's death and was sent from Oyster Bay to Washington. It was held there until the Pope died and then was transmitted to Rome and given out to the press.

RECEIVED at   *July 20*

Dated *White House, Washington DC 20*
To *Hon B F Barnes*
            Actg Secy., OyBay NY

The message of condolence was left by Secy Hay with instructions to send it when Pope died. It was therefore transmitted and given to the press before arrival of your telegram.

Fr. B Loomis

(*TR Papers*, Series 1, Reel 35)

However, on July 21, 1903, it was reported that President Roosevelt, on being informed of the death of Pope Leo, dictated the following statement:

> OYSTER BAY, L.I., July 20 — ..."The President expressed his profound regret at the death of the venerable Pontiff, whose long career no less than his exalted character has commanded the respect of all Christendom. The President said that in uttering these sentiments he was giving expression to the feeling of all the people of the United States, wholly without regard to their religious faiths." (*NY Times*, July 21, 1903)

On July 22, the bookbinder's union announced that the President's action to reinstate W.A. Miller, assistant foreman in the Government Printing Office, after he had been dismissed, may cause a strike by every bookbinder in the Government Printing Office as well as members of its allied unions. (*NY Times*, July 23, 1903)

Also on July 22, 1903, the President had several guests at Sagamore Hill. Among them were Morris Belknap, the Republican nominee for Governor of Kentucky, who discussed with the President the political situation in Kentucky; Senator T.C. Platt of New York and ex-Senator and Mrs. Turner of Washington; Gov. and Mrs. Yates of Illinois, Ambassador Tower and Joseph Cannon, the future Speaker of the House of Representatives. With Mr. Turner the President discussed the work of the Alaskan Boundary Commission, of which Mr. Turner was a member. With Senator Platt and Mr. Cannon the President discussed the upcoming extraordinary session of Congress and the necessity of financial legislation...(*NY Times*, July 23, 1903)

On July 23, Cardinal Rampolla sent a telegram to Secretary of State Hay in Washington expressing thanks for the President's note of condolence.

TELEGRAM RECEIVED.

Rome, July 23, 1903.

John Hay,
    Secretary of State,
        Washington, D.C.

I have not failed to convey to the Sacred College the heartfelt sympathy expressed by you in the President's name on the occasion of His Holiness's death.

The Sacred College desires me to express to the President its deep and sincere gratitude for such a noble manifestation.

M. Card Rampolla

(TR Papers, Series 1, Reel 35)

This telegram was enclosed with a letter from Acting Secretary of State Loomis to Acting Secretary Barnes in Oyster Bay.

DEPARTMENT OF STATE,
WASHINGTON.

July 24, 1903.

B.F. Barnes, Esquire,
    Acting Secretary to the President,
        Oyster Bay, New York.

Sir:

I enclose for the President's information copy of Cardinal Rampolla's reply to the telegram of sympathy addressed to him by the Secretary of State, by the President's direction, on the occasion of the Pope's death.

I am, Sir,

Your obedient servant

J.B. Loomis
Acting Secretary

Enclosure:

From Cardinal Rampolla, telegram
        July 23, 1903

(TR Papers, Series 1, Reel 35)

On July 24, the President worked with Secretary Barnes on executive business.

OYSTER BAY, L.I., July 24 — ...President Roosevelt soon after his arrival began with Secretary Barnes to dispose of the business which had accumulated during his absence... *(NY Times*, July 25, 1903)

On July 25, Acting Secretary of State Adee wrote to Acting Secretary Barnes to request an appointment with the President for the new German Ambassador to the United States, Baron Speck von Sternberg.

DEPARTMENT OF STATE,
WASHINGTON.

July 25,1903.

B.F. Barnes, Esquire,
    Acting Secretary to the President
    Oyster Bay, New York.

Sir:

Baron Speck von Sternberg, who has recently been appointed Ambassador Extraordinary and Plenipotentiary of Germany to the United States, desires to know whether the President will appoint a time for his reception for the purpose of presenting his credential.

Requesting that you will advise me of the President's pleasure,

I am, Sir,

Your obedient servant

Alvey A. Adee

Acting Secretary.

(TR Papers, Series 1, Reel 35)

On July 27, Secretary Loomis telegraphed a report to Mr. Barnes regarding Baron von Sternberg.

1 wh	JM pc 34 Paid Govt	July 27/03

White House Washington DC 27

B F Barnes, Acting Secty   Oyster-Bay NY

Referring to Adees letter about Baron Sternbergs credentials as Ambassador, I have written to the Baron on the subject as suggested by The President saturday.

F B Loomis.

10:25 a

(TR Papers, Series 1, Reel 35)

Secretary Loomis telegraphed Mr. Barnes again on July 31 concerning the presentation of the Baron's credentials.

1 WH JM PC 34 Paid Govt   July 31/03

White House Washington DC 31

Hon. B F Barnes,   Acting Secty
                                   Oyster-Bay NY

Has the President announced his decision respecting an audience for receiving Baron Sternberg and his letters of credence as Ambassador.

F.B. Loomis.

10:25 a

(TR Papers, Series 1, Reel 35)

Later that same day Secretary Loomis telegraphed Mr. Barnes again regarding the Baron.

1 wh   jm pc 82 Paid Govt   July 27/03

White House Washington DC 31

Hon. B F Barnes,   Acting Secretary to the President
                                   Oyster-Bay NY.

            The Presidents letter respecting Sternberg received.
He does not state whether my suggestion for the formalities in connection with Sternbergs reception is approved. Would like to know definitely so I can communicate necessary details to Sternberg and Col. Symons. Please say to the President that I would like some time to take up the question of filling the vacancies at Antwerp and Cairo as many applications are being received.

F B Loomis.

1:10 PM

(TR Papers, Series 1, Reel 35)

Also on July 31, Baron von Sternberg wrote a letter addressed to Secretary Loeb. This letter was later cancelled by a telegraph from the Baron on August 1.

IMPERIAL GERMAN EMBASSY
~~WASHINGTON, D.C.~~

Terrace Hall
The Oveirs N. Fl
July 31. 1903

Dear Mr Loeb

Will you be so kind as to let me know when the train leaves Long Island city which would be most suitable for me to take for Oyster Bay when I come up to deliver my letters to the President. I intend to leave here on Monday August 3. and to take same train on Tuesday morning for Oyster Bay, in case it would suit the conveniences of the President to receive me on Tuesday next. Please send me a short wire –

With many thanks
yours sincerely

H Sternberg

(*TR Papers*, Series 1, Reel 35)

On August 1, the White House in Washington received a telegram from King Carlos of Portugal. The text of the telegram was telegraphed to Mr. Barnes in Oyster Bay.

2 wh ra pc 47 paid Govt   August 1/03

White House Washington DC 1

Hon. B F Barnes,   Acting Secretary Oyster-Bay NY

The following just received and referred to State Department Lisbon
Aug 1 President Roosevelt Washington. I had in this moment the
pleasure of drinking your health and the prosperity of American
Navy on board the Brooklyn. signed King of Portugal.

(*TR Papers*, Series 1, Reel 35)

On August 1, the vacationing Secretary Loeb wrote to his assistant, Mr. Barnes, in Oyster Bay.

ROGERS' ROCK HOTEL

ROGERS' ROCK

LAKE GEORGE, N.Y.

D.W. EASTON PROPRIETOR.

Aug. 1st 1903

My dear Mr. Barnes -

Your letter of the 29th is at hand.

I think the idea of the White House picture for fairs is an excellent one. I know, for instance, in the few cases where Mrs. Roosevelt has sent her signed photographs to fairs they were more appreciated than anything else sent, no matter of what value. But I dont think it would do, nor would she want to send her photograph out to all requests from fairs. Of course, there is always the risk if she sends the same article to every fair that some unappreciative and ill mannered person will criticize.

I am delighted to hear the good news about the President and that matters are going on well.

Tell Latta I approved and forwarded his voucher to Col. Crook.

Wood fires and (illegible) are comfortable here morning and evenings.

Remember me to all,

Sincerely yours,

Wm Loeb Jr

(*TR Papers*, Series 1, Reel 35)

Also on August 1, Baron Sternberg telegraphed Acting Secretary Barnes cancelling his letter of July 31.

3 ny yf pc 24 paid   August 1/03

Weirs NH

Barnes   Acting Secty   Oyster-Bay   NY

Thanks for letter please cancel my yesterdays letter and reserve accommodations at Octagon for sixth when does morning train leave Long Island City for Oyster-Bay

Sternberg

3:30 P

(*TR Papers*, Series 1, Reel 35)

On August 4, 1903 *The New York Times* reported,

> OYSTER BAY, L.I., Aug. 3 — In response to a message from the King of
> Portugal announcing that he had had the pleasure of drinking to the President's
> health and to the prosperity of the American Navy on board the cruiser
> Brooklyn at Lisbon, President Roosevelt sent the following cablegram:
>
>> " Oyster Bay, N.Y., Aug 1, 1903
>> "His Majesty, the King of Portugal, Lisbon:
>> "I most cordially reciprocate your Majesty's greeting, seeing in it the friend-
>> ly occasion which prompts it a renewed proof of the good will which unites the
>> two countries and peoples.
>>   "THEODORE ROOSEVELT."
>
> The heaviest mail which has needed the attention of the President since he
> came here accumulated between Saturday afternoon and this morning, and the
> President and Mr. Barnes spent a long time over it this morning... *(NY Times,*
> August 4, 1903)

In a letter dated August 4, Acting Secretary Loomis wrote to Acting Secretary Barnes
regarding the upcoming visit of Baron von Sternberg.

OFFICE OF
THE ASSISTANT SECRETARY

Department of State, Washington.

August 4, 1903.

Honorable B.F. Barnes,
          Acting Secretary to the President,
                    Oyster Bay, Long Island.

Dear Mr. Barnes:

I enclose herewith a copy of Baron Sternberg's
remarks which he will address to the President upon the occasion of
presenting his letters of credence on Friday next. I also enclose a
proposed draft of the President's reply to the German Ambassador.

Very truly yours,

Francis B. Loomis
Acting Secretary.

Enclosures:

Copy of remarks of the German Ambassador to be addressed to the President;
Proposed draft of the President's reply.

Also on August 4, two cables were telegraphed from Washington to Oyster Bay regarding the newly elected Pope. The first cable told who had been elected.

1 wh gi pc 28 paid Govt   August 4/03

Washington DC   4

The President   Oyster-Bay NY

Cardinal Sarto was elected Pope today. Age 68. This cable has just come to us from our Embassy at Rome.

F B Loomis

10:10 A

(TR Papers, Series 1, Reel 35)

The second announced the Pope's new title.

RECEIVED at   *8/4* 1903

Dated Washington *DC 4*
To *The President*
        Oyster Bay. NY

Our embassy cables from Rome that the new pope takes the title
of Pius tenth
        Francis B Loomis

(TR Papers, Series 1, Reel 35)

August 5, 1903 was a busy day for the President.

The President, with the assistance of Secretary Barnes, disposed of a large amount of executive business which had been sent here from the various departments at Washington. *(NY Times*, August 6, 1903)

Also on August 5, Secretary Loomis wrote to Acting Secretary Barnes regarding the final arrangements for Baron Speck von Sternberg's visit to Oyster Bay.

DEPARTMENT OF STATE.

WASHINGTON.

Aug. 5, 1903

Dear Mr. Barnes:

May I trouble you to ask someone to engage a two-seated carriage to meet the train which arrives from New York at Oyster Bay on Friday morning about ten o'clock. I want it for the purpose of conveying the German Minister and Col. Symons to the hotel and thence to the President's house.

I would also like to have one of the ordinary light carriages of the town for myself, for I shall precede them.

It is always our rule to send a carriage for an Ambassador in charge of a Military Aide, so I thought it might be well to mention the matter in advance in order to be sure to have one.

Sincerely yours,

FB. Loomis

Hon. B F. Barnes,
        Acting Secretary
        Oyster Bay, N.Y.

P.S. It may be well also for some one to engage a room at the hotel.

(TR Papers, Series 1, Reel 35)

On August 6, the President held another conference with Secretary of War Root. The Secretary of War was in the process of finishing the reorganization of the army under the general staff plan.

OYSTER BAY, L.I., Aug. 6 — ...The President and the Secretary of War discussed at length some points which have arisen regarding the operation of the General Staff of the Army...A few details of the work of the General Staff remain to be worked out, but Secretary Root hopes to see the new organization running smoothly before he sails for England...*(NY Times*, August 7, 1903)

On August 7, 1903, the new German Ambassador to the United States, Baron Speck von Sternberg, presented his credentials to the President at Sagamore Hill.

OYSTER BAY, N.Y., Aug. 7 — Baron Speck von Sternberg, who has been Minister Plenipotentiary of Germany to the United States since Ambassador von Holleben returned to Europe, and who recently, on the retirement of Mr. von Holleben, was elevated to the rank of Ambassador, to-day at Sagamore Hill presented to the President his credentials as Ambassador and was received formally in his new diplomatic rank.

Ambassador von Sternberg arrived in Oyster Bay at 10:04 o'clock from New York. He was received at the station by Secretary Barnes, representing President Roosevelt. Accompanying the Ambassador were Acting Secretary of State Francis B. Loomis and Col. Thomas W. Symons, Superintendent of Public Buildings and Grounds at Washington, and the military aide of the President.

Ambassador von Sternberg, accompanied by Col. Symons, was driven to the residence of J. West Roosevelt, while Secretary Loomis and Secretary Barnes proceeded directly to Sagamore Hill.

Col. Symons at 11 o'clock escorted the Ambassador, who was in full Court dress, to the President's country home...

...It was stated authoritatively to-day that the reception by the President of the German Ambassador at Sagamore Hill is not to be regarded as a precedent, although it is the first time in the history of the country that an Ambassador has presented his credentials to the President outside of Washington...*(NY Times,* August 8, 1903)

In a letter addressed August 8, a councilman from Massachusetts recommended to Secretary Loeb the name of a man interested in working as an agent for the Secret Service.

Commonwealth of Massachusetts,
Council Chamber,
Boston,

Aug. 8, 1903

Hon. William Loeb Jr.
        Sec'y to the President,
                Oyster Bay, N.Y.

Dear Billy:-
        I am again moved to remind you that there is a man in Massachusetts who wishes to be a member of the secret service. His name is D.F. Callahan. He has served in the army and navy and was a particularly gallant member of the Boston Fire. Dept. He has all kinds of recommendations for pluck and daring. I have written you about him before and was told there would be some vacancies in midsummer. The man was laid off from the Fire Dept. as the result of straining the muscles of his back while working on a ladder. He has now recovered and, subject of course to the usual physical examination,
        I can honestly and truly recommend him as about the best man for that sort of work, except our poor friend at Pittsfield, that I have ever met. He is just the type of that little postmaster Sullivan who was so quick in action at the Victor riot, if you recollect.
        Cordially yours,

Curtis Guild, Jr.

(TR Papers, Series 1, Reel 36)

An August 9 article describes the Executive Offices in detail as follows:

A large brick store has been finished off in the second storey and here, for the time, are the executive offices of the President of the United States. While the President himself is not here, it is through these little rooms that the public must reach him. A telegraph wire and telephone line connect this office with his residence. Another wire for telegraphing and another line for talking lead from here into the White House. Two stenographers are always on call. In this manner Mr. Roosevelt can keep in as close touch with the world as he wants to or he can hold it as he chooses at arm's length...The presidential offices "over the corner feed store opposite the dry goods store and just below that saloon" as one Oyster Bayan describes them are neat and clean but not ornate. There are a half a dozen small rooms with a large array of windows. The reception parlor into which visitors are ushered is not arrayed with a view to the encouragement of large delegations. It is ten by twelve feet in size, has bare floors, and white furnished walls. An electric bulb hangs pendant from the center of the ceiling. There are two windows and one door. The furniture consists of: one split bottomed chair, one rocking chair, a steam radiator, a pile of newspapers in the corner. The other rooms have rugs, desks, typewriting machines. There are no pictures on the walls and no books except a shelf of reference works over the secretary's desk... (*Cleveland Plain Dealer*, August 9, 1903).

FIGURE 17: Secretary Loeb and his assistants at work in Moore's Building.
Courtesy of Sagamore Hill

On August 10, 1903, *The New York Times* reprinted a letter containing the President's denunciation of mob lawlessness. The letter included a major statement of the President's views on the subject and its threat to liberty and justice.

> OYSTER BAY, Aug. 9 — In a letter, the publication of which was authorized to-day, President Roosevelt commends Gov. Winfield T. Durbin of Indiana for the attitude he assumed recently respecting lynching. The President also embraces the opportunity to express his own views in reference to lynching and mob violence generally, pointing out that mob violence is merely one form of Anarchy, and that Anarchy is the forerunner of tyranny. The President vigorously urges that the penalty for that crime which most frequently induces a resort to lynching shall be applied swiftly and surely, but by due process of the courts, so that it may be demonstrated " that the law is adequate to deal with crime by freeing it from every vestige of technicality and delay..." *(NY Times, August 10, 1903)*

On August 11, Secretary of War Root announced his intention to resign. It was agreed that the resignation, although tendered to the President at this time, would not be acted upon until after the next Congressional session. However, it gave the President the opportunity to appoint a new Secretary of War while Secretary Root was in London with the Alaskan Boundary Commission.

> OYSTER BAY, Aug. 11 — It is understood here that the resignation of Mr. Root will take effect about the 1st of January and that he will be succeeded, unless present plans miscarry, by Judge William H. Taft, now Governor of the Philippines.
>
> For a long time Secretary Root has desired, for pressing private reasons, to retire from the Cabinet. When Mr. Roosevelt became President, Secretary Root indicated his wish to leave the Cabinet within a year, but his friendship for the President was so staunch and his interest in pending questions before the War Department so deep that he was persuaded to remain for a longer period than he intended.
>
> Even now he has not indicated to the President just when he may leave the Cabinet, but he and the President have discussed the subject many times and have a mutual understanding regarding it...*(NY Times, August 12, 1903)*

Also on August 11, 1903, Attorney General Knox visited Sagamore Hill.

> OYSTER BAY, Aug. 11 — ...The announcement is made that the Attorney General came to discuss departmental matters with the President. One of these matters is the Littauer-Lyon glove contract case, one phase of which was referred by Secretary Root to the Attorney General with a view to having the Department of Justice recover, if possible, certain sums of money paid by the Government under the glove contract...*(NY Times, August 12, 1903)*

On August 12, 1903, the Senate Sub-Committee on Currency was in conference with the President at Sagamore Hill.

OYSTER BAY, N.Y., Aug. 12 — President Roosevelt has as his guests to-night at Sagamore Hill the members of the sub-committee of the Senate Committee of Finance, which is engaged in drafting a currency measure to be submitted to Congress next Fall. The sub-committee consists of Senators Aldrich, Rhode Island, Chairman; Platt, Connecticut; Allison, Iowa, and Spooner, Wisconsin.

Prior to the adjournment of Congress last Spring this sub-committee was appointed and authorized to sit during recess of Congress to study the financial situation and prepare a measure to meet the requirements of the situation, as the committee viewed it, for introduction when the Senate should reconvene...

...Desiring to consult with President Roosevelt regarding their work, the subcommittee came to Oyster Bay late this afternoon...

...The object of the committee is to ascertain the views of President Roosevelt with definiteness in order, if possible, to meet them in the framing of the measure. It is understood to be the desire of the President, that the bill should be ready for introduction at the extraordinary session which, the President has announced, he will call for Monday, Nov. 9...

...It can be said that the President is not wedded to any particular plan of currency reform, so-called, but desires simply that a practicable scheme be evolved and put into the form of legislation at an early date that will render the currency system of the country the more elastic and the less likely to be affected by the fluctuations of values or demands for money at crop moving seasons. In a general way his ideas have been presented in some of his speeches during recent months...*(NY Times*, August 13, 1903)

The topics under consideration during the conference were reported the following day.

OYSTER BAY, N.Y., Aug. 13 — President Roosevelt's conference with the members of the sub-committee of the Senate Finance Committee was not concluded until the small hours of this morning. The whole subject of financial legislation at the approaching session of Congress was discussed thoroughly.

Serious consideration was also given to the legislation to be proposed to Congress in approval of the Cuban reciprocity treaty ratified by the Senate last Spring.

The committee...did not even present a tentative draft of a currency bill to the President, although some propositions, which subsequently may be embodied in the measure, were reduced to concrete form. No definite conclusions as to the shape of the proposed legislation were reached. The conference related rather to methods of procedure in the work at hand than to the form of legislation...

...One fact of distinct importance was developed at the conference. While an extraordinary session of Congress in the Fall is assured, it has not been determined definitely whether it will be called to meet in October or November...

...The primary purpose of the extraordinary session will be to enact legislation making operative the Cuban reciprocity treaty, but financial legislation also will be pressed upon the attention of Congress soon after it convenes...

It is the hope of the committee to devise a genuinely elastic currency system

— a system that will expand when the necessity arises, and contract when the necessity shall have ceased to exist. The members of the committee fully realize the difficulty of their work, but it is their desire to prepare a measure that will commend itself to the best judgment of the country — the judgment of Democrats as well as Republicans...*(NY Times,* August 14, 1903)

On August 14, 1903, the President met with several other members of the Congress as well as the Cabinet to discuss the very same situation as was discussed during the conference of the previous two days.

OYSTER BAY, L.I., Aug. 14 — Financial legislation and other work of the proposed extraordinary session of Congress were discussed to-day by the President with several of his callers. The first arrivals were Secretaries Shaw and Hitchcock, respectively of the Treasury and Interior Departments. In addition to some departmental questions which they desired to bring to the President's attention, they considered with him the suggestions made by the members of the Senate Sub-Committee on Finance at their conference with the President...particularly with regard to an extraordinary session of Congress at a date earlier than Nov. 9.

Senator Cullom and Controller Ridgely also discussed the financial situation with the President, with the special reference to the necessity for currency legislation. Controller Ridgely talked over with the President some of the features of his annual report to Congress. The opinion is expressed frankly that it is going to be a difficult task to frame a financial measure that will be reasonably satisfactory to the exponents of the various schemes for improving the currency system. Thus far, practically the only proposition upon which nearly all seem to be agreed is that the proposed legislation should include a provision for the depositing of customs receipts in National banks...

...It was announced to-day that no definite conclusion regarding the date of the extraordinary session yet has been reached, and that no decision would be announced until the President shall have consulted members of both branches of Congress and others...*(NY Times,* August 15, 1903)

On August 15, the North Atlantic Fleet was positioned off Oyster Bay Harbor to be reviewed by the President on August 17.

OYSTER BAY, N.Y., Aug. 15 — The vessels of the North Atlantic fleet which will be reviewed and inspected by President Roosevelt on Monday came to anchor in the Sound off Lloyd's Neck Point at sundown this evening and lie in four long lines, reaching east and west for 2,000 yards...

...Arrangements have practically been completed for the review and inspection. The ceremony will occur in Long Island Sound, almost directly north of the entrance to Oyster Bay. It gives promise of being an imposing spectacle. President Roosevelt will review the fleet from the bridge of the auxiliary cruiser Mayflower...*(NY Times,* August 15, 1903)

In a press release from the Executive Offices, the events of the naval review were outlined.

The following vessels will take part in the naval review Monday, August 17: Kearsage, Alabama, Illinois, Baltimore, Texas, Olympia, Yankee, Prairie,Topeka, Panther, and a number of destroyers. The larger ships will be anchored in double column lines of bearing east and west at intervals of about one thousand yards. At 9:00 a.m. the Mayflower will pass in review, steaming to the head of the south column, then along the south side of that column between it and the torpedo flotilla, passing around its west end and steaming back along the north side of the north column, finally anchoring between the columns. After the Mayflower anchors the Flag Officers and Commanding Officers will call upon the President; later the President will return these visits.

At 1:30 p.m. the Mayflower will go to the eastward, followed by the fleet in single column. When the Mayflower stops, the fleet will pass in review, after which it will continue down the Sound and the Mayflower will return to Oyster Bay.

(TR Papers, Series 1, Reel 36)

On August 16, the President visited the fleet and attended church services aboard the battleship Kearsage.

OYSTER BAY, N.Y., Aug. 16 — With the North Atlantic fleet anchored off Oyster Bay this has been almost a fête day on the bay and Sound. Hundreds of pleasure boats, ranging through all the grades from the plebian rowboat to the aristocratic steam yacht, have been hovering about the fleet of great fighting machines throughout the day...

...Official formalities were begun at 9 o'clock this morning when Rear Admiral Barker, Commander in Chief of the fleet, accompanied by Capt. Hemphill of the Kearsage, and Flag Lieutenant E.W. Eberle, went in a barge to the Dolphin to pay his respects to Secretary of the Navy Moody...

...Shortly after 11 A.M. President Roosevelt arrived near the Kearsage in the naval yacht Sylph. Flag Lieut. Eberle put off in the steam barge to present to the President the Admiral's compliments, and to conduct him aboard the flagship. On board the Kearsage the President, as he came over the side, was received with honors due to the President of the United States. The band was paraded, the marines presented arms, the bugle sounded a fanfare, and the drums gave four ruffles. Then the band played "Hail to the Chief," and Admiral Barker received the President on the quarterdeck...

..When the President left the Kearsage at 1 P.M. the sides of all the ships were again manned and every honor was paid except the firing of the salute, which was omitted because his visit was unofficial and was made on a Sunday...*(NY Times*, August 17, 1903)

FIGURE 18: The battleship Kearsage, showing how beautifully the ship was outlined with her white-clad tars.
Courtesy of Theodore Roosevelt Collection, Harvard College Library

Later that day, August 16, the President spoke at the quarterly meeting of the Society of the Holy Name of Brooklyn and Long Island in front of St. Dominick's Roman Catholic Church in Oyster Bay. Decency of speech and conduct was the theme of his address. He was accompanied by Secretary Barnes.

> OYSTER BAY, N.Y., Aug. 16 — President Roosevelt delivered the principal address at the quarterly meeting of the Society of the Holy Name of Brooklyn and Long Island, held here this afternoon. Decency of speech and conduct constituted the theme of his address, which was enthusiastically applauded by an audience of more than 2,000 persons.
>
> During the afternoon special trains brought hundreds of members of the society to Oyster Bay from Brooklyn and Western Long Island. Threatening weather kept many away, but, although a light rain fell during the exercises, the crowd remained banked about the flag-decked-stand on a hill opposite St. Dominick's Roman Catholic Church.
>
> As President Roosevelt drove up to the stand in a closed carriage, accompanied by Capt. W.H. Brownson, Superintendent of the Naval Academy, Secretary Barnes, and a representative of the society, he was received with enthusiasm...*(NY Times, August 17, 1903)*

The same day, August 16, Secretary Loeb wrote to the President thanking him for his vacation.

Rogers' Rock Hotel
ROGERS' ROCK
LAKE GEORGE, N.Y.
D.W. EASTON PROPRIETOR.

August 16, 1903

My dear Mr. President -
Romeike sent me the enclosed. It is such an audacious
fake that it staggered me. I send it to you, so that if it should
come to your notice in any way you will know its source. It
purports to emanate from O.B.
I shall report for duty Monday, the 24th inst.
You do not know how grateful I am to you for my
holiday from which both Mrs. Loeb and I have received so much benefit.
With warm regards to Mrs. Roosevelt and the children, believe me
Faithfully yours,
Wm Loeb Jr.
The President
Oyster Bay NY

(*TR Papers*, Series 1, Reel 36)

On August 17, 1903 the much anticipated naval review of 1903 took place. Unfortunately, two destroyers crashed during a maneuver. Neither ship was badly damaged.

OYSTER BAY, Aug. 17 — President Theodore Roosevelt was the central figure to-day in one of the most notable naval reviews held in American waters since the civil war, and certainly the most imposing.

The splendid function was marred to a certain extent at the very end by an accident in which the torpedo boat destroyer Decatur was rammed by one of her sister craft, the Barry, during a daring evolution in which five of this type of craft were passing before the President's yacht Mayflower at a twenty-two-knot speed...

...This accident was the only marring feature of an imposing reminder to the President that he is Commander in Chief of one of the best navies in the world.

Twenty-one warships drawn up on the glassy waters outside the entrance to Oyster Bay in four splendid parallel columns, each two miles in length, and including an example of almost every type of the modern floating fighting machine, furnished a spectacle overwhelmingly suggestive of America's newly born sea power...

Flanking the President on either side, and exulting with him in the splendid display of the strenuous life, were the men highest in rank next to the Commander in Chief of the army and navy. Admiral Dewey was there and saw again the vessel in which he won one of the country's greatest battles, and he saw before him other vessels that had assisted his flagship on the inspiring occasion, and the cheers of the men on the yardarms recalled those that he heard in Manila Bay. Gen. Chaffee represented that other branch of the service that the Chief Executive wants made more powerful yet, and besides these were Secretary of the Navy Moody, Assistant Secretary Sanger, and groups of Rear Admirals, active and retired...

...the fleet was made up of the following vessels: The battleships Kearsage, Alabama, Illinois, and Texas; the cruisers Baltimore, Chicago, Olympia,

Yankee, Topeka, Prairie, Panther, Dolphin; the torpedo boat destroyers Truxton, Worden, Whipple, Lawrence, Stewart, Decatur, Bainbridge, Barry, Dale, and Chauncey.

The review took place two miles and a half off the entrance to Oyster Bay...

...A salute of 21 guns thundered out as the President's flag was unfurled...

...Slowly the Mayflower picked her way along the narrow channel and passed out into the open between Sandy Point and Rocky Point, and a little later was at the head of the lines of war vessels. The 4,000 men were at attention, strung along the yards, lining rails, superstructures, turrets, and tops...

...The Mayflower turned sharply from a northeasterly course and passed westerly down through the first lane formed by a line of torpedo boat destroyers and battleships, the latter line being headed by the Kearsage, the flagship of the fleet commander. There was a thunder of twenty-one guns from the glistening white mountain of steel while amid the booming of the guns could be heard the saluting ruffle of drums and notes of the bugles, and then burst out the strains of "Hail, Columbia..."

...Then the Mayflower passed in turn the ponderous Illinois, Alabama, Texas, and the other vessels of the battleship line, each vessel in turn saluting with twenty-one guns, following with cheers and the strains of "Hail, Columbia," or "The Star-Spangled Banner." The thousands of spectators took up the songs or the cheers in an excess of enthusiasm...

...Following luncheon began a series of official visits to the Rear Admirals commanding each of the divisions...

...It required two hours for the President to complete his round of visits, and at the end of his tour every ship in the fleet except the destroyers had saluted him twenty-five times, a total of 6,300 guns...*(NY Times, August 18, 1903)*

FIGURE 19: The President going from the Kearsage to the Alabama, accompanied by formal escort.
Courtesy of Theodore Roosevelt Collection, Harvard College Library

FIGURE 20: The President, during the Naval Review.
Courtesy of Theodore Roosevelt Collection, Harvard College Library

On August 19, "Questions of national concern were discussed...by the President with several callers. Currency legislation, the Panama Canal situation, the work of the extra-ordinary session of Congress and Federal appointments were among the topics of con-sideration." *(NY Times*, August 20, 1903)

On August 21, "Gov. Benjamin B. Odell of New York...had a three hours' conference with President Roosevelt at Sagamore Hill...he and the President incidentally discussed the political situation in both the city and the State of New York, but no definite con-clusions were reached..." *(NY Times*, August 22, 1903)

On August 22, in reply to a letter from Acting Secretary Barnes, Assistant Secretary of State Adee wrote to Mr. Barnes regarding the Foreign Settlement in Shanghai, China. The Chinese government, to the consternation of Britain and the United States, con-tended that they had the right to punish crimes committed within the Settlement.

Office of
Second Assistant Secretary

Department of State, Washington.

(Personal)   August 22, 1903

B.F. Barnes, Esq.,
     Acting Secretary to the President.
       Oyster Bay. N.Y.
Dear Sir:-
     I have your letter of the 20th, inclosing a clipping in regard to the Shanghai sedition cases and conveying the President's view as to the treatment of the matter by the American Consul or Minister.

     Please say to the President that I do not understand that the question of asylum or of the surrender of alleged fugitives from Chinese justice need be involved, so far as our dealing with the matter is concerned. The conditions seem wholly confined to the Foreign Settlement in Shanghai. Six Chinese subjects, engaged in the publication of a Chinese newspaper in the Settlement, were charged by the Taotai with printing incendiary articles inciting to rebellion against the Chinese government. According to the judicial practice of the Foreign Settlement, Chinese subjects accused of crimes or offenses committed in the Settlement are triable by a mixed court, composed of a Chinese judge with a foreign Assessor. The Taotai made an engagement with the Consuls that the men should be so tried and, if convicted, punished in the Settlement. The trial was had before a Chinese magistrate and a British Assessor. Two of the prisoners confessed, and were found guilty. The court has not yet awarded sentence. The Taotai demanded that the convicted men be delivered to him for <u>punishment</u> according to Chinese law. The Chinese Government has made the same demand upon the Diplomatic body in Peking, and through its Ministers abroad. The Chinese Minister communicated the demand to Mr. Loomis, while Mr. Conger telegraphed that it had been made and asked instructions.

     Sir Chentung and Mr. Conger have been told that our Minister is not competent to join in any order of surrender in disregard of or interference with the agreement that the men were to be tried and, if convicted, punished in the Settlement - the hope being expressed that those convicted should receive exemplary punishment, and the assurance being given that this Government had no desire or purpose to see the Foreign Settlement made an asylum for subversive conspiracy against the Chinese government.

     The British Government has instructed its Minister in Peking not to consent to the surrender of convicts and to endeavor to have them adequately punished in the Settlement.

I append, for the President's information, copies of a note which I sent to Sir Chentung on the 19th inst., and of a memorandum of a conversation on the subject which I had with him yesterday. I also send copies of the last two telegrams sent to Mr. Conger. Please say to the President, that the Secretary, Mr. Loomis and I have been treating the case, with frequent consultation, and with every desire to take an unassailable position which shall not make the United States a party to any surrender of these men to be dealt with according to Chinese methods.

Very respectfully,
Alvey A. Adee

(TR Papers, Series 1, Reel 36)

On August 23, "William Loeb, Jr., secretary to the President, returned...from a six weeks' vacation...Assistant Secretary Barnes left...for a...trip to Washington on some official business." *(NY Times*, August 24, 1903)

On August 25, it was officially announced that Secretary of War Root would resign, effective January 1904, that Governor Taft of the Philippines would replace him and that Gen. Wright would replace Taft as Governor of the Philippines.

OYSTER BAY, N.Y., Aug. 25 — President Roosevelt announced late this afternoon, following the official announcement of the formal resignation of Secretary of War Root, and of the selection of Gov. Gen. Taft of the Philippines to fill that portfolio, that he would appoint Gen. Luke E. Wright to succeed Judge Taft. Gen Wright is now Vice Governor of the Philippines and a member of the Philippine Commission...*(NY Times*, August 26, 1903)

On August 27, former Executive Secretary Cortelyou wrote to Secretary Loeb to remind him of the anniversary of President McKinley's death.

Department of Commerce and Labor
OFFICE OF THE SECRETARY
Washington

Personal.   August 27, 1903

Dear Mr. Loeb:

Not that you will not think of it, and with every apology for suggesting it, I write to call attention to the fact that the President may not wish to have any engagement for September 14, the anniversary of the late President's death.

Very sincerely yours,
Geo B Cortelyou

Hon. William Loeb, Jr.,
        Secretary to the President,
                Oyster Bay, New York.

(TR Papers, Series 1, Reel 36)

Also on the August 27, Chief John E. Wilkie of the Secret Service wrote to Secretary Loeb regarding the President's upcoming trip to Syracuse, New York.

TREASURY DEPARTMENT
OFFICE OF THE SECRETARY
WASHINGTON

August 27 1903.

Hon. William Loeb, Jr.,
      Secretary to the President,
         Oyster Bay, New York.

Dear Mr. Loeb:
      I note your desire to have four men accompany the Presidential party on the trip to Syracuse, and will instruct Operative Tyree to take Messrs. Taylor, Connell, and Sloan with him. Inspector Sutton, who will go up in advance of the party, will also be instructed to join the party on its arrival, thus making five men available for service during the visit.

Respectfully,

John E. Wilkie
Chief.

(TR Papers, Series 1, Reel 36)

On August 28, 1903, *The New York Times* reported that President Roosevelt sent warships to Beyroot, Syria.

OYSTER BAY, N.Y., Aug. 27 — President Roosevelt to-night issued orders that the European squadron, under command of Rear Admiral Cotton, should proceed immediately to Beyroot, Syria, to be in readiness to support any demand made by the United States on Turkey on account of the assassination of William C. Magelssen, United States Vice Consul at Beirut.

The President manifested anxious interest in the announcement of the assassination of Mr. Magelssen, the first information concerning which was conveyed to him by a representative of the Associated Press. Shortly afterward he received from Acting Secretary of State Loomis a telegram communicating to him Minister Leishman's cablegram announcing the murder and advising him of the steps already taken by the State Department.

The President to-night is in close communication with the department and will be kept advised fully of the details of the incident as they are ascertained.

For several days President Roosevelt has been following closely the situation in Turkey. With the country in such turmoil as now prevails, almost anything is likely to happen. With a view to considering the subject the more carefully, the President and Secretary of State Hay had arranged for a conference tomorrow at Sagamore Hill... *(NY Times*, August 28, 1903)

The following day, it was reported that although shots were fired at Mr. Magelssen, he was unharmed in the attack. However, because of the violence that had been occurring throughout the month in the Ottoman Empire, President Roosevelt did not rescind his order to the European squadron.

OYSTER BAY, N.Y., Aug. 28 — President Roosevelt was informed to-night by a representative of The Associated Press of the incorrectness of the report that Vice Consul Magelsson had been assassinated. The President expressed gratification that Mr. Magelsson had escaped without injury.

He announced, however, that no change at present would be made in the plans of this Government, and that the European Squadron, which he last night ordered to proceed immediately to Beirut, would continue to its ordered destination.

It can be said to-day that the President and Secretary of State Hay both regard it advisable, in view of the present state of unrest in Turkey, to have American war vessels in Turkish waters.

For a long time to-day, President Roosevelt and Mr. Hay were in conference at Sagamore Hill. They discussed every suggested phase of the situation in Turkey. At the conclusion of the conference Secretary Hay announced his intention of returning immediately to Washington.

The fact that Secretary Hay considers his presence in Washington necessary at this time indicates the serious view he takes of the Turkish situation. He had not expected to return to Washington for several weeks, but the developments in the Ottoman Empire in the past few days induced him to come to Oyster Bay for a conference with the President, after which it was deemed desirable by both that he should return to Washington at least for a couple of weeks...

...It can be said that it is the purpose of President Roosevelt to afford American citizens in the disturbed provinces of Turkey all the protection possible. For that reason and for others which may develop in a short time the decision is reached that no change will at present be made in the orders to the European Squadron. Admiral Cotton will proceed with his vessels to Turkish waters with the idea of fully safeguarding Americans and American interests...*(NY Times*, August 29, 1903)

On August 28, it was announced that Secretary of the Treasury Leslie Shaw had arrived in Oyster Bay to meet with the President regarding financial proposals for currency regulation.

OYSTER BAY, N.Y., Aug. 28 — Secretary of the Treasury Leslie M. Shaw arrived here to-night, and, after dining at the residence of a friend, proceeded to Sagamore Hill, where he will be a guest of the President until some time to-morrow.

For some time the Secretary has been collecting information from various sources on the subject of currency legislation, and this he desires to present to Mr. Roosevelt. Both the President and Secretary Shaw have been working to the same end, but along different lines. President Roosevelt has been in consultation with Representatives and Senators in Congress on the subject, and, in addition, has been in correspondence with individual bankers and associations of bankers in every part of the country and representing every phase of opinion. Secretary Shaw has been in personal consultation with financial authorities of both the West and the East. He and the President will compare notes with a view of ascertaining whether a basis of agreement on specific legislation is likely in the near future.

Secretary Shaw also desires to consult the President regarding a plan to relieve any temporary stringency in the money market. It is known that the Secretary has a plan in mind for the depositing of certain moneys of the Government in National bank depositories. This he will consider fully with President Roosevelt...*(NY Times*, August 29, 1903)

In the local paper the busy Executive Offices are described as follows:

The amount of work at the executive offices has compelled the entire force to work overtime, and since his return even Secretary Loeb has been forced to burn the midnight oil. The President's mail is greater than it has ever been before, and a large amount of State documents have been under consideration. Not withstanding the superior facilities afforded by a suite of rooms in Moore's block, the tremendous inflow of letters from all over the country has kept two secretaries, two stenographers, two copyists and one official telegrapher constantly busy. (*East Norwich Enterprise*, Aug 29, 1903)

On August 31, Chief Wilkie of the Secret Service reported to Secretary Loeb regarding the possibility of threats against the President.

TREASURY DEPARTMENT
OFFICE OF THE SECRETARY
WASHINGTON

Personal   August 27 1903.

Hon. William Loeb, Jr.,
        Secretary to the President,
        Oyster Bay, New York.

Dear Mr. Loeb:

        I beg to acknowledge receipt of your letter of August 29th, and in reply to advise you that the information received through the State Department from Baron Sternberg related to the movements of certain well-known anarchists, who have been making extensive plans for lecture tours.

        I was already in possession of all the information contained in Baron Sternberg's communication, and while all the persons referred to are "dangerous" in the sense that they are agitators, none of them is the sort of person who would indulge in a physical attack on the President or any other official.

My only regret is that the anarchist bill failed to become a law, as were it now in effect with the information we have accumulated I am quite sure we could bring successful prosecutions against a large number of the leading spirits in anarchistic circles, both in the East and in the West. Our sources of information are excellent, and should anything be reported that has a most remote appearance of a menace to the President, I will advise you by wire and give the necessary instructions to the men of this service who are detailed with the President.

Respectfully,

John E. Wilkie

Chief.

(TR Papers, Series 1, Reel 36)

On September 2, 1903, Henry Weilbrenner of Syosset was arrested at Sagamore Hill while making a persistent demand to see the President. He was armed with a fully loaded revolver. *(NY Times*, September 3, 1903)

On September 4, the President announced important changes in the policy of appointing consuls in the State Department. Consuls would now be appointed from within the ranks of the State Department.

> OYSTER BAY, N.Y., Sept. 4 — An important change of policy with respect to the making of appointments in the Consular Service has been decided upon by President Roosevelt. He discussed the change to-day with Assistant Secretary of State Francis B. Loomis.
>
> For many years it has been the practice of Presidents to appoint men to these positions substantially without reference to any previous experience they may have had. President Roosevelt, after consultation with Secretary Hay, Assistant Secretary Loomis, and others, has determined hereafter to appoint to important places in the Consular Service men who are already in the service, and who have had that experience and training in minor positions to render them more capable of filling places of higher grade and greater importance...*(NY Times*, September 5, 1903)

On September 5, 1903, the President's plans for Labor Day were announced.

> OYSTER BAY, N.Y., Sept. 5 — Arrangements have been perfected for President Roosevelt's trip to Syracuse, N.Y., where he goes to open the New York State Fair, deliver a Labor Day address, and review two parades.
>
> The President and his party, numbering twelve or fifteen persons including Secretary Loeb and several members of the executive staff, will leave Oyster Bay to-morrow night at 9 o'clock in a special train on the Long Island Railroad...

...Soon after his arrival at Syracuse the President will review the Labor Day parade. He will then return to his train and proceed to the State Fair grounds, where, after formally opening the exhibition, he will deliver an address...*(NY Times*, September 6, 1903)

On September 8, the President received the resignation of William M. Byrne, the United States District Attorney for Delaware.

OYSTER BAY, Sept. 8 — President Roosevelt this evening received the resignation of William Michael Byrne as United States District Attorney for Delaware. He will accept the resignation.

Several weeks ago District Attorney Byrne called on the President at Sagamore Hill and indicated his intention of resigning his office at an early date. His action, it is intimated, was purely voluntary.

Mr. Byrne has completed arrangements to establish a law practice in New York City, and he will remove soon to that city from Wilmington. President Roosevelt will not consider the appointment of Mr. Byrne's successor until he returns to Washington. *(NY Times*, September 9, 1903)

On September 9, the Zionists of Baltimore sent a letter and the Hebrew flag to the President at Oyster Bay. The full text of the letter from the Zionists was as follows:

EZRAS CHOVEVI ZION ASSOCIATION OF BALTIMORE

NATHAN SAUBER, PRES.

HARRY FREEDMAN, VICE. PRES.   ציון   A. SLUSKY, REC. SEC.

MOSES BLUM, TREASURER   S. SACHS, FIN. SECY.

BOARD OF TRUSTEES - J.L. ISAACS, N. GITTLESON, R. SEIF.
1110 EAST BALTIMORE STREET
Baltimore, Md., September 9th 1903.

*Honorable Theodore Roosevelt, President
of the United States.*

Highly esteemed Sir!

The Hebraic flag that our Committee has the sincere pleasure to present to you forthwith, has, we presume, more than a passing interest for a historian who appreciates that the former nation of the Hebrews and their flag will forever afford most gratifying sources for the careful reflection of the scholar and the humanitarian.

We as Hebrews love the White and Blue with the same ardor and affection with which we love the Red, White, and Blue, because as Zionists who firmly believe in the renationalization of a certain number of Hebrews, we maintain that when a peaceful day dawns for the majestic floating of the banner of the Israelites in Palestine, the Red, White and Blue of America may still be more cherished by the Israelites of America upon that historic rehabilitation of our race and emblem as distinct National factors.

The raising of the Hebrew standard will never be accomplished by the lowering of old glory, as the Hebrew banner of a contented people in Palestine will never be unfurled unless the civilized and humanitarian nations of the earth, with our own dear American people possibly leading, will fully recognize the justice and necessity of the Zionist solution of the Jewish question, and almost driven by irresistible logic and a high regard for the perpetuation of the Hebrews as a nation, may not ignore an emblem under whose inspiring folds so many brave deeds were performed by bravest men in the great past of the Jews.

As loyal American citizens, with a loyal love for the history of not only the American nation, but the noble clans of our race as well, we beg to present to a most loyal American President the sacred flag of Zion, and to assure you that you are the first ruler in the history of all the world who has ever been presented with such a cherished, as much tear-as battle-stained banner as this one is, while we acknowledge that the prompting motive for making this gift to you is based upon the sincere recognition as proud American citizens of your broad minded interest in the future welfare of our people and in our firm and sombre belief that there was once a great Canaan and a world-enlightening Jerusalem, both now wrecked and depopulated woefully, but destined, it seems, to be erected again, not through the flaming torch of warfare or the slimy walks of treason, but by peaceful agreement of the civilized Christian nations of the world. Fully believing that the liberal-minded Christian and Jewish people will promptly realize the priceless advantages to be reaped for all mankind from a National perpetuation of the scattered Jewish race on even greater and more durable basis than merely the practice of charity and religion in all corners of the earth, on the broader and additional basis of unselfish patriotism and a gallant future history of a reunited nation, and abiding with sublime faith in the prophecy of God and the indisputable lessons taught us in the Holy Book, we are most humbly assuring you of our highest and most affectionate regards

Yours very Sincerely and Respectfully
The flag Committee of the Ezras Chovevi Zion Assoc of Baltimore City
Solomon Herrsman, 300 O'Donnell Str., Chairman.
Louis Michel 629 Brune Str., Secretary
J.L. Isaacs
Adolph Sauber
D. Bernstein.

(TR Papers, Series 1, Reel 37)

On September 10, 1903, Secretary Loeb arranged for the purchase of some of the horses used in the service of the President and the Executive Offices.

OYSTER BAY, L.I., Sept. 10 — ...Secretary Loeb has purchased for the White House stable a team of handsome bright bay horses. They are fine looking animals, 16 hands high, but not quite perfectly match in color. They will be used for carriage work exclusively... *(NY Times*, September 11, 1903)

On September 12, 1903, the President abandoned the idea of an extraordinary session of Congress in October. Many Congressman were against this session, especially because a trip to Washington would interrupt their re-election campaigns.

OYSTER BAY, N.Y., Sept. 12 — After mature consideration and consultation, in person and by mail, with members of both the Senate and the House of Representatives, President Roosevelt has abandoned the suggestion that Congress be called into extraordinary session in October. The extraordinary session which he announced many months ago would be held this Fall will be called, according to present plans, to meet on Monday, Nov. 9, which was the date tentatively fixed some time ago. It is not expected that the formal call for the session will be issued until after the President shall have returned to Washington...*(NY Times*, September 13, 1903)

On September 12, Assistant Secretary of State Adee wrote to Secretary Loeb regarding the Russian evacuation of Manchuria.

OFFICE OF
SECOND ASSISTANT SECRETARY

Department of State, Washington.

September 12, 1903

Wm. Loeb Jr. Esq.,
    Secretary to the President.
    Oyster Bay. N.Y.

Dear Mr. Loeb:-
            Enclosed please find a copy of the new demands of the Russian Government in reference to the evacuation of Manchuria, which were handed to me today by the Japanese Minister and which I forward for the information of the President. The conditions are the same as those reported by Mr. Conger in his telegram of September 9th a copy of which you have.

Very truly yours,

Alvey A. Adee

Acting Secretary.

(TR Papers, Series 1, Reel 37)

On September 15, President Roosevelt sent a telegram to the National Irrigation Congress in Utah. In it he lauded the National Irrigation Law and those working to select projects for the reclamation of arid land. Furthermore, he stressed the importance of a forestry reserve policy. Without one, any irrigation policy would fail. Forestry management and irrigation policy were linked together and the President stressed that in matters of such national importance, immediate private interests must yield to the public good. *(NY Times, September 16, 1903)*

On September 16, President Roosevelt made a surprise visit to and tour of inspection of Ellis Island and immediately announced the appointment of a special commission of inquiry to look into allegations of all sorts of irregularities in the administration of the immigration facility. He toured the facility for more than five hours and held an impromptu immigration hearing for a Russian immigrant and her children. *(NY Times, September 17, 1903)*

On September 27, it was announced that President Roosevelt accepted the Jewish national flag, presented to him by the Zionists of Baltimore.

> BALTIMORE, Sept. 27 — President Roosevelt has accepted a Jewish flag from the Zionists of Baltimore. Louis Michel, a leader in the movement here, has received this letter:
>
> Oyster Bay, N.Y. Sept. 15
> Sir: The President directs me to acknowledge the receipt of your letter accompanying the Zion flag presented by your committee to the American Government. The President thanks you sincerely on behalf of the Government for your gift, which he will direct to be placed in an appropriate place. With assurances of his appreciation, I am, very truly yours,
>
> William Loeb, Jr.,
> Secretary to the President
> The letter was in response to a communication addressed to the President accompanying the flag by the Flag Committee of the Ezras Chovevi Zion Association of Baltimore City. *(NY Times, September 28, 1903)*

The President returned to Washington with his family and Secretary Loeb on September 28, 1903, after spending thirteen weeks in Oyster Bay. With the President's departure from Oyster Bay, the village returned to its more tranquil state.

> Sad it is to state that the colony of newspaper reporters who have made things merry in the quiet old village, will be no more for a time, its members having been ordered to more strenuous sections. It may be truthfully said that but for one insignificant reason the people of Oyster Bay will sincerely regret the departure of the reporters. They have been a source of infinite interest and amusement to the old-fashioned residents. It will be with a sigh of satisfaction, however, that the average citizen will feel that he may venture along the public road leading to The Cove without danger of being arrested as a possible assassin and written up in all the papers of the United States as having deep designs on the President's life...Something has to happen in Oyster Bay every day the President is there. That is a fixed policy with the reporters, even if it is not official. They must get busy in other directions when Secretary Loeb tells them there is "nothing doing." *(East Norwich Enterprise, Oct 3, 1903)*

The Summer of 1904

Although an election year, the summer of 1904 was not expected to be as busy as the one before. In fact, during this summer, President Roosevelt stayed in Oyster Bay for the shortest period of time because the President returned briefly to Washington from July 28 through August 20. Even before the President's departure from Washington it was announced that he would limit the number of visitors to Sagamore Hill.

> WASHINGTON, July 2 — Secretaries Hay and Hitchcock called at the White House to say good-bye to the President before his departure to Oyster Bay to-day. Secretary Elmer Dover of the Republican National Committee was at the station to see the President off.
>
> It is President Roosevelt's intention to make his Oyster Bay sojourn as free from official and political cares as possible. At the same time he will devote the necessary time daily required for the transaction of executive business. This routine will be gone through precisely as it is conducted at the executive offices of the White House. Sagamore Hill, however, is not to be as accessible to callers as the White House. It has been planned that comparatively few people will be received by the President. Official calls will be limited according to their importance. Such political callers as are sent to the President by Chairman Cortelyou of the Republican National Committee will be received. *(NY Times, July 3, 1904)*

On the same day as this announcement, the President returned home to Oyster Bay, accompanied by his wife, and the members of the executive staff.

> OYSTER BAY, L.I., July 2 — President Roosevelt received the Presidential salute when he reached his home here to-day. There were twenty-one "guns," but seventeen of them were large cannon crackers and the other four came from the mouth of a smooth-bore cannon, hurriedly brought into action because there were no more big firecrackers at hand. Otherwise the reception of the President was not without all due honor and included a warm welcome from his fellow-townmen...
>
> ...With the President were Secretary and Mrs. Loeb, Assistant Secretary Barnes, and the regular White House corps of clerks, stenographers, and messengers...*(NY Times, July 3, 1904)*

*FIGURE 21: The Welcoming Speech at Oyster Bay.
Courtesy of Sagamore Hill*

While the President vacationed in Oyster Bay, the White House in Washington was closed.

*Figure 22: Gone to Oyster Bay...Back in the Fall.
Courtesy of Sagamore Hill*

The White House is as dark as pitch to-night. With the President's departure the orders were given to close the old mansion up as much as possible until his return. The big electric light in the porch is no longer lighted, and there is not a gleam from any of the windows. The executive offices, which, since they were first occupied, have been open day and night, are nearly as dark as the mansion.

One or two watchmen at the door and the Executive Clerk Rudolph Forster are the only occupants. Mr. Forster remains on duty to attend to the President's mail. Visitors to the White House on applying to Mr. Forster receive cards to permit them to see the East Room. *(NY Times*, July 4, 1904)

On the Fourth of July, the President remained at home with his family. However, Secretary Loeb made two official announcements regarding the summer's activities.

OYSTER BAY, July 4 — President Roosevelt and his family celebrated the day with a picnic at Cove Neck, about six miles from Sagamore Hill...

...In the evening there was the usual big display of fireworks, an expert from the city firing the set pieces...

...It was positively announced to-day that Senator Fairbanks would arrive here on Saturday, coming directly here from Jackson, Mich., where he is to attend the celebration of the fiftieth anniversary of the formation of the Republican Party. How long he will be here is not known, but while here he will plan with the President for his part in the campaign and confer with him in regard to many matters.

Secretary Loeb issued the following official announcement to-night:

"The arrangements in effect at Oyster Bay this Summer will be the same as those made for President McKinley at Canton in 1900. No delegation or excursion party will be admitted to the grounds of Sagamore Hill, and any one having public business of importance must first secure an appointment through the President's secretary. All persons wishing to see the President on matters affecting the campaign will be referred to Chairman Cortelyou, as well as all communications on that subject. The regular business of the Administration will be carried on the same in Oyster Bay as if the President were in Washington." *(NY Times*, July 5, 1904)

On July 5, the President met with Senator Beveridge of Indiana. It is interesting to note that the article announcing this meeting stated that Sagamore Hill did not have a telegraph wire at this time. This shows convincingly that any telegraph sent or received by the President was done through the Executive offices at Moore's Building. Furthermore it shows that any important information that required the President's immediate attention was telephoned directly to him from the Executive offices. In this case, the Executive offices would relay to the President news from the Democratic Convention held in St. Louis, Missouri.

OYSTER BAY, July 5 — President Roosevelt took up some of the hard work of his campaign this morning. A horseback ride before breakfast along the Cove Road began the day for him. Shortly after the meal, Secretary Loeb arrived, and the two men were busy for some time with official business which had accumulated since the Executive offices were transferred from Washington to Oyster Bay. Among the matters taken up was a communication of the Armenians in America to the State Department in regard to the renewed slaughters by the Turks.

Senator Beveridge, who has been the guest of Joseph Sears, a neighbor of the President, called about noon and had a long conference with the President about the political situation in Indiana.

No special telegraph wire has been put up to Sagamore Hill, although Mr. Roosevelt is deeply interested in what is happening in the St. Louis Democratic camp. Bulletins will be telephoned from the Executive offices in the village...*(NY Times*, July 6, 1904)

On July 8, 1904, the President and Governor Odell of New York met at Sagamore Hill. This conference would practically decide who would be the Republican nominee for the governorship of New York. Wrangling between the President and Odell continued throughout the summer.

OYSTER BAY, July 8 — Gov. Odell and Mr. Barnes arrived here shortly after noon to-day, and after luncheon with the President and his family talked for three hours with Mr. Roosevelt on the piazza overlooking the bay. Gov. Odell later said that the conversation was confined to the business of politics. Gov. Odell was quite positive that he was not carrying away the name of the next Republican candidate for Governor. He called ridiculous the reports that he and Senator Platt were at odds and that his call was to have the President act as an arbitrator between them. Asked about Woodruff's candidacy he gave the suggestion that Mr. Woodruff would not be the candidate for Governor.

There was evidently some mistake as to the hour when Gov. Odell was expected to arrive. The President's wagon met the 10 o'clock train and then drove away. The Governor and Mr. Barnes had to hire a hack with an ancient horse, just able to drag them up to Sagamore Hill...*(NY Times*, July 9, 1904)

Also on July 8, the Chairman of the Republican National Committee, George B. Cortelyou, former Executive Secretary, wrote to Mr. Loeb, regarding campaign pictures of the President.

GEO. B. CORTELYOU,

CHAIRMAN.

Republican National Committee

Personal.

Washington, D.C.,
July 8, 1904.

My dear Mr. Loeb:

I send you enclosed a letter I have just receive from Mr. Harry P. Clinton, art editor of Collier's Weekly.

If some of these pictures can be taken in a way that will not embarrass the President too much I think it would be a good thing. They should be of a character, however, that will not invade his home life. The President playing tennis, riding horseback, etc., would be all right.

All these pictures should be submitted to you and approved before they are used. Just at this time if something of this sort can be done to gratify the wishes of Collier's Weekly it would not be a bad idea, and if done in a dignified way it would do good.

Will you communicate directly with Mr. Clinton on the subject?

Sincerely yours,

GeoB Cortelyou

Hon. Wm. Loeb, Jr.,
     Secretary to the President,
         Oyster Bay, N.Y.

Enclosure.

(TR Papers, Series 1, Reel 45)

Booker T. Washington, of the Tuskegee Institute, also wrote to Mr. Loeb on July 8.

BOOKER T. WASHINGTON, Principal.   WARREN LOGAN, Treasurer

The.....
TUSKEGEE NORMAL AND INDUSTRIAL INSTITUTE

.....Tuskegee, Alabama....

| For the Training of Colored | South Weymouth, Mass. |
| Young Men and Women | July 8, 1904. |

Personal

Dear Mr. Loeb:-

Sometime when you have the opportunity, I wish very much that you would call the enclosed marked copy of the New Orleans Picayune to the attention of the President; it contains a letter written sometime ago by Mrs. W.J. Behan of New Orleans against the teaching of the children of the South about the life of Abraham Lincoln. Mr. Behan is at present acting postmaster at New Orleans and is seeking permanent appointment at the hands of the President. Behan is also one of the leaders of the Lily White movement.

Yours very truly,

Booker T. Washington

(TR Papers, Series 1, Reel 45)

FIGURE 23: The President and his family are at Oyster Bay seeking rest and privacy.
Courtesy of Sagamore Hill

On July 9, 1904, Alton B. Parker was nominated on the first ballot to be the Democratic candidate for the Presidency. The President received the news from St. Louis via a telephone call from the Executive office's at Moore's Building.

> OYSTER BAY, L.I., July 9 — President Roosevelt received the first word of the choice of Judge Parker as his opponent in the coming National campaign shortly before 9 o'clock from Secretary Loeb, who telephoned the news received from St. Louis.
> The President then attended to official business for a few hours and devoted the remainder of the day to recreation. *(NY Times, July 10, 1904)*

On July 10, the State Department in Washington received an update from the American consular in Turkey regarding the outcome of the United States' demand that schools run by American teachers in Turkey have equal rights with other foreign run schools. Sending an American fleet to the region to secure these demands was a decision that the President would have to make from Oyster Bay.

> WASHINGTON, July 10 — The latest advices from Minister Leishman at Constantinople received at the State Department show that he is urging as

forcibly as possible that the Porte grant the demands made by the United States that educational institutions conducted by American teachers have equal rights with other foreign institutions. In this he is receiving the hearty support of the State Department, which is anxious that there shall be an early compliance with the Minister's demands.

So devious are the ways of Turkish diplomacy, however, that it is with difficulty that a prompt reply to the demands made by the United States can be secured.

The question of sending an American fleet to Turkish waters has not been settled finally. The President may decide that such a step should be resorted to with a view of inducing the Porte to comply with the demands of the United States. *(NY Times,* July 11, 1904)

In Oyster Bay on July 10, it was announced that Secretary Fairbanks, the Republican candidate for Vice-President would meet with the President to discuss strategy. They met the following day. Furthermore, it was announced that any comments that the President had regarding the platform adopted by the Democrats in St. Louis, would be made in his address on receiving the notification of his renomination. This address would deal with the issues between the two parties. *(NY Times,* July 11, 1904)

OYSTER BAY, N.Y., July 11 — President Roosevelt, Senator Fairbanks, and Chairman Cortelyou to-day held a conference that may continue through to-morrow.

Mr. Cortelyou arrived on the 10 o'clock train. He declined to discuss the Democratic platform, Judge Parker's telegram, or anything of a political nature.

The next to arrive was the Treasurer of the Republican National Committee, Cornelius N. Bliss...

...With the President and Chairman Cortelyou he held a three hours' discussion as to the ways and means of the coming campaign, and then rode back to the station in time to meet the 4:56 o'clock train, on which it was expected that the Republican candidate for the Vice Presidency would arrive...

...Senator Fairbanks arrived at 6:43 o'clock. He had nothing to say on any political subject, and his carriage went to Sagamore Hill at a rapid rate, as it was feared that he might be late for dinner...*(NY Times,* July 12, 1904)

On July 2, an editor from Leslie's Weekly wrote to Mr. Loeb concerning campaign pictures of the President.

LESLIE'S WEEKLY

225 Fourth Ave. xxxxxxxxxxx Ave. New York,

AUSTIN B. FLETCHER, PREST.

EDITORIAL DEPARTMENT.

JOHN A. SLEICHER, EDITOR

July 12, 1904.

Hon. William Loeb, Jr.,
    Secretary to the President,
        Oyster Bay, L.I., N.Y.

My Dear Secretary:-

I have arranged with Brown Brothers, representing H.C. White, a famous photographer, for the publication, in connection with the campaign and for the best possible purposes, of pictures of the President, his home, and his family, as far as the President deems it proper for this publicity to go. I believe myself that the more there is of this in a genteel, proper way, the better it will be for us in the campaign and I know that you will agree with me and I hope the President will also. Will you do the best you can for the operator, Mr. Wallace, and give him facilities as soon as you can, because this campaign is to be short and I want to make it lively.

Sincerely yours,

John A. Sleicher

(TR Papers, Series 1, Reel 45)

Also on July 12, after the conference between the President, Senator Fairbanks, and Chairman Cortelyou ended and the two men left, the beginning of a small embarrassing mix-up occurred due in part to Secretary Loeb. Furthermore, in the evening, the Executive offices lost electric, and consequently their telephone link to the outside world, due to a lightning strike.

OYSTER BAY, July 12 — Senator Fairbanks and Chairman Cortelyou left here to-day on the 12:20 o'clock train without giving even a hint as to the result of the conference held at the President's home...

...There were two men who came here to-day and showed no signs of feeling happy over their visit. They had not, however, climbed Sagamore Hill, and this was the cause of their grievance. M.T. Burke of Carbondale and Henry Herskovits of Plymouth, Penn., arrived early in the day, bearing a petition to the President asking him to look into and act on the labor situation in Colorado.

The petition bearers were sent here to represent the miners now in convention at Pittston, Penn. Their instructions were to place the petition in the hands of Mr. Roosevelt himself and to give it to no one else. Secretary Loeb told the miners' delegation that it was impossible to grant their request. He would carry the message to Mr. Roosevelt, and the handing of the petition to him, the direct representative of the President, would be the same as a personal delivery. He said, further, that the Government was carefully investigating affairs in Colorado.

The miners were obdurate. They must see the President or carry back to the convention the undelivered petition. They left thoroughly angry, saying that as they represented 255,000 voters, the discourtesy to which they had been subjected would cost Mr. Roosevelt dearly in votes. They regretted this, as they were themselves Republicans.

William H. Hunt, ex-Governor of Porto Rico and now a United States District Judge in Montana, called on the President to-day to make his final report on conditions in the island...

...Lightning burned out the electric connections in the Executive offices to-night, leaving Secretary Loeb and his force of clerks without light and destroying the telephone connections. A force of electricians have been put to work to repair the damage. *(NY Times,* July 13, 1904)

On July 13, 1904, Secretary Loeb attempted to explain why the delegation from the miners' convention was kept from meeting with the President.

OYSTER BAY, N.Y., July 13 — Union labor men are criticizing Secretary Loeb for his action in keeping the Pennsylvania miners' delegates yesterday from seeing the President. They claim that the miners offered to remain until a convenient time to see Mr. Roosevelt in order to hand him the petition in regard to the Colorado situation. They did not mean to take his time, they say, but wanted only to deliver the petition. Republicans here do not look favorably upon Mr. Loeb's action.

In answer to a telegram from John E. Barrett, editor of The Scranton (Penn.) Truth, asking Secretary Loeb if President Roosevelt had personally refused to see a committee of miners, as reported in some morning papers, Secretary Loeb to-day sent the following telegraphic reply:

"Many thanks for your telegram. The committee came here and insisted on seeing the President to present petition at a time when I could not arrange it for them.

The President did not know they were here. If they had sent word that they desired to see the President I should have been glad to arrange for them at some convenient time. As it was I offered to bring the petition to the personal attention of the President. Statement that the President had any knowledge of committee's presence in Oyster Bay is not true."

The President and Secretary Loeb were engaged to-day for several hours in the transaction of official business at Sagamore Hill, and a part of the time was devoted by the President to work in preparation of his speech to be delivered on July 27, when he receives the notification of his nomination. The President is preparing his speech with great care, and it promises to be an important utterance. No official visitors were received by the President to-day...*(NY Times,* July 14, 1904)

On July 14, Nicholas Butler, President of Columbia University, wrote to Secretary Loeb regarding the President's acceptance speech.

COLUMBIA UNIVERSITY
IN THE CITY OF NEW YORK

PRESIDENT'S ROOM   July 14, 1904.

Mr. William Loeb, Jr.,
        Secretary to the President,
                Oyster Bay, L.I.

Dear Mr. Loeb:

        I have your kind letter of the 12th and will come down to Oyster Bay on Saturday, the 16th, leaving by the 4:30 train from New York, which is due to reach Oyster bay at 5:43 P.M. I have the President's speech of acceptance and will go over it with the greatest care. Inasmuch as I could not put it back in your hands before Saturday, I hope it will be convenient to bring it with me when I come.

                Faithfully yours,

                Nicholas Murray Butler

(TR Papers, Series 1, Reel 45)

John Sleicher of Leslie's Weekly also wrote to Mr. Loeb on July 14, regarding a hate letter he had received which he perceived to be a threat against the President.

LESLIE'S WEEKLY

225 Fourth Ave. xxxxxxxxxxx AVE. NEW YORK,
                AUSTIN B. FLETCHER, PREST.

EDITORIAL DEPARTMENT.
JOHN A. SLEICHER, EDITOR

                July 14, 1904.

Hon. William Loeb, Jr.,
        Secretary to the President,
                Oyster Bay, L.I., N.Y.

My Dear Secretary:-

        I enclose, confidentially, a letter, just as it was received at this office. A man who would write such a dirty thing would be fit to assassinate a President. If in your judgement it is wise, you might turn it over to the Secret Service. Otherwise destroy it. I hardly think I would let the President see it.

                Sincerely yours,

                John A. Sleicher

(TR Papers, Series 1, Reel 45)

Also on July 14, Louis Hammerling wrote from Wilkes-Barre, PA to Secretary Loeb regarding the mix-up with the union miners.

𝕷ouis 𝕹. 𝕳ammerling
𝕺ffice 17 𝖂. 𝕸arket 𝕾t.,
𝖂ilkes-𝕭arre, 𝕻a.

July 14, 1904.

Hon. William Loeb, Jr.,
     Secretary to the President
        Oyster Bay, N.Y.

My dear Sir:

I notice by the papers that you are making explanations concerning not permitting the delegation from our neighborhood to see the President. In my judgement, it does not require any fear whatever, as the Central Labor Unions claim through their representatives that their delegation represented 250,000 mine workers, etc., affiliated with their union. I want to explain to you that it is not correct. The mine workers organization does not compel any local or branch to belong to the Central Labor Unions and very few do.

If Mr. Mitchell would be home, I would ask him to give out a statement to this effect, but I went before the Pittston Convention of Mine Workers, which is in session, and asked President T.D. Nicholls and Secretary John T. Dempsey if they had any knowledge of the delegation going to see the President. Mr. Nicholls replied that he had no knowledge whatever, so did Mr. Dempsey. He said, "If these parties wanted to see the President why did they not write for a date or take somebody with them who knows the President?" I thought at this time to write you and explain, and if you would kindly explain to the President that there is no fear in this whatever.

I shall take great pleasure and write an article to the United Mine Workers Journal, which is the official organ of the miners union, explaining as you did in your telegram to Mr. Barrett at Scranton, that the President did not know anything about the Committee and that the Committee was not sent by the miners to see the President.

Before Mr. Mitchell left for Europe, he told me, in Philadelphia, that he had his hands washed from the Colorado trouble and that the National Organization of the United Mine Workers will not give them any more money from their Treasury to assist them.

I also want to assure you that President Nicholls of District No. 1 and President Fahey of District No. 9 feel very kindly towards the President for his success. They told me that they shall be only too glad to see the President sometime and assure him their support.

Hoping that this is explained, and assuring you that I would do anything in my power for the success of the President, I am,

Very truly yours,

Louis N. Hammerling

P.S.:- I take this opportunity to show you that President Mitchell is willing to do anything to help for the success of the Republican Party. When Senator Quay died Senator Penrose wanted Mr. Mitchell's opinion and approval of a successor.

I enclose you a letter from Mr. Mitchell, which will self explain, and would greatly appreciate that you shall return the same to me.

(TR Papers, Series 1, Reel 45)

On July 15, 1904, the embarrassing mix-up between Secretary Loeb and the miners' delegation had been straightened out and the President agreed to meet with them to receive their petition. However, it would be some time before a mutually agreeable date was fixed for the meeting.

OYSTER BAY, N.Y., July 14 — Peace between the President and the union miners was made to-day through a telegram from the men and an answer to it by Mr. Roosevelt. Early in the day a message, signed by D.J. Davis, of the United Mine Workers of America, was received by the President, asking if he would receive the delegates of the order with their petition asking for Federal investigations in the labor situation in Colorado. The President replied that he would be pleased to receive the delegates at Sagamore Hill to-morrow or on Saturday, leaving the choice to them.

It is assumed that the delegates will be M.T. Burke and Henry Herscovitz, the men whom Secretary Loeb did not permit to go to Sagamore Hill on Tuesday, for the reason, it was explained, that they did not bear proper credentials and had not asked in advance for an appointment with the President.

Mr. Davis's telegram, dated Wilkesbarre, read, as follows: "Secretary Loeb: Will it be possible for a committee to see the President to present a petition which they failed to present previously because not properly accredited, and because they did not have an appointment?" This was answered in the affirmative, and Friday and Saturday were designated as the days most convenient for him to receive the delegates...

It was announced that a meeting of the Central Labor Unions of Luzerne and Lackawauna Counties would be held in Scranton on Sunday to listen to the report of the delegates who were sent to Oyster Bay to solicit aid from President Roosevelt in the settlement of the Colorado mining troubles. After Secretary Loeb's message had been received saying that the President would receive the delegation, a reply was sent to Mr. Loeb to-night stating that it would be impossible to arrange a date until after the meeting at Scranton. *(NY Times*, July 15, 1904)

On July 15, 1903 Senator Thomas Platt visited the President at Sagamore Hill. The miners' delegates notified Secretary Loeb that they would be unable to meet with the President on the days that Secretary Loeb had suggested. The rumor that the President had called a special meeting of his Cabinet in Washington was also officially denied.

OYSTER BAY, L.I., July 15 — ...The miners' delegates notified Secretary Loeb to-day that they would not be able to accept the invitation to call on the President to present their petition in regard to the Colorado labor troubles either to-day or to-morrow. They are to hold a meeting on Sunday to consider the matter, and the delegates would arrive early next week with proper credentials from their convention.

President Roosevelt has received a report from the board appointed a few weeks ago to consider the Government's control of wireless telegraph systems...Neither the report nor the recommendations contained in it will be made public for some time.

Reports from Washington to the effect that President Roosevelt had called a special meeting of his Cabinet to be held in Washington on July 28 were denied at the executive offices here. *(NY Times*, July 16, 1904)

On July 16, 1904, the President took his first horse-ride in the village of Oyster Bay for the summer. On this day the arrangements for the notification ceremony for the President's renomination were announced at the Executive offices.

OYSTER BAY, L.I., July 16 — President Roosevelt apparently has finished writing the speech which he will deliver on July 27, when he receives the formal notification of his nomination. With the exception of three hours, which he occupied in working with Secretary Loeb over official business, Mr. Roosevelt devoted the remainder of his day to recreation.

...Earlier in the day, accompanied by Mrs. Roosevelt, he took a long ride and passed through the village for the first time this season...As the two came at a gentle canter into the village they were at once recognized. The first to see them were some children on East Main Street...

...It was announced to-day in the executive offices that the arrangements for the formal notification at Sagamore Hill would be very simple. Speaker Joseph G. Cannon is to deliver the notification address, to which the President will respond. About 100 persons will be present, including the members of the committee. They will be entertained at luncheon on the veranda of the President's home.

To-day at Sagamore Hill was very quiet. No visitors having official business with the President were received...*(NY Times*, July 17, 1904)

Also on July 16, Secretary Loeb cabled a telegram to Assistant Secretary Forster in Washington regarding an invitation the President received to attend the Grand Army Encampment in Boston.

TELEGRAM.

𝔚hite house,
𝔚ashington.

Oyster Bay, N.Y.,
July 16, 1904.

Memorandum for Assistant Secretary Forster:
    Please let me know whether our files and records show if the President has definitely informed the representatives of the Grand Army encampment at Boston that he would not be present at the encampment.
            WM. LOEB, JR.,
                Secretary.

(TR Papers, Series 1, Reel 46)

On July 18, John Sleicher of Leslie's Weekly wrote to Mr. Loeb again regarding pictures for the upcoming notification ceremony and the Presidential campaign.

LESLIE'S WEEKLY
225 Fourth Ave. xxxxxxxxxxx Ave. NEW YORK,
AUSTIN B. FLETCHER, PREST.

EDITORIAL DEPARTMENT.
JOHN A. SLEICHER, EDITOR

July 18, 1904.

Hon. William Loeb, Jr.,
            Secretary to the President,
                        Oyster Bay, L.I., N.Y.
My Dear Secretary:-
                    I observe that the formal notification of the President will occur at Oyster Bay, July 27th. I hope that you will let the President's official weekly organ, Leslie's weekly, have a chance to do this thing up in the best shape. I think the President will be particularly pleased with the treatment we will give him in this matter, and am sorry that Mr. Wallace, whom I sent over with a letter to you, did not have a chance to get a few choice photographs that I could have used with good effect during the campaign. I wanted also to send some of them to the London illustrated weeklies with which we exchange and which have been asking

for the latest and best photographs of the President and his surroundings. I wish you might feel at liberty to ask the President if he will not name a time and place when and where Mr. Wallace can get these views at Oyster Bay. Perhaps after the notification on the 27th, facilities might be given him, or just before notification. The President, I believe, from what he said to me, realizes that the public has a great interest in him and in his family and believes it has a certain sort of right to this interest. That was the impression he left on my mind and I thought it was very sensible, under all the circumstances, but of course I do not want to intrude upon him or to presume upon his courtesy.

I hope you will take up this matter from my point of view and with the knowledge that we want to do the very best we can for the President.

Gov. Black has asked me to come up to Freedom and see him. Before I go there are some things that I would like to say to the President.

Sincerely yours,

John A. Sleicher

(TR Papers, Series 1, Reel 46)

In international affairs, Acting Secretary of State Loomis wrote to Mr. Loeb on July 18 regarding a plan to send an American gunboat to help protect fur seals from poaching.

DEPARTMENT OF STATE,
WASHINGTON.

July 18, 1904.

Sir:

For some days past, correspondence has been had by cable with the British Government concerning a plan, now being elaborated at the instance of the Russian and Japanese Governments, for the protection of fur-seal in the Russian group of the Commander Islands from poaching by British and Japanese vessels. It being the purpose of the British Government to send a gunboat to patrol the high seas in the neighborhood of the Commander group, and if agreeable to Russia, the territorial waters of those islands, for the purpose of arresting British poachers, the British Government has communicated the suggestion of Russia that the British gunboat so to be detailed shall report to the United States Government any American vessels found poaching in those waters.

The Secretary of Commerce and Labor, to whom this matter was duly referred, has made a counter-suggestion of the simultaneous detail of an American gunboat to patrol the waters in question in order to prevent seal-poaching by American vessels. The appended copy of Senator Metcalf's letter indicates the character of this counter-suggestion.

The matter has been brought to the attention of the British and Russian Governments by telegram to the American Ambassadors in London and St. Petersburg. Copies of these telegrams, of today's date, are appended.

The proposition thus made is brought to the notice of the President so that, if the British and Russian replies should be favorable, the timely detail of an American gunboat for the described service may be ordered by the President if he approves the arrangement.

It will be observed that the duty of the American gunboat is proposed to be confined to the preventive control of American poachers in the waters of the Commander Islands and does not embrace any surveillance whatever over Japanese poachers, nor any concern as to the operations of British poachers beyond the convenient communication to the British naval commander of any instances which may come under the notice of our vessel.

I am, Sir,

Your obedient servant

Francis B. Loomis
Acting Secretary of State.

Enclosures:
From Secretary of Commerce
and Labor, July 16, 1904.
Telegram to Ambassador at London, July 18, 1904.
Telegram to St. Petersburg, July 18, 1904.

Honorable William Loeb, jr.,
Secretary to the President.
(TR Papers, Series 1, Reel 46)

On July 18, it was announced that the delegates from the United Mine Workers of America would finally meet with the President the following day.

OYSTER BAY, July 18 — ...A delegation from the United Mine Workers of America, who recently finished their convention in Scranton, will meet the President by appointment to-morrow. After the trouble which arose when the last delegation called to talk over the Colorado situation, the President instructed Secretary Loeb to see to it that no such mistake occurred again. Consequently when the miners' convention passed a resolution asking for an interview with the President on the same subject which caused the turning down of Messrs. Burke and Herscovitz, Mr. Loeb lost no time in sending word to the convention that a delegation would be received at Sagamore Hill to-morrow...*(NY Times*, July 19, 1904)

On July 19, 1904, the long sought for meeting with the President took place at Sagamore Hill.

OYSTER BAY, July 19 — The representatives of the Wyoming Valley Labor Unions, Henry Herscovitz and M.T. Burke, finally had an audience to-night with President Roosevelt. With them came Frank E. McCafferty, the Eastern representative of the Western Federation of Miners, now at war with the mine owners in Colorado. Mr. McCafferty was invited to accompany the other two on account of his intimate knowledge of the situation in Colorado.

The visitors to-night are the same men who were "turned down" a week ago today when they came without appointment with the President. But the blame for the embarrassing incident has since been placed, according to Mr. Burke, who says it did not lay with the President. On the contrary, he said that after presenting the petition, they received all the assurances from Mr. Roosevelt that they could possibly expect.

The original appointment with the miners was for 2:30 o'clock this afternoon. The men travelled from Wilkesbarre, which they left at 2 o'clock this morning, and they missed their Oyster Bay connections. Secretary Loeb arranged another interview for 7 o'clock, and the labor men reached Sagamore Hill at 7:25 o'clock. The President delayed his dinner to talk to them and they left his residence at 8:04, entirely satisfied, they all said, with their talk...

According to Mr. Burke the trouble about the first interview arose in Pennsylvania or in the local Post Office. He said that after the Scranton convention, when the resolutions were passed which the President now has, Mr. Burke asked Mr. Andrews, the private secretary to Senator Penrose, to write to Mr. Loeb making an appointment with the President. Mr. Andrews wrote to him saying the letter had been sent, and on the strength of that the delegation came on.

When they arrived here Mr. Loeb knew nothing of the matter. He had never received the letter. Burke has since learned that the day after the delegation left here the letter from Andrews came to hand... *(NY Times, July 20, 1904)*

On July 19, Republican National Chairman Cortelyou wrote to Mr. Loeb regarding the President's decision to attend the Grand Army of the Republic's encampment at Boston.

GEO. B. CORTELYOU,
           CHAIRMAN.

Republican National Committee

Personal.

Washington, D.C.,
July 19, 1904.

My dear Mr. Loeb:

I have your letter of the 18th instant regarding the invitation for the President to attend the G.A.R. Encampment at Boston. As I look at it now, I do not think he should attend. Of course, I understand the strong arguments in favor of his going, but I am inclined to think that his general rule had better apply - that is, that he is not going to take part in any of these celebrations nor make any speeches during the campaign.

Four years ago, President McKinley had the same question presented to him when the encampment was held in Chicago. He met the question by sending them either a strong letter or a strong telegram. I shall look the matter up and try to send you a copy of the message he sent at that time.

Ex-Secretary Long has written me most strongly on this subject, urging that the President attend. I shall talk with the President about this when I come on to the notification.

Very sincerely yours,

Geo B Cortelyou

Hon. William Loeb, Jr.,
          Secretary to the President,
                    Oyster Bay, New York.

(TR Papers, Series 1, Reel 46)

On July 20, 1904, the meat packing employees of Chicago, who had been on strike for the past nine days, together with officials of the Meat Cutters' Union, and representatives of all the allied trades employed at the Stock Yards, agreed to end their strike and to submit their controversy to a board of arbiters. The President received this news with great satisfaction. Unfortunately, the talks later broke-down and the strike continued on. The President did not intervene publicly in the strike until he returned to Washington the following week.

OYSTER BAY, L.I., July 20 — ...Mr. Roosevelt received news of the settlement of the beef strike at 9:30 o'clock to-night. It was telephoned from the Executive offices. Secretary Loeb was with the President, and Mr. Roosevelt expressed great satisfaction at the settlement of the trouble. *(NY Times*, July 21, 1904)

As the President's personal secretary, Mr. Loeb also replied to some letters on behalf of the President. On July 20, 1904, *The New York Times* reprinted one such letter.

Mr. and Mrs. I.J. White of this city are in receipt of a letter from President Roosevelt through Secretary Loeb on the birth of their twelfth child, a son, on July 6. All the children are alive and in good health. President Roosevelt's message was in reply to a letter from Thomas Buxton, a son-in-law of Mr. and Mrs. White, apprising him of the birth of a twelfth child to the couple. The President's letter reads as follows:

Your letter of the 7th last, has been received and I beg to thank you in the President's behalf for writing.

May I ask you to be good enough to extend to Mr. and Mrs. White the President's congratulations and best wishes for themselves and the members of their family ? Very truly yours,
          WILLIAM LOEB,
                    Secretary to the President.
(NY Times, July 20, 1904)

On July 21, 1904 it was announced that the President's reply to the upcoming notification speech of Mr. Cannon was almost completed.

> OYSTER BAY, L.I., July 21 — ...The President and Secretary Loeb spent the evening revising the proofs of the reply to the notification speech which "Joe" Cannon will deliver on Wednesday. The speech contains about 3,000 words. *(NY Times,* July 22, 1904)

The President's return to Washington after the notification ceremony was also being planned. Both the Long Island Railroad and the Secret Service were notified by Secretary Loeb. On July 21, The Long Island Railroad wrote to Mr. Loeb regarding the arrangements.

THE LONG ISLAND RAILROAD COMPANY.
THE NEW YORK AND ROCKAWAY BEACH RAILWAY COMPANY.
THE MONTAUK STEAMBOAT COMPANY, LIMITED.

OFFICE OF ASSISTANT TO THE PRESIDENT

J. STANLEY-BROWN,
ASSISTANT TO THE PRESIDENT.

128 BROADWAY, NEW YORK, N.Y. July 21 1904.

Mr. Wm. Loeb, Jr.,
    Secretary to the President,
        Oyster Bay, L.I.
Dear Mr. Loeb:
            In the absence of Mr. Baldwin, who is still kept away
by illness, the details of the arrangement for the trip of the President
and party to Washington on 28th inst. will be taken care of by Vice
President & General Manager Potter, to whom I have handed your
letter of July 20th.
                        Very truly yours,
                        JStanley Brown

(TR Papers, Series 1, Reel 46)

On the same day, Chief Wilkie of the Secret Service wrote to Secretary Loeb.

TREASURY DEPARTMENT
OFFICE OF THE SECRETARY
WASHINGTON

Personal.   July 21 1904.

Hon. William Loeb, Jr.,
        Secretary to the President,
                Oyster Bay, Long Island.

Dear Mr. Loeb:

    I have your letter of July 20th, and will make the
necessary arrangements for the 28th.
    I am writing Tyree today, suggesting that it may be well
to arrange through you with the War Department to have the two horses and
buckboard taken away on the 28th, and the horses, without the buckboard,
returned in time to be of service for whatever date may be settled upon as the
return to Oyster Bay, And of which I am not yet advised.

                        Respectfully,

                        John E. Wilkie
                        Chief.

(TR Papers, Series 1, Reel 46)

Also on July 21, Third Assistant Secretary of State Herbert H.D. Peirce wrote to Mr.
Loeb regarding his investigation of charges of bribery in some American consulates in
China. He also wrote regarding the hostilities between Russia and Japan. It would not
be until September 14, 1904, that Mr. Peirce's report would be made public.

OFFICE OF
THIRD ASSISTANT SECRETARY.
DEPARTMENT OF STATE,
WASHINGTON.

                                        July 21, 1904.

Hon. William Loeb Jr.
        Secretary to the President
                Oyster Bay, N.Y.
Dear Sir:-

    I have arrived at Washington somewhat later than was understood
between Secretary Hay and me that I should do, but having been detained by the
quarantine of the ship I was on, going from Shanghai to Yokohama, I was unable
to reach Washington before.
    My report to the President upon my investigation of the consulates
will not be ready before the end of October, for the mass of documents constitut-
ing evidence on which it would be based is so great as to make it hardly possible

to properly prepare it in the spirit of even justice which I am sure the President requires and embody the whole in such a report as I know would be expected.

I have however been received in audience by the Emperor of Japan who gave expression to certain sentiments which he desired me to convey to the President, and I had an intimate and extremely confidential conversation with both Marquis Ito and Baron Komura, Minister for Foreign Affairs of Japan, both of whom gave me for communication to my Government an outline of the policy of Japan in the future and the latter in addition related to me succinctly the events which led up to the final declaration of hostilities between Japan and Russia.

I therefore write to ask you to be good enough to communicate these facts to the President and to ask him if he desires to receive me at Oyster Bay in order that I may convey to him the message of the Emperor and the statements of Marquis Ito and Baron Komura.

With kind regards,

Yours sincerely,

Herbert H. D. Peirce

Third Assistant Secretary

P. S. I note that the President is coming to Washington shortly but I suppose he would find it easier to give me time enough to relate what I have to tell him in Oyster Bay than here. It would suit me personally better to go there if I could as I am naturally impatient to see my boys who are in New England.

(*TR Papers*, Series 1, Reel 46)

Secretary Loeb was also busy making final preparations for the President's notification of his nomination as the Republican candidate at Sagamore Hill. On July 21, Acting Secretary of War Robert Shaw Oliver telegraphed Mr. Loeb regarding some of the decorative flags.

TELEGRAM.

𝔚𝔥𝔦𝔱𝔢 𝔥𝔬𝔲𝔰𝔢,
𝔚𝔞𝔰𝔥𝔦𝔫𝔤𝔱𝔬𝔫.

5 NY FG GI 35 Paid Govt.

DI — WASHINGTON, D.C, July 21, 1904.

Hon. William Loeb, Jr.,
            Secretary to the President,
                        Oyster Bay.

Twelve Army Post flags ten by twenty feet will be shipped to you from here today by express.

Robert Shaw Oliver

Acting Secretary of War.

12:10p.

(*TR Papers*, Series 1, Reel 46)

On July 22, 1904, the President received a number of visitors at Sagamore Hill. At this meeting, the Gubernatorial situation in New York State was discussed.

> OYSTER BAY, July 22 — The adherents of a number of party leaders took luncheon with the President this afternoon. Among them were William L. Ward of Portschester, National Committeeman from this State, who is an Odell man, but has been flirting with the Gubernatorial nomination; John A Sleicher, President of the Republican National Editorial Association, who is a Platt adherent; S.D. Coykendall of Kingston, the wealthy steamboat man and friend of Odell, and Charles S. Francis, editor of The Troy Times, who is very close to ex-Gov. Black. As usual, these gentlemen denied that they talked politics with the President, but they had considerable to say about the political situation in the State nevertheless...*(NY Times*, July 23, 1904)

Also on July 22 George Cortelyou, Republican National Chairman, wrote to Secretary Loeb regarding the New York Gubernatorial situation.

GEO. B. CORTELYOU,
        CHAIRMAN.

Republican National Committee

                                        Washington, D.C.,
                Personal.

                                        July 22, 1904.

My dear Mr. Secretary:

    I have your letter of the 19th instant, concerning the several organizations and individuals in New York State who are not on good terms with Chairman Odell and the State Committee, and have already taken such steps as I could. I shall give the matter further attention as soon as I get to New York.

                        Very truly yours,

                        GeoB Cortelyou

Hon. William Loeb, Jr.,
        Secretary to the President,
                Oyster Bay, New York.

(TR Papers, Series 1, Reel 46)

Chairman Cortelyou wrote to Secretary Loeb again on July 23.

GEO. B. CORTELYOU,

        CHAIRMAN.

𝕽epublican 𝕹ational 𝕮ommittee

Personal.   Washington, D.C.,

                                                            July 23, 1904.

My dear Mr. Secretary:

       Your letter of the 18th instant has been received, and in reply to your inquiry I beg to say that unless the letters to which you refer containing assurances of support are, in your judgement, of particular interest or of such a nature as to call attention by the Committee, I think it would be better not to send them on. Our own mail is almost overwhelming, and it will save both of us somewhat by not rehandling those cases in which the acknowledgement from your office is sufficient. I hope to receive, however, everything that you think it might be well for me to see.

       Referring to the second paragraph of your letter, Mr. Patrick Egan's letter was not found to be enclosed.

       Instead of regarding you as a necessary evil, as you suggest, I am glad to hear from you at all times and upon all subjects, as of course you know.

       With warm regards, believe me,

                          Very sincerely yours,

                          GeoB Cortelyou

Hon. William Loeb, Jr.,

       Secretary to the President,

              Oyster Bay, New York.

(TR Papers, Series 1, Reel 46)

On July 26, 1904, plans for the President's notification of his nomination as the Republican candidate were complete. The citizens of Oyster Bay were barred from Sagamore Hill but the village itself was already decorated.

      OYSTER BAY, July 26 — National Chairman Cortelyou arrived here this evening and was driven at once to Sagamore Hill, where the finishing touches were put on the plans that are to mark to-morrow's notification ceremonies, when the President will be officially informed that he was the choice of the Chicago Convention.

      The ceremonies will be marked by extreme simplicity, and will not occupy over an hour, being limited to "Uncle Joe" Cannon's address of notification and the President's speech of acceptance. In all about 150 persons will attend. The notification committee consists of one member of each State and Territory, and in addition there are a number of invited guests, men high in the counsels of the party and personal friends of the President. Such a display of frock coats and high hats will never have been seen in Oyster Bay. The committee and guests will leave Long Island City at 10:30 on a special train, which will run through to this place without stop, arriving here an hour later. Carriages, if enough can be found, will convey them over three miles to Sagamore Hill.

      The President will leave here Thursday morning at 9 o'clock on a special train. Mrs. Roosevelt will accompany the President to Washington. He will return to Oyster Bay about Aug. 20, and remain about a month.

In spite of the continued dissatisfaction at the methods of Secretary Loeb in disbarring them from any participation in the ceremonies of to-morrow, the loyal citizens hung flags from their houses to-day and the town is well dressed in bunting. To-night strings of Japanese lanterns are burning under the trees in many gardens and are swung in strings across the street, giving the place a gala appearance. Oyster Bay citizens may be "sore" but they do not let it interfere with their loyalty. The name of Loeb, however, is not very popular...
(NY Times, July 27, 1904)

The following day, July 27, 1904, President Roosevelt received the Republican party's formal notification that he had been nominated for the Presidency.

FIGURE 24: *The President and some of his distinguished guests at the Notification Ceremony at Sagamore Hill.*
Secretary Loeb is the first man on the left standing in the front row.
Courtesy of Theodore Roosevelt Collection, Harvard College Library

The list of guests at the notification ceremonies at Sagamore Hill included both Secretary Loeb and Assistant Secretary Barnes, as well as stenographer Maurice C. Latta. In fact, Secretary Loeb presented the other guests to the President and Mrs. Roosevelt as they arrived.

> OYSTER BAY, July 27 — President and Mrs. Roosevelt stood just within the door of their house and shook hands with the guests as they were presented by Secretary Loeb. *(NY Times*, July 28, 1904)

After receiving the nomination, the President received many telegrams of congratulations, including one from the Republicans of Missouri, forwarded to Oyster Bay from Washington.

TELEGRAM.

𝔚𝔥𝔦𝔱𝔢 𝔥𝔬𝔲𝔰𝔢, 𝔚𝔞𝔰𝔥𝔦𝔫𝔤𝔱𝔬𝔫.

5 WH RA GI 71 Paid Govt — 8:25p

White House Washington, D.C, July 27, 1904.

Hon. Wm. Loeb, Jr.,
Secretary to the President,
Oyster Bay.

Following just received: "St Joseph, Mo., July 27.
The President,
Washington.
The Republicans of Missouri, in State Convention assembled, congratulate Theodore Roosevelt on his unanimous nomination and pledges the republicans of Missouri to his earnest support, trusting to be able to deliver in November electoral vote of republicanized Missouri to Roosevelt and Fairbanks. — Richard Bartholdt, Temp. Chairman."

Rudolph Forster,
Asst. Secretary.

(TR Papers, Series 1, Reel 46)

On July 27, many newspapers protested Secretary Loeb's announcement that the President's speeches would only be released through the Associated Press.

TELEGRAM.

𝔚𝔥𝔦𝔱𝔢 𝔥𝔬𝔲𝔰𝔢, 𝔚𝔞𝔰𝔥𝔦𝔫𝔤𝔱𝔬𝔫.

4 NY AN GI 34 Paid — 12:09p
UN — New York, July 27, 1904.

Chairman Geo. B. Cortelyou,
        Oyster Bay.

In the name of the Evening Sun, I protest against Mr.
William Loeb's insisting that releases of speeches be made through
the Associated Press with which we have no affiliation.
William C. McCloy,
        For the Evening Sun.

(TR Papers, Series 1, Reel 46)

TELEGRAM.

𝔚𝔥𝔦𝔱𝔢 𝔥𝔬𝔲𝔰𝔢, 𝔚𝔞𝔰𝔥𝔦𝔫𝔤𝔱𝔬𝔫.

4 NY AN GI 39 Paid — 12:10p

NX — New York, July 27, 1904.

Hon. Wm. Loeb, Jr.,
        Secretary to the President,
                Oyster Bay.

Being informed that release to addresses will be given out through
the Associated Press and having no affiliation with that Association
we protest and respectfully ask that the release be given to this
Association simultaneously.

Publishers Press
J.B. Shale, President.

(TR Papers, Series 1, Reel 46)

On July 28, the President returned to Washington for a special meeting with his Cabinet.
He would return to Oyster Bay on August 20, 1904.

OYSTER BAY, July 28 — Amid the acclaims of a multitude of his townsmen
who gathered to bid him good-bye President Roosevelt left here at 10:30 to-
day for Washington, and the Summer capital has assumed its wonted aspect
again. The executive offices are closed, the secret service men and reporters
have departed, and even Sagamore Hill is empty save for the servants and the
younger children...(*NY Times*, July 29, 1904)

On August 19, 1904, the President's plans for his return to Oyster Bay were announced. Oddly, *The New York Times* states that the executive offices were to be located at the Bank Building. In all probability this is a mistake. However, the executive staff, during this short stay in Oyster Bay, may have occupied the smaller offices across the street from Moore's Building. This seems unlikely, but it is a possibility since these were used by the Executive Staff during the Summer of 1902.

> OYSTER BAY, L.I., Aug. 19 — When President Roosevelt returns here tomorrow there will be no demonstration on the part of the citizens of the town...
>
> ...The executive offices in the Bank Building will again be occupied by Secretary Loeb and his corps of assistants, and the affairs of the Government will be conducted from there during the next month while the President is in Oyster Bay.
>
> The President will receive at Sagamore Hill only those callers who made appointments through Secretary Loeb. The President will not receive political delegations, all such callers being referred to Secretary Cortelyou of the Republican National Committee. *(NY Times, August 20, 1904)*

On August 20, 1904, the President returned to Oyster Bay to the cheers of his townsmen.

> OYSTER BAY, Aug. 20 — When the President's train arrived here he found the station decorated with flags and an enthusiastic crowd present. The President was escorted from his car to his carriage. He was compelled to halt every few feet to acknowledge the cheers of citizens. Almost every one present carried a flag and waved it all the time. The President entered his carriage alone and was driven to Sagamore Hill immediately. *(NY Times, August 21, 1904)*

On August 21, 1904 the President met with Gen. G.B. Snyman, a noted Boer, and discussed with him the latter's plans to establish a Boer colony in Mexico on 90,000 acres acquired for the project. *(NY Times, August 22, 1904)*

Also on August 21, the Austro-Hungarian Ambassador Hengelmuller wrote to Secretary Loeb requesting an appointment for the former Speaker of the Hungarian house of representatives, Count Albert Apponyi.

T.R.'s Summer White House, Oyster Bay

Barharbor August 21 1904

Dear Sir

      *Count Albert Apponyi, until quite recently Speaker
of the Hungarian house of representatives and at all times one of the
most prominent figures in our political life, is to arrive in Newyork
on September 3 with some 50 members of the Hungarian Parliament
in order to attend the interparliamentary conference for international
arbitration in St. Louis. As I understand from Count Apponyi's
letter these gentlemen intend to go to Washington on Sept. 7th
where according to their knowledge they are to be received
in general audience by the President of the United States on the 8th.*
      *As I read in Friday's papers (clipping of which I
enclose) that the President has left for Oyster Bay and does not
intend to return to Washington before Sept. 20th I should be much
obliged if you would inform me whether my countrymen are not in
error when they expect to be received at the White House on the 8th.
At the same time I beg you to obtain for Count Apponyi, if possible,
an opportunity for paying his respects to the President in private
audience. He is most anxious to obtain this honor and being one of
the foremost men in Hungary I feel sure the President will be
interested and pleased in making his closer acquaintance.*
      *If the President should wish me personally to present
Count Apponyi I hold myself entirely to his disposition. It is my
present intention to meet my countrymen at a banquet in Newyork
on September 6th and I shall be obliged if you will let me know the
President's pleasure at your earliest convenience.*
        yours truly

      the Austro Hungarian Ambassador

      Hengelmuller

(TR Papers, Series 1, Reel 46)

Throughout the Summer of 1904, the war between Japan and Russia waged on cease-
lessly. The battles involved hundreds of thousands of men and gradually the Japanese
Army began to defeat the Russians. Although the war would not end until September
1905, the main concern for the Administration at this time was China's neutrality, especially since some of the fighting was occurring on Chinese territory.

    OYSTER BAY, Aug. 22 — President Roosevelt to-day enjoyed a period of rest
and recreation, uninterrupted either by public business or by callers.
    The President is deeply concerned over the situation in the Far East, partic-
ularly in regard to the preservation of the neutrality of that part of China not
included in the war zone. He realizes fully the seriousness of the complica-

tions which may develop at any moment and is keeping in close touch with events in the Orient, all information bearing upon the situation being communicated to him by the State Department.

Thus far only the press reports of the situation at Shanghai have been received at the Executive offices. *(NY Times,* August 23, 1904)

On August 24, 1904, the President held a conference with ex-Lieut. Gov. Woodruff at Sagamore Hill. The two men, along with Senator Platt and Gov. Odell agreed not to interfere in the nomination for the governorship of New York.

> Ex-Lieut. Gov. Woodruff, who spent the day at Oyster Bay yesterday upon invitation of President Roosevelt, announced on his return to the city last evening that the agreement made by Senator Platt, Gov. Odell, and himself that the Republican State Convention at Saratoga on Sept. 14 was to be left absolutely free to make its own choice of a candidate for Governor, meets with the hearty endorsement of the President. Neither the President nor any of the Federal appointees in the State acting for him, it is said, will attempt in any way to influence the action of the convention, either on the nomination for Governor or any other nomination. It is the opinion of the President, it is declared, that the most effective aid which can be rendered the Presidential ticket in New York will be for the party leaders to "keep their hands off" the State Convention and create enthusiasm among the delegates by giving them convincing proof that the ticket will be made up according to their best judgment and not by the dictation of any one man or even a coterie of leaders...*(NY Times,* August 25, 1904)

Also on August 24, 1904, Ex-Secretary of War Elihu Root announced from Sagamore Hill that he would not be a candidate for the Governorship of New York.

> OYSTER BAY, Aug. 24 — "My final word has been spoken. That I am to be considered in any sense in connection with the New York Governorship is out of the question."
>
> Ex-Secretary of War Elihu Root made this statement to-night while a visitor at President Roosevelt's home. Accompanying Chairman Cortelyou of the National Committee, Mr. Root arrived in Oyster Bay at 5:43 P.M. They will remain as guests at Sagamore Hill until to-morrow. They came to consider with the President Mr. Roosevelt's letter of acceptance of the nomination made by the Chicago Convention and to discuss with him various matters relating to the National campaign...*(NY Times,* August 25, 1904)

On August 26, the President met with Representative Lucius Littauer of the Twenty-fifth District of New York. It was also announced that the National Government would probably not take any action in the matter of the Western Federation of Miners.

> OYSTER BAY, N.Y., Aug. 26 — President Roosevelt has as his guest at Sagamore Hill to-night Lucius N. Littauer, representative from the Twenty-fifth District of New York...

...The President's letter of acceptance will be placed in the hands of a printer about Sept. 1. The letter will contain approximately 12,000 words.

The President has not received the representations said to have been forwarded to him by attorneys for the Western Federation of Miners, urging action by the National Government in the matter of the deportation of citizens from the disturbed district in Colorado. As the matter stands now, it is understood to be entirely improbable that any action will be taken by the National Government. *(NY Times*, August 27, 1904)

On August 26,   Mr. Forster forwarded a telegram from Minister Conger in China to Secretary Loeb regarding the extension of the Russo-Japanese War into China.

TELEGRAM.

White house,
Washington.

3 WH RA GI 91 Paid Govt — 10:25a

White House Washington, D.C, August 26, 1904.

Hon. Wm. Loeb, Jr.,
    Secretary to the President,
        Oyster Bay.

Following from Conger, Peking:

"Confidential. 25th. Russian minister informed me unofficially that Japanese course warrants extension of hostile zone anywhere in China and that Russia will no longer consider the Chinese Government neutral."

Rudolph Forster,
Acting Secretary.

(TR Papers, Series 1, Reel 47)

Also on August 27, Booker T. Washington wrote to Secretary Loeb in an effort to get a black man appointed to public office.

BOOKER T. WASHINGTON, Principal.   WARREN LOGAN, Treasurer

The.....
TUSKEGEE NORMAL AND INDUSTRIAL INSTITUTE

.....Tuskegee, Alabama....

For the Training of Colored
Young Men and Women

South Weymouth, Mass.   August 27, 1904.

Personal

Mr. Wm. Loeb, Jr.,
    Oyster Bay, N.Y.

My dear Mr. Loeb:-

I wonder if it will be possible to find another place anywhere
in the public service for a very worthy colored man in Chicago?
You will remember that when Mr. Jerome B. Peterson was
appointed from New York I said that it would help very much if
some good man could be appointed to some position from Chicago.

Yours truly,

Booker T. Washington

(*TR Papers*, Series 1, Reel 47)

On August 29, 1904, the President's letter accepting his renomination to the Presidency
was substantially finished.

OYSTER BAY, L.I., Aug. 29 — President Roosevelt devoted his time to-day
almost wholly to recreation. He transacted some official business with
Secretary Loeb, but the volume of Government matters was comparatively
light. Work on the letter of acceptance has been completed substantially, and
the document now is being transcribed in final form. It will be placed in the
hands of a printer in a day or two.
  In the next two or three days few visitors will be received at Sagamore Hill.
No engagements for callers have been made for callers to-day, though personal friends of the President are likely to arrange by telegraph to visit him on any
matter of importance. (*NY Times*, August 30, 1904)

As the fighting between the Russians and the Japanese intensified, the first signs that the world would look to Mr. Roosevelt as peacemaker were apparent with the arrival to New York of the Belgian delegation to the peace conference to be held at the St. Louis Exposition.

OYSTER BAY, Aug. 30 — Information was received at the executive offices here to-night of the arrival in New York to-day of M. Francotte, a delegate to the Peace Conference which is to be held in September at the St. Louis Exposition.

He is said to be the bearer of credentials from the King of Belgium to President Roosevelt, requesting the latter to use his good offices in the restoration of peace between Russia and Japan.

No engagement has been made for M. Francotte to see the President. The usual diplomatic proceedings would require that the bearer of a mission should call upon the Secretary of State first and make through him arrangements for an interview with the President. It is likely that this course of procedure will be followed in this instance. *(NY Times*, August 31, 1904)

The following day it was reported from Washington that no word had been received at the State Department of M. Francotte's mission.

WASHINGTON, Aug. 31 — At the State Department nothing has been heard from M. Francotte, one of the delegates from Belgium to the Peace Conference to be held at St. Louis next month, who is said to be the bearer of credentials to President Roosevelt from the King of Belgium requesting the President to use his good offices with a view to ending the war between Russia and Japan. The department has not been advised of the reported action of the King of Belgium in this matter.

If M. Francotte has been commissioned as reported it is probable that he will seek the services of Baron Moncheur, the Belgian Minister at Washington, by whom he would be presented to the Secretary of State.

The President will not be in Washington until Sept. 23, when M. Francotte could be presented through Baron Moncheur and deliver whatever message he may be charged with from the King of Belgium.

It is not believed that the time is opportune for making peace overtures to either belligerent, and it is very doubtful whether President Roosevelt, in view of what is known of the feeling at St. Petersburg, would undertake to offer his good offices at this time. *(NY Times*, September 1, 1904)

On August 31, 1904, the President's letter of acceptance was already delivered to be printed and it was announced that the President would now have more time to entertain visitors.

OYSTER BAY, L.I., Aug. 31 — ...Having transacted all business of pressing importance that has been pending since his arrival at Sagamore Hill, the President will give more time henceforth to visitors. Members of the International Arbitration Conference, which is to be held in St. Louis in the next ten days, will be received by the President at the White House on Sept. 24. The delegates will be the guests of the Nation while in this country, Congress having appropriated $50,000 for their entertainment.

The President's letter of acceptance was taken to New York last night by Assistant Secretary Barnes and placed in the hands of a printer. It will require several days to make it ready for distribution and publication. *(NY Times,* September 1, 1904)

On September 3, 1904, the usual routine of executive business was carried out on a rainy day.

OYSTER BAY, L.I., Sept. 3 — President Roosevelt had intended to go on a boating trip with Mrs. Roosevelt and his sons to-day, but the threatening weather deterred him. He remained at Sagamore Hill the greater part of the day.

He and Secretary Loeb transacted considerable business, the official mail being heavy. The matters brought to his attention related principally to department business...*(NY Times,* September 4, 1904)

On September 3, Mr. Loeb received a telegram regarding the arrival of Count Apponyi.

TELEGRAM.

𝔚𝔥𝔦𝔱𝔢 𝔥𝔬𝔲𝔰𝔢,
𝔚𝔞𝔰𝔥𝔦𝔫𝔤𝔱𝔬𝔫.

4 NY AN GI 36 Paid —- 4:15p

Bar Harbor, Me., Sept. 3.

Mr. Loeb,
      Secretary to President,
        Oyster Bay.

Count Apponyi arrived. Most grateful for opportunity offered to pay his respects at Oyster Bay, will eagerly avail himself of same. I arrive New York on sixth. Please wire whether I may bring him on seventh or eighth.

      Hengelmuller.

(TR Papers, Series 1, Reel 47)

On September 4, Secretary Loeb received another telegram confirming the arrival of Count Apponyi.

TELEGRAM.

𝕎𝕙𝕚𝕥𝕖 𝕙𝕠𝕦𝕤𝕖,
𝕎𝕒𝕤𝕙𝕚𝕟𝕘𝕥𝕠𝕟.

1 OH IZ GI 38 Paid.

Bar Harbor, Maine, Sept. 4.

Wm Loeb:

We will come to lunch Friday ninth by train as indicated in your telegram. Please express to the President my and Count Apponyi's best thanks for kind invitation.

Hengelmuller.

8:30p

(TR Papers, Series 1, Reel 47)

On September 5, 1904, National Chairman Cortelyou and Francis Leupp visited the President.

OYSTER BAY, N.Y., Sept. 5 — National Chairman George B. Cortelyou was in conference with President Roosevelt at Sagamore Hill to-night...He said he had come to Oyster Bay to take up with the President some details of the campaign, and would remain at Sagamore Hill until to-morrow morning, when he expects to return to New York.

Francis E. Leupp, who some time ago was commissioned by the President to make an investigation into certain Indian affairs, made a verbal report of his work to Mr. Roosevelt to-day. *(NY Times*, September 5, 1904)

Also on September 5, Ambassador Hengelmuller wrote to Secretary Loeb confirming his previous telegram.

IMPERIAL & ROYAL
AUSTRO HUNGARIAN EMBASSY
WASHINGTON

Barharbor Sept. 5 1904

Dear Mr Loeb

I beg to confirm my telegram of yesterday by which I informed you that I will come with Count Apponyi to Sagamore Hill on Friday the ninth taking train which leaves Long Island City at 11 AM.

Never having been at Oyster Bay I would be much obliged if you would write me a line to the Buckingham Hotel Newyork in order to let me know in what dress (town or country ?) the President expects us to come to lunch.

yours truly

Hengelmuller

(TR Papers, Series 1, Reel 47)

On September 6, 1904, the President received the results of Vermont's election. The results showed appreciable gains for the Republicans.

> OYSTER BAY, N.Y., Sept. 6 — President Roosevelt received returns to-night from the Vermont election. The Associate Press bulletins and private dispatches were received over the special telegraph wire in the Summer executive offices, and then transmitted to Sagamore Hill by Secretary Loeb by telephone...*(NY Times*, September 7, 1904)

Also on September 6, Attorney General Moody visited Sagamore Hill to describe the campaign situation in Vermont and Maine, having just returned from a tour of those areas.

> OYSTER BAY, L.I., Sept. 6 — Attorney General William H. Moody arrived here to-day to confer with the President regarding both Government and political matters in which they are interested. Mr. Moody had just returned from a campaign tour of Vermont and Maine, and desired to talk with the President about the situation in those States as he had observed it. On his arrival he was met at the station by one of the President's carriages and driven directly to Sagamore Hill.
>
> At luncheon the President entertained, in addition to Attorney General Moody, Congressman George J. Smith of the Twenty-fourth New York District, in which Judge Parker resides...
>
> ...On a late train this afternoon W.W. Thomas, United States Minister to Norway and Sweden came to Oyster Bay to pay his respects to President Roosevelt. Minister Thomas arrived in New York from Sweden to-day. *(NY Times*, September 7, 1904)

On September 9, 1904, the President met with the Ambassador to America from Austria-Hungary as well as Count Apponyi, Speaker of the Hungarian Diet (parliament.)

> OYSTER BAY, Sept. 9 — Baron Ladislaus Hengelmuller, Ambassador of Austria-Hungary to America, and Count Apponyi, leader of the Liberals in the lower house of the Hungarian Diet, were guests of President and Mrs. Roosevelt to-day. Count Apponyi, who intends to visit the St. Louis Exposition and to make a short tour of the country, desired to pay his respects to President Roosevelt, and his presentation to him to-day was arranged through the Austrian Embassy.
>
> The visit, it is asserted, was of no official significance. The Hungarian visitors were entertained at luncheon by the President and Mrs. Roosevelt. *(NY Times*, September 10, 1904)

On September 11, 1904, President Roosevelt's letter of acceptance of the Republican nomination for President was released to the newspapers. It was addressed to Mr. Cannon and was dated from Oyster Bay.

On September 12, Senator Fairbanks, the Vice Presidential nominee for the Republican Party visited Sagamore Hill en route to Saratoga to address the New York State Republican Convention.

OYSTER BAY, L.I., Sept. 12 — Senator Fairbanks is a guest to-night of President Roosevelt at Sagamore Hill. One of the President's carriages was awaiting him at the station, and he was driven directly to Sagamore Hill...

...Senator Fairbanks said that he had been on the move constantly since he came East, and that thus far the campaign work had been most agreeable. He declined to discuss in detail his political observations, but indicated that so far as he could ascertain the situation was quite satisfactory from his point of view. He said his visit to the President was of personal rather than of public interest. They would discuss many questions relating to the campaign, as he might not see the President again before the election...

...During their conference at Sagamore Hill the President and Senator Fairbanks received returns from the election in Maine. Bulletins were received over the special wire in the executive office. Only the most important dispatches were transmitted to the President and Senator Fairbanks by Secretary Loeb, who telephoned them to Sagamore Hill...*(NY Times,* September 13, 1904)

Also on September 12, Secretary Loeb received two letters from Forester Gifford Pinchot. Both were regarding forest reserves.

GIFFORD PINCHOT
1615 RHODE ISLAND AVENUE
WASHINGTON D C

September 12, 1904.

Hon. Wm. Loeb, Jr.,
    Secretary to the President.

My dear Mr. Loeb:

On my return to Washington I want to send you my best thanks for your note of September 6th from Oyster Bay. I am looking forward with much pleasure to seeing you and to going over the whole forest situation with the President as he has been good enough to suggest.

Very sincerely yours,

Gifford Pinchot

(TR Papers, Series 1, Reel 47)

During the beginning of September many telegrams were exchanged between Assistant Secretary of State Adee and Mr. Loeb regarding the Russian ship LENA. The ship had docked in San Francisco for repairs contrary to the wishes of the Japanese Government. The Japanese Government protested since the LENA was armed with weapons and an armed ship was not allowed to load, unload, or make repairs in a neutral port.

OFFICE OF
SECOND ASSISTANT SECRETARY.

ALVEY A. ADEE

Department of State,
Washington.

September 13, 1904.

Dear Mr. Loeb:

Referring to my telegram to the President this morning, reporting an interview with the Japanese Minister regarding the Russian steamer LENA, I enclose for the President's information a memorandum of the interview.

Very cordially,

Alvey A. Adee

William Loeb, Jr., Esquire,
Secretary to the President,
Oyster Bay, N.Y.

(TR Papers, Series 1, Reel 47)

The interparliamentary conference in St. Louis also sent a telegram to Secretary Loeb on September 13.

TELEGRAM.

White house,
Washington.

6 NY LV GI 32 Paid —— 12:22p Govt.

HU — St Louis, Mo., Sept. 13, 1904.

Wm. Loeb, Jr.,
Oyster Bay, N.Y.

Interparliamentary Conference will this morning adopt resolutions of respect and greeting to President, kindly advise President and consider answer to be read at tomorrow's meeting.

Richard Bartholdt.

(TR Papers, Series 1, Reel 47)

Later that same day, the resolution and greeting were telegraphed to Oyster Bay.

TELEGRAM.

𝔚𝔥𝔦𝔱𝔢 𝔥𝔬𝔲𝔰𝔢,
𝔚𝔞𝔰𝔥𝔦𝔫𝔤𝔱𝔬𝔫.

7 NY LV NE 75 Paid　Govt.

World's Fair, St. Louis, Mo., Sept. 13, 1904.

The President,
　　　　Oyster Bay, N.Y.

　　　The twelfth Interparliamentary Conference composed of the representatives of fifteen different parliaments at the commencement of its deliberations sends its respectful and cordial salutations to the President of the great American Republic. It considers itself most fortunate to have the opportunity of holding its sessions in a country whose chief magistrate is considered by all the nations a champion of international justice.
　　　　　　　　　Richard Bartholdt, President;
　　　　　　Dr. A. Gabot, General Secretary.

2 10 P.M.

(TR Papers, Series 1, Reel 47)

On September 14, 1904, in an announcement that shocked the State Department, President Roosevelt dismissed from office the United States Consul General at Canton, China. He was charged with taking bribes for issuing certificates to Chinese who desired to come to America.

　　　OYSTER BAY, L.I., Sept. 14 — Robert M. McWade, United States Consul General at Canton, China, was removed to-day from office by President Roosevelt. Charges made against him recently were investigated by Assistant Secretary Peirce, (*Assistant Secretary of State*) who went to the Orient to make an investigation of several of the United States Consulates in China and Japan. Secretary Peirce in his report strongly sustained the charges made against McWade, and the order for his dismissal went forward this afternoon.
　　　(NY Times, September 15, 1904)

Also on September 14, Nicholas Murray Butler, President of Columbia University wrote to Secretary Loeb regarding the President's letter of acceptance as well as his chances for re-election.

COLUMBIA UNIVERSITY
IN THE CITY OF NEW YORK

PRESIDENT'S ROOM   September 14, 1904.

William Loeb, Jr,
      Secretary to the President,
         Oyster Bay, L.I.

Dear Mr. Loeb:-

    I return Governor Pardee's letter, which I greatly enjoyed seeing. What times these are! Tell the President that his letter is in my judgement absolutely the best thing he has ever done whether considered as politics or as literature. The air here is filled with the shrieks of the dead and dying. I have known more or less intimately every presidential campaign since 1880, and I remember in a general way the fight of 1876. Never in my life have I seen so complete a collapse as that of our friends the enemy in the year of grace 1904. Look out for a perfect smash in November. I was in Paterson, N.J. last night and the local primary elections were being held. I dropped in at one of my old political stamping grounds and talked with a dozen or fifteen of the democratic workers. To my great surprise their political interest began and ended in a ward fight for alderman. Without exception they openly announced their intention of voting for Roosevelt for President. They told me that the same feeling is widespread among the working people of Paterson. I am afraid however that they will vote to send back Hughes to Congress unless the Republicans make a very strong nomination against him.

Always sincerely yours,

Nicholas Murray Butler

(TR Papers, Series 1, Reel 47)

Photographer Arthur Hewitt also wrote to Secretary Loeb on September 14 regarding the President's ban on picture taking.

ARTHUR HEWITT

MAKER OF PHOTOGRAPHS

22 East Twenty-First Street   *New York*

Dear Mr. Loeb,

    Is the ban still existing in the matter of photographing: magazines are beginning to want new pictures of the President for use at Election Time? I could come over this week and make some pictures; perhaps too Mrs. Roosevelt might wish some family pictures again this summer. Will you please ask her?

Most truly yours

Arthur Hewitt

Wm. Loeb Jr.
Secretary to the President.

(TR Papers, Series 1, Reel 47)

On September 15, the LENA question was settled. The captain of the Russian ship offered to disarm the vessel thus allowing the ship to remain in San Francisco without protest from the Japanese. Acting Secretary of State Adee telegraphed the captain's request to disarm to Russia's Minister Cassini.

TELEGRAM.

𝔚hite house, 𝔚ashington.

Bar Harbor, Maine, Sept. 15, 1904.

Acting Secretary Adee,
           State Department, Washn.

    I receive this very moment your telegram of the 14th. It is materially impossible to receive a reply from St. Petersburg to-day. I beg the President to allow a delay of 48 hours to receive instruction from my government.

              Cassini.

Memo for Secretary Loeb:
Secretary Adee says: "This refers to my telegram of yesterday in which I stated the President's desire to settle the Lena question to-day. The captain's request to disarm and my telegram this morning to Count Cassini supersede my telegram of the 14th, as I explained to Mr. Hansen to-day. Mr. Hansen admitted that the case was settled by the captain's request. I telegraphed the conditions to Cassini this afternoon at 4:30."

(Received from White House at 7:50 P.M.)

(TR Papers, Series 1, Reel 48)

Later on September 15, Secretary Loeb received a telegram regarding the Republican's nominee for Governor of New York.

TELEGRAM.

𝔚𝔥𝔦𝔱𝔢 𝔥𝔬𝔲𝔰𝔢, 𝔚𝔞𝔰𝔥𝔦𝔫𝔤𝔱𝔬𝔫.

6 NY LV GI 12 Paid — 3p

SG — Saratoga, N.Y., Sept. 15, 1904.

Hon. William Loeb, Jr.,
    Secretary to the President,
      Oyster Bay.

    Woodruff withdraws as candidate and Higgins nominated by acclamation on Woodruff's motion.

N.N. Stranahan.

(TR Papers, Series 1, Reel 48)

Although the President had agreed not to interfere in the politics of the gubernatorial election in New York, on September 15, he expressed his confidence in the nominee of the Republican State Convention.

    OYSTER BAY, Sept. 15 — President Roosevelt expressed himself this evening as pleased that Mr. Higgins had been named for Governor. Mr. Higgins was Chairman of the Finance Committee of the State Senate while Mr. Roosevelt was Governor. Their relations were very close, Mr. Roosevelt relying upon him in many ways, and throughout their association the President grew to have a steadily increasing respect for Mr. Higgins's character and ability.
    It was stated here to-day that persistent anti-convention efforts were made to draw President Roosevelt into the contest over the Republican Gubernatorial nomination, but that he has maintained that it would be improper for him to offer suggestions, and therefore refrained from participating in any way.
    The President, accompanied by Mrs. Roosevelt, took a horseback ride this morning. Returning, the President, with Secretary Loeb, disposed of a mass of public business. He had no engagements to-day to receive visitors. *(NY Times*, September 15, 1904)

Also on September 15, Booker T. Washington wrote to Secretary Loeb regarding the President's letter of acceptance.

BOOKER T. WASHINGTON, Principal.   WARREN LOGAN, Treasurer

The.....

TUSKEGEE NORMAL AND INDUSTRIAL INSTITUTE

For the Training of Colored
Young Men and Women

September 15, 1904.

Mr. William Loeb,
     Secretary to the President,
          Oyster Bay, Long Island, N.Y.

Dear Mr. Loeb:

    The enclosed abstract from the President's letter of
acceptance is so strong, fundamental and comprehensive, that I want
to arrange if possible, for it to have the very widest reading and
influence. With this in view, I wonder if it would be practicable and
proper for the President to sign this paper. I would then have the
sentence appear with the President's signature, in ~~practically~~ all of
the ~~two hundred and fifty~~ *best* Negro newspapers, in various parts of the
country. In addition, I would undertake to have the sentence put in
an attractive form for hanging upon the walls of offices or homes
and to see that it got into the sections of the country where it would
accomplish much good.

            Very truly yours,

         Booker T. Washington

Enc.

P.S. Perhaps it would be better to have the sentence re-written on White House
paper for lithographing purposes.

           B.T.W.

(TR Papers, Series 1, Reel 47)

On September 16 it was confirmed in Oyster Bay that the President would return to
Washington on September 22. Furthermore, the entire Executive force would return to
Washington with him on the same day. *(NY Times*, September 17, 1904)

On September 19, it was announced that the President would take an unusual route to
Washington.

OYSTER BAY, L.I., Sept. 19 — It has been decided that the naval yacht Sylph shall convey President Roosevelt and his family from Sagamore Hill to Jersey City next Thursday, when they start on their return trip to Washington. Heretofore on his trips to and from Washington the President traveled on a special train between Oyster Bay and Long Island City, he and his party crossing Manhattan in carriages.

The Sylph will arrive in Oyster Bay probably on Wednesday evening or early Thursday. The trip to Jersey City will consume about three hours. At Jersey City the President and his family will be joined by the remainder of the Presidential party, including the clerical force of the Summer Executive offices, and the entire party will take special cars attached to the 1:14 P.M. Pennsylvania train for Washington. It is possible in the event of heavy passenger traffic that the President's cars will be run as a special train...*(NY Times,* September 20, 1904)

On September 20, 1904 a crank, who wanted to help the President publish a book on heaven, was arrested while trying to gain access to Sagamore Hill.

OYSTER BAY, Sept. 20 — A man who is regarded by the Secret Service officers and by the authorities of Oyster Bay as a dangerous crank was arrested here shortly before noon to-day. He says he is J.E. Reeves. He is a roughly attired man, about forty years of age. He was making his way to Sagamore Hill when he was arrested. He told Secret Service Agent Tyree, who arrested him, that he wanted to see the President on important business.

Realizing from the man's manner that he was probably insane, Officer Tyree took him before Justice Franklin for examination. To the Justice Reeves said that six years ago he died in a Jersey City Hospital and went to heaven in an automobile. While there he received an important message for President Roosevelt, which he was directed to deliver personally...

...Justice Franklin, being convinced that the man was insane and very likely dangerous, deputized one of the Secret Service men to take him to Mineola, where an inquiry into the man's mental condition was held...*(NY Times,* September 21, 1904)

On September 22, the President returned to Washington. He would return to Oyster Bay only to cast his ballot in the Presidential Election.

Vacation over, President Roosevelt returned yesterday to active official life at Washington from Oyster Bay, reaching New York waters on the naval yacht Sylph and leaving the Pennsylvania Railroad station at Jersey City at 1:27 P.M. with all his family, except Miss Alice Roosevelt and his sons Theodore and Kermit...

...With the President were Mrs. Roosevelt and their children, Ethel, Archie, and Quentin; Secretary William Loeb and Mrs. Loeb, a governess, members of the executive office staff and Secret Service men...*(NY Times,* September 23, 1904)

On September 26, 1904, *The New York Times* reported the effects of the Executive Order issued by President Roosevelt regulating duties on imports . This "Executive Order," issued earlier in the year, allowed the President to, in effect, run the customs service himself. He began to suspend the operations of decisions of the Board of General Appraisers, the board that heard appeals from importers who felt that the duty levied on them by the Collector was inappropriate. He also suspended decisions by the Board and called for new hearings before the Board on the same issue. The President's personal activity in the customs administration also involved Secretary Loeb.

...About six weeks ago the Collector of Philadelphia, acting, it is said, under orders from Washington, classified an importation of pickled sheepskins at 20 per cent. The importer filed a protest, and Assistant Secretary Armstrong *(head of the Customs Division)* issued a circular of instruction to Collectors, informing them of the Philadelphia case and ordering them to follow the practice established in Philadelphia in classifying these goods. Immediately a howl of protest went up, especially from the leather-manufacturing centers in Massachusetts.

Senator Lodge's aid was enlisted, and on his representation, it is said, President Roosevelt, at Oyster Bay, directed Secretary Loeb to write a letter to Mr. Armstrong ordering him to peremptorily to withdraw his circular of instruction and take no further action in the case until he had discussed the matter personally with the President... *(NY Times*, September 26, 1904)

The Summer of 1905

On June 4, 1905, *The Washington Post* printed a long article on the career of Secretary Loeb. Of interest is the section detailing the Secretary's many duties.

...The many things that come under Mr. Loeb's supervision in his present office cannot be enumerated in small space. A comparatively recent task is that of a chief of police. In a way the personal safety of the President is intrusted to his care. At least the country would not hold him blameless for any accident that could have been avoided. There is a force of Secret Service officials and policemen, under the direction of the Secretary, kept on guard night and day. The routine of the President's life is controlled largely by his Secretary. Important matters occupy his attention so completely that he cannot be bothered with petty duties. When he comes to his desk in the morning the President does not know what are his engagements for the day. He finds awaiting him a sheet of note paper with the words "The President's Engagements" at the top, and below in neat typescript a list of fifteen or twenty appointments, which he is expected to meet. The average number of visitors to the Secretary's office is probably as high as 200, many of whom want to talk to the President. The requests of but few can be granted. Senators, members of the House, and certain officials are admitted without going through the Secretary's room. But practically every one who sees the President for the discussion of business does so on an appointment made by his Secretary. There are requests of an infinite variety, sufficient to tax the ingenuity of a dozen men, especially in view of the general policy pursued of returning courteous answers and of refusing, when these requests must be refused, so as not to give offense...

...It is realized by few what an amount of labor is involved for the Secretary to the President in planning his trips away from Washington. Every movement must be guarded. The itinerary of each trip, even if it be but a short one to New York, must be prepared in advance. There are a score of these trips annually. There are half a dozen now being arranged for at the White House offices. Then there is the flood of all kinds of letters, which sometimes run as high as 700 or 800 a day and rarely falls below 300 or 400. Many, to be sure, are referred to the Departments for action, but the outgoing mail, much of which is signed by the Secretary, amounts to about 5,000 pieces a month.

Secretary Loeb has a force of about fifty ushers, messengers, and clerks under his supervision...When the seat of government is temporarily removed from Washington, as occasionally happens during the absence of the President, he must make certain that the necessary facilities are installed...When the

President goes home in summer to Oyster Bay complete arrangements must be made, including the transfer of the clerical force. A great variety of detail must be anticipated...

...The thoroughness with which these various duties are performed is attested by their successful execution. So smoothly and quietly are such matters arranged that people in general rarely have any occasion to think what a vast number of details Secretary Loeb has to look after...(*The Washington Post*, June 4, 1905)

This was especially true during the summer of the year 1905 as it proved to be one of the most eventful in Roosevelt's administration. The President's successful effort to negotiate an end to the Russo-Japanese war this summer would later earn him the Nobel Peace Prize. The staff at Moore's Building was absolutely vital to the transmission of confidential telegrams between the President and the leaders and representatives of Russia and Japan. The first such telegram was sent by Rudolph Forster in Washington to Secretary Loeb in Oyster Bay. Mr. Forster transmitted a message from the Japanese Minister, Takahira.

TELEGRAM.

White house,
Washington.

June 28, 1905

Hon. Wm Loeb Jr.

　　Secy to the President

Takahira asks that following be transmitted to the President.

"Confidential. The Japanese Minister has the honor to inform the President that he received a telegram from his government to the effect that the Japanese Government highly appreciates the action so opportunely taken by the President, when the Russian Government expressed a desire for armistice, in order to ascertain their disposition as to the nature of the full powers to be given to their plenipotentiaries and the Japanese Government hopes that through his powerful influence, the Russian Government may be induced to equip their plenipotentiaries with the full powers of the regular form.

　　The Japanese Minister also received another telegram from the Japanese Government stating that until they are informed of the definite decision of the Russian Government as to whom the latter will appoint as their plenipotentiaries, the Japanese Government will not be in a position to announce officially the appointment of their own plenipotentiaries; further that the Japanese Government are desirous to know what reply (?) the President has received from the Russian Government as to the question of full powers concerning which the President sent instructions to the United States Ambassador to Russia on the 23ᵈ of June.

The Japanese Minister wishes, in view of the above telegrams, to request the President to ascertain whether the Japanese Government can now consider the appointment of Monsieur Nelidoff as one of their plenipotentiaries as definitely decided and also who will be another Russian plenipotentiary.

The Japanese Minister further begs to request the President, if he deems it proper, to obtain the assurances of the Russian Government in regard to the full powers and to inform them, if necessary, that the President has understood from Cassini that as the word plenipotentiary signifies, there can be no doubt that the Russian plenipotentiaries will be equipped with full powers of the regular form authorizing them to negotiate and conclude the terms of peace, subject to the ratification by the Emperor of Russia, and that the President has already informed the Japanese Government to that effect. The Japanese Minister also begs to add that owing to the time required in this manner in arriving at preliminary understandings, he is very much afraid Japanese Minister for foreign affairs (by name) may be unable to arrive at Washington for several days after August first!!

(TR Papers, Series 1, Reel 55)

On June 29, the American Ambassador to Russia, Mr. Meyer sent a telegram to Secretary of State Hay in Washington. A copy of this telegram was forwarded from Washington to Secretary Loeb.

TELEGRAM.

White house, Washington.

Received in cipher.
1 WH JM GI 526 Paid Govt —— 10 a.m.

White House Washington, D.C., June 29, 1905.

Hon. Wm. Loeb, Jr.,
   Secretary to the President,
      Oyster Bay.

   Following just received:

"St. Petersburg

Secretary of State,
      Washington.

   Lamsdorff informs me today Nelidoff may not be able to serve on account of ill-health. Telegraphed Paris in order to know definitely. If Nelidoff is unable to serve the Emperor will appoint immediately his successor of equal importance to serve as first plenipotentiary; stated it was their intention to have Rosen serve as Russian plenipotentiary. Lamsdorff asked if, in case the Emperor should desire a third plenipotentiary, would there be any objection? Will also desire to send sever-

al delegates as specialists on Eastern affairs. I called Lamsdorff's attention again
to the President's desire, as instructed in your cable of June 24th, that at the time
of the appointment by the Russian Government of their plenipotentiaries it shall be
stated that they are named as plenipotentiaries to negotiate and conclude a treaty of
peace with Japan. To this he agreed."

Meyer.

—I—

(TR Papers, Series 1, Reel 55)

In reply to Mr. Takahira's telegram of the 28th, and with the new information contained
in Mr. Meyer's telegram of the 29th, Secretary Loeb sent a telegram on June 29th to Mr.
Takahira via Assistant Secretary Forster in Washington. According to a hand written
note on the telegram itself, Mr. Forster personally delivered the telegram to Mr.
Takahira.

TELEGRAM.

White house,
Washington.

Received in cipher.
1 RV GI JM 347 Paid Govt.

Oyster Bay, N.Y., June 29, 1905. (Rec'd. 4:07 p.m.)

Hon. Rudolph Forster,
    Ass't. Sec'y. to the President,
      The White House,
        Washington, D.C.

Please deliver this dispatch immediately to Mr. Takahira:
"Russia will appoint Nelidoff and Rosen, but if Nelidoff's health will not permit
him to serve some one of equally high rank will be appointed. Russia may wish to
appoint a third plenipotentiary, but this is not certain. The President would like to
announce the names of the plenipotentiaries as having been appointed. He will
make the announcement provisionally, if Japan so wishes; that is, he will say that
Baron Komura and Mr. Takahira of Japan Ambassador Nelidoff and Baron Rosen
from Russia have been appointed. If the President does not hear to the contrary he
will make this announcement Monday. The President is happy to inform Mr.
Takahira that the Russian Government has agreed when it formally appoints the
plenipotentiaries to give them full powers to negotiate and conclude peace, and the
President will make this announcement himself when he announces the names of
the Russian and Japanese plenipotentiaries."

Wm. Loeb, Jr.,
Secretary.

Personally delivered   *4:30 p.m.*

R.F.

(TR Papers, Series 1, Reel 55)

By June 30th, as evidenced by the following internal telegram of Western Union, the State Department had already made inquiries regarding the Western Union telegraph facilities at Portsmouth, New Hampshire, the proposed site of the upcoming peace negotiations.

WESTERN UNION TELEGRAPH COMPANY.

Telegram   New York, June 30, 1905.

H.F. Taff,

     Manager, Washington, D.C.

Our wire facilities from Portsmouth, N.H., are good and we could augment them to any desired extent on short notice. We could, however, make up with our present wires at least seven day and fifteen night circuits for exclusive assignment to local business, and this would, doubtless, be ample for all the business that would develop.

     You may assure the State Department that we will do everything to meet every requirement in the line of telegraph facilities; for the purpose of preparing for the event, we should, of course, like early information when the matter is finally decided, and we will treat it in strict confidence, if desired.

R.C. Clowry,

President.

(TR Papers, Series 1, Reel 55)

On June 30, Assistant Secretary Forster wrote to Secretary Loeb regarding the dispatch that he had handed to Mr. Takahira the previous day.

Personal.

WHITE HOUSE,

WASHINGTON.

6 / 30 / 05

Memo for Secretary Loeb:

    The Japanese Minister, when I handed him your dispatch, said it was very satisfactory and that he would at once transmit it to his government.

R. Forster.

(TR Papers, Series 1, Reel 55)

On June 30, Assistant Secretary Forster telegraphed Secretary Loeb with a message from Mr. Takahira.

TELEGRAM.

Received in Cipher. 𝔚𝔥𝔦𝔱𝔢 𝔥𝔬𝔲𝔰𝔢,
𝔚𝔞𝔰𝔥𝔦𝔫𝔤𝔱𝔬𝔫.

3 WH.

The White House, Washington, D.C., June 30 — 9:15p

Hon. Wm. Loeb, Jr.,
      Secretary to the President,
            Oyster Bay, N.Y.

Minister Takahira asks that the following be transmitted confidentially to the President:

"The Japanese minister having telegraphed to his Government the message of the President of the 29th of June, has received, on the 30th, the following telegram in answer:

'You will say to the President that the Imperial Government highly appreciates the successful efforts of the President to obtain a formal assurance from the Russian Government to clothe their plenipotentiaries, when they are appointed, with the full powers to negotiate and conclude peace and that they have no objection to the suggestion of the President to announce the appointment of Japanese and Russian plenipotentiaries next Monday. You will add that the Imperial Government will also formally announce in Tokyo the appointment of their plenipotentiaries on the same day and that Baron Komura will leave for Washington about the seventh of July and arrive there on or about the first of August'".

Rudolph Forster,
      Asst. Secretary.

(TR Papers, Series 1, Reel 55)

About an hour later the same evening, Assistant Secretary Forster telegraphed Secretary Loeb with a telegraph he had just received from Ambassador Meyer in St. Petersburg.

TELEGRAM.

Received in Cipher. 𝔚𝔥𝔦𝔱𝔢 𝔥𝔬𝔲𝔰𝔢,
𝔚𝔞𝔰𝔥𝔦𝔫𝔤𝔱𝔬𝔫.

THE WHITE HOUSE Washington, D.C., June 30 — 10:20 p.m.

Hon. Wm. Loeb, Jr.,
      Secretary to the President,
            Oyster Bay

Following just received from St. Petersburg:

"Have received this evening note from Lamsdorff expressing the Emperor's satisfaction at learning the names of the two proposed Japanese plenipotentiaries. The Emperor has appointed as first plenipotentiary in the place of Nelidoff, the

(Russian representative ?), Mauravioff, former minister of justice, now Russian Ambassador at Rome and Rosen as second plenipotentiary. The Imperial Government furthermore reserves the right of naming others delegates for the examination of special questions which may be discussed in the course of the negotiations. Mauravioff as well as the special delegates will not fail to present themselves at Washington for the first days of August next — Meyer"

Rudolph Forster,
Asst. Secretary.

(TR Papers, Series 1, Reel 55)

Early in the morning on July 1, Secretary of State John Hay died. His wife telegraphed to Washington to inform the President.

TELEGRAM.

𝔚hite house,
𝔚ashington.

1 NY D GI 29 DH —- 8:45 a

Newbury, N.H., July 1, 1905.

The President:

   Mr. Hay died of a sudden heart failure at 12:25 this morning. His condition during the day had been perfectly satisfactory. The end came most unexpectedly.

Mrs. Hay.

(TR Papers, Series 1, Reel 55)

   The untimely death of Secretary of State Hay, on the weekend of the President's return to Oyster Bay demonstrated the Executive Office's importance to Roosevelt's presidency. Although Mrs. Hay's telegram was received at the White House in Washington, the Executive Offices in Oyster Bay were closed at that hour of the morning and they did not receive the telegram until later.

   When the announcement of Secretary Hay's death was received THE TIMES tried to notify President Roosevelt at his Oyster Bay home.
   It was said there that the executive offices of the President were closed and that there was no way of notifying him. *(NY Times*, July 1, 1905)

The President received the news of the Secretary's death from a newspaper correspondent.

> OYSTER BAY, L.I., July 1 — ...The first message announcing the death of Secretary Hay reached Oyster Bay long before the little town was astir, and was carried to Sagamore Hill by a newspaper correspondent. The President, who was in bed, was awakened, and came down to the library, where he received the news.
>
> The President immediately dispatched the following message of condolence to the widow of the dead statesman:

> Mrs. John Hay, Lake Sunapee:
> I cannot believe the dreadful news. Pray accept our deepest sympathy in your terrible bereavement. I do not know what to say to express my sorrow.
> THEODORE ROOSEVELT.

> It was not until this message had been sent that the President received the official announcement of Mr. Hay's death. It came in a message from Mrs. Hay, which was received at the Executive office in the town and at once telephoned to Sagamore Hill...Secretary Loeb, as soon as he heard of Mr. Hay's death, went to Sagamore Hill, where he remained for a couple of hours. Upon his return to the Executive offices here the statement expressing the President's grief was given out... *(NY Times,* July 2, 1905)

The same day, despite Secretary Hay's death, the business of making the preliminary arrangements for the peace conference continued. Assistant Secretary Forster telegraphed Secretary Loeb with another telegram from Ambassador Meyer.

TELEGRAM.

Received in Cipher. 𝔚𝔥𝔦𝔱𝔢 𝔥𝔬𝔲𝔰𝔢,
                    𝔚𝔞𝔰𝔥𝔦𝔫𝔤𝔱𝔬𝔫.

THE WHITE HOUSE Washington, D.C., July 1 — 8:55 a.m.

Hon. Wm. Loeb, Jr.,
        Secretary to the President,
            Oyster Bay, N.Y.
        Following just received

                        Petersburg

Secretary of State,

        Washington.

Following dated June 30th just received from Lamsdorff:

"By the fact of the nomination of the plenipotentiaries of the two countries and by the fixing of the date and the place of the meeting, the question of peace has reached a definite stage. Under these conditions I believe I should address myself to your excellency in begging you kindly to inform me if, conforming to the idea expressed by President Roosevelt, the Japanese Government does not consider that there is some ground to proceed at the present time to the conclusion of an armistice, of which the terms and conditions could be fixed by direct agreement between the commanders-in-chief of the two armies?" Meyer.

Rudolph Forster,
Assistant Secretary.

(*TR Papers*, Series 1, Reel 55)

The following day, July 2, Secretary Loeb telegraphed Assistant Secretary Forster in Washington with a message for Mr. Takahira. The message repeated the content of the telegrams of June 30 and July 1 from Ambassador Meyer and continued with a message from the President.

TELEGRAM.

CIPHER.

COPY.

𝔚𝔥𝔦𝔱𝔢 𝔥𝔬𝔲𝔰𝔢, 𝔚𝔞𝔰𝔥𝔦𝔫𝔤𝔱𝔬𝔫.

1RV. GI. JM. 944 - Paid Govt.   11:00 a.m.
Oyster-Bay, N.Y., July 2, 1905.
Hon. Rudolph Forster,
    Ass't. Sec'y. to the President,
      The White House.
        Washington, D.C.

Please deliver to Mr. Takahira the following dispatch:

The President has just received from the Russian Government the statement that owing to the ill-health of Monsieur Nelidoff it will substitute for him Ambassador Mauravieff now at Rome and formerly Minister of Justice. The Russian Government further states that it may nominate in addition to Baron Rosen, the second plenipotentiary, a third plenipotentiary and certain delegates to examine any special questions which may arise. The President has answered that of course each government can send an additional plenipotentiary and delegates if it so desires. The President has also received through Ambassador Meyer the following note from Count Lamsdorff:

'By the fact of the nomination of the plenipotentiaries of the two countries and by the fixing of the date and the place of the meeting, the question of peace has reached a definite stage. Under these conditions I believe I should address myself to your excellency in begging you kindly to inform me if, conforming to the idea expressed by President Roosevelt, the Japanese Government does not consider that there is some ground to proceed at the present time to the conclusion of an armistice, of which the terms and conditions could be fixed by direct agreement between the commanders-in-chief of the two armies.'

The President hopes that the Japanese Government will see its way clear to granting the Russian request and will authorize him to state to the Russian Government that the generals commanding the two armies may forthwith negotiate for an armistice, if this is the manner in which the Japanese Government thinks it proper the armistice should be carried on. The President has secured the acceptance by Russia of Washington, D.C., instead of The Hague as a meeting place and has secured the authorization by her to publish on Monday the fact that the Russian plenipotentiaries like the Japanese plenipotentiaries will be empowered to negotiate and conclude a treaty of peace subject to ratification by the respective home governments. From all the information the President can obtain both from St. Petersburg and from Paris he believes that Russia intends to make peace, and he is of the opinion that peace can be secured. He therefore thinks it very desirable that the request for the armistice if possible should be granted. Moreover the President understands that the rainy season is about to begin during which military operations would be very difficult, and if the President is correct about this the objection granting armistice would be minimized. The President has hitherto declined to consider any suggestions from the Russian Government about an armistice, but the negotiations have reached such a stage that he no longer feels at liberty to refuse to speak.

> Wm. Loeb, Jr.,
>   Secretary.

(TR Papers, Series 1, Reel 55)

Later that day, July 2, Secretary Loeb received another telegram from Assistant Secretary Forster in Washington. The telegram contained a telegram from Ambassador Meyer in St. Petersburg. It is interesting to note that it was no longer addressed to the Secretary of State.

TELEGRAM.

𝔚𝔥𝔦𝔱𝔢 𝔥𝔬𝔲𝔰𝔢,
Received in Cipher.   𝔚𝔞𝔰𝔥𝔦𝔫𝔤𝔱𝔬𝔫.

White House, Washington, D.C., July 2 — 9:15 p.m.
    Hon. Wm. Loeb, Jr.,
         Secretary to the President,
             Oyster Bay, N.Y.

    Following from Meyer, St. Petersburg:

    "Notified Lamsdorff at 2:30 o'clock p.m. that the President would announce on Monday the appointment of plenipotentiaries by name, stating that they would be clothed with full powers to negotiate and conclude treaty of peace subject to ratification by home governments. This action fully approved by him. Lamsdorff stated that this evening he would send me the names of the five delegates who would act as specialists on different subjects and would accompany the plenipotentiary Muravieff. As to the armistice Lamsdorff expressed himself as follows: That it was not meant as a direct proposition to Japan but to the President personally, the original idea and movement for peace being the President's. Now that plenipotentiaries, place and time of meeting have been all decided upon an armistice is the natural sequence. On that they want the benefit of the President's advice and action if feasible. Lamsdorff claims that if it should go out to the world that they had made a proposition to Japan and it was turned down it would give the wrong impression and injure them, besides they desire whatever the President may do in this armistice matter to be kept secret."

Rudolph Forster,
Assistant Secretary.

(TR Papers, Series 1, Reel 55)

That evening, a statement was given out by Secretary Loeb in Oyster Bay announcing the names of the representatives from the warring governments who would meet in the United States to negotiate a peace treaty.

> OYSTER BAY, July 2 — The names of the plenipotentiaries selected by the Russian and Japanese Governments for the purpose of negotiating peace between the two nations were made public to-day in the following statement given out at the executive office here by Secretary Loeb:
>
> "The President announces that the Russian and Japanese Governments have notified him that they have appointed the plenipotentiaries to meet here as soon after the 1st of August as possible.
>
> "The two Russian plenipotentiaries are Ambassador Muravieff, formerly Minister of Justice and now Ambassador at Rome, and Ambassador Rosen.
>
> "The Japanese plenipotentiaries are Baron Komura, now Minister of Foreign Affairs, and Minister Takahira. It is possible that each side may send one or more additional representatives.
>
> "The plenipotentiaries of both Russia and Japan will be intrusted with full power to negotiate and conclude a treaty of peace, subject, of course, to ratification by their respective governments."
>
> ...The President's announcement practically concludes the preliminary negotiations for peace... *(NY Times*, July 3, 1905)

On July 3, Mr. Takahira telegraphed Mr. Loeb, via Assistant Secretary Forster in Washington, with a message for the President. It is documented that Mr. Takahira gave the message to Mr. Forster on the letterhead of the Japanese legation in Washington. This was put into cipher and transmitted to Oyster Bay. An example of the method of cipher is as follows: the President = 55963 and Minister Takahira = 45623. The message, as printed below, is the deciphered version. It was deciphered in Oyster Bay at the Moore's Building and typed on White House letterhead. It was in this form that the President received the message. The President's replies, of course, required the same process to be performed in reverse.

TELEGRAM.

White house,
Washington.

Received in Cipher.

White House, Washington, D.C., July 3, 1905.

Hon. Wm. Loeb, Jr.,
    Secretary to the President,
        Oyster Bay, N.Y.

Mr. Takahira asks that following be sent to the President:

"The Japanese minister has the honor to inform the President that he has just received a telegram from Count Katsura, Minister-President and minister for foreign affairs ad interim as follows:

You are hereby instructed to inform the President that his imperial Majesty has appointed on the third of July Baron Komura, minister for foreign affairs, and Mr. Takahira, envoy extraordinary and minister plenipotentiary, as plenipotentiaries of Japan to meet with the plenipotentiaries of Russia for the purpose of negotiating and concluding peace."

Rudolph Forster,
    Asst. Secretary.

(TR Papers, Series 1, Reel 55)

On July 3, Secretary Loeb also received two telegrams from Ambassador Meyer which were forwarded to Oyster Bay from Washington. The first telegram was a description of the state of affairs within Russia.

TELEGRAM.

White house,
Washington.

Received in Cipher.

White House, Washington, D.C., July 3

Hon. Wm. Loeb, Jr.,
    Secretary to the President,
        Oyster Bay, N.Y.

Petersburg July 3.
Secretary of State —— Confidential to the President.
    I have believed heretofore that revolution in Russia improbable but events of the past week have altered conditions and aspects. Increasing strikes, the disturbances in Lodz, the arousing by the Socialists of both the marines in Libau, the sailors in Odessa to a successful mutiny shows progress made by the revolutionists. There is general dissatisfaction among the people over last mobilization; felt that these troops will refuse to act in case of disturbances.

Should Japan refuse armistice and inflict severe defeat on Russian army impossible to foretell what conditions and events might follow due to the state of mind of the people and the incompetency of the Government.

Meyer.

(TR Papers, Series 1, Reel 55)

The information contained in this first telegram convinced the President that no news of Russia's request for an armistice should be released because of the volatility of the situation in Russia. The second telegram related the names of the special delegates that Russia would send to the peace conference. This new information was then sent back to Secretary Forster in Washington to relay to Mr. Takahira.

TELEGRAM.

White house,
Washington.

3RV. GI JM   411 - Paid Govt.   3:55 p.m.
Oyster-Bay, N.Y., July 3, 1905.
Rudolph Forster,
    Ass't. Sec't'y, The White House.

Please deliver the following message to Mr. Takahira:

The President thanks you for your kind letter and cordially appreciates His Majesty's cable which he has personally answered. The President desires of course that no publicity at all should be given to the request for an armistice, and that if it is not granted the President asks that it be treated as a request of his and not of the Russian Government, which would certainly not wish to feel that it made a direct proposition to Japan and been turned down. So the President earnestly requests that no publicity whatever be given to this phase of the matter until final action is taken. The Russian Government has announced to the President that it will send five delegates to act as specialists on different subjects, who will accompany Ambassador Muravieff. Their names are as follows: Pokotiloff, Russian Minister at Peking; De Martens, Privy Councillor and permanent member of Cabinet Council of Foreign Affairs; Chipoff, Privy Councillor and Director of the Ministry of Finance; Major-General Iermoloff, Chief of Military Statistics; Captain Rousine, Naval.

Wm. Loeb, Jr.,

Secretary to the President

(TR Papers, Series 1, Reel 55)

On July 5, Czar Nicolas of Russia wrote to President Roosevelt. It is one of the few handwritten letters that the President received from royalty. It was, of course, delivered to Oyster Bay.

Peterhof.   *July 5/th 1905.*

(*Imperial Seal*)

Dear Mr. Roosevelt,

    I take the opportunity of Mr. Witte's departure for Washington to express to you my feelings of sincere friendship.

    Thanks to your initiative the Russian and Japanese delegates are going to meet in your country to discuss the possible terms of peace between both belligerents.

    I have instructed Mr. Witte, Secretary of State, and my ambassador in the United States Baron Rosen   —how far Russia's concessions can go towards meeting Japan's propositions.

    I need not tell you that I have full confidence that you will do all that lies in your power to bring the peace negotiations to a satisfactory conclusion.

               Believe me

               your's truly

               Nicolas

(*TR Papers*, Series 1, Subseries B, Reel 309)

On July 5, U.S. Ambassador in China , Mr. Rockhill, sent a telegram to Washington which was forwarded by Assistant Secretary Forster to Mr. Loeb in Oyster Bay.

TELEGRAM.

White house, Washington.

<u>Received in Cipher.</u>

Washington, D.C., July 5, 1905.

Hon. William Loeb, Jr.,
    Secretary to the President,
        Oyster Bay, N.Y.

    Following just received from Rockhill:
        "Peking, July 5.

    By special request of the Emperor of China I send the President the following strictly confidential message: "Ever since the beginning of the war between Japan and Russia we have been placed under great obligations by your excellency's kindness in urging upon China a careful observance of neutrality and in proclaiming to the whole world that   the territorial integrity of China must be preserved and that her sovereignty must not be injured. For this our Empire is truly most deeply grateful. Now we hear that Japan and Russia are also planning peace and that your honorable country has come forth as a mediator. Whatever terms may be agreed upon hereafter in treaty between Japan and Russia we earnestly hope that your excellency will remember your former words and secure peace; exerting your influence to protect territorial rights of China in Manchuria and all interest of China, preserving sovereignty complete without loss. The reputation of your honorable country for benevolence and justice will be thus spread abroad throughout the world, and we more than all will never forget your friendly feeling. In sending this telegram we earnestly pray for your excellency that your country may prosper and your people have peace."

I have urged Chinese Government not to seek participation peace negotiations as her sovereign rights could not be impaired thereat. Questions affecting them will presumably be discussed later on. I am now officially informed that China will not send representatives to Washington; will trust solely to the United States."

Rudolph Forster,
Assistant Secretary.

(TR Papers, Series 1, Reel 56)

The following day, the President sent a telegram in reply. The telegram was, of course, sent via the Executive Offices in Oyster Bay to the White House in Washington.

TELEGRAM.

The White House,

1 RV GI JM 148 Paid Govt.   11:50 a.m.

Washington.

Oyster Bay, N.Y., July 6, 1905.

Hon. Rudolph Forster,
    Ass't. Sc'y.
        The White House, Washington, D.C.

        Please have State Department cable following message from the President to Minister Rockhill:
            The United States will do all that it can to preserve the territorial integrity of China and to see that her sovereignty is not

injured in the coming peace negotiations, but all the United States is doing is to bring the two countries together. She has nothing to do with the actual negotiations themselves.

WM.LOEB,JR.,
Secretary.

(TR Papers, Series 1, Reel 56)

Later in the evening of July 6, Minister Takahira sent his government's response to the President's telegrams of July 2nd and 3rd. His message was brought to the White House where Assistant Secretary Forster telegraphed it to Mr. Loeb in Oyster Bay.

TELEGRAM.

𝖂𝖍𝖎𝖙𝖊 𝖍𝖔𝖚𝖘𝖊, 𝖂𝖆𝖘𝖍𝖎𝖓𝖌𝖙𝖔𝖓.

Received in Cipher.

The White House, Washington, D.C., July 6, 1905 —- 8 P.M.

Hon. Wm. Loeb, Jr.,
　　　Secretary to the President,
　　　　　Oyster Bay, N.Y.

Minister Takahira asks that the following be transmitted:

Confidential. In answer to the President's communications of the 2d and 3d instants the Japanese Minister begs to inform the President that he received from His Government the following telegram:

"You will thank the President most cordially for the great trouble and care he is taking in arranging all preliminaries and you will assure him that his wishes concerning non-publicity mentioned in your telegram of the 3d instant will be completely respected. Regarding his suggestion as to armistice you will say that a temporary cessation of arms at this time would only operate to the distinct disadvantage of Japan and corresponding advantage of Russia and Japanese Government are consequently persuaded that armistice at the present juncture instead of making for peace would have contrary effect. Again, Japan has no indication of Russia's disposition towards the conditions of peace, which Japan may consider indispensable, nor is there any way of obtaining definite information on that subject until the plenipotentiaries of the two powers meet and without information armistice can hardly be regarded as feasible. Accordingly the Japanese Government think that the question of armistice should await meeting and decision of such plenipotentiaries."

Rudolph Forster,
Assistant Secretary.

(TR Papers, Series 1, Reel 56)

The President, although he initially suggested Washington as the venue for the peace negotiations, decided to change the venue to Portsmouth, New Hampshire. Third Secretary of State Herbert H.D. Peirce sent a report to the President on July 6, regarding the preparations at Portsmouth, as well as the preparations for the historic meeting between the Russian and Japanese plenipotentiaries in Oyster Bay.

DEPARTMENT OF STATE,

WASHINGTON.

July 6, 1905.

The President,
> Oyster Bay, New York.

Mr. President:

As instructed by you, I have communicated with the Navy Department and with the authorities of the State of New Hampshire relative to the place of the sessions of the plenipotentiaries of Russia and Japan in their negotiations for peace and fitting reception of them by you, and have the honor to report to you as follows:

The Acting Secretary of the Navy informs me that the repairs upon the Mayflower will be completed before August first, so that she will be available for your use in entertaining the plenipotentiaries.

There appears to be no other vessel in our navy of equal character with the Sylph, nor are there any two yachts suitable for transporting the plenipotentiaries from New York to Oyster Bay. All of the vessels termed yachts in the navy appear to be converted into boats for conveying recruits to and from our ships, and it is reported to me that none of them are in suitable condition to convey the plenipotentiaries to Oyster Bay. The Acting Secretary of the Navy suggests that in lieu of this they be transported upon two of the small cruisers of the Cleveland type of about 3000 tons. He informs me that Admiral Sigsbee has three of these cruisers in his squadron and that without doubt, two would be available for the purpose. The alternative would appear to be to convey both parties upon the Sylph.

I venture to submit that, on leaving Oyster Bay for Portsmouth, the plenipotentiaries would avoid running the gauntlet of the newspaper reporters if they were conveyed by water to their destination, and for this purpose the Mayflower and the Dolphin would be admirably suited. In addition, this means of transportation would probably be more comfortable than the railway journey in summer which would have to be broken at Boston, and it would add to the honors with which the plenipotentiaries would be received. The decision as to which of these vessels, if employed for this purpose, should be designated for the Russian plenipotentiaries and which for those of Japan would require some little consideration, but, although one is somewhat larger than the other, both being the President's yachts, there could be no serious feeling of partiality in this question. If one of the cruisers above mentioned was detailed to convoy the two yachts to Portsmouth, this would add to the honors of their reception.

In connection with the selection of Portsmouth, I have the honor to enclose a copy of a letter received from Honorable Edward N. Pearson, Secretary of State of the State of New Hampshire, and also a pamphlet giving pictures of the Wentworth Hotel, and to say that in my opinion, the plenipotentiaries could be lodged, as suggested by Mr. Pearson, in opposite ends of the hotel without fear of offense to either. The Navy Yard is directly across the bay from the Wentworth House, and it would probably be more agreeable for the plenipotentiaries to go from their quarters to their place of meeting by steam or electric launch, which could easily be provided for by the Navy Department. It would, however, probably be well to provide land conveyance also in case of bad weather and to enable the representatives of the powers to enjoy the recreation of driving about the country at times when not in session.

The new building at the Navy Yard appears from the plans to offer every facility requisite for the sittings of the conferees. They are, however, unfurnished, but arrangements could be made for the hire of such furniture as may be needed without very great expense to this government.

I submit a copy of a communication from the President of the Western Union Telegraph Company, from which it appears that the telegraph facilities of Portsmouth are suitable for the needs of the occasion, as is also the railway communication between Portsmouth and Boston.

It would seem to be desirable that an inspection, both of the Wentworth House and such other hotel conditions as Portsmouth offers, as well as the Navy Yard, be made with a view to completing arrangements, and assuming Baron Rosen will find this selection of the meeting place acceptable, I have the honor to suggest that soon after the return of Mr. Adee, I be authorized to proceed to Portsmouth for this purpose.

I have the honor to be, Mr. President,
Your obedient servant

Herbert H. D. Peirce

(TR Papers, Series 1, Reel 56)

Returning to national politics, the announcement of John Hay's replacement was made from the Executive Offices as well.

> OYSTER BAY, July 6 — It is definitely known here that the post of Secretary of State left vacant by the death of John Hay has been offered by President Roosevelt to Elihu Root, formerly Secretary of War. The report that Mr. Root has accepted lacks official confirmation.
>
> There is every likelihood, however, that an official statement definitely announcing Mr. Root's appointment as Secretary of State will be issued from the Executive office here to-morrow...
>
> At the executive offices here it was said this evening by Secretary Loeb that a statement would in all probability be given out to-morrow morning announcing the appointment of Secretary Hay's successor.... *(NY Times,* July 7, 1905)

On July 7, Secretary Loeb received a telegram from Third Secretary of State Herbert Peirce regarding Baron Rosen's introduction to the President.

TELEGRAM.

𝕎hite house,
𝕎ashington.

3 W MS GI 108 Paid Govt — 3:32p

Washington, D.C., July 7.

Hon. William Loeb, Jr.,

      Oyster Bay, N.Y.

      Have just received a call from Baron Rosen, Russian Ambassador, who desires to know when and where the President will receive him. Please inquire of the President his pleasure in this particular and if the Ambassador is to be received at Oyster Bay, advise me how he can best reach there from New York. The Ambassador also desires to know whether he should go in uniform and if not in what costume, your personal advice on this subject will be appreciated. Please inform the President that Baron Rosen accepts Portsmouth for the meeting of the peace conference as entirely satisfactory.

           Herbert H.D. Peirce

(TR Papers, Series 1, Reel 56)

In an interesting aside from the preparations for the peace conference, on July 7, retired army general John Wilson wrote to Secretary Loeb regarding the St. Gaudens-Neiuman Inaugural medals commemorating President Roosevelt's inauguration.

Inaugural Committee
No. 1773 Mass. Ave., N.W.
WASHINGTON *July 7th 1905*

GEN. JOHN M. WILSON
      CHAIRMAN

Hon. William Loeb Jr

      Secretary to the President

          Oyster Bay, New York

My dear Mr. Loeb:

      The St. Gaudens-Neiuman Inaugural medals reached me this morning from Tiffany + co. the box containing the following:

      One gold medal for the President, one gold medal for the Vice President, and one hundred and twenty bronze medals.

      The bronze medals will be distributed as follows:
35 for the President; 82 for the Inaugural Committee; 3 for the Congressional, the War Dept. and the District Col. libraries.

Will you kindly inform me whether the President prefers that I should bring his on and deliver them personally when I come to New York, which I expect to do shortly, or that I should send them by express, or hold them here until he returns to Washington in the Autumn.

In case he prefers I should hold them here, until autumn, can I deliver at once the bronze medals to the members of the Inaugural Committee?

In this matter of the medals, I promptly approved every suggestion of Mr. St Gaudens and Mr. Neiuman.

Yours very cordially

John M. Wilson
Maj. Genl. U.S.A. Retired
Chairman

(TR Papers, Series 1, Reel 56)

After Secretary Loeb received, and subsequently, mailed these medals to various members of government, he received a multitude of letters thanking the President for being so thoughtful. Meanwhile, preparations for the meeting between the Russian and Japanese plenipotentiaries progressed. On or about July 8, Mr. Takahira requested Mr. Forster to make arrangements for him to meet with the President at Sagamore Hill. Mr. Forster relayed this request to Mr. Loeb. The invitation inviting Mr. Takahira to come to Oyster Bay on July 14 was mailed by Mr. Loeb on July 10. Some details of the upcoming conference were also announced from Washington on July 10.

WASHINGTON, July 10 — Orders have been issued for the Mayflower to join the Dolphin at Oyster Bay early in August to receive the plenipotentiaries. The latter will assemble in New York early in August, and be taken to Oyster Bay on two protected cruisers of the Cleveland type, to pay their respects to the President and be formally presented by him to each other. A cruiser will escort them when they sail on the Mayflower and Dolphin to Portsmouth...
(NY Times, July 11, 1905)

On July 11, Secretary Loeb received a copy of a telegram sent by Ambassador Meyer to the Secretary of State. It contained the first intimation that the senior Russian plenipotentiary, Muravieff, had taken ill.

TELEGRAM.

White house, Washington.

<u>Received in Cipher.</u>

White House, Washington, D.C., Received July 11 — 9:20 a.

Hon. Wm. Loeb, Jr.,
> Secretary to the President,
>> Oyster Bay.
> Following just received:

Petersburg.

Secretary of State:
> Cable received this morning. Have communicated contents
to Lamsdorff. Claims again that his so-called unfortunate phrase should not have
been misunderstood. Recognizes that the invitation for meeting of plenipotentiaries not made at instigation of either Japan or Russia; that Russia accepted if
Japan accepted, it requiring the consent of both. Not supposed to have known officially at that time Japan's decision.

> Russia's plenipotentiary and delegates will sail on KAISER WILLIAM, due
New York August first. Muravieff arrived here Sunday morning for instructions;
taken ill yesterday, causing Lamsdorff some concern, as plenipotentiary has just
come from a cure at Contrexville.

Meyer.

(TR Papers, Series 1, Reel 56)

On July 12, Second Assistant Secretary of State Alvey Adee sent a telegram to Secretary
Loeb regarding the plans for Baron Rosen to come to Oyster Bay the following day.

TELEGRAM.

White house, Washington.

3 W K GI 125 Paid Govt —1:06p

Washington, D.C., July 12, 1905.

Hon. William Loeb, Jr.,
> Oyster Bay, N.Y.

Am just in receipt of a communication from Acting Secretary of the Navy as to
the SYLPH, and a telegram from Baron Rosen informing me that he will be in
readiness. Mr. Peirce will meet Baron Rosen in New York to-morrow morning at
eight thirty and take him to the Sylph and accompany him to Oyster Bay, arriving
there about twelve fifteen, landing at the dock of Mrs. J. West Roosevelt and proceeding at once as instructed to the President's house. Baron Rosen is much gratified at the President's invitation to luncheon which he accepts with great pleasure.
Mr. Peirce also desires me to thank the President for his invitation with which he
has much gratification in complying.

Alvey A. Adee

(TR Papers, Series 1, Reel 56)

Later that evening, Secretary Loeb received a telegram containing a message from Mr. Takahira from Mr. Forster in Washington.

TELEGRAM.

𝔚hite house,
𝔚ashington.

<u>RECEIVED IN CIPHER.</u>

The White House,
Washington, D.C., July 12 —— 8 P.M.

Hon. Wm. Loeb, Jr.,
        Secretary to the President,
            Oyster Bay, N.Y.

Minister Takahira asks that following be transmitted to the President:

"The Japanese minister has learned from the Associated Press that Monsieur Pokotiloff, Russian minister to China will replace Monsieur Muravieff as Russian plenipotentiary, and the Press dispatch from Paris even goes so far as to state that Monsieur Muravieff has cancelled his reservation of passage to New York on board the KAISER WILHELM DER GROSSE. The Japanese minister conse-quently begs to request that the President would be good enough to ascertain whether the above report is correct, and if so, whether Baron Rosen or Monsieur Pokotiloff is to be considered as senior member of Russian Commission or whether some other person will be appointed as senior plenipotentiary and Monsieur Pokotiloff is coming simply as advisor as previously understood."

Rudolph Forster,
        Assistant Secretary.

—-I—-

(TR Papers, Series 1, Reel 56)

Also on July 12, Mr. wrote to Secretary Loeb to accept the President's invitation to lunch.

Legation of Japan,
Washington.

July 12. 1905

My dear Mr Secretary.

I have just received your kind letter of the 10th of July and it will give me a great honor to join the President's lunch on Friday at one o'clock. I will leave Long Island City at the hour suggested. I asked Mr. Forster to telegraph you of my acceptance of the President's invitation yesterday afternoon and I think you are undoubtedly aware of it by this time.

*With kind regards
Sincerely yours
K Takahira*

*Hon. William Loeb., Jr.,
        Oyster Bay. N.Y.*

(TR Papers, Series 1, Reel 56)

On July 13th, 1905, the President met with the Russian plenipotentiary, Baron Rosen. Third Secretary of State Peirce wrote to Secretary Loeb regarding the conversation with Baron Rosen on the return trip to New York City.

The Waldorf-Astoria

New York July 13, 1905

Hon. William M. Loeb,
      Secretary to the President,
         Oyster Bay, L.I.

Dear Mr. Loeb:

      On the trip back Baron Rosen said to me that he greatly desired to have some further talk with the President. He expressed himself as being satisfied there had been some early misunderstanding regarding Russia on the part of our Government, which he felt sure that he could set right to the mutual good relations and good understanding of our respective Governments. The Ambassador made a considerable point of this and spoke of it on my *and desired me to make it known to the President.* parting from him at his hotel. He said that he did not desire to trouble the President by making an appointment for a formal audience, but that he would greatly appreciate it if the President would inform him when he might come down to Oyster Bay again before the Peace Conference and have a brief talk with him.

      Baron Rosen informed me that Mr. Witte and the delegates to the conference will sail from Cherbourg July 26th.

      Regarding the dinner which the President proposes to give to the Plenipotentiaries, it is very desirable that I know as much in advance as possible who will be included, and Capt. Winslow has expressed to me a similar desire. I send you herewith a list of the Plenipotentiaries and delegates for your convenience and that of the President in this regard.

      My address for the next week will be York Harbor, Maine, this being but a half hour from Portsmouth, where I have to make the preliminary arrangements for the conference.

          Very sincerely yours,

Herbert H.D. Peirce

(TR Papers, Series 1, Reel 56)

In the morning of July 13, a copy of the telegram from Ambassador Meyer to the Secretary of State was telegraphed to Secretary Loeb in Oyster Bay.

TELEGRAM.

𝔚hite house, 𝔚ashington.

The White House, Washington, D.C., July 13, 1905 — 10a.

Hon. Wm. Loeb, Jr.,
    Secretary to the President,
        Oyster Bay, N.Y.

St. Petersburg.

Secretary of State:

Received official communication from Lamsdorff this morning that Witte has been appointed in the place of Muravieff on account of the latters health. Witte, furnished with the full requisite powers, sails from Cherbourg <u>Wednesday</u>, July <u>twenty-fifth</u>, due New York August first ——- Meyer.

(TR Papers, Series 1, Reel 56)

At 12:45 p.m. on July 13, Secretary Loeb transmitted the text of this telegram to Assistant Secretary Forster with the request that it be given to Mr. Takahira. According to a hand-written note on the bottom of the telegram, Mr. Forster delivered it to First Secretary Hioki, Mr. Takahira's secretary. Mr. Forster then sent a telegram to Mr. Loeb confirming this. *(TR Papers*, Series 1, Reel 56)

On the 14th, the President met with the Japanese Minister (and plenipotentiary) Takahira. Of no less importance, the President met with Theodore P. Shonts, Chairman of the Executive Committee of the Isthmian Canal Commission and John F. Stevens, the newly appointed chief engineer of the Panama Canal to discuss Canal details.

In an interesting aside from politics, the firm of "Heins and La Farge", architects, wrote to Secretary Loeb regarding repairs that were to be made at Sagamore Hill after the President returned to Washington.

HEINS & LA FARGE. ARCHITECTS.

30-32 EAST TWENTY-FIRST STREET

NEW YORK

G.L. HEINS.

C.GRANT LA FORGE   In re Roosevelt House.

July 14, 1905.

Hon. Wm. Loeb, Jr.,
        Secretary to the President,
                Oyster Bay, L.I.

Dear Sir:-
        Replying to your favor of the 13th
inst., the matter of the defective fireplace will be taken up with the
contractors before final certificate is issued. There are also some
small matters in connection with the woodwork which we wish to
have the builders rectify as soon as the President and his family
leave Sagamore Hill.
        Yours very truly,
                Heins & La Farge,
                        Per
                        Bush

(TR Papers, Series 1, Reel 56)

By July 17, Secretary Loeb left Oyster Bay for a vacation and Assistant Secretary B.F.
Barnes assumed the former's duties completely. On July 17, a telegram from
Ambassador Meyer to Assistant Secretary of State Adee was telegraphed to Oyster Bay.

TELEGRAM.

White house,

RECEIVED IN CIPHER.   # Washington.

The White House, Washington, D.C., July 16, 1905.
Received July 17 — 9:28a

Hon. B. F. Barnes,
        Acting Secretary to the President,
        O y s t e r B a y, N.Y.

Petersburg.

Adee,
        Washington.
        Confidential. Witte called on me this afternoon. Impressed with his character
and direct way of speaking; first man that really has been frank. Regrets Ito is
not coming as plenipotentiary; feels that they could have come to an immediate

understanding. Witte says that he has been opposed to war from the first and has desired peace. Everything now however, depends entirely on Japan's willingness to make such conditions as the Emperor and Russia can accept. Will do utmost within his instructions in order to bring about an agreement. Leaves for Paris Wednesday; sails Cherbourg twenty-sixth, due August first. Expressed great respect for the Japanese and much satisfaction in being able to go to the United States of America. Speaks French but not English.

Meyer.

(TR Papers, Series 1, Reel 56)

Also on July 17, Acting Secretary of State Adee sent to Mr. Barnes a note from the Chinese Minister for the President regarding the upcoming peace negotiations between Japan and Russia.

DEPARTMENT OF STATE,

Washington, July 17, 1905.

Benjamin F. Barnes, Esquire,
    Acting Secretary to the President,
        Oyster Bay, New York.

Sir:

    I enclose for the President's perusal a copy of a note from the Chinese Minister embodying a declaration by his Government that it will not recognize as valid, without the approval of China previously obtained, any provision affecting China that may be contained in a treaty of peace between Japan and Russia.

I am, Sir,

Your obedient servant

Alvey A. Adee

Acting Secretary.

Enclosure:

    From Chinese Minister,
        July 10, 1905.

(TR Papers, Series 1, Reel 56)

In a remarkable contrast with the modus operandi of today's papparazzi, the photographer Gotthelf Pach wrote to Mr. Barnes on July 18, requesting permission to photograph the historic visit of the   Russian and Japanese plenipotentiaries to Sagamore Hill.

Pach Bros.
New York

July 18 / 05

My dear Mr. Barnes:

The visit of the Peace Envoys to Sagamore Hill will of course be an event of International Import, and I write to ask if we cannot be present with a camera ready to immortalize it, photographically speaking, should occasion serve. Of course I understand it must be done very quietly and unobtrusively and you can rest assured we will handle the affair with all possible tact.

Trusting it will meet the President's approval, I am, with kind regard,

Yours very truly
Gotthelf Pach.

Mr. B. F. Barnes,
Secretary to the President
Oyster Bay
Long Island.

(TR Papers, Series 1, Reel 56)

On July 19, Acting Secretary of the Navy Darling telegraphed to the Executive Office in Oyster Bay to inform them that the Sylph had been ordered to proceed to Oyster Bay immediately. *(TR Papers*, Series 1, Reel 57)

On July 20, Assistant Secretary of State Peirce wrote to Secretary Loeb regarding final preparations for lodging in Portsmouth.

Portsmouth, N.H., July 20" 1905.

Hon. William Loeb,
    Secretary to the President,
        Oyster Bay,
            Long Island, N.Y.
My dear Mr. Loeb:-

            I have received from Hon. Calvin Page a letter (a copy of which I append) offering to the President the hospitalities of "The Wentworth" and "The Rockingham" Houses during the Peace Conference, and request you to kindly place the matter before the President.

Very sincerely yours,

Herbert H. D. Peirce
Third Assistant Secretary of State

(TR Papers, Series 1, Reel 57)

On July 21, Assistant Secretary of State Peirce wrote again to Secretary Loeb regarding final preparations for the State dinner on the Mayflower as well as other preparations for the peace conference.

Portsmouth, N.H., July 20" 1905.

Hon. William Loeb,
      Secretary to the President,
         Oyster Bay,
           Long Island, N.Y.

My dear Mr. Loeb:-
      Your letter of July 14" received by me on my return from a visit to the Governor of New Hampshire, who desired to confer with me in the White Mountains.

      I note the President's suggestion for the additional guests for the dinner on "The Mayflower." You ask me to advise you as to the date of the dinner. It seems to me that the date can hardly be fixed definitely earlier than the 4th, or perhaps better the 5th, of August. The Russian plenipotentiaries leave Cherbourg on July 26th, which would probably bring them to New York about the 2d or 3d if the ship is on time, and the officials would probably require a day in which to recover from the voyage.

      With regard to the capacity of "The Mayflower" to accommodate twenty-three at dinner, I have no doubt that she can do so comfortably; indeed I am very sure of this from my talk with the people in the Navy Department and with Commander Winslow, but in order to make sure I have telegraphed Commander Winslow inquiring.

      I thank you very much for the memorandum from Embassador Jusserand, which is extremely convenient for guidance. I note that a permanent buffet was placed at the disposal of the plenipotentiaries and delegates in Paris, and I propose a similar buffet at Portsmouth.

      The State of New Hampshire, as the President knows, confers its hospitalities to the parties, and this consists in giving them their rooms (which are sufficiently commodious and upon a satisfactory scale) and furnishing them also, of course, their meals.

      It would be necessary to transport them daily from "The Wentworth" where they will be lodged to the Navy Yard, and for this purpose water communication for fair weather can be provided by the Navy Yard itself; but the conditions of the harbor are such that this would only be available in fair weather, and it seems to me, therefore, that our government should provide means of transportation from "The Wentworth" House to the Navy Yard by land. I am now engaged in endeavoring to form an accurate estimate of the cost of this, and will advise you later. I had hoped to be able to do so in this letter, but the estimates have not yet been furnished to me.

Very sincerely yours,

Herbert H.D. Peirce
Third Assistant Secretary of State

(*TR Papers*, Series 1, Reel 57)

On July 22, Mr. Takahira wrote to Secretary Loeb regarding the arrival of Baron Komura, the first plenipotentiary of Japan.

Legation of Japan, Washington.

July 22nd, 1905.

Honorable William Loeb, Jr.,
         Secretary to the President.

My dear Mr. Loeb:

I beg to request that you will be good enough to inform the President that Baron Komura, the First Plenipotentiary of Japan, will arrive at New York on Tuesday the 25th instant. It is my intention to go to New York on Monday to meet him there and I am inclined to think that before Baron Komura will be presented to the President informally, as was suggested by him, I may be required to request a short audience with the President to speak with him on certain matters he mentioned to me the other day. In case I should decide to do so, I will telegraph you from New York asking the pleasure of the President as to the day and hour which may suit his convenience to receive me.

With kind regards, I am,

Very sincerely yours,

K. Takahira

(TR Papers, Series 1, Reel 57)

Also on July 22, a statement, presumably released by the Executive Offices, was made regarding the Panama Canal.

OYSTER BAY, July 22 — President Roosevelt after a conference with Secretary of State Root to-night authorized the statement in regard to the contemplated transfer of the Panama Canal work from the War Department to the Department of State that it had been determined to let it remain under the jurisdiction of Secretary of War Taft for the present... *(NY Times*, July 23, 1905)

On the same day, the *The New York Times* also reported that the President called for an extra session of Congress in order to get new legislation passed regarding the Panama Canal.

It was learned here to-day that a call for an extra session of Congress to convene on Nov. 11 will be issued from the executive office here within a few days. This action had been contemplated by the President for some time, but the date had not been definitely set until within the last two weeks.

After an explosion which killed at least 60 people on the gunboat Bennington, the President cabled the following telegram to Acting Secretary of the Navy, Charles H. Darling.

OYSTER BAY, L.I., July 22 — ..."Am inexpressibly shocked by disaster to Bennington. I assume as a matter of course that everything is being done for the survivors who are injured. Please let me know particulars as soon as possible." *(NY Times, July 23, 1905)*

On July 23, Mr. Barnes received a telegram from Baron Rosen regarding his arrival to Oyster Bay on the 31st of July.

TELEGRAM.

The White House, Washington.

2 NY NL HE 18 Paid 6 PM

Magnolia, Mass., July 23, 1905.

B.F. Barnes,
      Acting Secretary, Ex. Office, O.Bay, N.Y.

Will come down Monday July 31st by 11:02 A.M. train from Long Island City.
                    Rosen.

(TR Papers, Series 1, Reel 57)

On July 24, 1905, *The New York Times* reported that in order to facilitate the peace negotiations in Portsmouth, there would be "telephones and telegraph offices near at hand, so that the envoys may keep in close touch with their Governments and with Oyster Bay."

The telegraph facilities located at the Executive Offices were also at the disposal of visiting dignitaries. After President Roosevelt refused to   accept the resignation of Governor George R. Carter of Hawaii, the Governor sent a cable to the acting Governor of Hawaii, presumably from the Executive Offices.

Acting Governor Atkinson has received a cable dispatch from Gov. Carter at Oyster Bay, in which Mr. Carter says:
"I shall continue."
This dispatch is taken to mean that Gov. Carter will stay in office.
(NY Times, July 25, 1905)

Also on July 24, Acting Secretary of State Alvey sent a letter to Mr. Barnes in Oyster Bay regarding the Canton-Hankow Railway. The Chinese were making inquiries in an effort to buy out the American concession for the railway because of mismanagement by the American-China Development Company, a corporation of which the firm J.P. Morgan & Co. held the controlling interest.

DEPARTMENT OF STATE,
WASHINGTON.

Personal.   July 24, 1905.

My dear Mr. Barnes:

Complying with the President's direction in your telegram of the 23d, I have cabled Mr. Rockhill to send a full report as to desirability of Americans retaining Hankow railroad.

Cordially yours,

Alvey A. Adee

Hon. B.F. Barnes,
    Acting Secretary to the President,
        Oyster Bay, New York.

(TR Papers, Series 1, Reel 57)

On July 25, Assistant Secretary of State Peirce telegraphed Mr. Loeb asking if the President authorized him to use his discretion in making transportation arrangements to and from the Navy Yard for the plenipotentiaries. *(TR Papers*, Series 1, Reel 57)

In an important letter, Simon Wolf wrote to Secretary Loeb on July 25 asking for an appointment with the President. Mr. Wolf wished to plead the case of Russian Jewry before Plenipotentiary Witte. Mr. Wolf thought Mr. Witte would lend a sympathetic ear.

Washington D. C.
July 25.05.

My dear Mr. Loeb.

I would like to see the President without any one knowing it. Mr. Witte the Russian representative is secretly friendly to the Jews, I am anxious to meet him as the representative of our people, much can now be done not only for the Russian Jews in Russia and in the U. S. but also for Russia and the United States. Russia needs money and friends. We can supply both, thus help Russia internally, and relieve our Country of the unnatural inflow of Immigrants. Conditions are ripe, and judicious tact and diplomacy may solve a problem of great moment.

Sincerely yours

Simon Wolf

Hon Wm Loeb Jr.

(TR Papers, Series 1, Reel 57)

On July 26, Acting Secretary Adee telegraphed Acting Secretary Barnes in Oyster Bay with Minister Rockhill's response to the telegram of July 24.

DEPARTMENT OF STATE,
WASHINGTON.

July 26, 1905.

Dear Mr. Barnes:

    Answering your telegram of the 23d, I beg to communicate the following cable message which I received today from Mr. Rockhill in response to the instructions sent at the President's direction:

"Peking, July 25, 1905.

"Secretary of State,
      Washington.

" Your telegram of twenty-fourth. The concession for the Canton-Hankow Railway was originally secured with direct support and assistance of our Government and this legation. Principal inducement was absence of all political complications. This allayed also all foreign antagonism. Chinese, while seeking full control by purchase of the concession, do so because confidence in the Development Company is absolutely shaken through former sale to foreigners of the majority of shares of the company, employment non-Americans, extravagance, and general bad management. Government of China wishes the line built and regrets the necessity of expending such a large sum for the cancelling of the concession. Price fixed by the Development Company six millions three quarters, a sum vastly in excess of outlay of Company to date, plus liberal interest, is looked upon by all as excessively sharp practice of the shareholders. It is a blow to all our interests in China. It places our Government, which helped to secure the concession, in a false position. It serves to intensify anti-American feeling and aids our competitors in these markets. It has shaken belief in our business integrity. If consummated Americans will get no new concessions for years to come. I strongly urged that an arrangement be promptly reached with the Chinese and work begun and actively pushed under good management.

Rockhill."

I am, my dear Mr. Barnes,

Very cordially yours
Alvey A. Adee

Hon. B.F. Barnes,
      Acting Secretary to the President,
            Oyster Bay, New York.

(TR Papers, Series 1, Reel 57)

Early in the morning on July 26, Mr. Takahira telegraphed Mr. Barnes to inform him that he will take the 11:02 train from Long Island City to Oyster Bay. *(TR Papers, Series 1, Reel 57)*

Later that day, Acting Secretary of State Peirce telegraphed Mr. Barnes to determine if the President approved the final fixing of the date to receive the plenipotentiaries.

TELEGRAM.

The White House, Washington.

1 W B GI 31 Paid Govt —-12:18p

SD — Washington, D.C., July 26

Hon. B. F. Barnes,
Acting Secretary to the President,
Oyster Bay.

Does the President approve August fifth as date of reception and dinner to Peace plenipotentiaries and delegates?
Herbert H.D. Peirce.

(TR Papers, Series 1, Reel 57)

Also on July 26, Mr. Forster forwarded to Mr. Barnes a cablegram that was sent to Washington from Ambassador McCormick in Paris. The Ambassador reported that the Russian delegates had taken a hard line on the issue of paying Japan an indemnity for the war.

TELEGRAM.

White house, Washington.

RECEIVED IN CIPHER.

The White House, Washington, D.C., July 26 — 6 P.M.

Hon. B. F. Barnes,
Acting Secretary to the President,
Oyster Bay.

The following cablegram just received:

"Paris.

Secretary of State:

Witte called on me on Sunday and in course of conversation said that he would not even discuss a payment of indemnity with Japanese commissioners; that if the demand was made seriously and adhered to the length of his stay in the United States would be short. He repeated the assertion to me on the occasion of my return visit and made it in equally strong language to German Ambassador who expressed his surprise but left with the impression that Witte was firm in this position. Professor Martin held same attitude as chief commissioner in short talk I was able to have with him last evening. Much will depend upon the nature of counsel given by German Emperor at recent meeting ——McCormick."

Rudolph Forster,

Acting Secretary.

(TR Papers, Series 1, Reel 57)

Five minutes later, Ambassador McCormick cabled again.

TELEGRAM.

𝔚𝔥𝔦𝔱𝔢 𝔥𝔬𝔲𝔰𝔢,
𝔚𝔞𝔰𝔥𝔦𝔫𝔤𝔱𝔬𝔫.

RECEIVED IN CIPHER.

The White House, Washington, D.C., July 26, 1905 — 6:05p

Hon. B. F. Barnes,
    Acting Secretary to the President,
        Oyster Bay.
                        "Paris.

Secretary of State:

Witte expressed same view to Minister of Foreign Affairs in strongest language, and, as latter informed me today, showed no sign of being willing to yield anything on this point. Here, as elsewhere however, great faith is in the power of the President being able to bring the combatants together —— McCormick."

Rudolph Forster,
                        Acting Secretary.

(TR Papers, Series 1, Reel 57)

On July 27, the President met with the Japanese plenipotentiaries at Sagamore Hill. This meeting was considered to be very important in connection with the peace negotiations between Russia and Japan.

OYSTER BAY, July 27 — Baron Komura and Minister Takahira were received by President Roosevelt at Sagamore Hill to-day.

While the visit is looked upon as being of the utmost importance in connection with the peace negotiations the coming and going of the two envoys was most unostentatious. Baron Komura and Mr. Takahira arrived here a little after noon. At the station the President's carriage was in waiting. Minister

Takahira, who has been here often enough in the last fortnight to know his way about pretty well, conducted his colleague to the carriage...

While Secretary Barnes, after conferring with the President, announced that no statement on the conference would be made for publication at this time, it is not denied that matters of the gravest import came up for discussion...
(*NY Times*, July 28, 1905)

Also on July 27, Assistant Secretary of State Peirce wrote to Mr. Barnes in Oyster Bay with the final details of the reception of the plenipotentiaries in Oyster Bay.

DEPARTMENT OF STATE,
WASHINGTON.

July 27, 1905.

Honorable Benjamin F. Barnes,
    Secretary to the President,
        Oyster Bay, N.Y.

Dear Mr. Barnes:

I am leaving this afternoon for Portsmouth to complete arrangements for the peace conference there, and shall then return to New York to pay my respects to the plenipotentiaries there, and escort them to Oyster Bay and present them to the President. My movements will be as follows: I arrive at Boston Friday morning, July 28, and proceed thence to Portsmouth, making York Harbor, where my wife is at present located, my headquarters until August first, when I go to Portsmouth.

Until August first, letters and telegrams addressed to me at York Harbor, Maine, will reach me. On August first, my address will be The Rockingham House, Portsmouth, New Hampshire. Wednesday morning, August 2, I go to New York where my address will be The University Club. On Saturday morning, August 5, at 9 o'clock, the plenipotentiaries will commence to embark aboard the cruisers which are to convey them to Oyster Bay where they will arrive about one o'clock. I shall precede them on the Sylph and will at once go on board the Mayflower and report to the President. It would be a convenience if the President should be on board the Mayflower at one o'clock and the cruisers will not proceed up to their anchorage until they see the President's flag flying upon the Mayflower. I would suggest that the captains of the three cruisers, the Tacoma, Galveston and Chattanooga, might well be added to the list of the President's luncheon, which I note is substituted for the dinner at first intended.

After luncheon it would seem best that the Japanese should leave the Mayflower before the President, and then the President should take his departure, leaving the Russians on board.

I believe that arrangements so far as they can be conveniently directed from Washington are now complete.

Very sincerely yours,

Herbert H. D. Peirce
Third Assistant Secretary

(*TR Papers*, Series 1, Reel 57)

On July 28, H. Bussche of the German Embassy, sent a letter to Acting Secretary Barnes. Enclosed with the letter was a confidential telegram to the President from Emperor William of Germany.

IMPERIAL GERMAN EMBASSY.

Lenox, Mass.
28th of July 05

My dear Mr. Barnes.

Please communicate as soon as possible the enclosed telegramm from H.M. the German Emperor to the President and let me know by one word that you have received my letter.

Very sincerely yours

H. Bussche

(TR Papers, Series 1, Reel 57)

The enclosed telegram was as follows:

IMPERIAL GERMAN EMBASSY.

Telegramm

Just had interview with Emperor Nicolas. His Majesty quite collected, firm, of peaceful disposition. Is most deeply grateful to you for your offering to bring about peace, and most touched by your letter to him. He is most satisfied with Mr. Meyer whom he trusts completely. He hopes and trusts that your powerful personality and genial statesmanship will enable you to bring too exorbitant Japanese conditions down to sensible level.

This communication is strictly <u>confidential</u> only for you <u>personally</u>; and you will kindly not mention it till after conclusion of peace.

William I.R.

(TR Papers, Series 1, Reel 57)

On July 29, Minister Takahira wrote to Secretary Barnes regarding his visit to Sagamore Hill with Baron Komura two days earlier.

Legation of Japan,
Washington.

July 29th. 1905

B.F. Barnes Esq.
  Acting Secretary to the President
    Oyster Bay, N.Y.

Dear Sir,

When Baron Komura and I were at Sagamore Hill the other day, the former told the President that he brought the Imperial message with him and he would deliver it to the President on the occasion of the formal presentation. I now wish to know whether on that occasion the Japanese Plenipotentiaries and those of Russia are to be presented to the President on board the "Mayflower" in body and not separately. If so, I am afraid the occasion will not permit Baron Komura to deliver the message to the President, and in that case he will have to request the President to receive him once more for that purpose before the formal presentation. But as we have troubled the President too much, we should be pleased if there is a way to arrange the formal presentation in such a manner as to enable each party of the plenipotentiaries to deliver to the President any message that they might have brought from their Sovereign and also to present to him the members of their respective staff so that they (Japanese + Russian plenipotentiaries) shall be introduced to each other after the formal presentation conducted separately. I beg you will kindly take the President's instruction in this matter and inform me of the same.

Sincerely yours

K Takahira

(TR Papers, Series 1, Reel 57)

On July 30, Acting Secretary Barnes sent the President's reply to Emperor William to Mr. Bussche at the Imperial German Embassy in Massachusetts. Mr. Bussche forwarded the reply to the Emperor. *(TR Papers*, Series 1, Reel 57)

On July 31, one of the Russian ambassadors met with the President and it was
announced that Russia's other Ambassador would also come to Sagamore Hill before
the formal reception was held.

> OYSTER BAY, L.I., July 31 — Following a visit at Sagamore Hill to-day of
> Baron Rosen, the Russian Ambassador, it was formally announced to-day that
> M. Witte, Russia's other peace plenipotentiary, would follow the example of
> Baron Komura and pay a visit to President Roosevelt prior to the formal recep-
> tion of the envoys on Saturday. M. Witte, who is due in this country to-mor-
> row or Wednesday, will pay his respects to Mr. Roosevelt on Friday, Baron
> Rosen will accompany him, and the two envoys will take luncheon at
> Sagamore Hill... *(NY Times*, August 1, 1905)

On August 1, the President met with Attorney General Moody.

> OYSTER BAY, Aug. 1 —Attorney General Moody spent all day in conference
> with President Roosevelt at Sagamore Hill. Mr. Moody will not leave the
> President's home until to-morrow morning, when he will go direct to
> Washington.
> It is not denied here that the President and Mr. Moody are discussing the
> scandals which have developed in the Department of Agriculture, and which
> led to the visit of the Secretary of Agriculture Wilson to Sagamore Hill yester-
> day. Mr. Roosevelt is determined not only to drive grafters out of the depart-
> ment, but to send to jail any employee against whom criminal charges will
> hold... *(NY Times*, August 2, 1905)

Assistant Secretary of State Peirce wrote two letters to Acting Secretary Barnes on
August 1. Both were regarding the final arrangements for the presentation of the
plenipotentiaries of Russia and Japan to the President in Oyster Bay.

Portsmouth, N.H., August 1" 1905.

Hon. B.F. Barnes,
> Acting Secretary to the President,
> > Oyster Bay, N.Y.

My dear Mr. Barnes:-
> I am in receipt of your letter of July 29th, informing me of the
President's instructions to me to invite the Captains of the three cruisers Tacoma,
Dalveston and Chattanooga to luncheon on "The Mayflower" on the 5th inst., and
also Col. Charles S. Bromwell should be in attendance.
> I am in receipt of a telegram from Col. Bromwell asking me if I
can take him to Oyster Bay on the 5th, and have telegraphed him in reply that I
can do so on the "Sylph".
> I note the President wishes that I should arrange for the pres-
ence on "The Mayflower" of Mr. H.A. Strohmeyer, photographer of Arlington,
N.J. (*Underwood & Underwood*), Mr. Elmer E. Payne, of the Associated Press,
Mr. R.H. Hazard, of the Publishers Press Association, and Mr. H.J. Forman, of the
New York Sun Press Association, and that the press and photographic representation be limited to these four, and will make the appropriate arrangements to carry
out his wishes.

Regarding formal speeches, I will confer with the Russian and Japanese plenipotentiaries on Thursday in New York, and will advise you further on this matter.

I will leave here to-morrow morning at an early hour for New York, where my address will be "University Club".

Arrangements here are completed, and I see no reason to doubt that all will proceed smoothly, so far as my functions are concerned.

Very truly yours,

Herbert H. D. Peirce

Third Assistant Secretary of State.

(TR Papers, Series 1, Reel 57)

The second letter read as follows:

Portsmouth, N.H., August 1" 1905.

Hon. B.F. Barnes,
    Acting Secretary to the President,
      Oyster Bay, N.Y.

My dear Mr. Barnes:-

I am in receipt of your two letter of July 27th and July 31st, respectively, relating to the relative precedence of the Japanese and Russian plenipotentiaries, and am glad to know how the President has determined this matter.

In consultation with Mr. Adee, he had expressed his opinion to me that Baron Rosen and Mr. Takahira being the only persons formally accredited to our government, and Baron Rosen being accredited as ambassador, the Russians should have precedence; but I note that the President regards the two first plenipotentiaries as having the standing of ambassadors, although not specially accredited, and by consequence of Baron Komura being the first to arrive he will have precedence.

I will see to it that the President's instructions regarding this are carried out, and that the Japanese representatives shall be brought on board "The Mayflower" on the 5th inst. sufficiently in advance of the Russians to allow entirely separate presentation of the representatives of each country before they are presented to each other. I presume that one-half an hour would be a sufficient interval for this purpose.

Very truly yours,

Herbert H. D. Peirce

Third Assistant Secretary of State.

(TR Papers, Series 1, Reel 57)

On August 3, Acting Secretary Barnes received a telegram from Assistant Secretary of State Peirce stating Baron Rosen's views of which plenipotentiary should have precedence during the upcoming meetings.

TELEGRAM.

𝕎hite house,
𝕎ashington.

5 NY D GI 106 Collect Govt —3:15p

CP — New York, August 3, 1905.

The Acting Secretary to the President,
    Oyster Bay, N.Y.

Baron Rosen has just stated to me that while he accepts willingly the decision of the President as to the order of presentation to him he considers that in view of the decision of the Congress of Vienna that the resident and regularly accredited representative of a country takes precedence over special envoys and as he is an ambassador and Mr. Takahira a minister, on other occasions the Russians should be entitled to the precedence. Please present this view to the President and ask his instructions for my guidance in arrangements at Portsmouth.

Herbert H.D. Peirce.

(TR Papers, Series 1, Reel 57)

Also on August 3, Mr. Takahira wrote to Mr. Barnes enclosing a copy of the Imperial Message which Baron Komura intended to present to the President in Oyster Bay.

Hotel Majestic, New York City

August 3rd 1905

B.F. Barnes Esq.
Acting Secretary to the President
Oyster Bay, N.Y.

Dear Sir,

With reference to the Imperial message which Baron Komura intends to deliver to the President on the occasion of the formal presentation of the Japanese Plenipotentiaries, I beg herewith to enclose to you a copy of his address showing in what form the message will be delivered to its high destination. I wish you will be good enough to submit the enclosed copy to the President for his perusal. I should be indebted by your kindly furnishing me with a copy of the President's reply, sometime after the presentation, if it suits his pleasure to give it through Baron Komura on that occasion.

Very Sincerely Yours
K Takahira

(TR Papers, Series 1, Reel 57)

On August 3rd and 4th, 1905 President Roosevelt received many distinguished visitors. Among them were the British Ambassador, Sir Henry Mortimer Durand, M. Witte and Baron Rosen, the Russian plenipotentiaries, and a delegation of two Koreans. The two Koreans sought, and later received an audience with the President.

> OYSTER BAY, Aug. 3 — ...Mr. Yoon, who heads the Korean delegation, will seek an audience with President Roosevelt to-morrow to present him a memorial and voice a fervent plea on behalf of the Korean people that Mr. Roosevelt constitute himself the guardian of Korea's rights in the coming peace negotiations... *(NY Times,* August 4, 1905)

On August 4, Acting Secretary Barnes received two telegrams from Assistant Secretary of State Peirce. The first was a rough timetable for the arrival of the ships and plenipotentiaries to Oyster Bay.

TELEGRAM.

The White House, Washington.

2 NY QQ GI 65 Collect Govt —9:04a

BN — New York, August 4, 1905.

Hon. B. F. Barnes,
    Secretary to the President,
      Oyster Bay.

Admirals Sigsbee and Coghland invited, Evans at sea MAYFLOWER can come into lower bay Japanese will come on board when President's flag shown on MAYFLOWER. Expect it to be about one o clock. Russians follow in half hour. I come on board to present officials. Mayflower will send launch for President.

Herbert H.D. Peirce.

(TR Papers, Series 1, Reel 57)

The second informed Mr. Barnes that only Baron Komura would deliver a short message to the President from the Japanese Emperor.

TELEGRAM.

The White House,
Washington.

9 NY D GI 40 Paid —2:38p

P — New York, August 4, 1905.

Hon. B. F. Barnes:

Baron Rosen informs me that it is not the intention of the Russian plenipotentiaries to make any formal speeches tomorrow. Baron Komura informs me that he has a brief message from the Emperor of Japan to communicate to the President.

Herbert H.D. Peirce.

(TR Papers, Series 1, Reel 57)

On August 4, Assistant Secretary of State Alvey Adee wrote to Acting Secretary Barnes relaying the text of a telegram from American Minister in China, W.W. Rockhill. A boycott of American goods by Chinese merchants prompted the telegram. It was suggested that the boycott was used by the Chinese Authorities to force the American Government and J.P. Morgan to surrender the Canton-Hankow Railway concession.

OFFICE OF
SECOND ASSISTANT SECRETARY

ALVEY A. ADEE.

Department of State,
Washington.

Personal.   August 4, 1905.

Dear Mr. Barnes:

I should be glad to know the President's wishes with regard to Mr. Rockhill's telegram of today which has been sent to you by wire, but which I confirm as follows:

"Peking, August 4, 1905.
Can I inform Chinese Government that under provision Article 15th, our treaty 1858, we will hold it responsible for any losses sustained by our trade for its failure to stop present organized movement interfering therewith. The United States Consul-General at Shanghai reports danger movement against us may shortly extend to stevedores. I am always urging on Foreign Office publication proclamations forbidding movement, but it is supine. Movement pleases it as effective means to coerce us. Agitation in American politics confirms belief. Send instructions. Who is Secretary of State? Is letter of the President of the United States June 24 in regard to Chinese passports authentic?
ROCKHILL.

I enclose copy of the Circular to Diplomatic and Consular Officers of

June 26th, on which the President's letter of June 24th was based. Mr. Rockhill probably refers to some newspaper publication he has seen, as he hardly had time to receive the Circular.

Very truly yours,

Alvey A. Adee

Hon. B.F. Barnes,
    Acting Secretary to the President,
        Oyster Bay, N.Y.

(TR Papers, Series 1, Reel 57)

On August 5, 1905, *The New York Times* reported the announcement made by Secretary Barnes regarding the schedule of the upcoming peace negotiations.

OYSTER BAY, Aug. 4 — The peace envoys will start for Portsmouth to-day. All arrangements for the official reception of them by the President and formal presentation of them to one another were completed this evening.

According to announcement made at the Executive Offices by Secretary Barnes, the President will board the naval yacht Mayflower, on which the ceremony will take place, at about 1 P.M. to-morrow. The Mayflower, which arrived here to-day and is anchored in the outer bay, will send one of her launches to the J. West Roosevelt pier for the President.

The moment the President sets foot on the deck of the Mayflower his flag will be broken out under the main truck of the naval yacht, and her guns will boom out the Presidential salute of twenty-one guns.

By that time the United States cruiser Tacoma, bearing the Japanese envoys and the Chattanooga, with the Russian peace mission aboard, will have arrived in the inlet. On account of their greater draught the cruiser will be compelled to anchor some distance out in the Sound.

The dispatch boat Dolphin, which will take the Japanese delegation to Portsmouth, is due here some time before morning, and the cruiser Galveston, which will convoy the Dolphin and the Mayflower to Portsmouth, will be in waiting when the vessels bearing the two delegations arrive.

The Tacoma will fly the Japanese flag at the main truck and the Russian Ambassador's flag will fly on the Chattanooga. As each vessel comes to anchor an Ambassadorial salute of nineteen guns will be fired from the Galveston.

As soon as the President's flag is shown on the Mayflower the Japanese plenipotentiaries will start from the Tacoma amid the booming of the Ambassadorial salute from the cruiser, which will be repeated from the Mayflower as they board that vessel. On board the Mayflower Third Assistant Secretary of State Peirce, who will arrive here in the morning on the naval yacht Sylph, will formally present them to the President, into whose hands they will then place any official messages from the Mikado of which they may be the bearers.

The Russian plenipotentiaries will follow, and after their separate presentation to the President the plenipotentiaries and their respective suites will be presented to each other by the President. The presentation will take place on the magnificently fitted cabin of the Mayflower.

The formal introduction will be followed by a luncheon, at which the President will do the honors. On either side of him will be seated Baron

Komura and Minister Takahira and M. Witte and Baron Rosen. There will be about twenty-five guests...After the luncheon the President will go ashore. The Japanese will leave the Mayflower a few moments later.

The Russians will stay on board the yacht, which is to carry them to Portsmouth. Baron Komura, Minster Takahira and their suite will then board the Dolphin, on which they are to travel to the place selected for the peace negotiations.

The Sylph will carry Mr. Peirce, several American officials, and the newspaper men to Portsmouth. The trip will be made very slowly, with a view to making the landing at Portsmouth Navy Yard at 10 o'clock Monday morning. *(NY Times, August 5, 1905)*

History was made on August 5, 1905, when the events outlined by Secretary Barnes took place in Oyster Bay.

Figure 25: The President and the plenipotentiaries of Japan and Russia meet for the first time aboard the Mayflower anchored in Oyster Bay.
Courtesy of Theodore Roosevelt Collection, Harvard College Library

Despite the flurry of diplomatic activity with regard to the Russian-Japanese negoti-ations, the President also responded to a request from leaders in Louisiana that the U.S. Government take full control of the fight against the yellow fever. Upon receipt of this request, the President immediately sent a telegram from the Executive Offices to the Surgeon General, requesting that he take control of the yellow fever situation at New Orleans on behalf of the Federal Government. *(NY Times*, August 5, 1905)

On August 7, J.P. Morgan visited Sagamore Hill to "discuss with the President the latest efforts...by the Chinese Government to buy out the American concession for the Canton-Hankow Railway...little in the way of conclusive information was obtainable at the exec-utive offices here regarding Mr. Morgan's talk with the President." *(NY Times*, August 8, 1905) Baron Kentaro Kaneko, a Japanese financier also visited with the President on August 7. *The New York Times*, August 8, 1905 reported that "He declined to discuss the purpose of his visit. At the executive office it was said that the call was purely social."

On August 9, 1905, the itinerary of the President's trip to Wilkesbarre, PA was announced at the Executive Office. *(NY Times*, August 10, 1905.) The President also received a telegram from Assistant Secretary of State Peirce announcing that the Russian and Japanese plenipotentiaries held their first session in conference. *(TR Papers*, Series 1, Reel 58)

On August 12, 1905, it was announced at the executive office that the trial of the Plunger, a new naval submarine, would take place in Oyster Bay the following week and that the President would attend the trial. *(NY Times*, August 13, 1905.)

Also on August 12, Acting Secretary Barnes received a telegram from Assistant Secretary Forster in Washington. Mr. Forster's telegram contained the text of a telegram from Minister Rockhill in China regarding the Canton-Hankow Railway con-cession. It informed the President that the decision to cancel the concession was made by a local viceroy and not the Chinese Foreign Office.

TELEGRAM.
RECEIVED IN CIPHER.

𝔚𝔥𝔦𝔱𝔢 𝔥𝔬𝔲𝔰𝔢,
𝔚𝔞𝔰𝔥𝔦𝔫𝔤𝔱𝔬𝔫.

The White House, Washington, D.C., August 12, 1905 — 12:15p

Hon. B. F. Barnes,
    Acting Secretary to the President,
        O y s t e r B a y.
    Following cablegram received:

"Peking, August 12.

Inform President in reply to his telegram received eighth instant that Foreign Office disclaims any knowledge cancelling concession and contract and of negoti-ations by Chinese minister at Washington. It says matter was placed by the Throne in the hands of Viceroy Chang Chih Tung, scope of whose authority is not known at Foreign Office. It is disposed to consider arrangement referred to only an incomplete outline. Foreign Office promises definite information in a few days which I will cable. —Rockhill".

Rudolph Forster,
Assistant Secretary.

(TR Papers, Series 1, Reel 58)

On August 14, Acting Secretary Barnes cabled Acting Secretary of State Adee with the President's reply to Mr. Rockhill's telegram.

TELEGRAM.

The White House,

RECEIVED IN CIPHER.

Washington.

Oyster-Bay, N.Y., August 14, 1905.

Hon. Alvey A. Adee,
    Acting Secretary of State,
        Washington, D.C.

President desires substantially the following dispatch sent minister Rockhill in response to his cable: "The President very much dissatisfied with the action of the foreign office. It would certainly seem that you should make the strongest representations in a manner which would not be misunderstood, saying that the American government expects the Chinese government to reverse the action of the local viceroy. The President wishes to know if you fully understand the gravity of the situation. Your first cable showed a complete misapprehension of the facts. Surely the Chinese government cannot intend to make this government hostile to it, and yet they are taking every means to do this. In your first cable you laid stress upon the blow it would be to American interests in the Orient to have this concession canceled. The President does not see how we can submit to such a blow, especially as the concession was largely obtained through the action of the government as stated in your first cable. The Chinese government must be made to understand the gravity of the situation."

B.F. Barnes,
Acting Secretary.

(Received 9:45 p.m.)

(TR Papers, Series 1, Reel 58)

Minister Rockhill cabled to Washington shortly thereafter. His reply was cabled to Mr. Barnes in Oyster Bay by Assistant Secretary Forster.

TELEGRAM.
RECEIVED IN CIPHER.

White house,
Washington.

The White House, Washington, D.C., August 14, 1905 — 11:20a
Hon. B. F. Barnes,
   Acting Secretary to the President,
   Oyster Bay, N.Y.

The following cable has just been received:
"Peking, 14.

Foreign Office in the course of conversation yesterday disclaimed again any knowledge of facts about canceled Hankow - Canton concession. I have received today a despatch from the Foreign Office saying that it had made inquiry concerning the settlement referred to in President's despatch to me. Foreign Office states that last year and this year the Grand Council sent to Viceroy Chang Chih Tung three confidential letters of instructions from the Emperor directing him to devise means to regain the control of the railway. Viceroy then memorialized Emperor that the Chinese minister at Washington be authorized to act jointly with him and his request was approved. Foreign Office, therefore, concludes Chinese minister has acted within authority."
                    Rudolph Forster,
                        Assistant Secretary.

(TR Papers, Series 1, Reel 58)

On August 15, Assistant Secretary Forster cabled Mr. Barnes with a telegram from Mr. Rockhill in Peking. The cable reported on the conditions in China resulting from the boycott.

TELEGRAM.

RECEIVED IN CIPHER.

White house,
Washington.

The White House, Washington, D.C., August 15 — 12 Noon.
Hon. B. F. Barnes,
   Acting Secretary to the President,
   Oyster Bay.
The following cable just received:
"Peking, 15th, 1905.

Your cable received 13th. Reports of consuls show Shanghai and Canton only localities seriously affected by boycott; in all others, conditions normal or only agitation. Tientsin business brighter than usual. Shanghai reports heavy losses, will take a long time to regain lost ground. All foreign interests are affected and the movement becoming anti-foreign. Consular Corps (has ordered?) Diplomatic Corps take action. Most Chinese merchants want boycott abandoned. Canton losses to date not fifty thousand dollars. I have asked a degradation leader movement Shanghai, who hold rank prefect. I have declined also further discussion of the treaty until movement suppressed. Foreign Office apparently apathetic; measures of provincial authorities inadequate. On the whole apprehension for the future is greater than losses sustained. Movement dangerous precedent if not broken. — Rockhill."

Rudolph Forster,
Assistant Secretary.

(TR Papers, Series 1, Reel 58)

Shortly after this telegram was received in Washington, Acting Secretary of State Adee telephoned Mr. Forster at the White House.

DEPARTMENT OF STATE

Second Assistant Secretary's Room.

MEMORANDUM.

Aug. 15, 1905.

Dear Mr. Forster:

  Referring to my telephone message of a few moments ago, I beg you to communicate the accompanying paraphrase to Mr. Barnes by wire. If it meets the President's approval, I think it would be well to have it given to the press from Oyster Bay.

Alvey Adee

(TR Papers, Series 1, Reel 58)

The statement to which Mr. Adee refers reported briefly the effects of the Chinese boycott of American goods in China. It was a paraphrase of Mr. Rockhill's telegram of the same day.

Statement for the press.

  A telegram from Minister Rockhill, received at the State Department this afternoon, says that reports from the several Consulates in China indicate that Shanghai and Canton are the only localities where the boycott has assumed serious proportions. In the other trading ports conditions are normal, though agitation exists in some of them. At Tientsin, for instance, business is reported as being unusually bright. At Shanghai, heavy losses are reported, adversely affecting foreign interests, and the movement appears not to be limited to American trade, but to be assuming an anti-foreign character. Most of the Chinese merchants wish the boycott abandoned. At Canton, it is believed the losses to American trade so far do not exceed fifty thousand dollars. The foreign office and the provincial authorities appear to be apathetic, and the steps taken by them are inadequate.

(*TR Papers*, Series 1, Reel 58)

Also on July 15, Oscar Straus wrote to the President regarding his meeting with the Russian plenipotentiaries Baron Rosen and M. Witte. The meeting took place the previous day, July 14, in Portsmouth. Probably this meeting took place because Simon Wolf's request on July 25 to meet with the President in secret was granted.

At the RR. Station

From Boston en route
from Portsmouth N.H.
15 Aug. 1905.

My Dear Mr President

I have just returned from Portsmouth where last evening together with (illegible) *Schiff, Isaac Seligman, Mr. Lewisohn and Adolf Kraus, President of the B'nei B'rith we had a three hours conference with M. de Witte, and Baron Rosen, the latter aiding in interpreting.*

We were called to this conference to discuss with M. de Witte the status of the Russian Jews and how to better their condition. Contrary to press reports this conference had nothing to with finances, the subject was not referred to.

We had a plain straight talk and Witte was equally straight out in his statements. He explained how acute and abnormal was the condition of the Jews and in his account of the causes which have produced this abnormal status he did not mince matters in arraigning the internal conditions and medieval backwardness of the Russian people. He agreed with us that the Russian Jewish question could only be settled in Russia, as it involved 7 million souls and that they should be accorded their civil rights. We differed in the question as to the immediate or gradual emancipation - he claiming the Russian masses might create disturbances if the former plan was followed. That the Council of Ministers had agreed in the principle of equal rights but because of opposition on the part of some people, they remitted the entire subject to the National Assembly soon to be convoked. It is needless to trouble you with the lines of argument and with the details of our insistence upon equal rights - no more no less - and without delay. M. Witte suggested further conference in New York prior to his departure.

The Peace Negotiations - From sources quite reliable on the Russian side, I learn the Peace Negotiations will fail. I understand even the Emperor is jealous of Witte's prestige and that his hands are practically tied unless the unexpected happens, that the Japanese make concessions that are not in the realm of probability, and that this task has been given him to break him and discredit him even among the liberals.

In my opinion it is yet possible for you to induce an agreement. If you would have it known to the plenipotentiaries that after they have concluded their labors and before final adjournment you desired them to call upon you to express to them your sentiments upon the results of their weighty labors. In some such way, which you will know best how to invoke, you will have an opportunity of bringing the two countries to so instruct their plenipotentiaries so that by mutual concessions peace will be obtained out of deference to you and for the peace of the world.

In the event a break practically comes such an invitation will keep the conference alive until your sentiments will have awakened the respective countries to the gravity of their responsibilities in renewed war. This is only a crude suggestion for your consideration. I am en route for the Maine woods. With cordial regards - Faithfully yours

Oscar S. Straus

(*TR Papers*, Series 1, Reel 58)

The following day, August 16, Mr. Straus telegraphed Mr. Barnes asking him to give his letter to the President. (*TR Papers*, Series 1, Reel 58)

Inasmuch as Secretary Loeb was on vacation,   *The New York Times* reported that Secretary Barnes was busy working with the President.

> President Roosevelt was back in time to transact official business with Secretary Barnes this afternoon. (*NY Times*, August 15, 1905)

On August 16, 1905, it was announced that "President Roosevelt has pledged the full support of the Administration for the enactment of a law providing for Federal supervision of life insurance." (*NY Times*, August 17, 1905.) It was also reported that "Assistant Secretary of the Treasury Charles H. Keep, Chairman of the Keep Commission, which was appointed to investigate the business methods of Government departments and inaugurate reforms, called on President Roosevelt at Sagamore Hill..." (*NY Times*, August 17, 1905.)

On August 17, it was announced that "Edwin H. Conger, who at present is the United States Ambassador to Mexico, soon will surrender that post to accept a special mission and go back to Peking...It is expected that the official announcement of Ambassador Conger's new mission will be forthcoming very shortly...Mr. Conger is to go to Peking...to look into the tangled relations which have arisen between this country and China over the interpretation of the Exclusion act, the resulting boycott of American goods in China, and the dispute over the Canton-Hankow railroad concession... (*NY Times*, August 18, 1905.)

Secretary Barnes received a telegram on July 17 regarding the Canton-Hankow railway from Minister Rockhill in Peking.

TELEGRAM.

RECEIVED IN CIPHER.

𝔚𝔥𝔦𝔱𝔢 𝔥𝔬𝔲𝔰𝔢, 𝔚𝔞𝔰𝔥𝔦𝔫𝔤𝔱𝔬𝔫.

The White House, Washington, D.C., August 17, 1905.

Hon. B. F. Barnes,
    Acting Secretary to the President,

Following just received: "Peking August 17 — Received 3 p.m.

Your telegram received. Conger despatches number 1797, 1809, 1829 show situation to date of my telegram of July 25th, which states facts and opinions known here. I know practically nothing American Company position. Barclay Parsons told me last spring sum six three quarters millions fixed by his Company to quote gauge Chinese opposition. Yesterday Foreign Office wrote saying it had been advised on fifth instant settlement made by Chinese minister with shareholders was approved by Imperial edict, probably within last few days. Official protest against carrying out pending your instructions on the ground failure of Foreign Office to report against previously to the Legation. See Conger's number 1797.

British minister informed me yesterday Hong Kong Government has agreed to lend Viceroy Chang eleven hundred thousand pounds sterling to pay American Company and British capitalists will lend him three million pounds sterling for building railroad under British control. American and German money offered pay Americans but declined.

I beg judgment general situation be suspended until all the facts in the case ascertained. Foreign Office showing usual weakness but no desire to create hostility. I am reporting fully by mail.

Your telegram sixteenth received. Rockhill."

Rudolph Forster,
            Assistant Secretary.

(TR Papers, Series 1, Reel 58)

About one hour later, Mr. Forster cabled Mr. Barnes again with a telegram from the Chinese Minister who in turn was communicating a telegram from the Chinese Foreign Office regarding the Canton-Hankow railway.

TELEGRAM.

RECEIVED IN CIPHER.

𝔚𝔥𝔦𝔱𝔢 𝔥𝔬𝔲𝔰𝔢,
𝔚𝔞𝔰𝔥𝔦𝔫𝔤𝔱𝔬𝔫.

The White House, Washington, D.C., August 17 —4p.

Hon. B. F. Barnes,
    Acting Secretary to the President,
        Oyster Bay.

The Chinese Minister communicates the following telegram from the Chinese Foreign Office, and asks that it be laid before the President:

"From Peking, August 14, 1905.

To Chinese Minister Liang, Washington. The Grand Council of State, which has just transmitted to this office copies of three Imperial Decrees issued this year and last with reference to the Hankow - Canton railway authorizing Chang Chih Tung to take all necessary measures for the regaining of the control of the railway, states that, China having given Viceroy Chang authority to do what is necessary in this matter, and Imperial sanction having been given to the request of Viceroy Chang presented in a special memorial that Chen Tung Liang Cheng act jointly with him, Minister Liang, therefore, has authority to do what is necessary in this matter.
    You will please act in accordance with this telegraphic instruction.

(signed) Waiwu Pu."
                    Alvey A. Adee
                Rudolph Forster,
                    Assistant Secretary.

(TR Papers, Series 1, Reel 58)

Also on August 17, it was announced that "Postmaster General George Bruce Cortelyou and Mrs. Cortelyou paid a visit...to Sagamore Hill, where they were entertained at luncheon by the President and Mrs. Roosevelt...this revived the rumor...that Mr. Cortelyou was slated to succeed Secretary Shaw as head of the Treasury Department...Mr. Cortelyou said that while calling upon the President he had recommended the appointment of Mrs. W.Y. Atkinson as Postmaster of Newnan, Ga. The appointment of Mrs. Atkinson was announced by Secretary Barnes after Mr. Cortelyou left. *(NY Times*, August 18, 1905.)

On August 18, Ambassador Meyer cabled the sticking point in the negotiations between the Russians and Japanese.

TELEGRAM.

RECEIVED IN CIPHER.

White House,
Washington.

WH — Washington, D.C., August 18, 1905 — 9:35p

Hon. B. F. Barnes,
Acting Secretary to the President,
Oyster Bay.

Following just received from:

"St Petersburg

Confidential for the President: The Czar today in conversation with a prominent diplomat, whose name I will not mention now, said peace for Russia was impossible if Japan held to her demands of an indemnity or the cession of territory.

Meyer."

Rudolph Forster,
Assistant Secretary.

(*TR Papers*, Series 1, Reel 58)

On August 19, Mr. O'Loughlin *(of the State Department)* telegraphed to Mr. Barnes from New Hampshire with additional details of the negotiations.

TELEGRAM.

RECEIVED IN CIPHER.

The White House,
Washington.

Hotel Wentworth, New Castle, N.H., August 19 — 3:32p

Hon. B. F. Barnes,
Assistant Secretary,
Oyster Bay.

As you are probably aware, Saghalin and indemnity principal questions; others said to be capable of adjustment. Russians talking earnestly about dividing Saghalin, retaining northern portion, which valueless, Japan holding southern portion where fisheries, agriculture. Such compromise possible. Russians insist won't pay indemnity though might pay something for part Saghalin, prisoners, and other like expenses. Best Japanese opinion five hundred millions minimum.

O'Loughlin.

(*TR Papers*, Series 1, Reel 58)

Although the President was engaged on a daily basis in the peace negotiations between the Russians and the Japanese, it was not until August 19, 1905 that he forcefully intervened to break a deadlock in the negotiations.

OYSTER BAY, Aug. 19 — For an hour to-day the center of activity in the negotiations to end the war in the Far East shifted from Portsmouth to Sagamore Hill.

For that space of time this evening President Roosevelt, in conference with Baron Rosen, the Russian Ambassador at Washington and junior Russian peace envoy, used all the influence which is his and every plea at his command in an effort to turn the tide and pave the way toward peace between Russia and Japan...

It is known, moreover, that the President did not trust to his persuasive powers alone in urging the Russian envoys through Baron Rosen to do all in their power to bring about peace. Mr. Roosevelt, when he asked Baron Rosen to come to Sagamore Hill for a conference, did not do so merely for the purpose of discussing the desirability from Russia's point of view of an early peace, even though it might prove bitter to Russia to pay the price.

The President was enabled to place before the Russian envoy certain inducements, substantial enough to be worthy of Russia's consideration, which may end the differences which have arisen between the envoys of Russia and Japan.

In connection with this, it is significant that the visit of Baron Rosen followed closely upon the one paid at Sagamore Hill last night by Baron Kaneko, who, while he apparently holds no official position, is believed to be a personal representative of the Mikado in this country.

Until the present time President Roosevelt has refrained from any action, even by indirection, that might be construed as interference in the work of the plenipotentiaries. He announced at the beginning of the negotiations that, neither by word nor act, would he participate in the proceedings of the conference, although he made it perfectly clear to the envoys of both Russia and Japan that he would be ready, at any time, to assist them in a proper way in the great work which they had been designated by their respective Emperors to undertake.

In anticipation, however, of the failure of the envoys to agree upon certain of the articles and in the expectation that he might be appealed to by one side or the other before the conclusion of the conference, the President has been in communication with the great neutral powers. His purpose was to enlist their support in a final effort to secure an honorable peace...Tremendous and world-wide pressure is being brought to bear upon the Governments at St. Petersburg and Tokio not to permit the conference to fail...

Through Mr. Griscom, the American Minister at Tokio, the President has also been working, but it cannot be ascertained whether or not his efforts have been directed toward a reduction of the demands of Japan...

Baron Kaneko has been keeping in close touch with President Roosevelt since the peace negotiations were begun. For the fourth time in as many weeks and for the second time within a week he was in conference with the President last evening. Neither he nor the President would disclose the nature of their interview, but the Baron had scarcely started for New York before the

President's interest in the negotiations became active. He sent an important communication to M. Witte and Baron Rosen. Secretary Peirce's reply to the message was communicated to the President by telephone from the executive office in Oyster Bay village.

Then ensued a long-distance conference between the President and the Russian envoys, the messages being transmitted through Secretary Barnes here and through Mr. Peirce at Portsmouth. The President invited Baron Rosen to come to Sagamore Hill in order that he might present to him for consideration of the Russian mission a proposition of the highest importance. The invitation of the President was accepted and the details were soon arranged... *(NY Times,* August 20, 1905)

On August 20 Ambassador Meyer again cabled regarding the Czar's opinion of Japan's demands.

TELEGRAM.

RECEIVED IN CIPHER.

𝔚𝔥𝔦𝔱𝔢 𝔥𝔬𝔲𝔰𝔢, 𝔚𝔞𝔰𝔥𝔦𝔫𝔤𝔱𝔬𝔫.

The White House Washington, D.C., August 20 — 2:45p

Hon. B. F. Barnes,
    Acting Secretary to the President,
      O y s t e r   B a y.

Following just received:

          "St. Petersburg.

I have it from absolutely reliable source that the Czar considers the Japanese demands as to limitation of naval force in the east and the surrender of interned ships are made to humiliate Russia before the world. The Czar added that it was uncalled for as they had no navy and in the future would have no winter port and that the interned vessels were absolutely unimportant to Japan. Some query as to whether these requests were instigated by England — Meyer."

          Rudolph Forster,
          Assistant Secretary.

(TR Papers, Series 1, Reel 58)

Later the same day, Mr. O'Laughlin cabled from Portsmouth.

TELEGRAM.

𝕿𝖍𝖊 𝖂𝖍𝖎𝖙𝖊 𝕳𝖔𝖚𝖘𝖊,

𝖂𝖆𝖘𝖍𝖎𝖓𝖌𝖙𝖔𝖓.

The Hotel Wentworth, Portsmouth, N.H., Aug. 20, 1905.

Hon. B. F. Barnes,
          Asst Secretary to the President, Oyster Bay, N.Y.

Am informed authoritatively Witte earnestly recommended concessions. Czar adopted unyielding attitude. Presume Meyer could reinforce Witte's arguments.

                              O'Loughlin.

(TR Papers, Series 1, Reel 58)

The President's suggestion that Russia and Japan agree to arbitration was announced in *The New York Times* on August 21, 1905. Although this suggestion did not immediately break the deadlock, it would later become the pivotal compromise of the peace negotiations. From Portsmouth the following was reported by *The New York Times*.

PORTSMOUTH, N.H., Aug. 20 — The Associated Press is able to announce that the proposition of President Roosevelt, which was to-day communicated through Baron Rosen to M. Witte and transmitted by the latter to Emperor Nicholas, is based upon the principle of arbitration.

Whether the proposal contemplates arbitration of all the articles upon which the plenipotentiaries have failed to agree or only of the question of indemnity cannot be stated with positiveness, but it is more than probable that it relates only to indemnity or to indemnity and the cession of Sakhalin... *(NY Times,* August 21, 1905.)

From Oyster Bay, the report was more guarded as to what occurred between Baron Rosen and the President.

OYSTER BAY, Aug. 20 — Official dispatches believed to have a vital bearing on the peace negotiations arrived at the executive office here to-day. Some of these dispatches are believed to have come from Portsmouth and others from foreign Governments. The contents of all have been carefully guarded. President Roosevelt has determined to withhold for the present any information regarding what passed between him and Baron Rosen yesterday.

It is stated here to-night, however, that President Roosevelt has received practical assurances from both sides that the session on Tuesday will not be the end of the peace conference. It is now believed that the envoys will spend further time in a discussion which, it is hoped, may do away with the minor differences. In the meantime, it is understood, the neutral powers, with whom Mr. Roosevelt is said to have a practical understanding, will bring all the pressure at their command to bear on the Governments at Tokio and St. Petersburg in an effort to bring about peace.

It is not expected here that the President will receive further visits from either Russian or Japanese representatives prior to the meeting of the conferees on Tuesday. There is ground for the belief that the Japanese plenipotentiaries were cognizant of the details of the President's final effort to prevent a rupture of the conference and are prepared, so far as their Government is concerned, to carry into effect the proposition he submitted to the Russian envoys. No intimation of the nature of that proposition has been given here. *(NY Times,* August 21, 1905.)

While the plenipotentiaries waited for their respective Governments to respond to the President's suggestion, rumors were rampant throughout the world. *The London Times* reported that the President did not suggest arbitration at all, that the President did not intervene in the negotiations and that no message was sent to the Russian Government. *The London Times* also reported that the Czar was against giving any further concessions to the Japanese *(NY Times,* August 20, 1905). However, the Japanese government did eventually contact the President regarding some concessions that they were willing to make to the Russians.

OYSTER BAY, Aug. 21 — It is believed that Japan has consented to modify her demands on Russia.

Another visit to the President was paid to-day by Baron Kaneko, who is now generally regarded as the confidential representative in the United States of the Tokio Government, and this time the visit was not at the President's invitation. Arrangements for it, on Baron Kaneko's initiative, were made by telephone at a late hour last night. This is regarded as indicating some new decision in Tokio in response to representations made by the President.

...President Roosevelt again tendered his good offices to Japan and notified Baron Kaneko that he would summon one of the Russian envoys...At the same time Baron Kaneko was asked to sound his Government as to whether in the interest of peace certain concessions could not be made by Japan that would enable Russia to conclude a treaty with less damage to her national honor.

There seems to be little room for doubt that Baron Kaneko to-day brought the President Japan's answer, and that this was drawn up at the Cabinet meeting which was held in Tokio yesterday.

Following Baron Kaneko's visit, President Roosevelt had his acting secretary, Mr. Barnes, with him for two hours. In addition to the matter which the Baron had presented to him the President received and considered an accumulation of dispatches and letters. The replies to these were forwarded in the afternoon. Late in the day important messages were received from Portsmouth, the responses to which occupied the President's attention for a considerable time.

Not the slightest indication of the character of the correspondence was permitted to become public. The President maintains that if any publication is made concerning the peace negotiations it must be authorized by representatives of one of the powers directly interested... *(NY Times,* August 22, 1905)

Perhaps one of the most important messages sent between the President and the Russian plenipotentiaries was delivered in "secret" by a messenger from the executive office in Oyster Bay. The arrangements to meet this messenger were made on August 21 between Assistant Secretary of State Peirce and Acting Secretary Barnes.

TELEGRAM.

𝔚𝔥𝔦𝔱𝔢 𝔥𝔬𝔲𝔰𝔢,
𝔚𝔞𝔰𝔥𝔦𝔫𝔤𝔱𝔬𝔫.

Hotel Wentworth, New Castle, N.H., Aug. 21.

Hon. B. F. Barnes,
    Acting Secretary.

Telegram received. I will meet the President's messenger tomorrow (Tuesday) morning at the Rockingham Hotel, Portsmouth, where I will take a room, as I have some times done before, for the transaction of business in the city of Portsmouth, and will then take the message to M. Witte. I regret exceedingly the publicity of the last message but the newspaper men inform me that they had received their news from Oyster Bay or New York by telephone. Certainly no reporter received anything from me on the subject. I was absolutely mute. I deeply regret not having a cipher, but had not foreseen the possibility of any communication of a confidential character. I can telegraph Washington by private wire and obtain a code in twenty-four hours if the President desires. Please ask his instructions. Can you inform me at what hour the messenger will arrive in Portsmouth? Let him inquire for me on his arrival.
                    H.H.D. Peirce.
(TR Papers, Series 1, Reel 58)

A handwritten note on the top of this telegram records the answer cabled to Mr. Peirce by Mr. Barnes. It reads "<u>Ansd</u> - Messenger will arrive 10:45 am - Nothing whatever has been made public here - President directs that you obtain cipher at once."
(TR Papers, Series 1, Reel 58)

In reply, Mr Peirce cabled the following telegram to Mr. Barnes.

TELEGRAM.

𝔗𝔥𝔢 𝔚𝔥𝔦𝔱𝔢 𝔥𝔬𝔲𝔰𝔢,

𝔚𝔞𝔰𝔥𝔦𝔫𝔤𝔱𝔬𝔫.

Hotel Wentworth, N.H., August 21.

Hon. B. F. Barnes,
    Acting Secretary.

Will meet messenger at Rockingham on arrival. Will wire for code immediately. Am wholly at loss to understand how message got out, certainly not from me.

H.H.D. Peirce.

(TR Papers, Series 1, Reel 58)

The stenographer later returned to Oyster Bay with the Russian response to the President's overtures. The report of the stenographer's trip was given from both Portsmouth, his destination and Oyster Bay.

PORTSMOUTH, N.H. Aug 22.—- The Associated Press is now in a position to reveal substantially the suggestion of President Roosevelt for breaking the dead-lock in the peace negotiations and rescuing the conference from failure. His solution would ingeniously permit the satisfaction of the Japanese demand for reimbursement for the cost of the war and at the same time enable Russia to face the world with the declaration that she had not ceded a foot of territory or paid a kopec of war tribute.

The solution...consists of   an agreement by Russia to repurchase the possession of either all or half of the Island of Sakhalin, now in the military occupation of Japan, for a sum the amount of which, if the two countries cannot agree, shall be decided by some method of arbitration hereafter to be determined. The purchase money, together with the sum Japan would obtain from the cession of the Chinese Eastern Railroad and the payment for the maintenance of the Russian prisoners in Japan, would, it is estimated, about equal her bill for the cost of the war...

...It seems practically certain, though this cannot be affirmed positively, that the President to-day was able to give M. Witte substantial assurance that Japan would be willing to accept such a compromise...

...It was the President's message to M. Witte which caused the sensation of the day. Early in the morning had come the official announcement that the meeting of the conference which was to have been held to-day had been postponed until to-morrow at 9:30 o'clock. The reason assigned was that the protocols for submission at the sitting had not been completed. But a few hours later the true reason leaked out.

J.L.McGrew, one of the stenographers attached to the executive office at Oyster Bay, had arrived with a communication from the President for the Russian plenipotentiaries. Mr. Witte and Baron de Rosen had left the hotel, ostensibly for a ride in an auto car to York Beach, but instead had quietly slipped over to the conference building at the navy yard to receive the message from Assistant Secretary Peirce. The most elaborate precautions had been taken to insure secrecy, but it leaked out through a "tip" from New York.

From 12:10 until 1:10 M. Witte and Baron de Rosen remained at the conference building with Mr. Peirce. All those present decline to make any statements regarding what transpired at the navy yard, even refusing to admit that any importance attached to the matter. M. Witte would only admit that he had gone to the building "to send a message," and Baron de Rosen and Mr. Peirce absolutely refused to make any statement.

Mr. McGrew took the 3:25 train to Boston, whence, according to reports, he took the Merchants' Limited, after first inquiring at the intelligence office for the connections to Oyster Bay. He probably carried the Russian reply to the President.

This reply, it is believed, was prepared by M. Witte and Baron de Rosen after Mr. Peirce had delivered to them the President's message. A suggestion is made that during the stay at the navy yard the Russian plenipotentiaries were in direct contact with the President by telegraph, but there is nothing to substantiate this, and under the circumstances it appears unlikely.

Mr. Roosevelt's message to M. Witte and Baron Rosen is believed to have been the result of his interview yesterday at Oyster Bay with Baron Kaneko, who has acted as the President's medium of communication with the Tokio Government. *(NY Times*, August 23, 1905)

The news from Oyster Bay was of no less importance.

OYSTER BAY, Aug. 22.—- The adjournment to-day of the session of the peace conference at Portsmouth is believed to be directly due to the representations made by President Roosevelt, and it is predicted with some measure of certainty that the meeting of the envoys scheduled for to-morrow will not be the final one.

The messenger who conferred at Portsmouth to-day with Mr. Peirce is John L. McGrew, one of the White House stenographers, now attached to the staff of the executive office here. Mr. McGrew left Oyster Bay on an afternoon train yesterday shortly after the President had had Secretary Barnes with him for two hours, which time was entirely devoted to the consideration of dispatches from Portsmouth and from foreign Governments in relation to the peace negotiations.

It is known here that the adjournment of the session of the conference to-day was in accordance with assurances received by the President from Baron Rosen and Baron Kaneko.

With such evidence to show that his good offices are bearing fruit, President Roosevelt is known to look forward to the developments at Portsmouth with greater hope than at any time since the envoys of the warring nations met. *(NY Times*, August 23, 1905)

That a "secret" messenger was discovered by the press was a great embarrassment to Mr. Peirce. The head of the Associated Press sent a telegram to Oyster Bay in an effort to exonerate him.

TELEGRAM.

The White House, Washington.

1 NY D GI 59 Paid — 8:55a

WH. Hotel Wentworth, Portsmouth N.H., August 22/23.

Hon. B. F. Barnes,
    Acting Secretary.

Confidential. In most solemn fashion I assure you Mr. Peirce neither directly nor indirectly was in any way responsible for our despatches this afternoon. He had not the slightest intimation that anything had leaked out until he saw it in the paper. We did not get our tip in Portsmouth. This is for your information.

> Howard Thompson,
>   In charge Associated Press at Portsmouth.

(TR Papers, Series 1, Reel 58)

Mr. Barnes also received a telegram from Ambassador Meyer forwarded to Oyster Bay via Assistant Secretary Forster in the White House.

TELEGRAM.

RECEIVED IN CIPHER.

The White House, Washington.

The White House Washington, D.C., August 22 — 12:25p

Hon. B. F. Barnes,
    Acting Secretary to the President,
        O y s t e r   B a y.

Following just received: "St. Petersburg.

Wire the President the Emperor away for the day at maneuvers. Lamsdorff informs me has an appointment with his majesty this evening; on his return he will notify me immediately when the Czar can receive me — Meyer."

> Rudolph Forster,
>   Assistant Secretary.

(TR Papers, Series 1, Reel 58)

On August 23, Assistant Secretary of State Peirce attempted to explain the press's ability to uncover the "secret" messenger the President had sent.

TELEGRAM.

RECEIVED IN CIPHER.

𝔚𝔥𝔦𝔱𝔢 𝔥𝔬𝔲𝔰𝔢, 𝔚𝔞𝔰𝔥𝔦𝔫𝔤𝔱𝔬𝔫.

Hotel Wentworth, Portsmouth, N.H., August 23 — 9:30a

Hon. B. F. Barnes,
    Secretary to the President,
        Oyster Bay.

Please explain to the President that, while I am deeply chagrined at the account of the Associated Press, the truth of which I have denied, I am absolutely sure that nothing has been communicated by or through me or by reason of my knowledge or that of any other near me. A friend closely associated with journalism today said to me that I am incurring the hostility of the press by my reticence; that the envoys themselves give more information than I do. He advised me to try and conciliate the correspondents in some way. On this account I am surrounded by a horde of correspondents who not only importune, but spy upon every movement of my own and of the plenipotentiaries. Through an error, click of the telegraph overheard is noted and reported, and conclusions drawn from the smallest deviation of the daily course of action. Nothing this morning was successfully spied out until the messenger was leaving. The Associated Press representatives assure me they got their information from New York. Associated Press agent here says he had a description of messenger before his departure from Oyster Bay and identified him at station at Portsmouth on his return journey —— H. H. D. Peirce.

(TR Papers, Series 1, Reel 58)

The same day Mr. Peirce also wrote a letter to Mr. Barnes reiterating his blamelessness in another leak.

DEPARTMENT OF STATE.
WASHINGTON.

Navy Yard, Portsmouth, August 23rd, 1905.

Honorable B.F. Barnes,
    Acting Secretary to the President,
        Oyster Bay, New York.

Dear Mr. Barnes:

    I regret more than I can tell that again the press has got on to the fact of the President having communicated with the envoys, but, as I telegraphed you in cypher last night, I am absolutely not responsible for any disclosures. The secret was kept by me absolutely and until the report ap-

peared in the evening papers, I had supposed we had succeeded in escaping the lynx eyes of these reporters, who
seem to have organized themselves into a very efficient detective force. As you know, the statements published by the
press were all erroneous, and I have categorically denied
that of the Associated Press as well as that contained in the
Boston Herald, and I send you herewith marked copies of the
Boston Herald and Boston Globe containing my denial, which
please call to the President's attention. I trust he exonerates
me from blame in this matter, concerning which I am
more distressed than I can tell you. The truth of the matter
is that I have really incurred no little hostility on the
part of the newspaper men here by my reticence regarding all
that goes on.

                        Yours sincerely,

                        Herbert H. D. Peirce

(TR Papers, Series 1, Reel 58)

Also on August 23 Ambassador Meyer cabled that he had received an audience with the
Czar. This cable was forwarded to Mr. Barnes via Mr. Forster in Washington.

TELEGRAM.

RECEIVED IN CIPHER.

White house, Washington.

The White House, Washington, D.C., August 23 —- 10:20a.

Hon. B. F. Barnes,
    Acting Secretary to the President,
        Oyster Bay.

    Following just received.

            "St. Petersburg.

The Czar received me in Peterhof at 4 p.m. Said he would welcome peace which
he believed to be honorable and lasting, but reiterates that Russia will not pay any war
indemnity whatever. In that, his conscience tells him he is right and he feels sure he
has the support of the nation. Appreciates that their naval arm has been cut off, but
still has an army which has endurance, opposed to Japanese army, which latter army
is thousands of miles from St. Petersburg. He added, if necessary I will join the army
myself and go to front. Claims that it should not be forgotten that the Japanese commenced hostilities; that they now have obtained all that they went to war for and a

great deal more. He is unwilling to pay a substantial sum for half of Sakhalien
would be?
as it (Would notwithstanding ?) interpreted as a war indemnity differently expressed.
He said I should prefer to lose territory temporarily than to humiliate the country by
paying a war indemnity as though a vanquished nation, Russia is not in the position of
France in 1870. The Czar told me he had received yesterday telegram from German
Emperor urging peace; read me his reply in which he said peace was impossible if
Japan insisted upon any war indemnity. Closeted with the Emperor two hours, at the
end of which time he informed me of the terms on which he would conclude peace.
Acceptance of the eight points substantially agreed upon by the plenipotentiaries at
Portsmouth, (No ?) payment of war indemnity but a liberal and generous payment
for care and maintenance of Russian prisoners but not such a sum as could be inter-
preted for a war indemnity, withdrawal of Japan's claims for interned ships and limitation of naval power in the Pacific, Russia to possess north half of Saghalien while
Japan to retain southern half (that portion which formerly belonged to Japan). The
Emperor instructed me to express his thanks and full appreciation to the President for
the efforts that he had made in behalf of peace — Meyer."

> Rudolph Forster
> Assistant Secretary.

(TR Papers, Series 1, Reel 58)

On August 24, 1905,   *The New York Times* reported that Ambassador Meyer had an
audience with the Czar.

> St. Petersburg, Aug 23.— The prospects of peace, which yesterday had
> almost vanished, were considerably improved to-day by optimistic newspaper
> messages from Portsmouth. Later, when it became known that the American
> Ambassador, Mr. Meyer, had gone to Peterhof, hopes of a settlement again arose.
> Exactly what occurred during the audience with the Czar is not yet known.
> Mr. Meyer probably will decline to say anything until a statement has been
> made by President Roosevelt. *(NY Times*, August 24, 1905)

> Oyster Bay, Aug. 23. — A lengthy cipher message from St. Petersburg,
> addressed to the President and believed to have been sent by Mr. Meyer,
> Ambassador to Russia, arrived at the Executive Office here at a late hour this
> evening.
> The contents of the message are not known here, but it is believed to contain
> a communication from the Czar which may decide the question of peace or war.
> A long cablegram was sent to Ambassador Meyer by the President late
> Monday. It contained instructions that representations, on behalf of President
> Roosevelt, be made directly to the Russian Emperor. There is reason for the
> belief that those representations were communicated yesterday to the Russian
> envoys at Portsmouth through the President's messenger.
> As a result of the instructions he received, Ambassador Meyer had a special
> audience of Emperor Nicholas to-day at Peterhof. *(NY Times*, August 24, 1905)

On August 24, Ambassador Meyer cabled again regarding his discussions with the Czar. The cable was forwarded to Mr. Barnes by Assistant Secretary Forster.

TELEGRAM.

RECEIVED IN CIPHER.

White house, Washington.

2 WR Fd Ne Paid.

White House, Washington, August 24, 05.

Hon. B. F. Barnes,
   Acting Secretary to the President,
      Oyster Bay.

"St. Petersburg. Notify President that his second cable has been forwarded to Czar. Let me know if his was sent before or after the arrival of mine. I discussed for two hours with Czar yesterday Saghalin and payment of substantial sum for north half. Tried to commit him to maximum amount he would be willing to pay. Emperor repeatedly stated that he had given his word publicly not to pay war indemnity of any kind or surrender Russian soil. It was only after I got him to acknowledge that lower half of Saghalin had been, like Port Arthur, merely temporary Russian territory, that he agreed to a division of Saghalin. I think moreover that by negotiation Russia might consent to pay land value of north half of Saghalin on same basis as Alaska was sold to us. Discussed it with Czar (after he absolutely refused to pay substantial sum) but he said how can the value be ascertained. Shies at it and fears Russians would consider any payment dishonorable. Claims he must act according to his conscience on this matter. Can you advise me of probable amount of money Japan has now on deposit in United States? Meyer."

Rudolph Forster,

Assistant Secretary.

(TR Papers, Series 1, Reel 58)

The pages of *The New York Times* of August 25, 1905 were filled with news from St. Petersburg, Portsmouth, and Oyster Bay. Although no further progress was reported, the Czar did not refuse further negotiations nor did he rule out further concessions. At this point in time, everyone recognized that the President's personal intervention was crucial to the peace negotiations.

   PORTSMOUTH, N.H., Aug. 24 — THE NEW YORK TIMES'S correspondent was informed this evening on absolutely reliable authority that Assistant Secretary Peirce handed a personal message to M. Witte from President Roosevelt this morning before the Russian envoy left for Magnolia Beach.

In the message the President urged M. Witte to accept the terms offered by Baron Komura yesterday. He did not specify any sum of money to be paid by Russia, but simply urged the compromise on half the Island of Sakhalin and payment for the expenses incurred by Japan on behalf of the Russian prisoners.

PORTSMOUTH, N.H., Aug 25 — ...The result of Ambassador Meyer's audience at Peterhof on Wednesday was unsatisfactory, but at least it was not a rebuff. It left the door open, and within a few hours after the receipt at Oyster Bay of Mr. Meyer's account of his audience the President had sent a new appeal through M. Witte, who received it from Mr. Peirce about 3 o'clock yesterday morning.

The Emperor had already, in effect, declined the proposed compromise offered by Japan. He had refused it because under a disguise so thin that, as the Russians say, even a child would not be deceived, Japan offered to withdraw the article asking remuneration for the cost of the war on condition that Russia repurchase from Japan the northern part of Sakhalin at a fixed price of 1,200,000,000 yen ($600,000,000)...

Had Japan not inserted the sum, had that been left for future adjustment, the proposition would undoubtedly have proved more palatable. And The Associated Press is in a position to state that the divergence in the compromise as suggested by the President and as offered by Japan at the conference touched this very point. The President did not suggest any price or the fixing of a price, and it is believed, although this cannot be affirmed, that his latest effort is to secure the consent of the Czar to agree to accept the Japanese proposition with the amount subject to future adjustment by an arbitration board, or otherwise.

OYSTER BAY, N.Y., Aug 24 — The cipher message which was received at the executive office here from Ambassador Meyer was translated this morning and sent to President Roosevelt shortly after noon.

"The President has determined not to make the text of the message public for the present," said Acting Secretary Barnes, in answer to a question.

"What does the President think about the outlook to-day?" was asked.

"There seems to be some doubt about the outcome," was the reply, "but the outlook may brighten in a day or two. It has been good and bad alternately for the last few days."

In addition to Ambassador Meyer's report, important advices from Portsmouth reached the President to-day. They were regarded as so urgent that as soon as they were received at the executive office they were carried to Sagamore Hill by a trusted clerk.

The utmost secrecy is manifested regarding the communications not the slightest intimation of the nature of their contents being allowed to become public.

It is quite certain now, in addition to making a direct appeal to the Russian Emperor, President Roosevelt has communicated with the Japanese Government. Whether the appeal was made directly to the Emperor of Japan, as in the case of Emperor Nicolas, cannot be ascertained.

(NY Times, August 25, 1905)

The effort to achieve an agreement continued daily, with the President in constant contact with both the Russians and the Japanese, through the many telegrams sent from and received by the Executive office.

ST. PETERSBURG, Saturday, Aug. 26 — According to information coming from a member of the imperial family, a dispatch was sent to M. Witte yesterday which is considered at Peterhof as offering a decided hope for peace...

...Everybody in St. Petersburg is awaiting the developments of to-day and hoping that a compromise is being effected, the most likely basis of which, it is believed, would be no indemnity, but a payment for Sakhalin, the amount to be left for future adjustment...

...After seeing Foreign Minister Lamsdorff on Thursday afternoon, Mr. Meyer, the American Ambassador, sent another long dispatch to President Roosevelt. It is impossible to learn the nature of this dispatch, the embassy declining to make any statement regarding it.

Up to 8 o'clock last evening Ambassador Meyer had received no message from the President. The idea that President Roosevelt might again communicate with the Emperor through the Ambassador finds credence in certain official quarters...

OYSTER BAY, Aug. 25 — Baron Kaneko to-day paid another visit to Sagamore Hill, where for over an hour he conferred with President Roosevelt. The Baron's last previous visit proved the forerunner of concessions on the part of the Mikado's Government. To-day Baron Kaneko declared emphatically that he was not the bearer of any new communication from the Mikado to Mr. Roosevelt, and, moreover, that Japan had delivered her ultimatum and could make no further concessions, much as she desired peace...

...There is ground for the statement that President Roosevelt asked Baron Kaneko to call on him for the purpose of communicating to him the contents of lengthy cipher messages received yesterday and again to-day from Ambassador Meyer at St. Petersburg. The messages are supposed to have contained the Czar's answer to the representations made by the President.

Following Baron Kaneko's visit there was great activity in the executive office. The wires from there were humming with messages, which several attachés of the executive staff were kept busy codifying. One of these messages is believed to have been directed to Ambassador Meyer, and others to Secretary Peirce at Portsmouth. President Roosevelt is in practically constant communication with the St. Petersburg and Tokio Governments. By both of the warring nations his good offices have been sought and his efforts to bring their plenipotentiaries into accord are unremitting. *(NY Times*, August 26, 1905)

As if international diplomacy was not enough, on August 25, the President was aboard an experimental submarine (the "Plunger") as it maneuvered in the waters of Oyster Bay.

Despite official denials that he intended to risk his life in a submarine, President Roosevelt shortly after 3 o'clock this afternoon went aboard the Holland type submarine boat commanded by Lieut. Charles Preston Nelson and remained under water off Oyster Bay for fifty-five minutes. *(NY Times*, August 26, 1905)

...In well informed quarters there is an impression that the President's experience on board the Plunger will usher in a new era of this important branch of the navy which up to this time is said to have received rather stepmotherly treatment at the hands of the naval authorities. Announcement was made yesterday of at least one reform that will be inaugurated at once.

Up to the present time men who are performing work on board the submarine boats — duties that require a high degree of both courage and skill — have been carried on the navy rolls as on shore duty. Under this system they receive about 25 per cent. less in wages than the men regularly assigned to duty on the naval ships, and also come behind them in the matter of promotion. On Monday an order will be issued by the Navy Department on the initiative of the President, placing the men employed on the submarines on the regular roll with the men doing duty on shipboard. *(NY Times*, August 27, 1905)

Although the President found time to dive beneath the waves, the negotiations between Russia and Japan continued. On August 26, the President received the Czar's reply to his proposals.

OYSTER BAY, Aug. 26 — President Roosevelt to-day received a dispatch from Ambassador Meyer giving an account of his interview with Count Lamsdorff.

Russia, it is understood, proposes to divide Sakhalin with Japan, but reiterates her earlier refusal to make any payment to Japan except a reasonable sum for the maintenance of the prisoners.

The President is still continuing his efforts with both powers in the interest of peace.

PORTSMOUTH, N.H., Aug. 26 — Half of Sakhalin and 100,000,000 rubles ($50,000,000) are the most that Russia will consent to concede. The President has so far failed entirely to sway the Czar from his original determination.

To-day's session of the conference was barren. But for Baron Komura it would have ended the negotiations. M. Witte and Baron Rosen were ready to terminate the conference then and there, but Baron Komura asked for another sitting, and one will be held on Monday...

...Since Wednesday President Roosevelt had been making strenuous efforts through Ambassador Meyer to induce the Czar to accept Japan's terms without specifying the sum of money to be paid. The fact that the President had failed was made apparent by the Lamsdorff statement and other telegrams from St. Petersburg and by the result of to-day's conference. In spite of the official denial, the Russians here say they know that the Lamsdorff dispatch was genuine and that it was sent out for the purpose of showing that Russia was firm in regard to the indemnity question...

ST. PETERSBURG, Sunday, Aug. 27 — ...Emperor Nicholas, after carefully weighing the consequences of his act, has said his last word. Russia will make no financial contribution to Japan in any form whatsoever, and unless Japan accedes to President Roosevelt's appeals for a compromise his efforts will have proved unavailing.

Mr. Meyer, the American Ambassador, yesterday informed President Roosevelt of Russia's ultimatum. Russia agrees to cede the southern half of the Island of Sakhalin and to pay Japan for the maintenance of the prisoners of war, but nothing more. Russia declares that she has met Japan more than half way and has proved to the world the sincerity of her desire for peace, but that she would rather fight on then pay a cent of indemnity. On this point Russia has not changed her opinion one hair's breadth.

Yesterday morning Mr. Meyer received his latest communication from President Roosevelt, and, as a result, called on Foreign Minister Lamsdorff later in the day. What final proposal was contained in the President's communication it is impossible to learn accurately, but there is reason to believe that it was a compromise on the basis of Russia paying Japan for Sakhalin.

Russia's final answer was communicated to Ambassador Meyer, who at once informed the President. (*NY Times*, August 27, 1905)

Also on August 26, a telegram from Minister Rockhill regarding the boycott in China was directed to Secretary Loeb in Oyster Bay.

TELEGRAM.

White house, Washington.

150
1 WH JM GI   Paid Govt — 10:50a.

The White House, Washington, D.C., August 26.

Hon. Wm. Loeb, Jr.,
    Secretary to the President,
        Oyster Bay.   Peking August 26.

Secretary of State:
    26th. Shanghai reports signs of gradual subsiding, Canton likewise. Chinese piece goods merchants Shanghai strongly opposing boycott and have taken steps through the viceroy Tientsin which I think breaks it as far as piece goods, our principal import is concerned. No trouble reported elsewhere except Amoy where boycott is only partial cause present agitation. Both Peking government and viceroy are taking action against the movement each time more emphatically under constant and great pressure from legation. My opinion is that if I went Shanghai the agitators would be encouraged and movement strengthened. I am (receiving ?) reports of causes every mail. May I wait to see situation develop before I carry out instructions? Principal danger of the agitation is that it may become anti-foreign and lead to violence.

Rockhill.

(*TR Papers*, Series 1, Reel 58)

Meanwhile, the peace negotiations entered their final phase the following day as everyone waited for word from the Japanese Government. No further concessions were expected from them and the Russian plenipotentiaries were preparing to return home.

PORTSMOUTH, N.H., Aug. 27 — After a long conference between Mr. Takahira and M. Witte in the latter's room this evening it was announced that the conference would be resumed on Tuesday at 4 P.M. instead of tomorrow, as planned. No new proposition by Mr. Takahira was advanced at this interview.

This last expedient was, it is believed, resorted to because of the apparent utter hopelessness of the situation. At the meeting yesterday the Japanese became alarmed over the imminence of a rupture. The hour of secret and unrecorded session between the four envoys, with even the secretaries banished from the room, marked the abandonment of diplomatic pretenses and the laying of all the cards on the table. It resulted in the demonstration to Baron Komura and Mr. Takahira that the Russians were determined to break off the negotiations unless the Japanese gave in.

Baron Komura's request at that time for a further conference to-morrow was, it is understood, based on the hope that the Mikado's Government might be induced to compromise...

...At the meeting yesterday M. Witte and Baron Komura discussed the situation fully to see if anything could be done. At the conclusion of the discussion M. Witte informed Baron Komura that it would be useless for Japan to make any new proposals which included an indemnity in any shape or form, as he had said his last word upon that subject and would not discuss it again.

After the meeting yesterday Baron Komura cabled the result of his private conversation with M. Witte to Tokio and stated that the negotiations would be broken off on Monday unless the Japanese made some new proposal. Up to a late hour this evening the reply had not arrived...

...One of the leading Russians said to-night that the Russians believed the dispatches from Tokio would contain no new proposal, but merely the formal authorization to the Japanese envoys to break off negotiations. The Japanese credentials do not authorize them to break off negotiations without direct instructions from Tokio.

The last hope of peace is that the Mikado may give in before Tuesday...

...The official explanation given out with regard to the postponement until Tuesday is that it is to enable all the formalities to be properly gone through with.

It is reported late to-night that the postponement is due to the President making a final effort to bring about peace...

...Assistant Secretary Peirce, after the announcement of the decision to adjourn to Tuesday, saw both M. Witte and Mr. Takahira and then sent a long cipher message to the President...

...The conference room has ceased to be a place for negotiations. It is simply the place where the Emperors of the warring countries exchange their communications by the hands of their envoys. And upon the point of indemnity under any disguise Emperor Nicholas has given the Japanese Emperor his last word...

...Whether the President has renewed his efforts cannot be ascertained here.

ST. PETERSBURG, Aug. 27 — The Czar's final reply to President Roosevelt was conveyed through Ambassador Meyer yesterday. It is an unqualified refusal to entertain the demand for an indemnity...

(NY Times, August 28, 1905)

On August 27, Mr. O'Loughlin sent a telegram for the President to Assistant Secretary Barnes regarding the state of the negotiations in Portsmouth. It is clear from the telegram that they were on the verge of breaking down.

TELEGRAM.

RECEIVED IN CIPHER.

White house, Washington.

Hotel Wentworth, New Castle, N.H., August 27, 1905 — 6:30p

Hon. B. F. Barnes,
    Assistant Secretary,
      Oyster Bay, N.Y..

Unless you induce adjournment until Wednesday fear tomorrow will be last meeting. Japanese friend states Komura make no concessions. Policy his Government fixed. Instructions Witte division Sakhaline last word Czar. If Japan could be induced leave question money out treaty, permit financial settlement private arrangement, adjustment possible. Czar believes question one principle. Important eliminate through Meyer within couple days, not at once, as despatches show stubbornness of Czar.

O'Loughlin.

(TR Papers, Series 1, Reel 58)

Also on August 27, Minister Rockhill cabled again regarding the situation in China.

TELEGRAM.

RECEIVED IN CIPHER.

𝔚𝔥𝔦𝔱𝔢 𝔥𝔬𝔲𝔰𝔢,
𝔚𝔞𝔰𝔥𝔦𝔫𝔤𝔱𝔬𝔫.

2 WH FD GI 141 Paid Govt ——8:45p.

WHH —- Washington, August 27.

Hon. Wm. Loeb, Jr.,
    Secretary to the President,
      Oyster Bay.

Peking, August 27.

Secretary of State:

Twenty-seventh. Received yesterday a dispatch from the Foreign Office in reply to my last three in reference to boycott. It says that the movement was started by the traders. The Government assumes no responsibility, decline to punish ring-leader fear of disorder. Have taken action as proof of friendship. Telegraph instructions have been sent again to publish proclamations explaining matters and authorities to urge the people to attend to their own private affairs; if any disturbances they must be stopped. Wants discussion of terms of treaty resumed and settled by which the grievance will be removed.

It is my intention to insist on our points and also complete suppression the agitation before the resumption of any discussion concerning the treaty. Do you approve my action?

Rockhill.

(TR Papers, Series 1, Reel 58)

On August 28, the negotiations had reached a critical stage. The importance given to the communications of the day is reflected in Assistant Secretary Peirce's telegram to Mr. Barnes in Oyster Bay.

TELEGRAM.

The White House,

Washington.

6 NY D GI 43 Paid Govt — 2:35p

Navy Yard, Portsmouth, N.H., August 28.

B. F. Barnes,
    Secretary to the President,
        Oyster Bay.

Is the President likely to telegraph me today? If so I will keep wire up between Oyster Bay and Navy Yard until five o'clock and Oyster Bay and the Wentworth after that hour.

H. H. D. Peirce

(TR Papers, Series 1, Reel 58)

Later in the day it was expected that the Japanese Government would begin to make some concessions.

A Special to the New York Times
PORTSMOUTH, N.H., Aug 28 — A message has been received from Tokio as a result of which arrangements have been made for beginning the meeting of the conference to-morrow at 9:30 in the morning instead of in the afternoon, as originally planned. The message contains a proposition not for the waiving of the indemnity but for its material reduction...
...The Japanese here are bitterly disappointed. They believe that now that the Tokio Government has begun to yield to pressure it will continue to do so until the Russians have succeeded in gaining all they want. They have no expectation that the Russians will consent to a mere reduction of the indemnity and they look for a further adjournment and for further recessions by the Mikado.

By The Associated Press
PORTSMOUTH, N.H., Aug 28 — Tomorrow morning Baron Komura, acting upon instructions received from Tokio as a result of to-day's meeting of the Cabinet and the Elder Statesmen under the Presidency of the Emperor, will submit to M. Witte a new basis of compromise, and that compromise, it is firmly believed to-night, will insure peace.
The revelation contained in The Associated Press announcement to-day that Japan had already informed Emperor Nicholas through President Roosevelt

and Ambassador Meyer that she was ready to waive the question of indemnity and submit the price to be paid for the northern half of Sakhalin to the judgement of a mixed commission but prepared the way for Japan's backdown upon the main issue...

...M. Witte by consummate skill in conceding all the demands of Japan involving the real issues of the war had maneuvered his adversaries into a position where, unless they abandoned the claim for indemnity, they could be held responsible for continuing the war for money. The Japanese, by now forgoing the demand for indemnity, practically turn the tables upon Russia and shift the burden back to her shoulders if she does not consent to submit a minor issue to the impartial judgment of a tribunal. *(NY Times*, August 29, 1905)

While these concessions were being made by the Japanese, President Roosevelt was again discussing the Hankow Railroad Concession with J.P. Morgan at Sagamore Hill. Inasmuch as many European countries were competing with the United States for spheres of influence in China, the continued American ownership of the Hankow concession by Mr. Morgan's American-China Development Company, was vitally important to America's continued influence in the region. The meeting held on August 28 was intended to convince Mr. Morgan that the Hankow concession should not be sold to the Chinese but should instead remain in American hands.

OYSTER BAY, Aug. 28 — The controversy now in progress between the Chinese Government and the American owners over control of the Canton-Hankow Railroad concession was the subject of an important conference today between President Roosevelt and J. Pierpont Morgan.

This is the second time Mr. Morgan has come to see the President about the Chinese railroad concession within a month...

...For some time the Chinese have made every effort to gain possession of the Hankow concession, which is owned by the America-China Development Company, a concern now controlled by the firm of J.P. Morgan & Co. For several months the Peking authorities with this end in view have managed to make things so unpleasant for the American owners that not a few of them, Mr. Morgan among them, have been only too anxious to get rid of their holdings.

President Roosevelt, on the other hand, to whom it is a matter of vital concern that the Hankow concession should remain in the hands of its American owners, not only for the advantage it would afford American commerce, but for the prestige it would give this country in that part of the world, has been bringing all the influence at his command to bear on Mr. Morgan, with a view of preventing the surrender of the concession.

In this attitude the President has been borne out by Edwin H. Conger, who for many years, until last April, was United States Minister at Peking...

...When Mr. Conger...visited Sagamore Hill several days ago, the President conferred with him on the Hankow matter. Mr. Conger advised him that the surrender of the concession by the company at this time would be a serious blow to American prestige and American interests in that part of the world...

...Subsequent to Mr. Morgan's departure a statement was given out by Secretary Loeb at the Executive offices here in which it was said that the President and Mr. Morgan had discussed the Canton-Hankow Railroad concession, but that "no conclusion had been reached." It is therefore believed here that when the Directors of the American-Chinese Development Company meet to-morrow final action in the matter of the sale will be postponed. *(NY Times*, August 29, 1905)

On August 29, the President sent a letter by special delivery to Mr. Peirce in Portsmouth.

TELEGRAM.

The White House, Washington.

RECEIVED IN CIPHER.

Portsmouth, N.H., August 29 —— 11:25a

William Loeb, Jr.,
 Secretary to the President,
  Oyster Bay.

 Special delivery letter not received. Conference which was postponed until late this afternoon was, late last night, appointed for this morning, now in session.

Herbert H. D. Peirce.

(TR Papers, Series 1, Reel 58)

Shortly after this telegram was cabled, Mr. Peirce sent another.

TELEGRAM.

The White House,

Washington.

RECEIVED IN CIPHER.

Portsmouth, N.H., August 29 —— 11:50a

Hon. Wm. Loeb, Jr.,
 Secretary to the President,
  Oyster Bay.

 Letter received. Delivered and read by Baron Komura. I am awaiting a reply which I will telegraph immediately after its receipt.

H. H. D. Peirce.

(TR Papers, Series 1, Reel 58)

All the negotiators could do now was wait.

Despite the meeting between J.P. Morgan and the President, the stockholders of the American-China Development Company decided to sell the concession to the Chinese Government for $6,750,000. It was rumored that the Japanese were behind the Chinese Government in its attempt to buy the concession and that there was a conspiracy between the U.S., China, and Japan. *(NY Times,* August 30,1905)

OYSTER BAY, Aug. 29 — Following the conference at Sagamore Hill yesterday between President Roosevelt and J. Pierpont Morgan, it was announced at the Executive office here this afternoon that the controversy between the Chinese Government and the American owners over the Canton-Hankow Railroad concession is about to be terminated by the formal surrender of the concession to the Peking authorities...The public announcement was made through the following official statement given out by Secretary Loeb:

"After full discussion with Mr. Morgan it was decided to accept the offer of the Chinese Government to pay $6,750,000 as an indemnity for the cancellation of the contract for the building of the Hankow-Canton Railway. The imperial Chinese Government having canceled the contract, and at the same time expressed a willingness to pay any damage, it left only the question of the indemnity, and as a satisfactory amount having been offered the stockholders have agreed to accept the same.

"Mr. Morgan has consulted with the Administration, and shown every desire to do what American interests in the Orient demanded, and only consented to the arrangement proposed by the Chinese Government in view of the fact that the attitude of the Chinese Government rendered it obvious that there was no other course which he could take with due regard to the interest of the stockholders he represented..."

Though the statement had been in readiness at the executive office since early this morning, it was not given out until about ten minutes after the President had received official confirmation of the peace envoys' agreement at Portsmouth in a dispatch from Third Assistant Secretary of State Peirce. Both announcements were made at the same time. *(NY Times,* August 30, 1905)

That same day, August 29, the Russians and the Japanese made peace.

PORTSMOUTH, N.H., Aug. 29 — Russia's only victory of the war was won to-day at Portsmouth. Despairing and broken hearted, Baron Komura obeyed the direct orders of the Mikado and conceded every point for which the Russians have contended.

The surrender was made, not at Portsmouth, not by Baron Komura and Minister Takahira, who opposed it to the last moment — it was made yesterday in Tokio by Marquis Ito and the three other Elder Statesmen. The war is practically at an end and the peace terms are agreed upon.

No indemnity is to be paid. Only the cost of keeping Russian prisoners is to be reimbursed to Japan. The Russians had determined that that should not exceed $50,000,000 but they did not have to name their maximum...

...The Japanese will also pay Russia for the cost of keeping the few prisoners she has taken.

There is no sale of Sakhalin. The Japanese are to restore to Russia the northern half of the island without taking any money for it. Permission to the Japanese to retain the southern half was given by the orders of the Czar to M. Witte. The envoy himself would never have consented to it but for that...

...When on Aug. 18, Baron Komura cabled to the Mikado urging some concessions be made, he had no idea of the extent to which those concessions would go. The later Japanese concessions he has opposed...

...Herbert H.D. Peirce, Third Assistant Secretary of State, the President's representative at the conference, was the first person outside the conference room to be informed of the "Peace of Portsmouth." For half an hour he was the only one besides the plenipotentiaries and their secretaries who knew it. By agreement the plenipotentiaries decided that the first message announcing the conclusion of peace should be sent to President Roosevelt at Oyster Bay, and, in the hope that he might receive the news even before Tokio or St. Petersburg, held the official bulletin for half an hour. *(NY Times, August 30, 1905)*

The news of the peace took the President completely by surprise.

OYSTER BAY, Aug, 29 — President Roosevelt received his first news of the agreement between the envoys of Russia and Japan on terms of peace at 12:50 o'clock this afternoon.

The President was in the library at Sagamore Hill dictating letters having an important bearing on the peace negotiations.

The telephone rang, Secretary Loeb dropped his pen and stepped up to receive his message, and the next moment Mr. Roosevelt knew that the efforts in which he had set his heart had finally borne fruit.

The President hesitated for a while and asked Mr. Loeb to repeat the message to him. His next move was to inform Mrs. Roosevelt and the children of the happy news.

Confirmation of the preliminary report did not reach the President until two hours later, when the following official dispatch from Third Assistant Secretary of State Peirce was received at the executive office here and at once forwarded to Sagamore Hill:

"The plenipotentiaries of Japan have withdrawn their claim for the reimbursement of war expenses and an agreement has been reached as to a partition of the Island of Sakhalin. All minor points have been definitely settled. The plenipotentiaries will now proceed to the discussion of details."

It can be stated authoritatively that the news came as a great surprise to the President. While Mr. Roosevelt never had entirely given up hope that a peaceful solution would be reached at Portsmouth, as is witnessed by the fact that he still was continuing his efforts when the peace message came, he had not been optimistic, and at any rate had not expected an agreement to come so soon.

While the news was still being discussed the following message was received from M. Witte and Baron Rosen, the Russian envoys:

"We have the honor to inform you that we have reached an agreement with the plenipotentiaries of Japan. To you history will award the glory of having taken the generous initiative in bringing about this conference, whose labors will now probably result in establishing a peace honorable to both sides."

The President's answer was as follows:

I cannot too strongly express my congratulations to you and to the entire civilized world upon the agreement reached between you and plenipotentiaries of Japan, and upon the fact that thereby a peace has been secured just and honorable to both sides.

THEODORE ROOSEVELT.

A response was also sent by the President to the dispatch received this afternoon from Baron Komura. The text of the message was not disclosed...

...Besides the message from the Russian and Japanese envoys, congratulations literally poured into Sagamore Hill last night. Some came by wire, and Mr. Roosevelt all evening was kept busy at the telephone receiving messages of congratulation.

The local paper gave a slightly different account.

In his library at Sagamore Hill President Roosevelt received the official announcement that the Russian and Japanese plenipotentiaries at Portsmouth had reached an agreement and would proceed at once to conclude the terms of a treaty of peace...Mr. Loeb, secretary to the president, who was engaged with him at the moment in work on the peace negotiations, answered the call.

"What?" he eagerly inquired as the message was given him.

The message was repeated.

He manifested so much excitement and incredulity that the president inquired, "What is it?"

"It is announced in an official bulletin from Portsmouth," replied Secretary Loeb, "that the plenipotentiaries have agreed on all points of difference and will proceed at once to negotiate a treaty of peace."

"That is fine—splendid!" exclaimed the president. "But, " as a doubt passed through his mind, "Do you think it is authentic?"

"It is a perfectly definite statement," Mr. Loeb responded.

(*East Norwich Pilot*, Sept 2, 1905.)

FIGURE 26: The President cutting wood on the grounds of Oyster Bay.
Courtesy of Sagamore Hill

Roosevelt's pivotal position in the negotiations was immediately recognized by the world's leaders. The Executive office became the hub of activity, receiving all the many messages of congratulations and passing on the most important ones to the President.

OYSTER BAY, Aug. 30 — Theodore Roosevelt, the peacemaker, to-day received his tribute from the world for the share he has had in ending the war between Russia and Japan and preventing further bloodshed in the Far East.

While the telegraph wires leading into this little village on the shores of the Sound, which has played such an important part in the history of the last few weeks, were humming with congratulatory messages from the mighty ones of the world, and while the instrument in the little telegraph room at the executive office was spelling out its ceaseless story of praise, the President might have been seen dressed in khaki and carrying an axe, striding down the wooded slope near his summer home...

...Two hours later, at 9 o'clock in the morning, Secretary Loeb arrived at Sagamore Hill for his daily session of executive business with the President. He carried a handbag filled with congratulations from the crowned heads of Europe, from men occupying exalted places in State and Church the world over, and letters that came from men and women in humbler station.

On learning at Sagamore Hill that Mr. Roosevelt was out in the woods, Mr. Loeb went to look for him, and found the President half hidden behind a pile of wood. Mr. Loeb put the handbag down on a stump and fished out a bundle of telegrams which he handed to Mr. Roosevelt. Thus it was that the man on whom is centered the gaze of the world received the official thanks of the world...

...There was hardly a minute's let up to-day in the flow of messages. Secretary Loeb said this afternoon that fully 900 messages had been received.

Among the first messages to arrive were those from King Edward and Emperor William. They came over the Executive telegraph wire almost simultaneously yesterday afternoon. The message from President Loubet of France, whose good offices with those of King Edward and the Kaiser were exercised in the interest of peace at the request of Mr. Roosevelt, did not reach Oyster Bay until this afternoon.

The President spent the whole forenoon, after the Executive business had been disposed of, in dictating answers to messages of congratulations. Hundreds of the telegrams and messages the President may never read himself...

...On behalf of the President, it was said to-day that the place for the signing of the treaty would be a matter for the envoys themselves to settle. (*NY Times*, August 31, 1905)

On September 1, 1905 *The New York Times* announced that an armistice had been agreed upon by the plenipotentiaries and the fighting between Russia and Japan would end. The flood of messages to the Executive office continued endlessly.

OYSTER BAY, L.I., Aug. 31 — Most remarkable of the many messages received by President Roosevelt to-day was one from the Czar of Russia, showing how glad that ruler is that the President succeeded in his effort to

make peace. The cablegram is dated at Peterhof yesterday and reads:
"President Roosevelt:

" Accept my congratulations and warmest thanks for having brought the peace negotiations to a successful conclusion owing to your personal energetic efforts. My country will gratefully recognize the great part you have played in the Portsmouth peace conference.

NICHOLAS."

...The dispatch is regarded as one of the most remarkable of its kind ever sent by the head of one nation to that of another.

The Executive office force here is swamped by the messages of congratulating the President, and it will be many days before acknowledgements can be sent out. It is impossible for President Roosevelt himself to respond to the felicitations of his friends everywhere, but the sender of each message will receive a response.

Among the other messages of congratulations, the President received a message from Franz Joseph, Emperor of Austria-Hungary and the Empress Dowager of China. It was also announced from Oyster Bay on August 31, 1905 that President Roosevelt signed an executive order fixing the salaries of the members of the Advisory Board of Engineers of the Isthmian Canal. This board would later decide the Panama Canal's method of construction, sea-level or lock.

On September 1, 1905, the Executive office received a dispatch from W.W. Rockhill, United States Minister to China. The dispatch informed the President that an Imperial edict had been issued commanding the Chinese viceroys and governors to put down a six week old boycott of American goods by Chinese merchants. The power to put down such a boycott rested with the Chinese Government alone and many exchanges were made between the State Department and the Chinese Minister at Washington to try and resolve the situation. The dispatch also informed the President that the situation in Shanghai was improving. Also on September 1, Assistant Secretary of State Francis Loomis visited Sagamore Hill. He would resign from his post in the coming weeks *(NY Times*, September 2, 1905)

On September 3, 1905, *The New York Times* announced that the peace treaty was approved by the peace envoys and was expected to be signed the following day, September 4, 1905.

After a delay of nearly six days, the President finally received a cable of thanks from the Japanese Government on September 3, 1905.

OYSTER BAY, Sept. 3 — A belated cable message from the Mikado expressing his appreciation of the work done by President Roosevelt in bringing about peace between Russia and Japan reached the Executive office here to-day.

To-day's message came in reply to the congratulations sent to the Mikado by the President through Baron Komura immediately after the agreement at Portsmouth last Tuesday. It was dated yesterday.

The dispatch came over the Formosa-Fuchow route, the other cable lines to Japan having been put out of commission by a typhoon. This accounts for the long time which elapsed in the exchange of messages.

The Mikado's message came in over the special Executive wire at 12:40 o'clock this afternoon, as follows:

"Tokio, Sept 3.

"The President: I have received with gratification your message of congratulation conveyed through our plenipotentiaries, and thank you warmly for it.

"To your disinterested and unremitting efforts in the interest of peace and humanity I attach the high value which is their due, and assure you of my grateful appreciation of the distinguished part you have taken in the establishment of peace, based upon principles essential to the permanent welfare and tranquility of the Far East.

"MUTSUHITO."

(NY Times, September 4, 1905)

On September 4, 1905, it was announced that Assistant Secretary of State Loomis had resigned and his replacement would be Robert Bacon.

Official announcement was made at the Executive office here to-day of the appointment of Robert Bacon, who has been prominent in Wall Street as a financier, Director of banks, railways, and industrial organizations, and a former member of the banking firm of J.P. Morgan & Co., as Assistant Secretary of State to succeed Francis B. Loomis. At the same time it was made known that Loomis resigned some time ago.

Mr. Bacon...at the moment his appointment was announced by Secretary Loeb was being entertained at luncheon at Sagamore Hill by the President and Mrs. Roosevelt. His arrival here was unheralded. His name was not announced by Mr. Loeb with that of the other visitors of the day this morning...

...At the executive office it was said to-night that no provision had been made for the political future of Mr. Loomis. *(NY Times*, September 5, 1905)

On September 5, the Treaty of Portsmouth was signed and the plenipotentiaries of Russia sent a telegram of thanks to the President.

TELEGRAM.

White house,
Washington.

1 NY D GI 101 Paid —— 9:17a

Hotel Wentworth, New Castle, N.H. Sept 5/6

The President:

We have the honor to inform you that we have this day signed the treaty of peace with Japan. It is not for us to thank you for what you have done in the cause of peace as your noble and generous efforts have been fittingly acknowledged by our august sovereign. We can only express to you, Mr. President, and to the people of the United States, our personal sentiments of profound gratitude for the cordial reception you have done us the honor to extend to us and which we have met with at the hands of the people of this country.

Witte,

Rosen.

(TR Papers, Series 1, Reel 59)

On September 6, the preliminary arrangements were made for the Russian and Japanese plenipotentiaries to visit the President, albeit separately, at Sagamore Hill.

TELEGRAM.

The White House,

Washington.

3 NY QQ GI 43 Paid — Govt — 9:30 a

Portsmouth, N.H. Sept. 6, 1905.

Hon. Wm. Loeb,
  Secretary to the President,
    Oyster Bay.

Inexact only to save wording. Envoys train leaves Long Island City at 5:43 p.m. Will telegraph them again reciting <u>our</u> departure from Long Island City and arrangements for return from Oyster Bay.

Herbert H. D. Peirce.

(TR Papers, Series 1, Reel 59)

In response to the announced peace accord, the Japanese people rioted in Tokyo. Ambassador Griscom cabled the Secretary of State with this new development. This cable was then forwarded, via Secretary Loeb, to the President.

TELEGRAM.

𝔚𝔥𝔦𝔱𝔢 𝔥𝔬𝔲𝔰𝔢,
𝔚𝔞𝔰𝔥𝔦𝔫𝔤𝔱𝔬𝔫.

1 WH JM GI 172 Paid Govt — 11:08a

WH — Washington, D.C. Sept. 6.

Hon. Wm. Loeb,
   Secretary,
      Oyster Bay.

Tokio

Secretary of State:

September 5 — 11p. Considerable rioting occurred in Tokyo today when the police endeavored to prevent mass meeting protesting against so called humiliating terms of peace, police being obliged to use swords; some severe injuries inflicted but without fatalities. Mob attacked the house of Home Minister and also set fire to part of the Foreign Office and damaged premises of the pro-government newspaper. Three mobs numbering about one thousand each are now rioting through different districts, destroying Government property. The Government has been obliged to call out troops to assist police. A guard of fifty soldiers have been placed in this legation and the number is now being increased to two hundred owing to the attitude of the crowd. I do not anticipate trouble here but will leave the matter of guards to the discretion of the authorities. Several foreigners have been stoned in the streets. The other legations are similarly guarded.

Griscom.

(TR Papers, Series 1, Reel 59)

Also on September 6, Acting Secretary of State Adee, via Assistant Secretary Forster, cabled Secretary Loeb with the translated text of the telegraphic message of congratulations from the Emperor of China to the President.

TELEGRAM.

𝔚hite house, 𝔚ashington.

2 WH JM GI 280 Paid Govt — 4:35p

The White House, Washington, D.C. Sept. 6.

Hon. Wm. Loeb, Jr.,
    Secretary to the President,
        Oyster Bay.

      Secretary Adee sends over following communication with request that it be forwarded to you by wire:

IMPERIAL CHINESE LEGATION,
Amherst, Mass., September 5.

My dear Mr. Secretary:

      I have just received, through the Waiwu Pu, the Foreign Office at Peking, a telegraphic message addressed by the Emperor of China to the President of the United States, of which the enclosed is an English translation; and I beg that you will kindly transmit the same to its high destination.

                I am, my dear Mr. Secretary,

Very sincerely yours,

Chentung Liang-Cheng.

Honorable Alvey A. Adee,
    Acting Secretary of State.

The message from the Emperor Kuang Hsu immediately followed and was later released to the press.

TELEGRAM.

White house,
Washington.

The Emperor of China
To The President of the United States of America.

Greeting: The joyful tidings respecting the satisfactory
issue of the peace negotiations between Japan and Russia having
been received by all friendly Governments with profound gratification, we congratulate you, Mr. President, upon the success of your
efforts to bring the relations of the neighboring powers concerned
into harmony and to promote the welfare of mankind. With the cessation of hostilities and the establishment of a good understanding
we earnestly hope that all nations will hereafter enjoy the fruits
of peace without interruption, to the end that the three Manchurian
provinces of China may be blessed with complete tranquility and
lasting welfare, to the benefit of the whole world.

Her Majesty, the Empress Dowager of China, being mindful of
the friendly relations that have always subsisted between China
and the United States desires to join us in offering you hearty
felicitations for your grand achievement.

Rudolph Forster.

(TR Papers, Series 1, Reel 59)

On September 7, the President of the Long Island Railroad wrote a letter to Secretary Loeb confirming the travel arrangements of the Russian plenipotentiaries to Oyster Bay.

THE LONG ISLAND RAILROAD COMPANY

OFFICE OF THE PRESIDENT AND GENERAL MANAGER.

RALPH PETERS
  PRESIDENT AND GEN. MANAGER.

LONG ISLAND CITY, N. Y.   September 7, 1905.

Mr. William Loeb, Jr.,
    Secretary to the President,
        Oyster Bay, L.I.

My dear Mr. Loeb:-

Your message in connection with furnishing a special car for the Russian Peace Plenipotentiaries on Saturday evening, received and understood, and we will take pleasure in providing the service.

Yours truly,

Ralph Peters
President & General Manager.

(TR Papers, Series 1, Reel 59)

Also on September 7, a little mix-up occurred when Assistant Secretary of State Peirce's secretary inadvertently sent a telegram meant for the Russian plenipotentiaries to the Japanese instead.

TELEGRAM.

The White House,

Washington.

5 NY D GI 90 Paid —— 12:30 p
                    New York, Sept. 7, 1905.
Mr. B.F. Barnes, Assistant Secretary:

Secretary Peirce informed us Tuesday evening that the President invited Baron Komura and myself to luncheon on Saturday and we have to go to Oyster Bay by the SYLPH leaving at 10 oclock from New York Yacht Club. Baron Komura now received another telegram from Mr. Peirce that we have to go to Oyster Bay by the President's private car leaving Long Island City at 5:43 Saturday p.m. Will you kindly inform me whether we are invited to luncheon or dinner. As for us, either arrangement is perfectly agreeable.

K. Takahira,
Waldorf Astoria.

(TR Papers, Series 1, Reel 59)

Mr. Peirce was notified of the error and telegraphed to Mr. Loeb that he had corrected the mistake.

TELEGRAM.

The White House,

Washington.

15 NY ZJ GI 35 Collect Govt —- 8:35 p

Portsmouth, N.H. Sept. 7.

Hon. Wm. Loeb,
    Secretary to the President,
        Oyster Bay.

    Evidently my secretary to whom I dictated telegrams to Baron Komura and Baron Rosen confused the two. Have corrected error by telegram.

        Herbert H. D. Peirce.

(TR Papers, Series 1, Reel 59)

Shortly thereafter, Mr. Peirce cabled again with a further clarification.

TELEGRAM.

𝕸𝖍𝖎𝖙𝖊 𝖍𝖔𝖚𝖘𝖊, 𝖂𝖆𝖘𝖍𝖎𝖓𝖌𝖙𝖔𝖓.

16 NY UW GI 71 Paid —— 9:15p Govt.

Portsmouth, N.H. September 7.

Hon. Wm. Loeb,
    Secretary to the President,
      Oyster Bay.

Find my secretary in the rush of final movements of envoys sent duplicate of my telegram to Witte to Komura instead Rosen. Have telegraphed to Rosen making arrangements for dinner Saturday clear and have telegraphed Komura that telegram sent to him was an error and that he is expected at luncheon as first stated by me. Deeply regret error.

Herbert H. D. Peirce.

(TR Papers, Series 1, Reel 59)

Finally on September 8, Mr. Peirce wrote a long letter to Mr. Loeb explaining exactly why the mix-up had occurred.

DEPARTMENT OF STATE,
WASHINGTON.

September 8, 1905.

My dear Mr. Loeb:

I am more chagrined than I can express at the unfortunate contretemps in connection with the President's luncheon and dinner, which has occurred to mar at the very end the performance of my duties in connection with the Peace Plenipotentiaries.

My Secretary here had proved himself so exact and efficient in following my instructions that I had believed I could entirely rely on him in the transmission of telegrams dictated by me.

There was considerable rush of business immediately following the signing of the treaty and to save time I dictated a telegram to Mr. Witte conveying the President's invitation to him, and gave my secretary instructions to dispatch the message both to the Waldorf and St. Regis, and to transmit the same message to Baron Rosen at both hotels. I did this as it had been left somewhat uncertain to which of these two hotels the Russians would go.

On examining my secretary's memorandum I find that he had made the remark that the telegram was to go to both hotels but had not stated Baron Rosen's name, and it appears that he sent this telegram to Mr. Witte at the St. Regis and duplicated it to Baron Komura at the Waldorf.

I cannot tell you how much I deplore this accident and I trust that you will make the President understand my explanation, which may in some measure mitigate in his mind the gravity if not the blunder itself, at least of the appearance of carelessness.

We have all been under considerable strain here keeping ourselves ready to act at a moment's notice, often upon conflicting orders, at all hours of the day and night, and heretofore everything has gone with perfect smoothness.

At this moment I am in receipt of your telegram making it apparent that the telegraph operator has mistaken the word "hour" for "our", making the context read "our departure" instead of "hour of departure" as I wrote it. This is a minor error which my telegram of this morning will have explained satisfactorily to you.

Very sincerely yours,

Herbert H. D. Peirce

Hon. William Loeb, Jr.,
    Secretary to the President,
    Oyster Bay, N.Y.

(TR Papers, Series 1, Reel 59)

During the following week, the President's attention was also focused on the growing troubles in the Government Printing Office, which began on September 4, 1905.

OYSTER BAY, N.Y., Sept. 8 — For insubordination in disobeying his orders, President Roosevelt to-day ordered the summary and immediate removal of F.W. Palmer, head of the Government Printing Office at Washington...

...Palmer's troubles grew out of the recent investigation of the contract for typesetting machines for the Government Printing Office. The contract was awarded to the Lanston Company, and the Mergenthaler Company, a rival concern, charged that unfair methods had been employed in making the award. During the investigation which followed two foremen in the department, Oscar

J. Ricketts and L.C. Hay, gave testimony which was unfavorable to Palmer. After the investigation had been closed Palmer proffered charges of insubordination against the two foremen, and ordered them to appear before him on Sept. 5 to show cause why they should not be removed from office.

When President Roosevelt learned of this he issued an order calling upon Palmer to tender his resignation to take effect on Sept. 15. Pending this the President issued an order prohibiting Palmer from issuing any order to the employees of the department or in any way interfering with the working of the Government Printing Office.

To-day the President was informed that Palmer nonetheless had ordered Ricketts and Hay to appear before him and answer charges to-morrow. Mr. Roosevelt then issued the order busting him at once.

WASHINGTON, Sept. 8 — When Foreman Oscar J. Ricketts this evening reached his home from the Government Printing Office he found Rudolph Forster, Assistant Secretary to the President, waiting for him with a message from Secretary Loeb directing him to take charge of the Government Printing Office at once. Mr. Forster stated that a message had come from Oyster Bay to notify Public Printer Palmer of his removal, and Mr. Forster on the way to Mr. Rickett's house had stopped at Mr. Palmer's residence and told him of the President's action. *(NY Times, September 9, 1905)*

Also on September 8, the President met with Vice President Charles Warren Fairbanks.

The Vice President arrived from New York on the 12:20 P.M. train, and was met at the station by a confidential messenger of the President, who escorted him to one of the Executive carriages in waiting. *(NY Times, September 9, 1905)*

The President was also asked to intervene in the award given by Chairman Shonts of the Panama Canal Commission to the J.E. Markel company of Omaha to feed and care for the Panama canal employees. Local bidders asserted that the award indicated collusion and that they would consequently withdraw their own bids with the intention of invalidating the award to Markel by withdrawing competition. *(NY Times, September 9, 1905)*

On September 9, the President had as his guests both the Japanese and Russian plenipotentiaries.

President Roosevelt entertained the peace plenipotentiaries of Russia and Japan at Sagamore Hill. Baron Komura and Minister Takahira, the Mikado's envoys, were the guests at the luncheon. M. Witte and Baron Rosen, the Russian envoys, dined at Sagamore Hill this evening...

...The first one to greet the *(Japanese)* envoys at the President's home was Secretary Loeb, who received them in the library. A moment later the President and Mrs. Roosevelt came in. *(NY Times, September 10, 1905)*

The peace dividend for the United States was clear the following day when the Czar announced that duties on certain goods from the U.S. would be lowered.

OYSTER BAY, Sept. 10 — The text of a communication from the Czar, presented to President Roosevelt by M. Witte yesterday, was made public this evening. The communication reads as follows:

"Some years ago, in consequence of a misunderstanding in the interpretation of the most-favored-nation clause, there were established in Russia on several articles of American production custom duties on a higher scale than those levied on the same articles when imported from other countries.

"His Majesty the Emperor of Russia has commanded me to inform the President of the United States that he has been pleased to order the discontinuance of the levying of such higher duties on American products in order that henceforth the American manufacturers should pay the same duties as importers from other countries." *(NY Times, September 11, 1905)*

On September 10, the President authorized the publication of the report given by the Keep Commission. This commission investigated charges of irregularities in the Government Printing Office. *(NY Times, September 11, 1905)*

On September 11, Sir Chentung Liang-Cheng, the Chinese Minister at Washington wrote to Secretary Loeb requesting an appointment to meet with the President. The Chinese Minister would visit the President in Oyster Bay on September 18.

IMPERIAL CHINESE LEGATION
WASHINGTON

Amherst, Mass.

11th September 1905.

My dear Mr Secretary,

Mr Wang Tai-sieh a member of our Foreign Office who was sent by my Government to confer with me on special matters, and to watch the Peace Conference of Portsmouth, is desirous of paying his respects to the President before he returns to China. Mr Wang is an important official in the Court at Peking, and I think it would be of benefit to both countries, especially at this time, for him to have the honor of being presented to the President. I shall accompany Mr. Wang to Oyster Bay should the President be so gracious as to receive him. And we will only take a few minutes of the President's time. We shall leave here Thursday afternoon arriving at the Hotel Manhattan New York City, Friday morning the 15th remaining there over Saturday.

Respectfully waiting for the President's pleasure, and thanking you, Mr Secretary, for your kind service, believe me

Yours faithfully
Chentung Liangcheng

Hon. William Loeb Jr.
Secretary to the President

(TR Papers, Series 1, Reel 59)

The meeting of the members of the international board of consulting engineers of the Panama Canal also took place at Sagamore Hill on September 11, 1905. At this meeting the President learned the views of the board members and expressed his wishes to them regarding the manner in which the canal should be built. He also urged them to come to their decision quickly. (September 12, 1905) The text of the President's address to the board was released on September 17, 1905.

The President's remarks on the occasion of the engineers' visit to Oyster Bay were made public to-day. In part he said:

"What I am about to say must be considered in the light of suggestion, not as direction. I have named you, because, in my judgement, you are especially fitted to serve as advisors in planning the greatest engineering work the world has ever seen, and I expect you to advise me, not what you think I want to hear, but what you think I ought to hear.

"There are two or three considerations which I trust you will steadily keep before your minds in coming to a conclusion as to the proper type of canal. I hope that ultimately it will prove possible to build a sea level canal. Such a canal would undoubtedly be best in the end, if feasible, and I feel that one of the chief advantages of the Panama route is that ultimately a sea level canal will be a possibility. But while paying due heed to the ideal perfectibility of the scheme from an engineer's standpoint, remember the need of having a plan which shall provide for the immediate building of a canal on the safest terms and in the shortest possible time.

"If to build a sea level canal will but slightly increase the risk then, of course, it is preferable. But if to adopt the plan of a sea level canal means to incur hazard, and to insure indefinite delay, then it is not preferable. If the advantages and disadvantages are closely balanced I expect you to say so.

"I desire also to know whether, if you recommend a high level multi-lock canal, it will be possible after it is completed, to turn it into or substitute for it, in time, a sea level canal, without interrupting the traffic upon it. Two of the prime considerations to be kept steadily in mind are:

"1. The utmost practical speed of construction.

"2. Practical certainty that the plan proposed will be feasible; that it can be carried out with the minimum risk.

"The quantity of work and the amount of work should be minimized as far as possible. There may be good reason why the delay incident to the adoption of a plan for an ideal canal should be incurred, but if there is not, then I hope to see the canal constructed on a system which will bring to the nearest possible date in the future the time when it is practicable to take the first ship across the Isthmus; that is, which will in the shortest time possible secure a Panama waterway between the oceans, of such a character as to guarantee permanent and ample communication for the greatest ships of our navy and for the larger steamships on either the Atlantic or the Pacific. The delay in transit of the vessels owing to additional locks would be of small consequence when compared with the shortening the time for the construction of the canal or diminishing the risks in its construction.

"Finally, I urge upon you the necessity of as great expedition in coming to a decision as is compatible with the thoroughness in considering the conditions."
(NY Times, Sept. 17, 1905)

On September 13, the President received the special report of Theodore Shonts, Chairman of the Isthmian Canal Commission, on the complaints made...in connection with the...award of the commissary concessions on the Isthmus. *(NY Times, September 14, 1905)* After receiving the report, the President approved of the concession award to Jacob E. Markel and released the report's text. *(NY Times, September 15, 1905)*

On September 13, a fabricated interview with the President appeared in a French paper. The President immediately sent a scathing telegram denouncing the interview.

OYSTER BAY, Sept. 13 — By the President's direction copies of a scathing telegram addressed to Gaston Charles Richard, a correspondent of the Petit Parisien, were given out to the newspaper men here to-day.

An alleged interview with the President appeared in the Petit Parisien to-day, and it was telegraphed back to several newspapers in this country. In this interview the President is quoted freely expressing his views regarding the peace and as asserting that he advised Japan to forego her demand for an indemnity...

...There is some mystery about the interview printed in the Petit Parisien. It seems that it was signed, not by M. Richard, but by M. Legardére, also of the Petit Parisien, who came to Oyster Bay with M. Richard, but did not go inside the President's house. It is suggested that Richard wrote the dispatch and Legardére signed it.

M. Richard sailed for Europe yesterday. Following is the telegram which Secretary Loeb addressed to him, and which will presumably be telegraphed on to Paris:

" Gaston Richard, Hotel Lafayette, New York, N.Y.:

"The President directs me to say to you that the alleged interview with him published in this morning's papers is not only an absolute fabrication, wholly without basis of truth, but that your conduct in obtaining permission to see him under false pretenses is thoroughly dishonorable.

"When you came to see the President you informed him that you were the grandson of Marshal Augereau; that you had been at the Battle of Mukden with the Russian Army and with the Japanese Army afterward; that you understood thoroughly that you could have no interview of any kind, and that you simply wished to pay respects to him. Under these circumstances the President received you and listened to your account of your experiences with the Japanese and Russians, and spoke to you also of the deeds of Marshal Augereau and of Napoleon's other Generals.

"The President had no conversation with you about the terms of the peace, and your account of your alleged interview with him is a fabrication from beginning to end, without any foundation in fact, and both your untruthfulness and your obtaining permission to see him under false pretenses the President considers highly dishonorable.

"WILLIAM LOEB, Jr., Secretary."

Also on September 13, Baron Rosen visited with the President at Sagamore Hill.

Ambassador Rosen came to Sagamore Hill to-day and was in conference with the President for about an hour.

Baron Rosen declined to discuss his mission, but it is understood that it was in regard to a readjustment of the commercial relations between the United States and Russia, following the repeal of the retaliatory duties imposed on certain classes of American goods imported into Russia...

...The following message sent to the President by M. Witte prior to his departure yesterday was given out at the Executive Office to-day:

New York, Sept. 12, 1905

President Roosevelt:

Before leaving the hospitable soil of the United States, I beg in my own name and on behalf of my fellow workers to offer my heartfelt thanks to you, Mr. President, to the Government of the United States, and the whole American Nation for the cordial welcome given to us on our arrival, and the uniform courtesy shown us during our sojourn here, the memory of which will live in our hearts forever.

WITTE

On September 13, the President postponed a hearing of the charges against William S. Leib, Assistant Treasurer at Philadelphia, until his return to Washington. Leib was charged with violating the order of President Roosevelt prohibiting Federal office holders from taking part in politics and that he had created public scandal by his activity in political matters. *(NY Times*, September 14, 1905)

After the arrest of two brothers in Nicaragua, President Roosevelt directed that no demonstration against Nicaragua be taken until further notice.

OYSTER BAY, Sept. 15 — A misapprehension has arisen as to the action of the Government in the case of William C. Albers and his brother, who are confined in prison in Ocatel, Nicaragua. It is said here by authority of President Roosevelt that no demonstration against Nicaragua is to be made at this time.

It appears from the official correspondence that the Albers brothers are under arrest in Ocatel for an alleged violation of the law of Nicaragua and for contempt of court...the President directed that the usual steps be taken to insure absolute fair and impartial treatment at the trial of the prisoners. *(NY Times*, September 16, 1905)

It was announced on September 18, 1905, that President Roosevelt would visit New Orleans, despite the South's battle against yellow fever and the quarantine regulations some States had imposed on visitors returning from that city. *(NY Times*, September 19, 1905)

Also on September 18, it was announced that China sought to gain control of the entire Canton-Hankow Railroad from foreign powers.

OYSTER BAY, Sept. 18 — The claim of a group of Belgian capitalists, who at one time controlled the American syndicate which owned the Canton-Hankow concession recently surrendered to the Chinese Government, for second right to that concession will be ignored at Peking...

...Moreover, the Chinese Government is entertaining a plan by which before long the northern extension of the Canton-Hankow line, terminating in the capital of China, is to be wrested from foreign control.

The statement that the claim of the Belgians will be ignored is made on the authority of Sir Chentung Liang-Cheng, the Chinese Minister at Washington, who paid a visit to President Roosevelt at Sagamore Hill this afternoon. Sir Liang was accompanied by Wang Tai Hsie, who was sent to this country shortly before the Russo-Japanese peace negotiations began...

...To bring about the connection between Peking and Canton, the southern metropolis of the Chinese Empire, it will be necessary to extend the Canton-Hankow line some 800 miles. This line is now covered by a concession which was granted in 1896 to the same Belgian syndicate that originally held the controlling interest in the Canton-Hankow concession, and, recently after its surrender by the Morgan syndicate, claimed title to it from the Chinese Government. The French and Russian legations in Peking were instrumental in obtaining the concession for the Belgian syndicate, and it is known that the Russo-Chinese Bank, which was organized by M. Witte, and is really believed to be merely an agency for the Russian Government, advanced the money necessary for the construction of the 300 miles of the road southward from Peking...

...King Leopold of Belgium is said to be heavily interested in the alleged Belgian syndicate, and it is likely that in the carrying out of the Chinese Government's plans, as outlined to-day by Sir Liang, the King's worst fears, as voiced by him to Mr. Morgan, regarding the danger of the Western enterprise in China receiving a death blow through the schemes of China and Japan, would come to be realized in the near future. *(NY Times*, September 19, 1905)

Also on September 18, Secretary Taft, in a cablegram from Tokyo, conveyed to the President the assurances of the Japanese Government that the recent riots in Japan were not anti-American demonstrations. The text of the dispatch was made public by direction of the President. *(NY Times*, September 19, 1905)

The Pennsylvania Railroad Company wrote to Secretary Loeb on September 18 to confirm the itinerary of the President's departure from Oyster Bay.

The Pennsylvania Railroad Company
Office of the President

General Office
Broad Street Station   *Philadelphia,*

September 18th, 1905.

My dear Mr. Loeb:

Supplementing my letter to you of the 14th instant, all arrangements have been made to provide two of our best horse and carriage cars for President Roosevelt's shipment from Oyster Bay to Washington on Thursday, September 28th. The cars will be sent to Oyster Bay on the 27th instant, to be moved on the 28th, when loaded, on the following schedule:

Lve. Oyster Bay, Long Island R.R.,		8.10 A.M.
Arr. Long Island City, "		9.05 A.M.
Special float to Jersey City.		
Arr. Jersey City,	about	11.00 A.M.
Lve. Jersey City, Pennsylvania R.R.,		12.44 P.M.
Arr. Washington, "		6.10 P.M.

I enclose herewith the necessary transportation for the shipment. In case you should require transportation for more than four attendants, please let me know.

Yours very truly,

(illegible)
Assistant to the President

Mr. Wm. Loeb, Jr.,
Secretary to the President,
Oyster Bay, N.Y.

(TR Papers, Series 1, Reel 58)

On September 20 and September 21, an extremely important meeting took place at Sagamore Hill in which future legislation to regulate life insurance companies was discussed.

OYSTER BAY, Sept. 20 — An important conference is on at Sagamore Hill to-night, with the recent disclosure before the investigating committee in New York regarding campaign contributions by the insurance companies as the foremost topic of discussion. The conferees are President Roosevelt, Secretary of State Elihu Root, ex-Ambassador Joseph H. Choate, United States Senator Henry Cabot Lodge, and Postmaster General George Bruce Cortelyou.

There is every reason to believe that to-night's conference will be far reaching in its results as affecting future legislation to regulate life insurance companies...

...It is now learned that the President is determined that the whole weight of the Administration must be thrown in the balance to bring about such legislation as will correct abuses of the nature just brought to light. Nor, is it said, will these recommendations be confined in scope to cover only insurance companies or corporations of a fiduciary character. They will, it is believed, be broad enough to provide the initiative for legislative enactment which would place under the ban campaign contributions solicited from any corporation or individual in a position to be affected by National legislation or by the policy of one or other of the political parties...

...That President Roosevelt felt keenly the accusations made on the eve of the last election by ex-Judge Alton B. Parker, then Democratic candidate for President, is generally remembered. Mr. Parker then declared that George B. Cortelyou, as Chairman of the Republican National Committee, had received enormous campaign contributions from corporations from all over the country. The spirited reply made by Mr. Roosevelt through the press contained, however, no denial that such contributions had flowed freely to the Republican campaign coffers of which Mr. Cortelyou was custodian in chief...

...Mr. Cortelyou would be in an excellent position to tell President Roosevelt exactly where the funds, mounting into the millions, which furnished the sinews of war to the Republican Party, came from and what proportion was furnished by corporations engaged in life insurance or in business that involved the trusteeship of funds for others...*(NY Times,* September 21, 1905)

OYSTER BAY, Sept. 21 — The conference held by President Roosevelt, Secretary of State Root, Senator Henry Cabot Lodge, and Joseph H. Choate, beginning last night, was brought to a close this forenoon.

Not until some time after the conferees had left Sagamore Hill did it become evident how desirous every one was of keeping the account of the conference secret and to get away without being questioned.

The newspaper correspondents who wanted to interview the President's distinguished visitors expected them to take the train from Oyster Bay Station, as the President's visitors usually do. At noon they learned that Messrs. Root, Lodge, and Choate had left on a train departing from Syosset at 10:51 A.M....

...It is the first time on record that any of the President's visitors, no matter how important their mission, has taken such great pains to avoid the newspaper men. The matter caused the more surprise as it had been confidently expected that the President would make some public utterance in advance of his message to Congress to define his attitude against the recent disclosures made before the Insurance Investigating Committee regarding campaign contributions. In the absence of any such utterance it is assumed here that Mr. Roosevelt had been discouraged by his advisers from publishing his views in any way at the present time.

At the executive office Secretary Loeb threw cold water on the suggestion that the insurance disclosures had been discussed.

"You might just as well say that the Mother Goose stories were discussed," he said.

"Was it the story about the goose that laid the golden eggs?" asked one correspondent.

Mr. Loeb merely laughed...

(NY Times, September 22, 1905)

At the same meeting the troubling conditions in Venezuela were discussed as well.

Among State Department matters that came up for discussion on the visit of Secretary Root to Sagamore Hill has been the relation of Venezuela with this and other countries.

It is said that Judge W.T. Calhoun, who was sent to Venezuela by President Roosevelt to investigate conditions there, has found that they are more alarming than anybody in Administration circles is willing to admit...

...In the recent difficulties of Venezuela with her several creditors among the nations of Europe, and when those nations resorted to coercive methods to enforce their claims, the Monroe Doctrine was brought into play by the United States Government, with the result that the United States in a way became a guarantor of Venezuela's good behavior.

Recently Castro has been buying guns instead of making the stipulated payments on the national debt. It is now rumored that Germany and France, who are interested in various railway and cable and telegraph concessions in Venezuela, have had enough trouble to warrant them in appealing to the United States, and that as a result some drastic action on the part of the United States may become necessary. It is not unlikely that the Congress may be asked by the President to look into the situation.

The financial condition of Santo Domingo, for which country the United States, under similar conditions, became financial administrator by virtue of a modus vivendi which provides that the United States shall pay the claims out of the custom house receipts, was also discussed. *(NY Times,* September 22, 1905)

Also on September 22, it was reported that a note from Czar Nicholas had been received notifying the President of the Czar's intentions to call a second peace conference at The Hague.

OYSTER BAY, Sept. 21 — Official announcement was made at the executive office here to-day of the receipt of a note from the Czar formally notifying the President of his intention to call a second peace conference at The Hague with a view to supplementing the work accomplished by the first conference held three years ago on the Czar's initiative.

In the statement authorized by the President, it was explained that Baron Rosen, when he visited Sagamore Hill on Sept. 13, had informed Mr. Roosevelt of the Czar's intention. *(NY Times,* September 22, 1905)

Also on September 22, Chief John Wilkie of the Secret Service wrote to Secretary Loeb to confirm that arrangements would be ready for the President's return to Washington.

TREASURY DEPARTMENT
OFFICE OF THE SECRETARY
WASHINGTON

Personal.

September 22 1905.

Hon. William Loeb, Jr.,
    Secretary to the President,

        Oyster Bay, New York.

My dear Mr. Loeb:

    I beg to acknowledge the receipt of your letter of September 21st, advising me the date of the return of the President and party to Washington. The usual precautionary arrangements will be made.

    Respectfully,

John E. Wilkie

Chief.

(TR Papers, Series 1, Reel 58)

As the yellow fever continued to spread throughout New Orleans, the President's plans to visit the city were placed in jeopardy and it was announced that his visit there might be postponed entirely.

OYSTER BAY, Sept. 23 — Arrangements for the trip of President Roosevelt through the South practically have been completed, excepts as relates to his visit to New Orleans and Little Rock, Ark. On account of the prevalence of yellow fever in New Orleans, it is not unlikely that the President may defer his visit to that city until later, in which event he would visit Little Rock at the same time...

...It was announced officially to-night that if the quarantine regulations of other States should prevent the President's entrance into Arkansas or his return to Washington by rail, after having visited New Orleans, he may consider the plan of making New Orleans the final stop on his trip and returning from there to Washington by sea. However, no definite plans have been made for the New Orleans and Little Rock portion of the trip, and they will not be completed perhaps for two weeks. *(NY Times, Sept. 24, 1905)*

The following day it was announced from the Executive Offices that "...The President, Mrs. Roosevelt, and members of their family, Secretary and Mrs. Loeb and the members of the executive work force" would leave Oyster Bay and return to Washington on September 30, 1905. *(NY Times, September 25, 1905)*

FIGURE 27: All Roads Lead To Oyster Bay.
Courtesy of Sagamore Hill

The Summer of 1906

The summer of the year 1906 began as usual, with the President's return to Oyster Bay. Final plans were confirmed in a letter by Chief Wilkie of the Secret Service on June 30.

TREASURY DEPARTMENT
OFFICE OF THE SECRETARY
WASHINGTON

Personal.

June 30, 1906.

Hon. William Loeb, Jr.,
        Secretary to the President,
                White House.

Sir:

    I beg to acknowledge the receipt of your letter of June 29th, relating to the President's trip to Oyster Bay and enclosing photographs of Gessler Rosseau.
    All arrangements have been made by this office with reference to the President's trip, and a sufficient detail at Oyster Bay to properly protect him while there.

Respectfully,

John E. Wilkie

Chief.

(*TR Papers*, Series 1, Reel 65)

The Executive Staff arrived with him on July 1 and the Executive Office was re-opened the day following his arrival.

> OYSTER BAY, July 1 — President Roosevelt is at Sagamore Hill for the summer...His journey from Washington ended with the three-mile drive to Sagamore Hill, where he remained throughout the day...
> ...Secretary Loeb left the party at Long Island City to meet Mrs. Loeb from Albany. They reached the Wright cottage, which they are to occupy for the summer, in the afternoon.
> The executive offices over Moore's grocery and provision store have been fitted up for work, and the necessary executive business will begin there tomorrow morning. *(NY Times, July 2, 1906)*

The following day was a restful one for the President but not for Secretary Loeb. He was busy revising the plans of the local committee for the upcoming Fourth of July celebration. *(NY Times, July 3, 1906)*

> OYSTER BAY, N.Y., July 2 — President Roosevelt has had his first day's rest and complete relaxation from official cares since Congress assembled last December. All work was barred from Sagamore Hill to-day. The routine of official business was conducted at the executive offices in Oyster Bay by Secretary Loeb without the aid of his chief, and without even using the direct telephone between his desk and the library at the President's house... *(NY Times, July 3, 1906)*

On July 4, the Emperor of Japan, Mutsuhito, wrote a letter thanking the President for his offer to aid the famine stricken in Northern Japan. The letter was written in Japanese calligraphy and attached to it was a translation in English.

Translation

(Imperial Seal)

The President of the United States of America.

Great and Good Friend:

When I learned that you had in great sympathy and good will, invited the American Public to come to the aid and succour of the famine stricken people of my northeastern Provinces, I hastened to express to you, through my Representative at Washington, my deep sense of gratitude.

The very generous and substantial contributions subscribed and collected by different American individuals and organizations and especially by the American National

Red Cross and the Christian Herald, were duly received by the local authorities concerned through the kindness of the State Department, and were, with great care, distributed among the distressed in such a manner as to faithfully carry out the noble intentions of those who so liberally responded to your appeal. I need hardly assure you that by this means the most serious effects of the calamity were greatly mitigated.

Now that the immediate danger has been removed, I wish to assure you that I have been very deeply touched and gratified by the high example of international good will and friendship displayed by the people of the United States and that the memory of it will always be warmly cherished by me.

I remain, Mr. President, with the best wishes for your continued well being.

Your sincere Friend
Signed: Mutsuhito.

Imperial Palace, Tokio,
the fourth day of the seventh month
of the thirty-ninth year of Meiji.

(TR Papers, Series 1, Subseries B, Reel 309)

On July 5 it was announced that the President had declined an invitation of William Hoge to attend a reception for William J. Bryan at Madison Square Garden.

OYSTER BAY, N.Y., July 5 — President Roosevelt will not preside at the reception which the Commercial Travelers' Anti-Trust League is to tender to William J. Bryan at Madison Square Garden...
...The complimentary letter of William Hoge, President of the League...was received and answered by Mr. Loeb.
The President had determined some time ago to refuse all proffered engagements this Summer, and Secretary Loeb needed no further consultation in sending a declination. *(NY Times,* July 6, 1906)

On July 6, John Wilkie, chief of the Secret Service, wrote to Secretary Loeb regarding the charge of battery made against Secret Service Agent Sloan.

TREASURY DEPARTMENT
OFFICE OF THE SECRETARY
WASHINGTON

July 6, 1906.

Dear Mr. Loeb:

With reference to the "battery" case against Agent Sloan, which I believe is set for Monday. I am wondering if it would not be just as well for the Assistant United States Attorney at Brooklyn, Mr. Chatfield, to look after Sloan's interests in the justice court. As far as I am personally concerned I would be perfectly willing to have Sloan go into court and plead guilty and pay his fine, but we must take into consideration the moral effect, and it seems to me, should have it distinctly understood by everybody that the government stands by its agents. It is for that reason that I suggest Mr. Chatfield's services be enlisted. Sloan can easily get him on the telephone and I am sure he will be only too glad to go into the matter. While I am in some doubt as to whether or not the prosecuting witness will show up in court, it is just as well to be prepared. This particular photographer is an old offender, has made himself obnoxious on many occasions, and unless we take a firm stand now there is no telling what trouble we might be brewing for ourselves for the future. You know the tribe, and you readily see they would attempt to run over us if given the slightest opening.

Of course I regret that the incident occurred, but from Sloan's report it seems to me that the camera man got what was coming to him and I think the only serious mistake made was in not destroying his camera, or in taking out the plate holder and exposing the plates.

With kindest regards, believe me,

Sincerely yours,

John E. Wilkie
Chief.

Hon. William Loeb, Jr.,
    Secretary to the President,
      Oyster Bay, N.Y.

On July 7, the President met with Secretary Taft to discuss plans to increase the efficiency of the army. The number of army posts was reduced while the posts that remained were made larger. *(NY Times*, July 8, 1906)

On July 8, Secretary Loeb received a telegram from Chief Wilkie regarding Agent Sloan's battery case.

TELEGRAM.

The White House,

Washington.

Washington, D.C.,
July 8 —— 3p

Wm. Loeb, Jr.,
    Secretary to the President,
        Oyster Bay.

Editorial and letter received. Considering the fact that the photographer was insulting and aggressive and that there was acute provocation for Sloan's action as an individual entirely apart from his official position, do you not think in fairness to him he should be represented by counsel to protect his interests, which are to a large degree our interests.

Editorial in POST here applauds his action and I have seen no unfavorable comment in any paper except the WORLD.

If the President feels that Sloan was seriously at fault in the matter and that his reputation at the Bay is likely to cause unpleasant comment, I will, with reluctance, withdraw him.

Please let me know what you decide to do.

John E. Wilkie.

(TR Papers, Series 1, Reel 65)

As mentioned earlier, the President's appointments were announced by Secretary Loeb at the Executive Office. The Summer of 1906 was no exception.

OYSTER BAY, L.I., July 9 — President Roosevelt took up his correspondence soon after 9 o'clock to-day, an hour earlier than usual, and finished by noon. When Secretary Loeb returned from Sagamore Hill he announced that the President had appointed Charles Earle Solicitor to the Department of Commerce and Labor...

...The President also authorized the announcement of the appointment of Richard K. Campbell as Chief of the new Bureau of Naturalization.
(NY Times, July 10, 1906)

In fact, many new appointments were filled early in the Summer of 1906.

> OYSTER BAY, L.I., July 11 — Secretary Loeb went to Sagamore Hill at 9
> o'clock to-day and did not return until 1:30 o'clock. In this time the President
> signed more than 150 commissions. The diplomatic and consular officers
> were commissioned under a new law reorganizing that service. *(NY Times,*
> July 12, 1906)

Secretary Loeb was also quite adroit at deflecting the inquiries of reporters, especially
when the President's reputation for being receptive to Republican statesmen was at stake.

> OYSTER BAY, N.Y., July 13 — Lemuel Eli Quigg, the Republican statesman
> who is opposed to the rule of Chairman Herbert Parsons over the County
> Committee of New York, came to Oyster Bay to-day...
> ...The Platt-Odell offensive and defensive alliance is known to be no favorite
> at Sagamore Hill, but the diplomatic abilities of Mr. Quigg, it was thought at
> first, might persuade the President to grant an interview...
> "Will the President see Mr. Quigg?" Secretary Loeb was asked at the exec-
> utive offices.
> "The President and his family have just sailed on the Sylph bent on a picnic
> to Eaton's Neck," was the reply.
> "Otherwise, of course," suggested the reported.
> "Otherwise, of course," Mr. Loeb caught him up, without giving him a
> chance to finish. And then Mr. Loeb smiled. *(NY Times,* July 14, 1906)

President Roosevelt, known to favor the expansion of forest reserves and for the preservation of America's environmental heritage established at least two reserves during the
summer of 1906. The proclamations creating the Heppner Forest Reserve in Oregon
and the Pinnacles Forest Reserve in California were signed in Oyster Bay on July 18,
1906. Presumably, these proclamations were announced at the Executive Office.
(NY Times, July 19, 1906)

On July 19, 1906, President Roosevelt, from Oyster Bay, ordered Secretary Taft to
direct all Federal officers in charge of public works to detect and punish violations of
the 1892 law which limited the work day to a maximum of eight hours. *(NY Times,* July
20, 1906)

On July 23, 1906, a conference was held at Sagamore Hill by Republican leaders to discuss their party's platform.

> OYSTER BAY, L.I., July 23 — The Republican Congressional campaign next
> Fall will be conducted on a stand-pat platform...
> ...This plan of campaign was outlined to-day when the President gave a lun-
> cheon in honor of Speaker Cannon, Representative James S. Sherman of New
> York, Chairman of the Republican Congressional Committee, and
> Representative Loudenslager of New Jersey, and McKinley of Illinois, respec-
> tively Secretary and Treasurer of the committee. The luncheon and conference

lasted for over an hour, and when it had concluded the President's guests were in good humor.

Secretary Loeb, on behalf of the President, gave out this statement: "The plans of the Congressional campaign were gone over thoroughly, and the President expressed himself as being in entire accord with the ideas of the committee." *(NY Times*, July 24, 1906)

On July 24, the first announcements were also made that the President would review the entire Atlantic Fleet off Oyster Bay on September 3. Four of the newest armored cruisers, scheduled for the Asiatic service would also be reviewed. This would be the largest fleet of battleships, armored carriers, and torpedo craft ever assembled under the American flag up to that time.

On July 25, Chief of the Office of Administration for the Panama Canal, W. Leon Pepperman, wrote to Secretary Loeb regarding the employment of Chinese laborers in the Canal Zone.

CHAIRMAN OF COMMISSION: THEODORE P. SHONTS	ISTHMIAN CANAL AFFAIRS	GENERAL AUDITOR: ERNEST S. BENSON

OFFICE OF ADMINISTRATION

GENERAL PURCHASING OFFICER:
DAVID W. ROSS

PANAMA CANAL BUILDING

CHIEF OF OFFICE:
W. LEON PEPPERMAN

DISBURSING OFFICER:
JAMES G. JESTER

WASHINGTON, D. C.

July 25, 1906

My Dear Mr. Loeb:

I am in receipt of a telegram from the Secretary of War, reading as follows:

"Send to the President copies of Chinese contracts and all papers. Also of all applications to furnish Chinese laborers."

In accordance therewith I send you herewith copy of a form of contract drawn by Mr. Paul Charlton, Law Officer in the War Department, accompanied by his memorandum thereon, and the opinion of the Attorney-General.

The views of the Isthmian Canal Commission as to the employment of Chinese are set forth in the attached copy of a letter from Chairman Shonts to the Secretary of War, dated May 16th, reviewing the labor situation on the Isthmus.

A later expression of the views of the Commission is set forth in a cablegram from Chairman Shonts to the Secretary of War, of this date, copy of which is hereto attached.

I also inclose herewith copy of a communication from Chief Engineer Stevens to Mr. Shonts, dated May 4, 1906, relative to the employment of Chinese.

Very truly yours,

WLeonPepperman

Mr. William Loeb Jr.,
    Secretary to the President,
        Oyster Bay, N.Y.

Inclosure. As stated.

P.S. I also inclose herewith a list of some of the persons

(TR Papers, Series 1, Reel 66)

On July 30, a letter written by Secretary Loeb was reprinted in the *The New York Times*.

> PEORIA, ILL., July 30 — Another announcement from President Roosevelt
> that he will not be a candidate for re-election is made in a letter received to-
> day by Mrs. L.A. Kinney from Secretary Loeb, writing for the President.
>   The letter is dated July 26 and declares:
>
> "I would say that the President has nothing to add to the statement issued on
> the night of the election in 1904. His decision as announced at that time is
> irrevocable." *(NY Times,* July 31, 1906)

On July 31, Senator Charles Dick of Ohio and Elmer Dover, Secretary of the
Republican National Committee visited Sagamore Hill to discuss the political situation
in Ohio. The President expressed a desire for "harmony" in the coming Congressional
campaign and this support would "have decided weight in the Republican situation in
Ohio." *(NY Times,* August 1, 1906)

Also on July 31, the Pennsylvania Railroad Company sent to Secretary Loeb an explanation of their charges for the President's trip from Washington to Oyster Bay.

The Pennsylvania Railroad Company
Office of the President

General Office
Broad Street Station   *Philadelphia,*

                                                    July 31, 1906.

My dear Mr. Loeb:

          Your favor of the 26th instant was duly received, but I have
delayed replying until I could have an opportunity to confer fully with
our people on the subject.

          I find that the bill for the President's special train be-
tween Washington and Oyster Bay, July 1st, which is returned herewith,
was made up on the regular basis that is charged for the handling of
all special passenger trains over our lines. For your information,
I may say that the rate for this special train service is $3.00 per
mile for distances less than 100 miles, and $2.00 per mile for distances
greater than 100 miles. While the Pullman bill is not analyzed in
detail, I find that the charge is made up as follows:

          Private car "Columbia", one day's service $ 75.00
          12-section drawing-room sleeping car "Cynwyd",   75.00
          Commissary supplies, based on actual cost plus
               20% to cover service,   20.29
                              Total, $150.29

The explanation of the Pullman charge is as follows:

Where private cars are chartered for a one-day run, the rate is $75.00; where chartered for two days or more the rate is $50.00 per day; where chartered for 30 days or more, the rate is $45.00 per day. For special sleeping cars the charter rate is $45.00 per day, with a minimum of three days, unless the full capacity of the car at regular berth rates is less, when the latter rate is charged, as was done in this case for car "Cynwyd". For more than thirty days the rate is $40.00 per day.

I believe that you will find that the rate of $2.00 per mile
handling
is the customary rate charged by railroads generally for ʌ a special train of this character. Trusting that I have given you full information on the points desired, and with my best wishes to you for a pleasant summer, I remain,

Yours very truly,

(illegible)
Assistant to the President.

Mr. Wm. Loeb, Jr.,
Secretary to the President,
Oyster Bay, L.I.

(TR Papers, Series 1, Reel 66)

On August 8, President Roosevelt rescinded the order which gave Sundays off to the employees of the U.S. Immigration Service at Ellis Island. When closed on Sundays, hundreds of new immigrants arriving Saturday night or Sunday had to remain on board their ships until Monday morning. *(NY Times*, August 9, 1906)

On August 9, the President met with representatives of the Standard Oil Company to discuss the matter of its controversy with the Department of the Interior regarding oil line leases in the Indian Territory. *(NY Times*, August 10, 1906)

On August 11, 1906, it was reported that a lawsuit was filed against Secretary Loeb.

Miss Nadage Doree is the author of a book called "Jesus's Christianity. By a Jewess." Last Winter she stood in front of St. John's Church, in Washington, and as the congregation filed out handed the members circulars urging them to read the volume. When she tried to give President Roosevelt one of the leaflets she was arrested. Now she is suing Secretary Loeb for $50,000 because, she says, he caused her arrest. Mr. Loeb said at Oyster Bay yesterday that the Washington police had arrested the woman, and that he had had nothing to do with it.

Samuel Bernstein, a clerk in the law office of K. Henry Rosenberg, served Mr. Loeb with the summons at Oyster Bay yesterday. The President's Secretary is directed to make any answer to the suit within twenty days in New

York City. Either Attorney General Moody or one of his subordinates in the Department of Justice will appear for the defendant.

The circular which Miss Doree gave out appealed to every one, especially the President of the United States, to stop the massacres in Russia. It asked the President what he would do if his son or daughter were burned alive.

The complaint in the suit says that Miss Doree was imprisoned and then released without a hearing before a Magistrate. It is said that Miss Doree made an unsuccessful effort to see President Roosevelt at Oyster Bay last Summer. *(NY Times*, August 11, 1906)

On August 13, 1906, President Roosevelt met with Representative James S. Sherman of New York in order to review the "campaign textbook," a book which outlined the Republican party's past performance and the reasons why it should remain in power. *(NY Times*, August 14, 1906)

On August 16, Chief Wilkie of the Secret Service wrote a three page letter to Secretary Loeb. It addressed Mr. Loeb's complaints about the new Secret Service men stationed in Oyster Bay.

TREASURY DEPARTMENT
OFFICE OF THE SECRETARY
WASHINGTON

August 17, 1906.

Dear Mr. Loeb:

I have heard with some concern that there is dissatisfaction over the fact that several of the men at
Oyster Bay this year are new men on the detail.

While it is true that Sommer, Tate and Eberstein
are new men at the Bay, they are experienced men in the
service. In making the detail this year I was particularly careful to select not only experienced and dependable
men but also men who never indulge in liquor to any extent.
Last year I disciplined three of the men who were detailed there for having used intoxicants when off duty and
there was some complaint among the residents of Oyster
Bay, with whom these men came in contact, over their
conduct. I was particularly anxious this year that there
should not be the slightest cause for complaint on this
ground, and the detail was so arranged that there would
always be on duty at the house at least one man of the
pair who had been there before and knew the usages
and requirements. It comes, therefore, as a distinct

disappointment and causes me no little chagrin to know that there is even the slightest dissatisfaction with the representatives of this service.

So far as I have been advised, with the single exception of the Sloan Le Gendre incident on the day of the President's arrival, there has been nothing to mar the serenity of the work. Even had I been inclined to send to the Bay this year the same men identically who were there last year, it would have been absolutely impossible. Three of them are engaged on special investigations which have been continuously conducted for more than six months and which promise to last at least as much longer, and are in such condition that to abandon them would be out of the question.

I was much surprised to hear that some of the men had been smoking while on duty at night. While I understand perfectly the strong desire that would exist for a pipe or cigar during the long watches of the night, I consider that smoking while on duty at the President's residence is entirely improper and Mr. Moran, who goes up to the Bay tomorrow, will carry instructions from me to Sloan and Connell prohibiting smoking at the Hill. I have wired Operative Sloan for a full report on the situation and trust that when it is received I may find it possible to make some adjustment that will meet the requirements of the situation. In the meantime, I would be glad to hear from you personally and frankly what you think about the men who are up there this year and whether you have seen anything to indicate that there has been any laxity or inattention or that they have failed in any way to properly provide for an efficient guard.

With sincere regards I am, as always,

Respectfully yours,

John E. Wilkie

Chief.

Hon. William Loeb, Jr.,
    Secretary to the President,
    Oyster Bay, N.Y.

(*TR Papers*, Series 1, Reel 67)

On August 21, Charles Bonaparte wrote to Secretary Loeb regarding the upcoming naval review which was to take place off Oyster Bay.

hotel
Aspinwall

O. D. SEAVEY

WINTER:

MAGNOLIA SPRINGS HOTEL,　　LENOX, MASS., *Aug. 21* 1906

MAGNOLIA SPRINGS,
FLORIDA.

My dear Mr. Loeb,

I sent your first letter and telegram in hebus "Mayflower" and "Sylph" to Admiral Converse, who was then Acting Secretary, and your second letter to Mr. Newberry, who had succeeded him: doubtless you have heard ere this from all of them.

Am I right in supposing that the "Sylph" is to act as a tender to the "Mayflower," and follow the latter as she passes through the fleet? This was my understanding of your letter, but did not say so tolidem verbis. I suppose it is intended that Mrs. Newberry shall receive the other ladies on board the "Sylph," and be, in some sort, a chaperone for the party, as she will be the lady most prominently identified with the Navy on board: let me know if I am right as to this.

Is there any objection to having three or four extra officers assigned to the "Sylph" to give the ladies information and answer their questions? I think this will be advisable, if there is no reason contra, for it will undoubtedly add to their (i.e. the ladies') pleasure. You understand, of course, that the "Dolphin" will be on hand, and will be ready for any service which may be required of her on the day of the review.

Believe me,
as ever,
Yours most truly,
Charles J. Bonaparte

Wm. Loeb Jr., Esq.,
Secretary to the President,
Oyster Bay, L.I.
New York.

On August 22, insurgents in Cuba achieved their first victory against the Cuban Government in the Province of Pinar del Rio. The city of San Luis was taken and this would become an important base for future operations. The official word from Oyster Bay was that the President had not given the events in Cuba any serious consideration.

> OYSTER BAY, L.I., Aug. 22 — At the Executive offices to-day it was stated that President Roosevelt has received no information whatever on the Cuban revolution, that the President has taken no action on the matter and has given the subject no thought. *(NY Times,* August 23, 1906)

However, by August 24, President Palma of Cuba would request guns and ammunition from the M. Hartley Company and its American supplier, The Union Metallic Cartridge Company. Union Metallic, unable to meet Cuba's request for 5,000,000 rifle ball cartridges, requested that the U.S. Government, with President Roosevelt's permission, "loan" them the necessary cartridges. The request was made in a letter to Secretary Loeb, dated August 24, as well as the following memorandum written in Oyster Bay.

> WHITE HOUSE,
> WASHINGTON.
>
> Oyster Bay, N.Y.,
> August 24, 1906.
>
> By telephone from W.J. Bruff, President, Union Metallic Cartridge Co., 315 Broadway, New York:
>   We are sending to the Cuban Government by to-morrow's steamer 10,000 guns, but no ammunition. We have made the following proposition to the Ordnance Department of the Army: we want to borrow one to five millions of cartridges from the Government and give a bond to replace them with expressly made ammunition of the same quality, under inspection and supervision of a Government officer. The Ordnance Department is stated to have said that they would bring the matter before the President. Mr. Bruff asks to be informed as soon as possible of the President's decision. He will come out this afternoon if it is desired. His phone No. is 2137-Worth.

(TR Papers, Series 1, Reel 67)

In a controversial announcement which took most of the English speaking world by surprise, the President indorsed the Carnegie spelling reform movement and adopted simplified spelling methods. The changes adopted by the President were ridiculed in many places, especially in Great Britain.

OYSTER BAY, L.I., Aug. 24 — President Roosevelt has indorsed the Carnegie spelling reform movement. He issued orders to-day to Public Printer Stillings that hereafter all messages from the President and all other documents from the White House shall be printed in accordance with the recommendation of the Spelling Reform Committee headed by Brander Matthews, Professor of English in Columbia University.

This committee has published a list of 300 words in which the spelling is reformed. This list contains such words as "thru" and "tho" as the spelling for "through" and "though." The President's official sanction of this reform movement is regarded as the most effective and speediest method of inaugurating the new system of spelling throughout the country.

Not only will the printed documents emanating from the President utilize the reform spelling, but his correspondence also will be spelled in the new style. Secretary Loeb has sent for the list of words which have been reformed, and upon its arrival will order all correspondence of the President and of the executive force of the White House spelled in accordance therewith. As the Spelling Reform Committee shall adopt new reforms they will be added to the President's list and also to that of the Public Printer. *(NY Times*, August 25, 1906)

On August 25, President Roosevelt issued a proclamation from Oyster Bay appealing for aid from all Americans for the people of earthquake stricken Chile. Chile had suffered an earthquake in Valparaiso earlier that week. *(NY Times*, August 26, 1906)

On August 27, Secretary Loeb cabled Acting Secretary of War Ainsworth regarding the request of the Union Metallic Cartridge Company to borrow ammunition. Mr. Ainsworth's response was cabled as a memo to Secretary Loeb by Assistant Secretary N.P. Webster in Washington.

TELEGRAM.

The White House,

Washington.

MEMO. FOR SECRETARY LOEB:

General Ainsworth says they have nothing from the Cuban Government and nothing from Hartley and Graham stating that the request was made by the Cuban Government but yesterday that State Department said the Cuban Chargé had been there with a dispatch saying that the Cuban Government desired the President to have Hartley and Graham deliver 5,000,000 rounds of ammunition, so we can safely say that it was done at the request of the Cuban Government. The Ordnance Department sent the following telegram to Hartley yesterday:

"By direction of the President Ordnance Department will deliver at your expense 5,000,000 ball cartridges, model 1898 on following conditions:

'Sworn statement that your Company is acting on request of Cuban Government accompanied by sworn copy of such order or request from that Government. This is to be presented by this Department to State Department so that latter may inform Cuban Government. This Department will then order 2,000,000 ball cartridges, model 1898, to be placed on board cars at Frankford and 3,000,000 at Rock Island."

Gen. Ainsworth also says that issue of 5,000,000 1898 ammunition will deplete our store of that model for issue to Navy and Militia to such extent that orders for 5,000,000 ammunition at Frankfort will have to be revoked. Manufacture stopped, machines taken down, new ones set up, material not required for 1898 ammunition thrown away.

Webster.

August 27 ——— 11:33a

(TR Papers, Series 1, Reel 67)

Later that day, Mr. Ainsworth cabled again regarding the same matter.

TELEGRAM.

𝕎𝕙𝕚𝕥𝕖 𝕙𝕠𝕦𝕤𝕖,
𝕎𝕒𝕤𝕙𝕚𝕟𝕘𝕥𝕠𝕟.

2 DI SY GI 762 Paid Govt ——5:40 p

DI — Washington, D.C. August 27.

Hon. Wm. Loeb, Jr.,
    Secretary to the President,
        Oyster Bay.

Reference your telegram of to-day Acting Chief of Ordnance says he can spare two million cartridges on terms proposed by Union Metallic Cartridge Company, million and a half to be furnished from Frankford Arsenal, and half million from Rock Island. He has been directed to make this delivery immediately and to waive statement as to request of Cuban Government required by your telegram of August twenty-five. He says that delay in complying with President's instructions is entirely due to failure of Cartridge Company to act on instructions sent them under your telegram of August twenty-five...
...Acting Chief of Ordnance also reports that immediately on receipt of your two telegrams of August twenty-five he telegraphed orders to Frankford

and Rock Island Arsenals to make ammunition ready for immediate shipment
and have cars ready to receive it as soon as cartridge company should be
heard from. Cartridge Company has conducted all its correspondence
with Chief of Ordnance. Request of cartridge company was first brought
to my attention August twenty-fourth and was acted upon after conference
with Chief of Staff, I regarded it at the time as a commercial transaction that did not require action by the President, especially as Texas difficulty was then pressing. I regret that request was not telegraphed
President, as I now see it should have been done and as it would have been
if its character had not been lost sight of through preoccupation and
anxiety growing out of Texas affair. I agree with Acting Chief of
 Ordnance however, that all the delay in carrying out President's instructions
of August twenty-five has been due to failure of Cartridge Company either
to respond to telegram sent them or to act upon instructions given
them. They now have opportunity to obtain immediately two million
rounds on their own terms of exchange and three million more on Ordnance
Department terms. Ordnance Department assures me there will be
no delay except through failure of Cartridge Company to put up certified
check give shipping instructions and accept Ordnance Department terms
if more than two million rounds are wanted. Please lay this before the President.

Ainsworth,
Acting Secretary of War.

(TR Papers, Series 1, Reel 67)

On August 27, a Mr. Untermyer, a representative of the International Policy Holders'
Committee, Trustees of the Mutual Life Insurance Company, visited with Secretary
Loeb. After 40,000 letters mailed to Mutual Life policy holders were returned because
of incorrect addresses, Mr. Untermyer "asked Secretary Loeb if it would not be possible to have the Postmaster General issue an order to Postmasters to have every effort
made in the local offices to find the persons to whom the International Committee's
mail was addressed. Such orders are not uncommon in the Post Office Department in
cases where it appears that substantial difficulty is experienced in reaching a large number of persons through the mails, and accordingly the order was issued as desired." *(NY
Times*, August 28, 1906)

On August 27, the Professor Brander Matthews, Chairman of the Simplified Spelling
Board responded to the President's order to use the board's recommendations.

> "The President's order came as an entire surprise to me. I am sure that I did
> not even send him any of the documents published by the board, and did not
> have any idea that he was interested in the subject, even, until a request for our
> list of recommended spellings was received from Secretary Loeb." *(NY Times*,
> August 28, 1906)

On August 28, the President's order regarding simplified spelling was extended to all
departments of the Federal Government. *(NY Times*, August 29, 1906) The first use of
the simplified spelling in a government document occurred at the Executive Office in
Oyster Bay.

OYSTER BAY, Aug. 28 — President Roosevelt's correspondence is now spelled in accordance with the recommendation of the Carnegie Spelling Reform Board.

An official list of the 300 reformed words reached the Executive office yesterday and the letters which were mailed yesterday afternoon were written in accordance with it. This list will be the official dictionary of the executive staff from now on, and when the committee adds new words to the list its recommendations are to be adopted immediately.

Secretary Taft received the first letter from President Roosevelt written in the reformed spelling. The letter pertained to the business of the Government, which fact rendered its publication impossible. *(NY Times*, August 29, 1906)

In response to statements wrongly attributed to the President regarding the Cuban revolution, Secretary Loeb issued a response which restated that the President had not made public any of his positions regarding the situation in Cuba.

OYSTER BAY, L.I., Aug. 28 — In view of public statements that President Roosevelt had made known his intended policy toward Cuba in the present revolution in that island Secretary Loeb said to-day that any such statements were entirely without foundation, as the President had indicated to no one any determination in the matter. *(NY Times*, August 29, 1906)

In an unusual move by the President, on August 29, it was announced from the Executive Office that the President would politely interfere in the gubernatorial campaign of New York State. By giving his support to Congressman Herbert Parsons, Chairman of the Republican County Committee, the President in effect endorsed Charles E. Hughes for Governor. Mr. Hughes was also endorsed by the Odell-Platt-Quigg party machine, the nemesis of Mr. Parsons, but this endorsement was merely to get the sitting Governor Higgins to resign. The Odell-Platt-Quigg machine had no intention of actually naming Hughes as Governor.

...The announcement from Oyster Bay came in the form of a statement from Secretary Loeb, as follows:

"Secretary Loeb said to-day that Congressman Herbert Parsons, Chairman of the New York County Republican Committee, would lunch with President Roosevelt on Friday, and that the President's interview with Mr. Parsons has no further political significance than that of expressing the President's cordial sympathy with the purposes and methods for which Congressman Parsons stands in public life and which the President believes must obtain in the Republican Party if the Republican Party is to fulfill its full measure of usefulness to the Nation.

The President does not regard it as his business under ordinary conditions to interfere in State or local contests. He thinks that such interference is not only not desired, but would be resented by the people. But he has made no secret of his cordial sympathy with men like

Congressman Parsons, Chairman of the Republican County Committee; with men like James W. Wadsworth, Jr., Speaker of the New York State Assembly, who stand not only as individuals but as types of many other men like them who have gone into politics with the intention of rendering disinterested, honest, common sense service to the public as a whole, and with whom the President as a citizen cordially sympathizes."

...The President's action was taken after a careful study of the New York situation made by Postmaster General Cortelyou, Henry W. Taft, brother of the Secretary of War, and Secretary Loeb. *(NY Times,* August 30, 1906)

Hughes would later receive the Republican nomination for Governor.

On September 1, 1906, two days before President Roosevelt reviewed the entire Atlantic Fleet off Oyster Bay, most of the ships to be reviewed were already stationed near Oyster Bay. This was the largest naval review in the history of the United States up to that time with over forty five vessels reviewed. The review was also witnessed by at least 100,000 spectators who viewed the event from small craft. Others lined the beaches at Lloyd Neck, Centre Island, and Bayville to catch a glimpse of the display from the shore.

    The fleet of battleships, armored cruisers, protected cruisers, torpedo boats, submarines, and naval auxiliaries which President Roosevelt will review in Oyster Bay to-morrow morning were assembling all day yesterday in Smithtown and Huntington Bays in Long Island Sound...the naval yacht Mayflower, from the deck of which President Roosevelt will review the fleet, sailed from the Navy Yard for Oyster Bay yesterday morning...*(NY Times,* September 2, 1906)

However, as preparations for the naval review were being completed, the situation in Cuba grew worse with each passing day.

TELEGRAM.

The White House,

Washington.

1 WH JM GI 100 Paid Govt ——— 9:22a

                Washington, D.C. September 1, 1906.

Hon. Wm. Loeb, Jr.,
    Secretary to the President,
        Oyster Bay.

                        Havana Aug. 31.

The Secretary of State:
    Persistent talk of friction between President and Vice President. I am advised by Secretary of State President strongly opposed to any compromise although reliable private advices indicate President not avers to effecting amicable settlement with insurrectionists. Vice President

and President Senate said to favor adjusting matter with rebels in order to prevent possible united States interference. No general change military situation Pinar del Rio province. Government reports victory yesterday over forces <u>Asbert</u> near Camp Florida, Havana province. Unofficial advices that outbreak has spread to Santiago province.

Sleeper, Chargé.

(TR Papers, Series 1, Reel 67)

Another cable from American Chargé d' Affaires Sleeper was received on September 2.

TELEGRAM.

𝔚𝔥𝔦𝔱𝔢 𝔥𝔬𝔲𝔰𝔢,
𝔚𝔞𝔰𝔥𝔦𝔫𝔤𝔱𝔬𝔫.

1 WH JM NE 90 Paid Govt   10 35 AM

Washington, D.C. Sept. 2, 1906.

Hon. Wm. Loeb, Jr.,
Secretary to the President,

Havana, September 1, to Secretary of State, Washington:

Santiago consulate telegraphs no disturbances yet, Santiago Province, but may be unless insurrection soon quelled. Trouble reported in Camaguay Province to-day. Government states it is nothing more than incursion of rebel band from Santa Clara Province.

Confidential and private. Have reliable private information secret meeting to-night between representatives government and liberal party to endeavor to arrange basis for settlement difficulties.

Sleeper, Chargé.

(TR Papers, Series 1, Reel 67)

The details of the naval review's choreography were also outlined in the press on September 2.

> As the Mayflower, with the President on board, is sighted, the entire fleet will fire the Presidential salute of twenty-one guns, and immediately (*after*) this ceremony ends the Mayflower will proceed to the head of the second or central column, and the review will be under way. The Mayflower will steam along the south side of the central column...

...As the President's yacht passes along the line of ships, each ship, beginning with the Maine, will fire the Presidential salute, timing the salute so that it will be begun when the stern of the Mayflower has passed well clear of the saluting point. The salute will be given only when the Mayflower passes the first time. As soon as the Mayflower has anchored after the review the flag officers of the fleet will pay their respects to the President, after which the commanding officers of the vessels will board the Mayflower for the same purpose.

During the review all of the ships will be "full dressed," and at night they will be illuminated...*(NY Times*, September 2, 1906)

The event took place according to plan, except for an early morning drizzle. Secretary Loeb accompanied the President aboard the Presidential yacht, Mayflower, during the review.

OYSTER BAY, Sept. 3 — With twice a hundred guns booming out a salute to the Nation's Chief, President Roosevelt reviewed the Atlantic Fleet of these United States in Long Island Sound, near his home to-day.

It was a picturesque and an impressive spectacle. Twelve great battleships, eight powerful cruisers, four monitors, twelve destroyers and torpedo boats, five auxiliary cruisers, three submarines, and a troopship — forty-five craft in all, a ship of war for every State in the Union — lay in three long columns within sight of the Sound's green shore, while the President's yacht, Mayflower, with Mr. Roosevelt aboard, steamed between them. Never had so formidable a fleet been assembled in these waters. Rarely has a more powerful naval aggregation been gathered anywhere in the world in time of peace...

...President Roosevelt, accompanied by Secretary Loeb, left the pier at Sagamore Hill at 10:30 o'clock. Just as he reached the landing stage a heavy downpour of rain set in, and as he stepped out of his carriage the Secretary raised an umbrella. The President wore a high silk hat and long rain coat. From another carriage, close behind, stepped Mrs. Roosevelt, with the Secretary of the Navy, Mr. Bonaparte...

...A launch load of officials and invited guests had already boarded the Mayflower when, at 10:55 o'clock, the Presidential party arrived. The trip from Sagamore Hill had been a rapid one. In the launch the President sat amidships, all unmindful of the rain which was beating into his face and careless of the umbrella with which Secretary Loeb endeavored to shield him. As he hove in sight there came a burst of cheering from a little group of yachts and excursion craft which hung about the spot where, just off Lloyd Neck, rode the Mayflower, Sylph, and Dolphin...

...It was still raining when the Mayflower was reached, but the President, without waiting for his umbrella bearer, mounted the gangway and stepped over the side... *(NY Times*, September 4, 1906)

In summary, "It was a great day for Oyster Bay, a great day for the navy, and, last, but not least, it was a great day for President Roosevelt." *(NY Times*, September 4, 1906)

FIGURE 28: *Some of the battleships and armored cruisers of the North Atlantic Fleet in the Long Island Sound for the Naval Review. Courtesy Theodore Roosevelt Collection, Harvard College Library*

*FIGURE 29: Admiral Evans, the President, and Secretary Loeb aboard the Mayflower
during the Naval Review.
Courtesy Theodore Roosevelt Collection, Harvard College Library*

*FIGURE 30: Admirals Brownson, Davis, Evans, the President, and Secretary Loeb
aboard the Mayflower during the Naval Review.
Courtesy Theodore Roosevelt Collection, Harvard College Library*

In one of the first cases involving the extradition of a prisoner from a foreign country where no treaty existed between that country and the United States, President Roosevelt appointed official representatives to travel to Tangier to bring the fugitive, Paul O. Stensland, to justice. Mr. Stensland was the President of the Milwaukee Avenue State Bank, in Chicago, and was charged with stealing $1,500,000 from that institution. The authorization for the arrest of Mr. Stensland on charges of embezzlement was sent both by cable, presumably from the Executive Office, and by mail.. *(NY Times*, September 7, 1906)

Also on September 6, President Roosevelt directed several executive departments to resume a study of the Newfoundland fishing dispute. A new treaty defining the rights of American fisherman was the desired outcome of the resumption of the year-long study. *(NY Times*, September 7, 1906)

On September 7, Postmaster General Cortelyou and his family were the luncheon guests of Secretary Loeb at his Oyster Bay residence. *(NY Times*, September 7, 1906)

On September 8, President Roosevelt spoke at Christ Episcopal Church in Oyster Bay in honor of its two hundredth anniversary celebration. The keynote of the President's speech "was that the wealth of the Nation must not be disregarded, but looked upon as the basis for spiritual development, clean living, and civic virtues." *(NY Times*, September 9, 1906)

Also on September 8, Chargé d'Affairs Sleeper cabled to the Secretary of State informing him of the situation of the rebellion in Cuba. This cable was forwarded to Secretary Loeb.

TELEGRAM.

White house,
Washington.

1 WH JM GI 120 Paid Govt ——5p

The White House, Washington, D.C. Sept. 8.

Hon. Wm. Loeb, Jr.,
      Secretary,
            Oyster Bay.

The Secretary of State:

September 8th. General Manager Western Railway in conversation this morning stated the following:

"Besides culverts destroyed between San Luis and Pinar del Rio, reported my telegram of yesterday, telegraph wires between Herradure and San Juan y Martinez cut; freight train stopt at Lasovas by main body of rebels, line cut and other culverts destroyed. Troop train coming after freight train, with 250 men, two armored cars and two machine guns, on arriving near Lasovas was attacked by rebels and returned to the Palacios. It is clear that Government cannot give us any escort for our trains sufficiently strong to enable us to continue the service and it will be necessary to suspend traffic beyond San Cristobal. I propose seeing the President today to so inform him."

Sleeper,

Chargé.

(TR Papers, Series 1, Reel 68)

In just under an hour, at 5:45 P.M., another cable arrived at Oyster Bay requesting immediate American naval aid because the Cuban Government was unable to put down the resistance.

TELEGRAM.

𝔚hite house,
𝔚ashington.

White House, Washington, D.C.   September 8.

Hon. Wm. Loeb, Jr.,
    Secretary to the President,
        Oyster Bay.

ABSOLUTELY CONFIDENTIAL. Secretary of State Cuba has requested me in name of President Palma to ask President Roosevelt send immediately two vessels, one to Havana, other to Cienfuegos. They must come at once. Government forces are unable quell rebellion. The Government is unable to protect life and property. President Palma will convene Congress next Friday and Congress will ask for our forcible intervention. It must be kept secret and confidential that Palma asked for vessels. No one here except President, Secretary of State and myself know about it. Very anxiously awaiting answer. Send answer to Steinhart.

N.P.W.

Received 5:45p

(TR Papers, Series 1, Reel 68)

By 8 P.M. the United States was preparing to send warships to Cuba.

TELEGRAM.

𝕳𝖍𝖎𝖙𝖊 𝖍𝖔𝖚𝖘𝖊,
𝕳𝖆𝖘𝖍𝖎𝖓𝖌𝖙𝖔𝖓.

RECEIVED IN CIPHER.

The White House, Washington, D.C. Sept. 8.

Hon. Wm. Loeb, Jr.,
   Secretary to the President,
     Oyster Bay.

Admiral Converse, Acting Secretary of the Navy, sends following:

The DESMOINES and TACOMA or another vessel of that class are at
Norfolk and will start as soon as they can be operated, probably 24 to
36 hours. If other force is needed the MINNEAPOLIS , CLEVELAND or DENVER
can be added immediately or the coast defense monitors all are ready.
Have you any special instructions ?"

N.P.W.

(TR Papers, Series 1, Reel 68)

Five minutes later Mr. Sleeper cabled again.

TELEGRAM.

𝕳𝖍𝖎𝖙𝖊 𝖍𝖔𝖚𝖘𝖊,
𝕳𝖆𝖘𝖍𝖎𝖓𝖌𝖙𝖔𝖓.

4 WH RA GI 72 Paid Govt ——8:05p

The White House, Washington, D.C. Sept. 8.

Hon. Wm. Loeb, Jr.,
   Secretary to the President,
     Oyster Bay.

"Havana

Secretary State:

Unofficially informed emissary from Veterans to Pino Guerra
relative to temporary suspension hostilities thus far unsuccessful.
At noon today armored train again proceeded westward from Palacios

protecting passenger train, probably not get beyond Consolacion del
Sur, where numerous rebels destroying wires and track. No information
obtainable from Pinar del Rio. Guerra reported having made detour
and being near Consolacion del Sur.

Sleeper,
Chargé.

N.P. Webster.

(TR Papers, Series 1, Reel 68)

On September 9, Secretary Loeb received a copy of a telegram to the Secretary of State
informing him that the insurrection in Cuba had spread.

TELEGRAM.

𝔚𝔥𝔦𝔱𝔢 𝔥𝔬𝔲𝔰𝔢,
𝔚𝔞𝔰𝔥𝔦𝔫𝔤𝔱𝔬𝔫.

1 WH JM NE 110 Govt —— *11:20 am*

Washington, D.C. Sept. 9, 1906.

Hon. Wm. Loeb, Jr.,
      Secretary to the President, O. Bay.

Havana. Secretary of State, Washington: Following cable just
received from Consul Santiago de Cuba: Telegram received to-day
from our consular agent at Manzanillo says revolutionary movement
started here last night. Report will follow. I have received information of a reliable character that there are two thousand men
in this city and vicinity fully equipped to revolt. I cannot find
out who is at the head of the movement. The situation here appears
more critical than at any time since the beginning." Am informed
that President now intends convene Congress on 14th instant.

Sleeper, Charge.

(TR Papers, Series 1, Reel 68)

By evening, Secretary Loeb had received two more telegrams, both from the White
House with messages from Admiral Converse.

TELEGRAM.

The White House,

Washington.

The White House, Washington, D.C. Sept. 9, 1906.

Hon. Wm. Loeb, Jr.,

　　Admiral Converse says the DENVER past the capes of Virginia about noon bound for Havana; will be intercepted by wireless and directed to go to Key West and await orders. Other vessel will be held ready to sail tomorrow afternoon.

N.P. Webster.

(TR Papers, Series 1, Reel 68)

TELEGRAM.

The White House,

Washington.

Memo for Secretary Loeb:

　　Admiral Converse says Commandant at Navy Yard Norfolk reports that he will coal Des Moines and Tacoma with despatch and report to the Department by telegraph to-day what hour they will be ready to sail. The first ready for sea will be directed to go to Cienfuegos; the second to Havana.

W H　Sept. 9, 1906.

(TR Papers, Series 1, Reel 68)

As the insurrection in Cuba grew larger, the U.S. Government began to take the first open steps toward intervening in that island's crisis as allowed under the terms of the Platt amendment. The following days saw an escalation in American military activity near the island. This activity was carried out under detailed instructions from the President in Oyster Bay.

WASHINGTON, Sept. 11 — The cruiser Des Moines, which sailed from Norfolk yesterday, is going to Cuba. This is not stated officially, but is known to be the case. It is said that she is going there to protect American interests, but it is known that her mission involves more than that. She is to take President Palma off the island in case the situation there becomes desperate. This purpose is not admitted by the officials at the Navy Department. The statement comes from other reliable sources.

Such an incident, of course, would be the first step toward intervention. President Palma can obtain American aid if he asks for it, but he will not ask until he has exhausted every other resource.

The mission of the Des Moines indicates that the seriousness of the situation in Cuba has not been fully revealed. Officially, the American Government has been confident of Palma's ability to crush the insurrection, but the belief is growing that the revolutionists are making much greater headway than has been admitted or supposed...

...The critical situation in Cuba is absorbing the attention of the Government to the exclusion of all other foreign topics, as is indicated by the activity of the officials in the State, Navy, and War Departments. The President is keeping in close touch with every development of the revolutionary movement in Cuba. The officials here, indeed, are even in receipt of detailed instructions from the President as to what they shall do. *(NY Times*, September 12, 1906)

These instructions were conveyed to the various departments via the telegraph at the Executive Office and the responses were conveyed to the President via the Executive Secretary.

On September 11, Mr. Loeb received a copy of a cable that Mr. Steinhart cabled from Havana to the Secretary of State.

TELEGRAM.

𝔚𝔥𝔦𝔱𝔢 𝔥𝔬𝔲𝔰𝔢,
𝔚𝔞𝔰𝔥𝔦𝔫𝔤𝔱𝔬𝔫.

RECEIVED IN CIPHER.

The White House, Washington, D.C. Sept. 11.

Hon. Wm. Loeb, Jr.,
    Secretary to the President,
        Oyster Bay.

"Havana, September 10, 1906.

Secretary of State:
    Your cable received and directly communicated to the President who asks ships remain for a considerable time to give security to foreigners in Island of Cuba, and says that he will do as much as pos-

sible with his forces to put down insurrection, but if unable to conquer
or compromise, Cuban Congress will indicate kind of intervention desirable. I appreciate reluctance on our part to intervene, especially in
view of Secretary Root's recent statements. Few, however, understand
Cuban situation and a less number are able to appreciate the same. This is,
of course, without any reference to superior authority. Palma applied
public funds in public works and public education but not in purchase
war materials. Insurrectionists for a considerable time prepared for
present condition hence Government's apparent weakness at the commencement. Yesterday's defeat of rebels gives the Government hope.
Attempts useless from the start.

Steinhart."

(TR Papers, Series 1, Reel 68)

Later that morning, Mr. Loeb received another copy of a cable that Mr. Sleeper cabled
from Havana to the Secretary of State.

TELEGRAM.

𝕎hite house,
𝕎ashington.

2 WH JM GI 135 Paid Govt — 10:40a

The White House, Washington, D.C. Sept. 11.

Hon. Wm. Loeb, Jr.,
    Secretary to the President,
        Oyster Bay.

RECEIVED IN CIPHER.
Havana.

Secretary of State:

September 10. President refuses to suspend hostilities. Veterans
consider this breach of faith; state will make no further efforts
in behalf of peace. Will publish manifesto making entire situation
public.

Sleeper,
    Chargé.

(TR Papers, Series 1, Reel 68)

In an interesting and representative letter written to Secretary Loeb by J. Sloat Fasset
on September 11, Mr. Loeb's influence and involvement in New York State politics is
readily observed.

J. SLOAT FASSET
EMIRA, N Y

PERSONAL AND
CONFIDENTIAL.

September 11th, 1906.

Hon. William Loeb, Jr.,
    Oyster Bay, New York.

My dear Loeb:

First, with reference to Bostelmann: I want to thank you very much. That was quite a problem for me to take care of, and I think with your kind help we have solved it.

Now, with reference to the State convention: Of course if Higgins controls that State Convention the Mongin delegation, which is entirely correct and has every right behind it, will be thrown out, and I will be defeated for State Committeemen by our good friend Senator Tulley. I have not the slightest thought that Odell can be re-established in power by any sort of accident. I would not be for that one minute, and I would co-operate cordially in anything to crush Odell, and Higgins too; but your program involves Higgins' success in the convention, which involves my getting hit over the head. Now, if you can fix it so that I shall have fair play in the Seneca county contest, that is all I want. I am as much in earnest to do up that man Odell as anybody in this world is; but Higgins has been so unspeakably mean and aggressive toward me, with no reason whatever, that I cannot contemplate his succeeding with very great complacency. I notice what you say, and of course will regard it as absolutely confidential. The only salvation for us is Hughes. I gave an interview six weeks ago in which I said in effect that I was not worrying about the nomination, for when the time came we were just as sure to nominate Hughes as we were to meet. I am inclined to think it is likely to take that turn. I do not know where there could be a conflict unless it would be in the organization of the convention, and that will largely be determined on by the State Committee, and if a decent man is chosen as temporary Chairman, and as a permanent Chairman, by the State Committee, I should think that there would be no need for a contest. The State Committee, as at present organized, would turn down Odell provided I and my immediate friends co-operate in that direction, but we cannot do that, Will, if it is going to mean that we are going to be punished and persecuted by Higgins.

I just present these thoughts to you for your consideration, with the further assurance that of course I will go just as far as possible to do everything that the President wants done, when he wants it done and as he wants it done. I would like to be given a steer as far ahead as possible.

With best greetings, as always,

Yours very truly,

J. S. Fassett

P.S. I am returning you herewith the letter from Commissioner Leupp, re Bostelmann.

(TR Papers, Series 1, Reel 68)

Inasmuch as the Congress had just passed a new law concerning the meat packing industry, there was a considerable amount of confusion regarding the new regulations. On September 12, 1906 Senator Hopkins of Illinois and James E. Wilson, general manager for the Nelson-Morris Packing Company of Chicago, who represented all of the Chicago packing houses before Congress, visited the President in Oyster Bay. "They came to see the President regarding the controversy between the packers and the Department of Agriculture as to the construction of the new law as it applies to labels." *(NY Times,* September 13, 1906)

On September 12, 1906, Secretary Loeb met with Edward Butler to discuss local politics.

> Edward H. Butler, proprietor of The Buffalo Evening News and generally recognized as a leader of the anti-Benjamin B.Odell forces in that city, was a visitor at Oyster Bay to-day. Mr. Butler, who has just returned from Europe, held a conference with Secretary Loeb for the purpose of getting posted on the political situation in the State. *(NY Times,* September 13, 1906)

Secretary Loeb also received a copy of a cable from Mr. Steinhart in Havana to the Secretary of State.

TELEGRAM.

𝔚hite house, 𝔚ashington.

RECEIVED IN CIPHER.

The White House,
   Washington, D.C. September 12, 1906.

Hon. Wm. Loeb, Jr.,
  Secretary to the President,
   Oyster Bay.

               "Havana, September 12, 1906.

Secretary of State:

  Your cable 11th received and instructions complied with, except publication with regard to Herald article which it would be best let alone for the present. My opinion is that a message reading as follows should at once be cabled to our Chargé d'affairs here to be communicated to President Palma and if possible given at the same time to the press:
  "'The President of the United States directs me to communicate to you that he regrets present state of affairs in Cuba and directs me further to say that you must use in the most effective manner all the resources at your command to quell the present revolt or else in the end

intervention on the part of the United States of America becomes a necessity, which, for the sake of your country, must be avoided.'"

I have used as far as possible your own phraseology and I believe if so sent, will have a favorable result in Cuban Congress next Friday. All <u>reference</u> to make a compromise or like ideas must be omitted. Is most important that the dignity of Government is upheld to guarantee its future stability.

Steinhart."

—I—

(TR Papers, Series 1, Reel 68)

Later, Secretary Loeb received a copy of a cable from Mr. Sleeper in Havana to the Secretary of State.

TELEGRAM.

𝔚hite house,
𝔚ashington.

The White House, Washington, D.C. September 12.

Hon. Wm. Loeb, Jr.,
    Secretary to the President,
        Oyster Bay, N.Y.

    Following just received:
"Havana.

Secretary of State:

In short conversation with President this afternoon I urged American citizens and interests be furnished all protection possible. Many Americans have complained to legation that the protection already requested has not been afforded. In reply to an inquiry as to ability Government to crush rebellion he replied evasively.

Cruiser DENVER has just arrived. Please instruct me fully.

Sleeper, Chargé."

N.P. Webster.

—I—

9:45p

(TR Papers, Series 1, Reel 68)

By this time it was clear that American intervention was imminent. In a second cable from Mr. Steinhart, the Cuban Government's request for American intervention was delivered to the President.

TELEGRAM.

White house,
Washington.

CIPHER.

Hon. Wm. Loeb, Jr.,

The following just received:

"Havana.

"Assistant Secretary of State,

"Secretary of State Republic of Cuba at 3:40 to-day delivered to me memorandum in his own handwriting a translation of which follows and is transmitted notwithstanding previous secret instructions on the subject:

"'The rebellion has increased in the provinces of Santa Clara, Havana, and Pinar del Rio and the Cuban Government has no elements to contend it, to defend the towns and prevent rebels from destroying property. President Estrada Palma asks for American intervention and begs that President Roosevelt send to Havana with the greatest secrecy and rapidity two or three thousand men to avoid any catastrophe in the Capitol. The intervention asked should not be made public until the American troops are in Havana. The situation is grave and any delay may produce a massacre of citizens in Havana. '

(signed) "Steinhart."

Webster.

(TR Papers, Series 1, Reel 68)

The telegrams between the President and Assistant Secretary of State Bacon in Cuba, although unknown to the newspapers, show that the President was firmly in control of the situation. On September 12, 1906, the President ordered additional warships to Havana.

To Robert Bacon   Roosevelt Mss.
Telegram   Oyster Bay, September 12, 1906

Hurry instructions to Navy Department to send at once additional ships to Havana and to get as many marines on them as possible. We should have a large force of marines in Havana at the earliest possible moment on any vessels able to carry them...Come here on Friday without fail and see that Assistant Secretary Newberry or Secretary Bonaparte comes at the same time.

(The Letters of Theodore Roosevelt)

From Washington, *The New York Times* reported the various movements of vessels and the likely actions to be taken by the President.

WASHINGTON, Sept. 12 — President Roosevelt is keenly alive to the progress of the revolutionary movement in Cuba and the responsibility of the United States in case the conditions grow worse and intervention becomes necessary.

The President's policy of preparedness for any emergency was announced at the State Department to-day. It is shown by the arrival at Havana to-night of the cruiser Denver. The gunboat Marietta will reach Cienfuegos some time to-morrow. The cruiser Des Moines will remain at Key West until further orders.

In making public these facts Acting Secretary of State Bacon said that there was no disposition on the part of this Government to make a demonstration in Cuban waters, but the insurrection had attained such proportions that it had become necessary to take steps for the protection of American interests in Cuba.

It is known that the President will not intervene unless it appears absolutely necessary, yet steps have been taken which would make such intervention effective. The ships that have been sent to Cuba are to be there for the purpose only of protecting American interests and furnishing asylum for Americans who may be in danger. Actual intervention would mean the use of the army, and all the available forces would be needed...

...The messages to the State Department from Mr. Sleeper, Chargé at Havana, and other American representatives in Cuba, which are supposed to have told of conditions requiring that prompt action be taken to safeguard Americans and their property, will not be discussed by officials of the State or Navy Departments. It is admitted, however, that all these messages have been forwarded, upon their receipt, to President Roosevelt at Oyster Bay, who has personally directed the policy of the United States concerning the Cuban outbreak. *(NY Times, September 13, 1906)*

On September 13, a detachment of 120 armed American sailors from the cruiser Denver landed at Havana without orders from Washington. The landing followed a conference in Havana between President Palma, American Chargé d'Affaires Sleeper, and Commander Colwell of the Denver. When President Roosevelt received the news from Havana that sailors had landed, they were immediately ordered to return to the Denver. The President first sent a telegram to Secretary of the Navy Bonaparte and a similar one to Acting Secretary of State Bacon regarding the incident.

To Robert Bacon   Roosevelt Mss.
Telegram   Oyster Bay, September 13, 1906

You had no business to direct the landing of those troops without specific authority from here. They are not to be employed in keeping general order without our authority. Notify me immediately if they cannot be taken to the American Legation with the field pieces and kept there. Scrupulous care is to be taken to avoid bloodshed. Remember that unless you are directed otherwise from here the forces are only to be used to protect American life and property.

(The Letters of Theodore Roosevelt)

The New York Times reported that there was no official information relative to the landing of the sailors.

> OYSTER BAY, N.Y., Sept 13 — It is stated that no official information has been received here relative to the landing by the armored cruiser Denver of a detachment of sailors at Havana, or their recall to their vessel under orders from Washington. It is also said that no orders had been sent from here concerning the incident. *(NY Times, September 14, 1906)*

However, Acting Secretary of State Bacon, after receiving the President's telegram of the 13th, telegraphed Chargé d'Affairs Sleeper, ordering him to withdraw the troops. After Mr. Sleeper had done so, he reported his action to Acting Secretary of State Bacon. A copy of this telegram was cabled to Secretary Loeb on September 14.

TELEGRAM.

𝔚𝔥𝔦𝔱𝔢 𝔥𝔬𝔲𝔰𝔢, 𝔚𝔞𝔰𝔥𝔦𝔫𝔤𝔱𝔬𝔫.

2 WH JM GI   70 Paid Govt ———- 10a

The White House, Washington, D.C. Sept. 14.

Hon. Wm. Loeb, Jr.,
    Secretary to the President,
        Oyster Bay, N.Y.

"Havana 14.

Secretary of State:

September 13, 12p. On receipt of your confidential cable of this evening instructing me under no circumstances to request landing of any armed force, I immediately requested Captain Colwell, who had already landed a force as per my cable of this afternoon to withdraw it.

Sleeper,
Chargé.

(TR Papers, Series 1, Reel 68)

Either Chargé d'Affaires Sleeper was unaware of the President's desire to avoid confrontation or "he lost his head." *(NY Times, September 14, 1906)* Also on September 13, it was announced that the Cuban situation would be discussed the following day at a conference at Sagamore Hill between the President, Secretary of War Taft, Acting Secretary of State Bacon, and Secretary of the Navy Bonaparte. *(NY Times*, September 14, 1906) On September 14, but prior to the conference at Sagamore Hill, Secretary Loeb received a cable from Assistant Secretary of State Adee. This telegram reiterated the United States' rights and obligations under the Treaty of Peace and the Treaty with Cuba, dated May 22, 1903.

TELEGRAM.

The White House,

Washington.

Hon. Wm. Loeb, Jr:

Following are the pertinent treaty articles defining President's power and duty regarding maintenance of adequate government in Cuba:

Article 1, Treaty of Peace, Paris 1898. Spain relinquishes all claim of sovereignty over and title to Cuba. And as the Island is, upon its evacuation by Spain, to be occupied by the United States, the United States will, so long as such occupation shall last, assume and discharge the obligations that may under international law result from the fact of its occupation, for the protection of life and property.

Article 3 Treaty with Cuba, May 22, 1903. The Government of Cuba consents that the United States may exercise the right to intervene for the preservation of Cuban independence, the maintenance of a government adequate for the protection of life, property, and individual liberty, and for discharging the obligations with respect to Cuba imposed by the treaty of Paris on the United States, now to be assumed and undertaken by the Government of Cuba.

Full text of first treaty in treaty compilation 1904. Text of latter treaty mailed you tonight.

Adee.

(TR Papers, Series 1, Reel 68)

These important excerpts from the treaties were used during the conference at Sagamore Hill on September 14, to formulate the letter to the Cuban Minister to the United States. As a result of this conference Secretary of War Taft and Acting Secretary of State Bacon were appointed as special representatives to Cuba with orders to thoroughly investigate the situation and to give such aid as was necessary to end the fighting.

OYSTER BAY, N.Y., Sept. 14 — As the result of a six-hour conference at Sagamore Hill to-day between President Roosevelt, Secretary of War Taft, Secretary of the Navy Bonaparte, and Acting Secretary of State Bacon, Mssrs.

Taft and Bacon will start at once for Cuba as the special representatives of the American Government. It will be their mission to make a thorough investigation and to render such aid as may be necessary to the task of bringing about an immediate cessation of hostilities and the permanent pacification of the island, which is declared by the President to be imperative.

They will proceed to Key West and sail from that port to Havana on a warship. They will leave Washington on Sunday.

This decision was made public by means of the following letter to Señor Quesada, the Cuban Minister to the United States, which was given out by Secretary Loeb at 10:30 P.M.

> Oyster Bay, N.Y., Sept. 14, 1906
> My Dear Señor Quesada:
>
> In this crisis in the affairs of the Republic of Cuba I write you not merely because you are the Minister of Cuba accredited to this Government, but because you and I were intimately drawn together at the time when the United States intervened in the affairs of Cuba with the result of making her an independent nation.
>
> You know how sincere my affection and admiration and regard for Cuba are. You know that I never have done and never shall do anything in reference to Cuba save with such regard for her welfare. You also know the pride I felt because it came to me as President to withdraw the American troops from the Island of Cuba and officially to proclaim her independence and to wish her godspeed in her career as a free republic.
>
> I desire now through you to say a word of solemn warning to your people, whose earnest well wisher I am. For seven years Cuba has been in a condition of profound peace and of steadily growing prosperity. For four years this peace and prosperity have obtained under her own independent government. Her peace, prosperity, and independence are now menaced; for of all the possible evils that can befall Cuba, the worst is the evil of anarchy into which civil war and revolutionary disturbances will assuredly throw her...
>
> ...Under the treaty with your Government I, as President of the United States, have a duty in this matter which I cannot shirk. The third article of that treaty explicitly confers upon the United States the right to intervene for the maintenance in Cuba of a Government adequate for the protection of life, property, and individual liberty.
>
> The treaty conferring this right is the supreme law of the land, and furnishes me with the right and the means of fulfilling the obligation that I am under to protect American interests. The information at hand shows that the social bonds throughout the island have been so relaxed that life, property, and individual liberty are no longer safe...
>
> ...I am sending to Havana the Secretary of War, Mr. Taft and the Assistant Secretary of State, Mr. Bacon, as the special representatives of this Government...

...It was 3:30 o'clock when the conference began at Sagamore Hill and 9:30 o'clock when it was over. Secretary Taft and Secretary Bonaparte left on the 10:03 train, racing to the station in an automobile. Assistant Secretary Bacon went to the executive offices with the President's secretary and remained there until the Roosevelt letter was given to the reporters who were awaiting it...*(NY Times*, September 15, 1906)

During the conference, several important telegrams were received in Oyster Bay regarding the situation in Cuba. The first telegram was from Mr. Sleeper to the Secretary of State. Mr. Sleeper wanted to make certain that the mistake with the Denver was not repeated by the Marietta in Cienfuegos.

TELEGRAM.

The White House,

Washington.

7 WH JM GI 107 Paid Govt ——4:45p

The White House, Washington, D.C.
September 14.

Hon. Wm. Loeb, Jr.,
    Secretary to the President,
        Oyster Bay.

Havana.

Secretary of State:

September 14. Owing to report that troops have been disembarked from MARIETTA at Cienfuegos, I framed following cable to consul there:
    "If troops have been disembarked from MARIETTA without specific orders from Washington, please request reembarkation at once. Please advise me immediately and fully."
    Not sent because telegraph <u>instructions</u> reports wires cut. Will send later if communication reestablished unless instructed to contrary by you.

Sleeper,
Chargé.

(TR Papers, Series 1, Reel 68)

Assistant Secretary of State Adee telegraphed Mr. Loeb regarding this telegram two hours later.

TELEGRAM.

The White House,

Washington.

8 NY RA GI 93 Paid Govt.

White House, Washington, D.C. Sept. 14.

Hon. Wm. Loeb, Jr.,

    Oyster Bay, N.Y.

Concerning Sleeper's telegram of to-day reporting the instructions he attempted to send to the MARIETTA, should he not be cabled not to send such a telegram ? Sleeper does not comprehend that conditions are different at Cienfuegos, where valuable estates are being burned and the duty to protect property from actual destruction may be paramount. Sleeper might be told that the MARIETTA receives orders direct from Washington.

I shall be accessible all this evening and night.

Adee.

6:45p

(TR Papers, Series 1, Reel 68)

In one of the most significant telegrams sent during the Cuban crises, Mr. Steinhart reported to the Secretary of State, that the Government of Cuba intended to resign, thus leaving behind a state of anarchy. It is interesting to note that in this telegram simplified spelling is used.

TELEGRAM.

White house, Washington.

6 WH JM GI   Paid Govt.

The White House, Washington, D.C. September 14.

Hon. Wm. Loeb, Jr.,
    Secretary to the President,
        Oyster Bay, N.Y.

Havana, September 14.

Secretary of State:

President Palma has resolved not to continue at the head of the Government and is ready to present his resignation even tho the present disturbances should cease at once. The vice president has resolved not to accept the office. Cabinet ministers have declared that they will previously resign. Under these conditions it is impossible that Congress will meet for the lack of a proper person to convoke same to designate a new president. The consequence will be absence of legal power and therefore the prevailing state of anarchy will continue unless the Government of the United States will adopt the measures necessary to avoid this danger. The foregoing must remain secret and confidential until the President of the United States takes action. With reference to the disembarkation of force by the commander of DENVER upon request of the Chargé d'affaires, and now by him countermanded, which landing was contrary to my opinion until American life and proper actually in danger. President Palma desires me to say that their return to ships adds serious complications for him and for his Government. Reply as soon as possible.

Steinhart.

(TR Papers, Series 1, Reel 68)

On September 15, Mr. Sleeper cabled to the Secretary of State again regarding the disembarkation of troops from the Marietta at Cienfuegos. The telegram was forwarded to Mr. Loeb.

TELEGRAM.

The White House,

Washington.

2 WH RA GI 93 Paid Govt ——5:50p

White House, Washington, D.C. Sept. 15.

Hon. Wm. Loeb:

Havana, September 15.

Secretary of State:

Following message just received from Consul Cienfuegos: "Marietta
is here. Do you request commander to land men for protection of
sugar estates ? Answer commander Marietta immediately."

I replied as follows: "Not without specific instructions from
Washington. Have cabled your message State Department and will telegraph
you further as soon as possible."

Please instruct legation or Marietta fully immediately. Telegraph
communication with Cienfuegos reestablished.

Sleeper,
Chargé.

(TR Papers, Series 1, Reel 68)

Three hours later, Mr. Sleeper cabled again.

TELEGRAM.

The White House,

Washington.

3 WH RA GI 101 Paid Govt ——8:45p

The White House, Washington, D.C. September 15.

Hon. Wm. Loeb, Jr.:

Havana, September 15.

Secretary of State:

Encounter last night between forces rural guard and rebels. Havana
province vicinity Mazzora. Government advises rebels dispersed, altho
reliable unofficial reports to the contrary. Also encounter near
Santo Domingo, Santa Clara province, result unknown. Guerra said to be
moving toward Havana. Two bridges burnt between towns of Guanajay and
Cabanas, Pinar del Rio province.

U. S. S. DESMOINES and DIXIE arrived today. Since publication President's letter more hopeful tone possibility peace. Business interests greatly relieved. Government sympathizers also friends revolution all manifest confidence in fairness attitude American Government.

Sleeper,
Chargé.

(TR Papers, Series 1, Reel 68)

The announcement that Secretary Taft and Secretary Bacon would travel to Cuba, as well as the arrival of more American warships to Havana, prodded the Cuban Government and the rebels to issue orders suspending hostilities. However, the hostilities continued nonetheless.

HAVANA, Sept. 16 — The Government this evening is making final strenuous efforts to restore peace in Cuba and thus avoid any kind of American intervention. The object of these endeavors, it is stated, is that the Government may be able to say by the time the Secretary of War Taft and Acting Secretary of State Bacon arrive that peace has already been arranged and that therefore there is no need for the American Government's intervention, either to restore peace or insure permanent tranquility.

WASHINGTON, Sept. 16 — The announcement from Havana that the Government has declared an armistice was expected here...

...There is no question that the Havana officials are extremely worried over the turn of affairs since Friday. They were anxious to have armed intervention, because that would necessarily imply the crushing of the rebellion by American soldiers. The last thing they expected or desired was peaceful intervention with its accompaniment of a full investigation...

...The insurgents...welcomed an investigation...implying that the administration has more to lose by a full investigation...

...According to all the obtainable information this is the fact. A full showdown before Mr. Taft would, it was expected, reveal that the Palma Government, while it had made the island prosperous commercially, had held control politically by despotic means, that the elections were farces, and that the majorities did not rule., This is not by any means giving the insurgents the whole of the argument. Palma's rule seems to have been beneficial in an economic way, and if the hungry ex-soldiers who lead the opposition should get into control their rule might be worse for Cuba. The question, however, is not which rule is the more desirable, but whether, on a plain showing of facts before the arbitrator, Mr. Taft might not have to present a report which would leave Palma no course but to get out of office and take his whole administration with him...

...Mr. Taft left here to-day fully determined to act, not as a mere investigator, but also as an arbitrator. Armed intervention would follow immediately on the rejection of whatever plan of arbitration he proposed...*(NY Times,* September 17, 1906)

On September 17, 1906 General Castillo, the commander of the insurgents sent a letter to Mr. Sleeper, the American Chargé d'Affaires expressing his disposition to "suspend hostilities in order to facilitate peace efforts, provided these are based on new general elections, with guarantees of justice and legality, and on the resignation of the present forced administration and guarantees that the peace be lasting." *(NY Times, September 18, 1906)* It was also announced from Washington that the United States would protect British as well as American interests in Cuba. In Oyster Bay, the President met with a delegation of manufacturers from Germany who sought relief from restrictive legislation in American custom houses against imports from Germany. The President advised them to present a detailed complaint to officials in the State and Treasury Departments in Washington. *(NY Times, September 18, 1906)*

On September 18, M.R. Spelman, President of the Colonial Sugars Company, owner of sugar plantations in Cuba, sent a telegram to Secretary Loeb in Oyster Bay. In it he repeated a telegram he had received from workers on his plantation in Cuba.

TELEGRAM.

The White House,

Washington.

1 NY VV GI 70 Paid —— 11:05a

16 Broad Street, New York, September 18, 1906.

Wm. Loeb, Jr.,
   Secretary,
      Oyster Bay.

Following just received from Cienfuegos, dated this morning:

"Prompt action commander Fullam and presence his men undoubtedly saved Constancia last night. Insurgent general Collado burned Esperanza American property adjoining us this morning. Threatens completely destroy Constancia. Present force can protect sugar house only. Reinforcements needed quickly."

This for the President's information with the request that it be repeated to Assistant Secretary Bacon en route to Cuba.

M.R. Spelman,
President, Colonial Sugars Company.

(TR Papers, Series 1, Reel 68)

Assistant Secretary of State Adee cabled to Secretary Loeb in reply to Spelman's telegram.

TELEGRAM.

The White House,

Washington.

2 WH JM GI 99   Paid Govt —— 4p

The White House, Washington, D.C. September 18.

Wm. Loeb, Jr.,
      Oyster Bay, N.Y.

     Please say to the President that Spellman's telegram based on a despatch from Cienfuegos dated this morning is important because indicating that the local insurgents disregard the announced suspension of hostilities. The DIXIE having arrived at Cienfuegos with marines it would seem proper to reinforce detachment at Constancia, Soledad and neighboring plantations. I suggest that, if approved, orders go directly to Navy Department from Oyster Bay to avoid delay.
     Mr. Bacon being now at sea I shall endeavor to reach him by wireless and repeat Spellman's telegram to him.

Alvey A. Adee.

(TR Papers, Series 1, Reel 68)

An hour and a half later, Assistant Secretary of State Adee sent a cable to Oyster Bay based upon his cable in reply to Mr. Spelman.

TELEGRAM.

The White House,

Washington.

3 WH FD NE   89 Paid Govt Chg State Dept   5 23 PM

The White House, Washington, D.C. Sept. 18, 1906.

Wm. Loeb, Jr.,
    O. Bay.

After consultation with Navy Department I have sent following
telegram to Spelman: "Your telegram to Mr. Loeb referred to
Washington. Dixie arrived Cienfuegos this morning with additional
marines. Representatives of estates should lay complaints and facts
before senior naval officer who is instructed to land force necessary
to protect American property." Admiral Converse says Dixie has
ample men to reinforce guards upon the facts being shown to the senior
naval officer, Fullam, who will be cabled in accordance with the
President's direction.

Adee.

(TR Papers, Series 1, Reel 68)

Upon their arrival to Cuba on September 19, Messrs. Taft and Bacon immediately
conferred with members of the Cuban Government. President Palma made it clear that
he would rather resign than concede to any of the demands made by the Revolutionists.

HAVANA, Sept. 19 — Messrs. Taft and Bacon have had long conversations
with President Palma, Vice President Mendez Capote, Secretary of State
O'Farrill, the Presidents of the Moderate and Liberal Parties, and other leaders. Both President Palma and Vice President Mendez Capote said the
Government was absolutely opposed to any plan which involved a new general election. The President said he would resign if it were ordered, adding that
no members of the Government would be willing to concede this point under
any circumstances. *(NY Times*, September 20, 1906)

Despite the flurry of activity regarding the Cuban crisis, the President opened several
Indian lands in the West for settlement.

OYSTER BAY, N.Y., Sept. 19 — President Roosevelt to-day issued a proclamation opening the Kiowa, Comanche, and Apache Indian lands in Oklahoma.

The Department of the Interior will announce the date for the reception of sealed bids under which the 505,000 acres of lands will be disposed of to settlers. *(NY Times,* September 20, 1906)

Meanwhile in Cuba, Secretary Taft and Assistant Secretary Bacon met again with the Cuban leaders.

HAVANA, Sept. 19 — A second day of conferences with the leaders of the factions of the Cuban conflict has not enabled Secretary of War Taft and Assistant Secretary of State Bacon to announce any plan for compromising the difficulty. So strenuous are the appeals of both the Liberal and Moderate leaders that the situation becomes increasingly complicated as the negotiations proceed.

However, Secretary Taft said to-night that he believed when they were brought face to face with the danger of losing their independence forever all patriotic Cubans would be willing to make concessions. Mr. Taft added that the United States peace emissaries were in a most delicate position. They had undertaken to hear all complaints, and until they had made themselves thoroughly conversant with the political turmoil in Cuba they could not express themselves freely in the conferences, fearing that possible misunderstandings might have a deterrent effect on the proceedings...

...Cuban, Spanish, American, and other business men are talking of uniting in a petition to Messrs. Taft and Bacon urging some radical form of intervention or else annexation... *(NY Times,* September 21, 1906)

With neither political party willing to yield in Cuba, and the insurgents advancing to surround Havana, Secretary Taft reported to the President that intervention of some sort was unavoidable.

HAVANA, Sept. 21 — I am reliably informed that Secretary Taft has reported to President Roosevelt that the situation is more serious than he had expected and that intervention of some sort is practically unavoidable.

The dead-lock continues. Neither political party will yield, and the revolutionists are advancing to surround Havana.

It is the general expectation among all classes that the United States will soon take definite action...It is not believed that the United States will annex the island, but it is thought that she will control it for some years.

The battleships Louisiana and Virginia and the cruisers Cleveland and Tacoma arrived this morning and the battleship New Jersey arrived this afternoon. With the cruisers Denver and Des Moines there are now seven United States warships in the harbor...

...The American mediators have now sifted the dispute and define it as a demand by the Insurrectionists for a new general election and an absolute rejection of the demand by the Government.

Messrs. Taft and Bacon have practically abandoned hope of finding a middle ground, and fear that a decision in favor of either side would result in no more than temporary tranquillity for the island. It is their belief that American occupation is the only way to end the civil warfare, and it is not denied that intervention must be followed by American sovereignty.

Secretary Taft has cabled to President Roosevelt regarding the gravity of the situation, and Mr. Roosevelt will, it is expected, dictate the future programme of his Commissioners...*(NY Times*, September 22, 1906)

Indeed, the President was in constant communication with Secretary Taft.

WASHINGTON, Sept. 21 — ...President Roosevelt is in personal and constant direction of the negotiations for a settlement of the difficulties. It was learned to-day that he had been in personal and direct telegraphic communication with President Palma before he sent Secretaries Taft and Bacon to Havana. He had sent several messages to the Cuban President and had received some replies. These replies not being satisfactory he sent Taft and Bacon down. Direct telegraphic communication has been established between Havana and Oyster Bay, in order that Secretary Taft may be able to promptly report to the President. *(NY Times*, September 22, 1906)

In reply to Secretary Taft, the President sent a telegram from the Executive Office on September 21, 1906 to Taft in Cuba.

To William Howard Taft   Roosevelt Mss.
Telegram   Oyster Bay, September 21, 1906

I approve entirely of your plan. I suggest, however, that if you have to land troops in Havana you will avoid the use of the word intervention and simply state that they are landed to save life and property in Havana. In view of what you say it is manifestly impossible for us to try and sustain Palma, and I doubt if it will be wise to try to keep him temporarily in office...In any event I authorize you to use your discretion, if you have to act so quickly that you cannot communicate with me, and in such case you can of course count upon my absolutely standing by you; but equally of course I desire if possible that you communicate with me before taking such final steps as will irrevocably commit us to intervention.

(*The Letters of Theodore Roosevelt*)

On September 22, Secretary Taft did indeed decide to land troops in Havana and preparations were immediately made for this there.

HAVANA, Sept. 22 — Fifteen hundred American marines and sailors are preparing to land in Havana to-night for transfer to Camp Columbia. The United Railways has two trains, with a total of thirty cars, waiting to transport the force.

When it became known that an armed American force was coming ashore it was said that forcible intervention was at hand. The object of landing the troops is stated to be in order to resist a possible attack on the city and to protect American lives and property should the rebels outside the city become dissatisfied with the condition of the peace negotiations and undertake to invade

Havana...

...Secretary of War Taft and Assistant Secretary of State Bacon and upward of a score of leaders of the revolution held a conference to-night, and it was later announced that the revolutionists had appointed a committee of seven to represent them in a conference. The leaders told Secretary Taft that all had agreed to abide by the judgement of this committee in any peace arrangements which it could make with the Government through the aid of the American commissioners...

...The first conference between the committee and Secretary Taft will be held to-morrow...

...Secretary Taft received a long cablegram direct from Oyster Bay to-day. It is understood that he was instructed by it to exhaust every resource in settling the difficulty without intervention, if possible. This was in response to the Secretary's pessimistic messages of yesterday...*(NY Times,* September 23, 1906)

In fact, the President sent two telegrams to Taft on September 22. The text of both telegrams follows:

To William Howard Taft   Roosevelt Mss.
Telegram   Oyster Bay, September 22, 1906

Much pleased with your telegram. Of course if continuance of Palma can be secured I think it would be best; but I am afraid you will find difficulties in the way.

To William Howard Taft   Roosevelt Mss.
Telegram   Oyster Bay, September 22, 1906

I repeat my entire approval of your proposal. Put in some temporary executive and then carry out the plan of action you outline in your cable...It is not only important to try to get them to come to an agreement but it is important from the standpoint of public sentiment here that we shall make it plain that we are exhausting every effort to come to an agreement before we intervene.

(The Letters of Theodore Roosevelt)

As reported earlier on September 23, Secretary Taft met with the committee of seven appointed by the Revolutionists.

HAVANA, Sept. 24 — ...The committee of leaders of the revolution conferred at length with Messrs. Taft and Bacon this afternoon and their final proposition was fully discussed. It varies little from the original revolutionary programe except that the insurgents have consented to withdraw the demand that President Palma resign.

Mr. Taft later called at the Palace with the rebel agreement fully outlined and discussed the situation with President Palma and leading Moderates, who evidently regret the necessity of making concessions to the rebels. *(NY Times,* September 25, 1906)

However, by September 25, President Palma had announced his intention to abdicate rather than yield to any of the terms presented by the Revolutionists.

> HAVANA, Sept. 25 — The Cuban Republic to-night stands on the verge of a second period of American intervention. The Moderate Party, which six weeks ago was in absolute control of every office in the island...is to-night determined to abdicate everything and compel the United States to intervene. In fact, every Government official from President Palma down is sincerely anxious to force such intervention rather than yield to any one of the terms offered by the Liberal Party and those in arms against the Government.
>
> It is declared on very high authority that intervention is certain and it is expected that the proclamation announcing it will be issued at Oyster Bay...
>
> ...It is just barely possible that President Roosevelt through Messrs. Taft and Bacon may yet arrange to establish the Liberals in control of the Cuban Government, but this is regarded only as the remotest sort of possibility. With either party installed in power there would remain a condition of deplorable unrest and to-night there appears nothing whatever to promise relief save full control by the United States...
>
> ...President Palma has called a special session of Congress for Friday, when he will present the resignations of himself and Vice President Mendez Capote. The Moderates, however, will not attend that session of Congress, for in a hurriedly called National Moderate Assembly this afternoon they decided unanimously simply to quit forthwith. They will not have anything more to do with the Government of Cuba, alleging that they have been unjustly treated by President Roosevelt's commissioners...*(NY Times*, September 26, 1906)

On September 25, President Roosevelt sent two lengthy telegrams from Oyster Bay to Secretary Taft at the American Legation over the direct wire from the legation to the cable office in the Executive Building. Excerpts from these telegrams follow:

To William Howard Taft   Roosevelt Mss.
Telegram   Oyster Bay, September 25, 1906

Am of course greatly concerned at news. If it is the obstinancy of Palma and the Moderates which is the cause of the trouble I greatly fear that the mobilization of the troops would only strengthen them in their course. Instead of my cabling direct to Palma I authorize you to sign for me and if in your judgement wise deliver the following:

President Palma.

I most earnestly ask that you sacrifice your own feeling on the altar of your country's good and yield to Mr. Taft's request by continuing in the Presidency a sufficient length of time to in his judgement inaugurate the new temporary government under which the arrangements for peace can be carried out...Under you for four years Cuba has been an independent republic. I adjure you for the sake of your own fair fame not so to conduct yourself that the responsibility if such there be for the death of the republic can be put at your door. I pray that you will act so that it shall appear that you at least have sacrificed yourself for your country and that when you leave office you leave your country still free...You will have done your part as a gentleman and a patriot if you act in this manner on the suggestion of Mr. Taft and I most earnestly beg you to do so.

THEODORE ROOSEVELT

I also authorize you to vary the phraseology of the above if you think it important. On the other hand point out to the insurgent chiefs that this is their last chance; that additional warships are coming; that the army is being mobilized, and that if we are obliged to intervene in Cuba now and act against the insurgents, that no matter what destruction they may temporarily cause and no matter how much delay there may be, the ultimate putting down of the insurrection is an absolute certainty...

(*The Letters of Theodore Roosevelt*)

The second telegram was as follows:

To William Howard Taft   Roosevelt Mss.
Telegram   Oyster Bay, September 25, 1906

I do not understand how conditions have changed so completely. It seems to me that the thing to do is to land the troops and temporarily assume the functions of government, but to say nothing about suppressing the insurrection; and on the contrary to have an agreement with the insurrecto leaders to the effect that we are merely taking Palma's place to do what they had said would be entirely satisfactory to them in their conversation with you. It seems to me that under the Platt Amendment it is at least doubtful whether the resignation of the regular government would not amount to substituting the hitherto insurrectionary party as the government *de facto*. At any rate I am inclined to think that unless you have reason to the contrary of which I am ignorant, it would be better to proceed with the insurrectos along the exact lines that you have proposed, simply notifying them that as Palma will not act we will appoint some man to act in his place...I do not believe we should, simply because Palma has turned sulky and will not act as a patriot, put ourselves in the place of his unpopular government and face all the likelihood of a long drawn out and very destructive guerilla warfare. Certainly I do not think this should be done unless we can make it clear that the insurrectos will not act reasonably. As I say, there may be reasons that I do not know why what I now suggest is not feasible, but if so I wish you to cable me.

(*The Letters of Theodore Roosevelt*)

According to *The New York Times* of September 26, the President sent orders to both the Department of the Navy to send more warships to Cuba and to the War Department to ready the army.

WASHINGTON, Sept. 25 — Three more battleships, three more cruisers, and 2,500 more marines have been ordered to Cuba.

The hopefulness was all blown out of the dispatches from Havana this morning by the receipt at the Navy Department of telegrams from Oyster Bay in which President Roosevelt directed the immediate sending of additional forces to Cuba...

...It is apparent that Secretary Taft and the President mean to exhaust the resources of the navy in making a show of force to the Cubans in order to influence them to come to some sort of agreement if possible, and that the army will not be called upon until the determination has been made to intervene...

...There were indications to-day at the War Department that orders had been received there also from Oyster Bay, but the most extreme reticence was maintained in regard to them...*(NY Times*, September 26, 1906)

An announcement was also made from the Executive Office in Oyster Bay that plans were being made to transfer troops to Cuba in the event that Secretary Taft's mission fails.

OYSTER BAY, N.Y., Sept. 25 — Plans for the transfer of troops to Cuba in the event of the failure of Secretary Taft's mission have been completed.

According to an announcement made here to-night, the transport ship Sumner, now lying at the New York Navy Yard, is in readiness for the immediate embarkation of troops.

Negotiations are already under way for the acquisition of merchant steamers to be used as transports should intervention in Cuba become necessary. *(NY Times*, September 26, 1906)

In a memorandum from M.C. Latta in Oyster Bay to Assistant Secretary Forster in Washington, approval was given for General Ainsworth to make pubic the preparations being made on the transport ship Sumner.

TELEGRAM.

The White House,

Washington.

Oyster Bay, N.Y. September 25, 1906.

Memorandum for Mr. Forster:

Please inform General Ainsworth that the President says it will be all right now to make public the fact that the transport Sumner has been ordered put in commission; that all that is necessary now in order to move troops, in case effort to bring peace fails, is to charter transports.

M.C. Latta.

(TR Papers, Series 1, Reel 68)

After an ultimatum by Secretary Taft threatening military rule in Cuba, the Moderate Party agreed to negotiate with a committee of the rebels and the Liberal Party.

HAVANA, Sept. 26 — The Moderates have agreed to appoint a committee to negotiate terms of peace with a committee of the rebels and the Liberals, leaving all points upon which no agreement is reached to the arbitration of the American Commissioners. The Moderates have abandoned a condition they first insisted on, that the rebels must lay down their arms before negotiations could commence.

It is tacitly understood by the committees of the two parties that unless an agreement is reached this week armed intervention will ensue...

...It has been agreed that at the extraordinary session of Congress called for Friday the resignation of President Palma shall be tabled pending these negotiations, with the hope of obviating the necessity of leaving his office.

It was an ultimatum issued by Messrs. Taft and Bacon that brought the Moderates to agree to these conciliatory plans. *(NY Times,* September 27, 1906)

On September 26, President Roosevelt cabled Havana three times in order to congratulate Secretary Taft on the news of the impending negotiations and to brief Taft on his desired course of action.

To William Howard Taft   Roosevelt Mss.
Telegram   Oyster Bay, September 26, 1906

Have just received your telegram of today. Am immensely pleased with it and am delighted with the way you are handling situation. You are doing just what I hoped would be done. Remember, however, that we are certain to be violently attacked in Congress not only by most of our open political opponents but by Republicans who have special cause to be jealous of either you or me and we should leave them as little room for attack as possible. Avoid the use of the word intervention in any proclamation or paper of yours and if possible place the landing of our sailors and marines on grounds of conservation of American interests emphasizing the temporary character of the landing and the hope that our keeping sailors, marines or troops in the Island will be but for a short time until a permanent government has been formed...Please consider whether it would not be well at first to limit as far as possible the places where we have to establish garrisons. I want to make it evident beyond possibility of doubt that we take no step we are not absolutely forced to by the situation and therefore avoid taking possession in appearance of the entire Island if that is possible...I sympathize most heartily with your abhorrence of the insurrectionary spirit and appreciate keenly the evil necessarily done by the recognition of the insurrectionary party into which we are forced, but this evil is not in the slightest degree due to any act of ours. On the contrary it is evident that only your going to Havana prevented that city and all of Cuba from falling immediately into the possession of the revolutionists. We have not caused the evil; we have simply dealt with it in the wisest possible manner under conditions as they have actually been.

To William Howard Taft   Roosevelt Mss.
Telegram   Oyster Bay, September 26, 1906

Have been thinking over your last telegram in connection with your previous
telegrams and letter. It is undoubtedly a very evil thing that the revolutionists
should be encouraged and the dreadful example afforded the island of success
in remedying wrongs by violence and treason to the government. If the Palma
government had shown any real capacity for self-defense and ability to sustain
itself and a sincere purpose to remedy the wrongs of which your telegrams
show that they have been guilty, I should have been inclined to stand by them
no matter to what extent, including armed intervention. But as things actually
are we do not have the chance of following any such course...Under such circumstances, as the least of two very serious evils it seems to me that we must
simply put ourselves for the time being in Palma's place, land a sufficient force
to insure order, and notify the insurgents that we will carry thru the program in
which you and they agreed, keeping control simply until this program can be
carried thru...I feel therefore that in ordering troops to land or issuing any
proclamation in my name, which of course I hereby authorize you to do, you
should base your action on the ground that organized government had disappeared and that order must be kept, and should avoid issuing an ultimatum to
the insurrectos or the use of phraseology saying that they are in revolt against
the United States until you have seen whether they will in good faith carry out
the agreement they have already made with you, you on your part carrying out
so much of the agreement as you had intended to have Palma carry out. Of
course there may be circumstances known to you which make this plan of
mine futile, and I am giving my views with the understanding that they come
from a man at a distance, who does not know the facts as you do on the ground.
If possible cable me fully; but if the crisis comes and has to be met I hereby
authorize you to do whatever in your discretion you deem best...

To William Howard Taft   Roosevelt Mss.
Telegram   Oyster Bay, September 26, 1906

Your second cable of today has been received. Things are certainly kaleido-
scopic and I must trust to your judgement on the ground how to meet each suc-
cessive change as it occurs. Let me repeat that if possible you base any action
in landing a force and taking possession of the government or restoring order
upon the need of protecting American interests, and avoid so long as it is possible the use of the word intervention or the use of terms that will imply that
the rebels are in the position of an insurrection against us...I think you understand thoroly what I mean, however, which is to do anything that is necessary
no matter how strong the course, but to try to do it in as gentle a way possible...
    ...On Friday morning I sail on the *Mayflower* at eleven o'clock, and will be
in Buzzards Bay at the target practice...If possible shape your action so that it
will not be necessary to cable me while I am at sea, altho I shall have wireless
telegraphy...

(*The Letters of Theodore Roosevelt*)

On September 26 it was announced from both Washington and Oyster Bay that President Roosevelt had given preliminary orders for the dispatch of troops to Cuba.

> WASHINGTON, Sept. 26 — ...President Roosevelt has issued the preliminary order looking to the dispatch of the land forces to Cuba to supplement the force of marines and bluejackets now at the disposal of Secretary Taft. He telegraphed to the War Department from Oyster Bay directing that immediate preparation be made to send an expedition of 6,000 men. *(NY Times, September 27, 1906)*

> OYSTER BAY, N.Y., Sept. 26 — While no order has yet been given for the mobilization of troops in anticipation of intervention in Cuba, it is learned here that preparations for such an eventuality have progressed so far that no time would be lost embarking troops should such a move become necessary. Whether or not the order directing the move is made depends entirely upon events in Havana.

> Assistant Secretary Latta said to-day that there was no immediate prospect of the issue of a Presidential proclamation declaring intervention in Cuba. *(NY Times, September 27, 1906)*

By September 27, it was clear that time was running out for the Cuban Government and that U.S. intervention was imminent.

> HAVANA, Sept. 27 — It is generally understood that if within the next twenty-four hours the warring factions have not come to some sort of an arrangement which gives hope that the present chaotic situation will soon end, the United States will intervene. Every one believes that there is no chance of such an agreement, and it is the general belief that to-day is the last of the independent Cuban Republic...

> ...The Moderate Party to-night decided to make a final effort to perpetuate the authority of the Palma administration by determining to reject the resignation of the President when it is presented to Congress to-morrow. When this decision was reached Secretary of War Taft and Assistant Secretary of State Bacon, the American Commissioners, had already concluded to intervene, but they agreed to await to-morrow's developments, as they are anxious to afford every opportunity to the Cubans to work out their own salvation.

> President Palma steadfastly refuses every solicitation of his friends to withdraw his resignation. In the cablegram he sent to President Roosevelt in response to the final urgent message from the American President that he remain at the helm in Cuba he expressed his warm appreciation of President Roosevelt's efforts to obtain peace for Cuba and the friendship he has always shown the Cuban people...

> ...The American Commissioners have little confidence in the seriousness of the intentions of politicians who have been vacillating and insincere throughout these nine days of futile negotiations. This being the situation, nobody is inclined to doubt to-night that within twenty-four hours Secretary Taft, by authority of the President of the United States, will proclaim himself Provisional Governor of Cuba. *(NY Times, September 27, 1906)*

On September 27, 1906 it was announced at the Executive Offices that the President would sail on the yacht Mayflower to visit the North Atlantic Fleet off the coast of Massachusetts.

> OYSTER BAY, N.Y., Sept. 27 — The President will depart before noon tomorrow for a stay of nearly forty-eight hours with the North Atlantic Fleet off Provincetown, Mass. The yacht Mayflower, on which he will make the journey from Oyster Bay to the Massachusetts coast, arrived here to-night.
>
> It had been suggested that in the event of conditions at Havana assuming what might be considered a really desperate status, Mr. Roosevelt's visit to the fleet might be abandoned or postponed. It was said at the executive offices to-night, however, that there did not seem to be any chance that a change of plans would be made.
>
> As the Mayflower and the ships of Admiral Evans's fleet are equipped with wireless telegraphy outlets, the journey does not mean that the President will be even for a brief time beyond the reach of his Commissioners in Cuba should they desire to consult him. *(NY Times*, September 28, 1906)

On September 28, the President, prior to leaving Oyster Bay, sent two telegrams to Secretary Taft. One more was sent to Taft from the Mayflower.

To William Howard Taft	Roosevelt Mss.
Telegram	Oyster Bay, September 28, 1906

Your telegram of September 27th received. It is very difficult for me from here to understand exactly the needs of the situation and therefore why one course is better than another. My offhand judgment is that it would be better to follow your first impulse and agree to the formation of a provisional government under a provisional president in spite of its not being constitutional. Upon my word I do not see that with Cuba in the position it is we need bother our heads much about the exact way in which the Cubans observe or do not observe so much of their own constitution as does not concern us. Certainly the constitution will come to an end if President Palma resigns and leaves his office while there is not a quorum of Congress to accept his resignation. Neither do I understand why the fact that the government is not within the Constitution, as you say, would alter our control of the situation for pacification. I think it would be a misfortune for us to undertake to form a provisional government if there was a fair chance of obtaining peace by allowing the Cubans themselves to form their own provisional government.

Remember that we have to do not only what is best for the island, but what we can get public sentiment in this country to support, and there will be very grave dissatisfaction here with our intervention unless we can show clearly that we have exhausted every method by which it is possible to obtain peace and the perpetuation of the government with some show of order prior to our taking control ourselves...I feel very strongly that any provisional government which offers any reasonable chance of securing peace should be tried and any scheme for such a provisional government encouraged before we take control of the government ourselves. I do not think that we should take such control except as a last resort, and after every other expedient for securing pacification has been attempted...

| To William Howard Taft | Roosevelt Mss. |
| Telegram | Oyster Bay, September 28, 1906 |

As you say matters change like a kaleidoscope, so any advice from me is apt to be just several hours late...if we have to intervene I shall not object to any additional proof that the intervention was inevitable. If it were possible to tide over affairs for two or three days until I could be back in Washington I should be glad. This is of course not essential. I am about to leave on the *Mayflower* for the battleship target practice, but can be reached constantly thru the wireless telegraph. It seems to me that it might be well under the circumstances to land an ample garrison of marines for Havana, probably to take possession of Moro Castle. I suppose this could be done with Palma's full consent. As far as possible, however, avoid the use of the word intervention, and if this is not possible and we have to name our own provisional government, then emphasize the fact that our action is only temporary and that we are landing troops to secure pacification and set the Cuban government going again. Do not, however, make any promise as to the withdrawal of the troops...

(*The Letters of Theodore Roosevelt*)

Secretary Taft's cables arrived to Oyster Bay and from there they were transmitted by Acting Secretary Latta to the Commandant at the Second Naval Station in Newport, Rhode Island. Although Mr. Roosevelt was at sea, Mr. Taft's telegrams were sent by wireless telegraphy from the Naval Station to the *Mayflower*. The President's replies were sent in the reverse direction to Assistant Secretary Latta at the Executive Office in Oyster Bay. From there, they were then forwarded to Secretary Taft in Cuba. The Executive Office was vital in maintaining the link between the President and Secretary Taft at this crucial moment.

TELEGRAM.

White house,
Washington.

The President   Oyster Bay, N.Y., September 28, 1906.
Care Commandant, Second Naval Station,
     Newport, Rhode Island.

     Please have following message from Secretary Taft transmitted to the President on board the Mayflower which left Oyster Bay about twelve o'clock to-day for target grounds:

"The President:

"Situation now likely to be this. Congress called at two P.M. will not have a quorum; President will wait until four and then will send word to me that Congress had not met, that he now presents his resignation to me and asks me to intervene to protect life and property. Shall land forces and proclaim in your name provisional government according to terms of former telegrams unless you direct otherwise. No other course seems open to Bacon and me. Merely landing troops without establishing provisional government would hardly result in insurgents giving up arms as we hope provisional government will.

TAFT."

M.C. LATTA,
Acting Secretary.

Official.

(TR Papers, Series 1, Reel 68)

Assistant Secretary Latta cabled the following to Mr. Taft at 9 P.M. on September 28.

TELEGRAM.

𝕿𝖍𝖊 𝖂𝖍𝖎𝖙𝖊 𝕳𝖔𝖚𝖘𝖊,

𝖂𝖆𝖘𝖍𝖎𝖓𝖌𝖙𝖔𝖓.

Oyster Bay, N.Y.,
September 28, 1906.

Taft, Havana

All your dispatches of today have been forwarded to the President by wireless, the following received from him prior to the receipt by him of your last cable including proclamation.

M.C. LATTA,
Acting Secretary.

(TR Papers, Series 1, Reel 68)

The telegram which Mr. Latta referred to was the following from the President. In it, the President replied to Secretary Taft with permission to land forces and establish a provisional government.

To William Howard Taft   Roosevelt Mss.
Telegram   Aboard the *Mayflower*, September 28, 1906

All right land forces and issue proclamation as suggested in my name, but if possible emphasize fact that you are landing only at Palma's request and because there is no Government left so that it is imperative to establish one and to land forces to protect life and property, also tell that the Government you form is only provisional and temporary until Cubans can form one for themselves. I suppose you will get insurgents to disperse by telling them you will carry out substantially the agreement to which they once before assented.

(*The Letters of Theodore Roosevelt*)

Unfortunately, when this cable was sent by Mr. Latta to Mr. Taft, the President had not yet received Mr. Taft's latest cable. That cable contained several messages including one containing the form of the proclamation which Mr. Taft would issue when he established the provisional government.

Executive Office,
Oyster Bay, Sept. 28th,
via Newport, R.I., 29th.

President,
U.S.S. Mayflower,
Provincetown, Mass.

In view of your telegram today shall not act until we have submitted the whole matter to you. Taft.

The President.

Situation entirely changed this morning. Zayas and some of the moderates have attempted to get together agreement to select Zayas or Senquilly or Menocal President, and Zayos came on to see whether we would object to the agreements. We said we would object to no agreement of any sort which would bring about peace, that we had no private opinion in compromise suggested by us, but they might make any agreement they chose if it only brought about peace.

Following this Menocal and Agramente called to ask in respect to the same thing and we said the same thing to them.

We then received a call from General (*illegible*) of the moderate party in which he said that the election of Zayas, or Senquilly or Menocal to succeed Palma was utterly absurd, that what the moderate party would do would be to convene congress, receive the resignation of President Palma and appoint a committee to ask him not to resign; that he would decline to reconsider; that they would then return to congress, break the quorum and disappear.

He said they wanted intervention, that there was no other solution. He told Steinhart while here that while the moderates wanted intervention, they did not want it to appear that they were asking for it.

The situation probably developed by Andrade will probably be consummated tonight or tomorrow morning, then action must follow.
Taft.

The President:

Following form of proclamation in case we must establish provisional government is suggested:

"To the People of Cuba.

"The failure of Congress to act on the irrevocable resignation of the President of the Republic of Cuba or to elect a successor at this time when great disorder prevails in the country, requires that, pursuant to a request of President Palma preferred to the President of the United States, the necessary steps be by this proclamation, in the name and by the authority of the President of the United States to restore order, protect life and property in the Island of Cuba and Islands and Keys adjacent thereto, and for this purpose to establish therein a Provisional Government.

"The Provisional Government hereby established will be maintained only long enough to restore order and peace and public confidence, and then hold such elections as may be necessary to determine those persons to whom the permanent Government of the Republic should be turned back.

"In so far as it is consistent with the nature of a provisional government the constitution of Cuba will be observed; it will be a Cuban government as far as possible, and the mere continuance of the one for which it is temporarily substituted. All the Executive Departments will be as under President Palma, the courts will continue to administer justice and all laws not in their nature applicable by the reason of the temporary and emergent character of the government.

"President Roosevelt has been most anxious to bring about peace under the constitutional government of Cuba, and has made every endeavor to avoid the present steps. Longer delay, however, would be dangerous.

"In view of the resignation of the Cabinet, until further notice, the heads of all departments of the central government will report to me for instruction, including General Alejandro Rodriguez in command of the Rural Guard and other regular government forces, and General Carlos Roloff, treasurer of Cuba.

"Until further notice the civil governors and Alcaldes will also report to me for instruction.

"...I ask all citizens and residents of Cuba to assist in the work of restoring order, tranquility, and public confidence. Signed William H. Taft, Secretary of War of the United States Provisional Government (Governor ?) of Cuba."

Havana. Cuba,
        September 28, 1906.

(TR Papers, Series 1, Reel 68)

By September 28 then, it was clear that Secretary Taft would appoint himself Military Governor of Cuba with a proclamation being issued the following day.

HAVANA, Sept. 28 — President Palma will start for New York to-morrow via Matanzas, leaving Secretary of War Taft in charge. It is assumed that Mr. Taft will declare himself Military Governor of Cuba. He has advised Gen.

Rodriguez, Chief of the military forces in Havana, and Gen. Agramonte, Chief of Police, to report to him and watch the city's safety.

Thirty American marines have been landed to guard the Treasury, and it is expected that more will be landed in the course of the night...

...Cuba's last hope of a avoiding American intervention disappeared to-night, when, after President Palma had refused to reconsider his resignation, the supporters of the Government decided not to attend the adjourned session of Congress at 9 P.M.

Cuba is without a President, a Vice-President, or Cabinet officers, and Congress has refused to appoint officials to take their places. The taking over of the Government by the United States therefore became inevitable...

...The proclamation to be issued to-day will be signed by Secretary Taft in virtue of the authority vested in him by President Roosevelt. It will appoint the Secretary provisional Military Governor of Cuba. He will immediately assume full control of the Government and retain it until he deems the country to be sufficiently pacified for civil government, whereupon he will call Beekman Winthrop, at present Governor of Porto Rico, to act as Civil Governor here...*(NY Times*, September 29, 1906)

The flurry of telegrams between President Roosevelt and Secretary Taft continued throughout the night of September 28 and into the early morning of September 29.

NEWPORT, R.I., Saturday, Sept. 29 — The Naval Station here was in constant communication with the President's yacht Mayflower, on which Mr. Roosevelt is traveling to Provincetown, from the time she passed through the Race, short-ly before 7 o'clock last night, until early this morning. The operators here sent a large number of dispatches to the Mayflower, presumably in regard to the Cuban situation...*(NY Times*, September 30, 1906)

The telegrams exchanged between President Roosevelt and Secretary Taft on September 29th gave the Secretary the final approval to establish the provisional government and to land marines at once.

To Maurice C. Latta   Roosevelt Mss.
Telegram   Aboard the *Mayflower*, September 29, 1906

Cable Taft as follows: President sends following by wireless
Two telegrams received. Am much pleased. Earnestly hope the Cuban parties can be persuaded themselves to agree on provisional government of some kind that will ensure peace...I approve the form of proclamation you suggest. If we must establish provisional government of course you can land force at any time no matter what government is inaugurated, if you think situation requires it and I suppose from what you say that such will be the case, but I earnestly hope you can persuade the parties themselves to agree on a temporary provi-sional government which if necessary we can supervise until the elections you have planned can be held.

(The Letters of Theodore Roosevelt)

Mr. Latta cabled another telegram from Mr. Taft to the President, this one enclosing President Palma's letter of resignation.

Just Received,-

Havana.

To President.

Congress will not elect a successor to Palma. An earnest effort has been made to agree upon a person and a compromise but it has failed. Congress meets at nine o'clock tonight and will not have a quorum. Palma will send a letter to us as follows:

> "The embarrassing position in which I have been placed on account
> of the non election of a person to succeed me in the office of
> President of the Republic, the irrevocable resignation which I
> have presented to Congress oblige me to submit to you the follow-
> ing:- It is absolutely essential for my peace of mind that I de-
> liver the national funds amounting to thirteen millions, six hun-
> dred and twenty five thousand, five hundred and thirty nine dol-
> lars, to a responsible person; that it is also of urgent necessi-
> ty to disband the militia hastily organized as an auxiliary force
> and the support of which daily costs the States many thousands of
> dollars; that it is not possible to discharge this militia so long
> as rebels do not disband it being of the highest importance
> that the latter be compelled to lay down their arms and all return
> quietly to their homes; that otherwise, Cuban social conditions
> will continue in their present chaotic state with all business
> paralyzed, the spirits of all troubled and restless, the lives and
> property of citizens at the mercy of anarchy and every one lacking
> confidence in the future. As a patriot and decided lover of peace
> and order, and anxious that the guarantees of all the
> inhabitants reign anew in Cuba, I have considered it my
> imperative duty to lay the above before you, so that the
> unfortunate condition through which my country passes may
> be terminated."

I shall surround treasury with marines tonight and should be glad to hear from you as early as possible tomorrow. If provisional government is established under a proclamation like that sent you should like to insert in it statement that the Cuban flag will still fly over all public buildings.

Taft.

Signed M.C. Latta,
Act'g Sec'y.

(TR Papers, Series 1, Reel 68)

Assistant Secretary Latta cabled the President's reply to Mr. Taft.

To Maurice C. Latta	Roosevelt Mss.
Telegram	Aboard the *Mayflower*, September 29, 1906

Cable Taft as follows:

Your cable containing Palma's message received. You have done all in your power to get Cubans to establish their own government. You can now do nothing but establish provisional government, as you suggest. I approve your proclamation with insertion of statement that the Cuban flag will fly over all public buildings. Land marines at once to guard treasury, and of course I presume also to take possession of forts and guard the water works. I hope you can convince the insurgents that it is to their interest to lay down arms at once as we intend immediately to hold a new election and that they will have practically all the advantages they would have had if Palma had gone into the original agreement to which they assented.

(*The Letters of Theodore Roosevelt*)

On September 29, 1906, William H. Taft, Secretary of War of the United States, declared himself Provisional Governor of Cuba. He issued the following proclamation, the text of which had been approved by the President in the telegram sent to Taft earlier in the same day:

"To the People of Cuba: The failure of Congress to act on the irrevocable resignation of the President of the Republic of Cuba or to elect a successor leaves the country without a Government at a time when great disorder prevails, and requires that, pursuant to the request of Mr. Palma, the necessary steps be taken in the name and by the authority of the President of the United States to restore order and protect life and property in the Island of Cuba and the islands and keys adjacent thereto, and for this purpose to establish therein a Provisional Government.

"The Provisional Government hereby established will be maintained only long enough to restore order, peace, and public confidence, by direction of and in the name of the President of the United States, and then to hold such elections as may be necessary to determine on those persons upon whom the permanent Government of the republic should be devolved.

"In so far as is consistent with the nature of the provisional Government established under the authority of the United States this will be a Cuban Government, conforming with the Constitution of Cuba. The Cuban flag will be hoisted as usual over the Government buildings of the island, all the executive departments and provincial and municipal governments, including that of the City of Havana, will continue to be administered as under the Cuban Republic; the courts will continue to administer justice, and all the laws not in their nature inapplicable by reason of the temporary and emergent character of the Government will be in force.

"President Roosevelt has been most anxious to bring about peace under the constitutional Government of Cuba, and he made every endeavor to avoid the present step. Longer delay, however, would be dangerous in view of the resignation of the Cabinet...

"...I ask all citizens and residents of Cuba to assist me in the work of restoring order, tranquility, and public confidence.

"WILLIAM H. TAFT,

"Secretary of War, United States; Provisional Governor of Cuba.

"Havana, Sept. 29, 1906."

Also on September 29, Mr. Taft cabled Oyster Bay requesting that six thousand troops should be sent to Cuba.

xxxxxxxxxxxxxxxxxxx Havana, September 29, 1906.

The President:

    Oyster Bay.

"Think that six thousand troops should come. This would be one expedition. Am hopeful that all difficulties can be composed but it would be wise to have that number of troops for occupation of Island. They can be used to garrison towns and the rural guard used for predatory bands that are quite certain to infest the Island no matter how complete and successful the surrender of the insurgents may be. There is possibility as suggested in my last telegram that we may have some difficulty with militia. All these things require in my judgement sending of troops. Plan I suggest contemplates release of marines and navy which will of course not wish to stay in the waters in such force as now.

TAFT."

Latta,

Acting Secretary.

(TR Papers, Series 1, Reel 68)

The text of this cable was sent to the President on board the Mayflower, passing Newport, R.I. with the additional information that the War Department was trying to reach the President all day.

President Roosevelt sent approval for the troops and his congratulations to Secretary Taft immediately upon returning to Oyster Bay on September 30.

To William Howard Taft   Roosevelt Mss.
Telegram   Oyster Bay, September 30, 1906

Have directed that the six thousand men go to you. You might announce that they are to relieve the sailors and marines. This might make it a little easier as regards any Cuban insurgents who may wish an excuse to be suspicious of our good faith...I congratulate you heartily upon the admirable way you handled the whole matter. It is another great public service you have rendered. Will you also congratulate Bacon most heartily for me upon what he has done? ...Have directed the State Department to continue Cuban foreign relations, consuls and ministers as if no change had occurred.

(*The Letters of Theodore Roosevelt*)

Later that same day, he returned to Washington.

OYSTER BAY, N.Y., Sept 30 — President Roosevelt returned to Oyster Bay on the Mayflower at 10:30 A.M. to-day. He had been afloat forty-eight hours and had witnessed the target practice of the North Atlantic Fleet off Cape Cod. The Mayflower dropped anchor at the entrance to Oyster Bay half an hour ahead of scheduled time. It is understood that the Cuban situation influenced the President to hasten his return.

Acting Secretary Latta went at once to Sagamore Hill with lengthy cables from Havana. He remained with the President throughout the day, and to-night announced that the President had no statement to make on the situation and that nothing in the dispatches received could be made public...

...Work at the "Summer capital" came to an end to-night. The executive staff, with the office outfit, will go to Washington with the President...

(*NY Times*, September 30, 1906)

The Summer of 1907

The arrival of the President for his Summer vacation in 1907, is described as follows:

> President Roosevelt is again at Sagamore Hill, Secretary Loeb is again at his suite of offices in the Moore Building with his corps of assistants, and Oyster Bay has been metamorphosed from an ordinary village to the seat of government of the greatest country on the face of the earth. This change took place on Wednesday afternoon, and so quietly did it occur that the usual routine of business was not disjointed in the least. Flags were displayed on many dwellings and business houses, and unusual activity was noticeable among the old occupants of the band wagon, to whom the Presidential salutation acts, not alone as nourishment, but as an inflator. The time of and the route of the President's arrival was not generally known but, a crowd gathered at the station at about three p.m., and waited until after five before the special train arrived. There was no roping out the ordinary citizens to make room for the parade of a few self-appointed masters of ceremonies, and every man, woman and child were afforded an equal opportunity to see their townsman, the President. (*Oyster Bay Guardian*, June 14, 1907)

The summer of 1907 was quite different from those that preceded it. Although the usual business of government continued from Sagamore Hill and Moore's Building, the President's schedule was not filled with international peace conferences or urgent crises. At the beginning of the summer, Secretary Loeb even predicted that the vacation of 1907 would be "very quiet." *(NY Times*, June 14, 1907)

> OYSTER BAY, L.I., June 13 — This was President Roosevelt's first day here of what he intends shall be his longest vacation at his old home since he became President. Secretary Loeb, who has rented a cottage for the season, says that this resting time of the President will be "very quiet." But Oyster Bay isn't quiet. It has just awakened for the year. The coming of Oyster Bay's most distinguished son starts the village on a round of commercial and social activity...
>
> ...The clerical staff of the President got settled this morning in its old quarters at the Moore building in the main street. The executive officers received a first visit from the "Woman in Blue," understood to be Mrs. Lucy Lee of Brooklyn. She examined the water front, and then went to the Executive offices, where she left her regards for the secret service men.
>
> The President spent most of the day reading over his mail with Secretary Loeb, unpacking, and helping in the arrangements of the household effects...*(NY Times*, June 14, 1907)

321

A small controversy erupted in the press on June 15 when Governor Terrell of Georgia and Commissioner Mitchell of the Georgia Commission accused the President of interrupting their speeches with calls of "Cut it short!" or "Cut it out!" during Georgia Day at Jamestown Exposition on June 13. Assistant Secretary Latta issued a statement denying this from the Executive office. *(NY Times,* June 15, 1907)

On June 15, 1907 the President received a long telegram from Governor Terrell of Georgia "relieving him of any responsibility in cutting the exercises short on Georgia Day, and giving him entire credit for the success of that occasion. The exercises were cut...because the review took longer than expected." *(NY Times,* June 16, 1907)

On June 15, 1907, the Chicago Board of Trade appealed to President Roosevelt to intervene to prevent a strike by the Western Union telegraphers. The appeal was sent by telegram, received presumably at Moore's Building and forwarded to the President at Sagamore Hill.

CHICAGO, June 15 — Interest in the threatened strike of the Western Union telegraphers led President Hiam N. Sager of the Board of Trade to-day to call a meeting of the Directors, who sent the following telegram to President Roosevelt, at Oyster Bay:

The Board of Trade especially requests the President of the United States to take such steps as in his judgment may seem advisable to avert impending disastrous interference with legitimate business by reason of the proposed telegraphers' strike. It is the judgment of this board that such strike would result in serious and widespread injury to the commerce of this country. *(NY Times,* June 16, 1907)

On June 16, it was announced that the President had referred all appeals regarding the impending telegraphers' strike to Commissioner of Labor Charles P. Neill.

OYSTER BAY, June 16 — President Roosevelt has referred to Commissioner of Labor Charles P. Neill, without comment, the various appeals which have been made to him by wire and mail to intervene to prevent the threatened telegraphers' strike.

The position is taken that no emergency exists, such as obtained at the time the President intervened in the anthracite coal strike, but, on the contrary, the situation presented is one where action by the Government, if taken at all, may properly be initiated and directed by the Bureau of Labor...*(NY Times,* June 17, 1907)

On June 18, 1907 Secretary Loeb issued a statement denying that President Roosevelt meddled in the New York apportionment fight.

OYSTER BAY, L.I., June 18 — A disclaimer of any activity on the part of President Roosevelt in the New York apportionment fight was made by Secretary Loeb to-day upon his return to the executive offices from Sagamore Hill. The secretary said:

"These statements that have been published in the newspapers, that the President has interfered in any way in the apportionment matter, are so absurd that it is hardly worth while to notice them. The President has not only taken no hand one way or the other, but he has not the slightest knowledge of either scheme of apportionment, and has not only never expressed any opinion, but has not been consulted about either plan. If he had been consulted he would, of course, have declined to express any opinion whatever concerning either." *(NY Times,* June 19, 1907)

The President met with U.S. Senator Albert Beveridge of Indiana on June 18, 1907. They discussed the proposed inheritance tax, a matter which interested the President and which the Senator was about to study. *(NY Times,* June 19, 1907)

On June 18, 1907, Sir Chentung Liang Cheng, the retiring Chinese Minister to the United States announced that he had received a message from Secretary of State Root. The message was regarding the indemnity charged to China for losses incurred by the United States Government and its citizen's private property resulting from the Boxer Rebellion. The President directed Secretary Root to inform the Chinese Minister that in the next annual message to Congress, the President would recommend that China be relieved of all obligation to pay the amount in excess of the final revised indemnity. The initial indemnity agreed upon was approximately $24,000,000 plus 4% interest. The revised indemnity was approximately $11,000,000. The President's recommendation, if approved by Congress, would thus save China a substantial sum of money. *(NY Times,* June 19, 1907)

FIGURE 31: A Luncheon at Sagamore Hill.
Courtesy Theodore Roosevelt Collection, Harvard College Library

On June 20, 1907, Frank Philbrick, a Cheyenne Indian from North Dakota who had worked for the President on his ranch, tried to see the President "on a matter of great importance to himself, which he wished the President to adjust, but was turned away by Secretary Loeb..." On the same day the President acted on a number of pardon cases and signed the commissions of some postmasters. *(NY Times, June 21, 1907)*

On June 21 it was reported that U.S. Labor Commissioner Neill succeeded in preventing the strike by the Western Union telegraphers.

> The efforts of United States Labor Commissioner Neill, who came here from Washington as the representative of President Roosevelt to investigate troubles between the telegraphers and the Western Union Company, led yesterday to a satisfactory settlement of the trouble, and the strike which had been voted against the Western Union Company and which would have involved, it is believed, the Postal Company as well, was averted. The strike was to have been called in San Francisco between June 24 and 28...*(NY Times, June 21, 1907)*

On June 24, 1907, President Roosevelt "instructed the Secretary of Commerce and Labor to have the Census Bureau make a special enumeration of the inhabitants of the proposed State of Oklahoma to determine the population of the proposed new State and its distribution among the territorial sub-divisions." *(NY Times, June 25, 1907)*

Also on June 24, President Roosevelt signed "the Dominican Treaty. The convention, which regulates customs matters between the United States and Santo Domingo, was negotiated Feb. 8 last, by the plenipotentiaries of the two countries, and has since been approved by the United States Senate and the legislative body of Santo Domingo. The President's signature is understood to be the last step necessary to make the convention operative." *(NY Times, June 25, 1907)*

On June 25, "Secretary Taft spent four hours with President Roosevelt...He said as he left Oyster Bay to return to the Yale Commencement that a number of important matters relative to Cuba, Panama, and the Philippines had been decided. The public announcement relative to these matters, he said, would come when the appropriate orders were issued on his return to Washington." *(NY Times, June 26, 1907)*

On June 27, "President Roosevelt...entertained a luncheon party which consisted of a member of his Cabinet, members of the Diplomatic Corps, representatives of the army and navy, and distinguished authors. Sir Chentung Liang-Cheng, the Chinese Minister, bore the personal thanks of his Emperor for the generosity of the United States in remitting the greater part of the Chinese indemnity." *(NY Times, June 28, 1907)*

On June 29, "In accordance with directions from President Roosevelt, Secretary Taft...instructed Gov. Magoon to purchase all the church property in Cuba in the diocese of Havana, according to the original recommendations. This action was taken despite strong protests from Cuba to the effect that the price asked by the Church was excessive and it would be a bad bargain to make the purchase." *(NY Times, June 30, 1907)*

In a letter from the Japanese Chamber of Commerce in Tokyo directed to President Roosevelt and the American Chambers of Commerce, the Japanese implied that they would boycott American goods if something wasn't done to ameliorate the tension between a section of the community in San Francisco and the Japanese residents there. This tension had exposed the Japanese residents and their property to serious danger. *(NY Times, July 1, 1907)*

On July 1, "President Roosevelt accepted the resignation of Postmaster W.R. Wilcox" of New York City. *(NY Times, July 2, 1907)*

On July 2, U.S. Congressman Herbert Parsons wrote to Secretary Loeb regarding his upcoming visit to Sagamore Hill. Mr. Parsons refers to Postmaster Wilcox and the man destined to replace him, Edward R. Morgan. Mr. Morgan would be appointed Postmaster of New York City on August 14, 1907.

HERBERT PARSONS

13 ᵀᴴ DISTRICT

NEW YORK

house of Representatives U.S.
Washington, D.C. at 52 William Street,
NEW YORK, N.Y.

July 2, 1907.

Hon. William Loeb, Jr.,
     Secretary to the President,
        Oyster Bay, N.Y.
Dear Mr. Loeb:

    I thank you for your letter of July 1st. It will, in fact, suit me much better to come on Friday, the 12th, rather than on Tuesday, the 9th. I shall certainly take the 8:50 train, among other things for the pleasure of riding out to Sagamore Hill with you. It will embarrass me somewhat to have Wilcox present. He will not echo any of my ideas and will be inclined to knock any of my suggestions, but I will make good use of the hours before he comes.

    There seems to be an intention on the part of some of the President's enemies to weaken me in the matter even if I should urge the appointment of Morgan, as anyone can tell by reading the news articles in The Sun. I am told that every Odell-Quigg man wants Morgan appointed. They could ask nothing better.

    ...The President will shortly receive a request from the business men of the 23rd Assembly District. Investigation will probably disclose that the meeting was held at Morgan's own political club in that district, was attended by political heelers and that a majority of the committee are the same. I believe that my classmate, ex-Assemblyman William H. Smith, who is a lawyer, Judge William H. Olmstead, and one or two other professional men are the moving spirits on the committee. I do not know that the President has heard from the Hon. George E. Bidwell, but Bidwell is strongly for Morgan.

                      Very truly yours,

                      Herbert Parsons

Enclosures.

(TR Papers, Series 1, Reel 75)

Mr. Parsons wrote to Secretary Loeb again on July 3.

HERBERT PARSONS

13 <u>TH</u> DISTRICT

NEW YORK

house of Representatives U.S.

Washington, D.C. at 52 William Street,

NEW YORK, N.Y.

July 3, 1907.

Hon. William Loeb, Jr.,
    Secretary to the President,
      Oyster Bay, N.Y.

My dear Mr. Loeb:

    Enclosed I return you the further letters in behalf of Mr. Morgan that came with your letter of July 2nd.

    Mr. Smith correctly states the situation in the last primary and at the time I was first elected President of the Republican County Committee. However, even some of those who now favor Mr. Morgan last summer put me wise to the fact that while Smith was for us there would be a question whether some of the Smith delegation from that district would not be against us. Even Quigg was helpful in our first battle. The fact is, however, that during the past year those men who have recently come into politics and are known as Parsons men have almost without exception had very inconsiderate treatment at the hands of Mr. Morgan.

    I cannot agree with the Postmaster-General that the appointment of Mr. Morgan rather than that of some other man would bring extra apportionment for New York. I suppose that no one questions that Postmaster Wilcox accomplished more for New York than Morgan could have done. From what I know of Mr. Morgan I should think he would be weakest where the Postmaster General would expect him to be the strongest.

    These letters remind me of an even superior lot of letters that were recently written in behalf of the re-appointment of a local public official. I never saw greater encomiums from a finer body of thoughtful and independent citizens who were confident they knew whereof they spoke. Morally I was certain that the man was a crook, as were others who really knew him. We could not prove it and so he was re-appointed. I allude to this not to denominate Morgan a crook, altho I may have heard as bad things as that said of him. There is a humor in the information contained in the letter of M.T. Richardson where he says he does not believe Morgan is a politician!

    I have carefully told Morgan's friends that I was carefully looking into the matter, as I am. I seem to be getting some information that has not been furnished the President.

        Very truly yours,

        Herbert Parsons

Enclosures.

(TR Papers, Series 1, Reel 75)

On July 4, 1907, Secretary Loeb gave out an official statement regarding the establishment of a Pacific Fleet. Many people assumed that the rumors stating that a new fleet would be stationed in the Pacific was in response to Japanese threats of a boycott of American goods. However, the eventual transglobal voyage of the "Great White Fleet" was clearly intended to show American naval strength to the entire world and to establish the United States as one of the pre-eminent naval powers.

OYSTER BAY, N.Y., July 4 — The basis of the reports that a fleet of American battleships is to be stationed in the Pacific is probably explained in an official statement made public at the Executive Offices here to-day...

...The official statement, as given out by Secretary Loeb, follows:

"There is no intention of sending a fleet at once to the Pacific. For the last two years the Administration has been perfecting its plans to arrange for a long ocean cruise of the battleship fleet, when a sufficient number of warships are gathered. This cruise may possibly be to the Pacific, but might possibly be only to the Mediterranean, or the South Atlantic. It may possibly take place this Winter, but, on the hand, it may not be convenient to arrange it until later. In any event, after a few months, the fleet will be brought back together to the Atlantic Coast."

"Whether the voyage is made or not, whether the fleet stays in the Atlantic or goes to the Pacific, will be determined simply as a matter of routine in the management and drill of the navy. It is now part of the settled policy of the Navy Department, in its effort to keep the navy up to the highest point of efficiency, always to keep the battleships together, maneuvering as a fleet composed of several squadrons, and it is desirable that this fleet should, from time to time, take a long voyage.

"The relations between the United States and all other powers never were more peaceful and friendly..." *(NY Times, July 5, 1907)*

On July 7, 1907, Rear Admiral Brownson made some additional comments regarding the contemplated movement of the Atlantic Battleship Fleet.

OYSTER BAY, July 7 — ...Admiral Brownson came to Oyster Bay on Friday to take luncheon with the President, professing entire ignorance of the new navy plans.

When he left Sagamore Hill to take the train for Washington the Admiral had one idea which he wished emphasized — that it was desirable and important to demonstrate to the world how quickly the American navy could transfer its fighting strength from one ocean to the other. This was distinctly an addition to the President's previous statement issued through Secretary Loeb, in which the object of the voyage was said to be to perfect the navy's training in fleet exercise on an extended scale, the purpose of the plan being for the benefit of the navy alone.

What came from President Roosevelt through Admiral Brownson is decidedly a different and much broader design. President Roosevelt has been consistent in advocating a large navy as the surest guarantee of peace between the United States and all foreign powers. Heretofore a large navy has been reckoned solely from the point of view of the number of ships, their tonnage, armor, guns, and fighting capacity. With this idea the American Navy has grown steadily, ship by ship.

In addition to the array of ships and tonnage, the President now proposes to give the world a somewhat startling demonstration of what the American Navy is capable of doing to protect either or both of the extended shore lines of the United States...

...While it is asserted with all possible emphasis that there is no foundation for apprehension of trouble, immediate or future, between the United States and Japan, the proposed demonstration with the fleet can be looked upon in no other light than that President Roosevelt intends to use the American Navy for exactly that purpose for which he has advocated its augmentation — a guarantee of international peace...*(NY Times*, July 8, 1907)

On July 8, 1907, it was announced from Washington that the government would issue injunctions and appoint receivers to bring down corporations in violation of the Sherman Anti-Trust Law. Until this point, the Government could merely impose fines against corporate violators. The new policy was recommended by Milton Purdy of the Department of Justice, accepted by Attorney General Bonaparte, and enthusiastically supported by President Roosevelt. The President's correspondence with Attorney General Bonaparte show the President's involvement in this new policy. *(NY Times*, July 9, 1907)

On July 9, 1907, "President Roosevelt...received the report of the Inter-State Commerce Commission setting forth the facts and the conclusions arrived at as a result of the investigation of E.H. Harriman's alleged stock manipulations...A copy of the report also has been sent to Attorney General Bonaparte, and the statement was made...by Secretary Loeb that Mr. Bonaparte's recommendations as to future proceedings by the Government in the matter doubtless would be awaited by the President before he directed any further move..." *(NY Times*, July 10, 1907)

On July 11, 1907, "Congressman Herbert Parsons...held a conference with President Roosevelt, presumably on the appointment of a Postmaster for this city *(New York City)* to succeed William R. Wilcox, who resigned to become a Utilities Commissioner. Mr. Wilcox himself had a conference with the President on the same subject a day or two ago." *(NY Times*, July 13, 1907)

On July 12, 1907, in an effort to determine the status of the relationship between Japan and the United States, the President met with Admiral Baron Yamamoto and Japanese Ambassador Aoki at Sagamore Hill. The political climate between Japan and the United States was uncertain and many analysts were predicting that war between the two countries was imminent, especially after the announcement that the Atlantic Fleet would be sent to the Pacific.

OYSTER BAY, L.I., July 12 — After the visit of Admiral Yamamoto and Japanese Ambassador Aoki to Sagamore Hill to-day President Roosevelt issued the following statement through Secretary Loeb:

"The President had a long interview with Admiral Baron Yamamoto, and it was most satisfactory in every way. It simply confirms (what had already been made clear by Ambassador Aoki) the thoroughly good understanding between the two Governments and the fundamental friendliness between the two nations." *(NY Times*, July 13, 1907)

On July 17, 1907, "President Roosevelt, Senator Hopkins of Illinois, and H.E. Miles, representing the Wisconsin Tariff Revision League, discussed the subject of tariff revision at luncheon at Sagamore Hill...Senator Hopkins, on leaving Oyster Bay, said that the conclusion was reached that no tariff revision should be undertaken until after the next Presidential election." *(NY Times*, July 18, 1907)

Rudolph Forster, Assistant Secretary in Oyster Bay, was by this time considered to be one of the most powerful man at the White House.

> WASHINGTON, July 18 — For the next sixty days the National Government will be run by proxy. With the departure of Secretary Cortelyou and Postmaster General Meyer from Washington for their Summer vacations, every responsible head of the Government is out of the city, and the weighty problems of state are being solved by the assistant Cabinet officers...
> ...The man who is all powerful at the White House during these hot days is Rudolph Forster, the assistant secretary to the President...It has been rumored that in the event of the retirement of Secretary Loeb next December Mr. Forster may go up one step higher. *(NY Times*, July 19, 1907)

On July 22, 1907 the age-old conflict between States' rights and the rights of the Federal Government flared anew as President Roosevelt began a legal contest to determine who had the ultimate authority to regulate the railroads.

> WASHINGTON, July 22 — President Roosevelt has sent Assistant Attorney General Sanford to Asheville to prepare for the important legal contest as to the scope of the Federal and State authorities over the railroads. It is now apparent that the controversy between the President and his legal advisors with the constitutional authorities who have taken issue with the policy of the Administration is to be carried to the Supreme Court of the United States for final settlement.
> This grows out of the decision of Judge Pritchard, who declared to-day at Asheville that the penalty clause of the North Carolina rate bill is unconstitutional and void...In this case the United States Supreme Court will have an opportunity to sustain the policy of the Administration as outlined by the President and Secretary Root.
> The President and Secretary Root have gone further in advocating an extension of the power of the Federal Government and depreciating the power of the States over common carriers than the most pronounced Federalists in the history of the country...*(NY Times*, July 23, 1907)

On July 23, Chief John Wilkie of the Secret Service wrote to Secretary Loeb regarding the possibility of members of certain anarchist societies attempting to assassinate the President or Secretary Taft.

TREASURY DEPARTMENT
OFFICE OF THE SECRETARY
WASHINGTON

July 23, 1907.

Dear Mr. Loeb:

I beg to acknowledge the receipt of your letter of July 22 enclosing Mr. Jenks' communication. The information in the possession of this office does not suggest any danger to either the President or Secretary Taft from any of the anarchist societies. An informant, who is in a position where he can get as much information as appears in the communication of Prof. Jenks, would certainly be able to get the names of those in the conspiracy and supply all of the information necessary to make a case.

The anarchist societies, as far as I have been able to ascertain, content themselves with talking about the removal of foreign rulers. There has been absolutely nothing in the last two years to cause the slightest suggestion of a "plot" against the President or any cabinet officer, and I am advised by an investigator who has been in close personal touch with the leading spirits, including the so called "terrorists," that any talk of a general meeting of a number of persons to formally decide upon the "removal" of the President or any other high official of this Government, is the veriest nonsense. Then too, we must give the radical branch of the Western Federation credit for having at least common sense, and it does not take much of a prophet to imagine the plight in which they would find themselves were there to be even a demonstration or attempt upon the life of the President or one of his cabinet officers following an adverse verdict at Boise. Every interest they have in the world would be centered in preventing an act of that kind.

We shall continue to make every effort to keep posted on the situation among the disaffected classes, and while our sources of information continue as satisfactory and dependable as they have been in the past, I shall have to ask that Mr. Jenks' informant be more specific before I can regard his information as worthy of serious consideration.

Respectfully,

John E. Wilkie

Chief.

Hon. William Loeb, Jr.,
     Secretary to the President.

On July 25, Mr. Wilkie wrote to Secretary Loeb regarding the President's trip to Provincetown.

TREASURY DEPARTMENT
OFFICE OF THE SECRETARY
WASHINGTON

July 25, 1907.

Dear Mr. Loeb:

I have your letter of July 24 relating to the Provincetown trip. I am leaving for the west today and do not expect to be back much before the last week of August. I think it can be arranged for Mr. Moran to go over and make a preliminary survey of the town, or, if he finds it impossible to get away, we will ask that Inspector Sutton make the trip, advising Mr. Sears in ample time so he can accompany whoever goes up.

Respectfully,

John E. Wilkie
Chief.

Hon. William Loeb, Jr.,
Secretary to the President.

(TR Papers, Series 1, Reel 75)

On July 29, 1907, "As the result of the visit to Sagamore Hill...of Acting Secretary of the Navy Newberry, President Roosevelt has informally approved the report of the board which investigated the disaster on the battleship Georgia, and indorsed a plan whereby a board of naval technical experts will be convened thoroughly to investigate the construction and operation of gun turrets on battleships with a view to providing every possible safeguard against explosions." *(NY Times, July 30, 1907)*

On July 31, 1907, the newly appointed territorial governor of New Mexico, George Curry, visited Sagamore Hill.

OYSTER BAY, July 31 — Radical reforms in the territorial government of New Mexico are to be inaugurated upon the arrival in Santa Fe of Gov. George Curry, who has just returned from the Philippines to assume that office. President Roosevelt conferred with Gov. Curry for two hours to-day, and sent him on his way thoroughly imbued with the necessity of ruling with an iron hand until the alleged tangle of intrigue and graft in New Mexico has been straightened out...

...Conferences on the situation in the Territories were continued at Sagamore Hill after the departure of Gov. Curry, as Chief Justice Kent of Arizona, and Federal Judge B.S. Rodey of Porto Rico, formerly Delegate in Congress from New Mexico, were luncheon guests of the President.

Judge Rodey told the President that the tax valuation in New Mexico had been outrageously juggled by the railroad and mining interests..." *(NY Times,* August 1, 1907)

On August 1, Secretary Loeb announced that there had been no change in plans for the Atlantic Fleet and that they were destined for the Pacific.

> OYSTER BAY, L.I., Aug. 1 — Secretary Loeb said to-day that there had been no change in the plans to send the Atlantic battleship fleet to the Pacific Ocean, and that the necessary preparations for the trip are now being made by the Navy Department. Upon their completion and approval by the President the voyage will be begun when the President gives the word.
>
> Mr. Loeb made this statement incidentally in saying that there is no foundation for the report that Secretary Metcalf had been or would be asked to resign from the Cabinet because of his announcement that the fleet will be in San Francisco Harbor in the near future. Mr. Loeb said there was no reason for criticizing Secretary Metcalf on account of his announcement. *(NY Times,* August 2, 1907)

On August 2, 1907, "President Roosevelt entertained at luncheon...Peter A. Jay of Rhode Island, the newly appointed Secretary to the American Embassy at Tokio, and Alfred W. Cooley, Assistant United States Attorney General. Mr. Cooley said he had several matters to go over with the President at the request of the Attorney General, and on leaving here said the President had discussed with him in a general way the North Carolina rate case." *(NY Times,* August 3, 1907)

On August 3, 1907, Judge Kenesaw M. Landis of the United States District Court...fined the Standard Oil Company $29,240,000, the extreme limit of the penalty fixed for the acceptance of illegal rebates. In the announcement he closes, so far as his court is concerned, what is regarded as the most important case against a trust in the history of the United States." *(NY Times,* August 4, 1907)

On August 4, 1907, it was reported that "the resolutions for an improvement in the present United States coinage and the enlargement of the Mint coin collection at Philadelphia, which were forwarded to President Roosevelt at Oyster Bay...by a committee of the American Numismatic Society...were favorably received, according to a letter received...by the secretary of the committee...from the President. The President says that he has called for a report on the resolutions from the Secretary of the Treasury..." *(NY Times,* August 5, 1907)

On August 7, William Taft, wrote to Secretary Loeb regarding the possible indictment of people who had furnished information leading to the fine levied against the Standard Oil Company.

WAR DEPARTMENT
WASHINGTON

Pointe-au-Pic, Canada,
August 7, 1907.

My dear Mr. Loeb:

This will introduce to you Mr. Shaw, a prominent lawyer of Chicago,
who is the counsel for the Chicago and Alton Road. He and Mr. Felton, the
President have just been to see me, and Shaw has made a statement to me which
I think in all fairness the President ought to hear, concerning the agreement
which was made between Shaw and Moody on one hand, and between Shaw and
Morrison as the District Attorney on the other, by which if the Chicago and
Alton officials furnished all the evidence in their power against the Standard Oil Company, ∧they should escape indictment. Judge Landis has called
the grand jury for the 14th of August and summoned witnesses to appear before it. My own judgement is that the President ought to request him,
through the District Attorney, to postpone this grand jury until the President can look into the question of whether in fact the agreement was made as
Mr. Shaw states, and then to consider the effect that the agreement ought to
have upon the prosecution of the Railroad Company.

Mr. Shaw will present this note in person and I hope you may be able to
arrange a meeting between him and the President, so that Shaw can state to
the President exactly what facts are as he knows them, and leave a memorandum of
them for future use.

Very sincerely yours,

Wm H. Taft

Hon. William Loeb, Jr.,
        Secretary to the President,
                Oyster Bay, New York.

(TR Papers, Series 1, Reel 76)

On August 9, 1907, "Attorney General Charles J. Bonaparte...went down to Oyster
Bay...and spent six hours in conference with President Roosevelt. At this conference,
Mr. Bonaparte admitted afterward, many subjects intimately concerning the Harriman
railroads and the Standard Oil Company were discussed...Among other things discussed
by the President and Mr. Bonaparte, according to the latter, was the prevalence of "land
frauds" in the West. There are a great many of these cases...and the President is much
interested in having them brought to light and the offenders criminally prosecuted..."
(NY Times, August 10, 1907)

On August 12, 1907, the New York Telegraphers Union announced that they would not strike until the results of a conference in Chicago between the Telegraphers' Union and the companies (Western Union and the Postal Company) were announced. It was hoped that the conference would effect a compromise acceptable to both sides thereby averting a general strike across the country. This conference was attended by United States Labor Commissioner Neill, President Samuel Gompers of the American Federation of Labor, and Ralph M. Easley of the National Civic Federation. It was rumored that President Roosevelt ordered Commissioner Neill to intervene but this was denied by Secretary Loeb in Oyster Bay.

> OYSTER BAY, L.I., Aug. 11 — President Roosevelt has not intervened in the strike, said Secretary Loeb to-night, when a dispatch from New York was shown to him asserting that United States Labor Commissioner Neill was proceeding to Chicago to effect a settlement of the telegraph strike at the direction of the President.
>
> Secretary Loeb said that the President had not requested Commissioner Neill to take action in the telegraph strike, nor had the Labor Commissioner communicated his plans to the President.
>
> Mr. Loeb added that Commissioner Neill had full authority to take whatever action he thought advisable in such matters. *(NY Times, August 12, 1907)*

Although the Presidential Election of 1908 was still more than one year away, the President had already begun preparations to insure that his preferred candidate, Secretary Taft, would become the Republican nominee.

> President Roosevelt, Secretary Taft, and Secretary Root will hold a conference to-day at Oyster Bay at which plans for the carrying on of the Taft Presidential boom and for the heading off, if possible, of the Hughes boom, will be discussed at length.
>
> Preparatory to the scheduled visit of Secretary Taft the President conferred yesterday with State Chairman Timothy L. Woodruff and William Barnes, Jr., as to the situation in New York State; with Republican National Committeeman Charles F. Brooker of Connecticut, and with the Fleischman brothers of Cincinnati.
>
> Mr. Taft will see the President to-day for the last time before taking his trip to the Philippines. While departmental matters are to be discussed to some extent, it is understood that the forthcoming National campaign will be the chief topic of conversation. *(NY Times, August 13, 1907)*

As the telegraphers' strike continued, at least in Chicago, the President continued to publicly deny any personal involvement in the negotiations to end it.

> OYSTER BAY, Aug. 14 — President Roosevelt will not concern himself personally with the telegraphers' strike according to the best information obtainable here to-night.
>
> Appeals to the President to take some action were received at the Executive office here to-day from Boards of Trade and commercial bodies in many cities. The applications were similar in character to those formulated yesterday by the

Chicago Board of Trade. Each emphasized the importance of direct action by the President.

These communications have been referred to Commissioner of Labor Charles P. Neill. It is understood that no instructions or recommendations have been forwarded to Neill. From the first he has been actively endeavoring to effect a settlement of the trouble. It is stated here that he has yet made no report to the President, nor has he received any messages from Mr. Roosevelt touching the matter at hand.

Mr. Neill's movements, however, have been closely followed, and while the direct statement is not made, the impression is given that in Mr. Neill's efforts the administration considers that the limit of its functions and authority in the matter is being exercised...*(NY Times*, August 15, 1907)

Also on August 14, 1907, President Roosevelt met with Assistant United States Attorney McHarg. It was agreed at this conference that the Federal investigations which were proceeding in New Mexico should be continued and that the Federal and Territorial offices could work together to weed out corruption and graft in the New Mexico Territory. *(NY Times*, August 15, 1907)

On August 23, 1907, it was announced that the Atlantic Fleet would indeed go to the Pacific in December.

> OYSTER BAY, N.Y., Aug. 23 — After President Roosevelt had held a long conference to-day with Assistant Secretary Newberry of the Navy Department, Rear Admiral W.H. Brownson, Chief of the Bureau of Navigation, and Rear Admiral Robley D. Evans, commander of the Atlantic Fleet, Secretary Loeb made formal announcement to-night that the Atlantic fleet will go to San Francisco some time in December, and that its route will be through the Straits of Megellan, and not the Suez Canal. The formal statement, issued after the conference between the President and Representatives of the Navy Department says:
>
> "A conference was held this afternoon between President Roosevelt, Assistant Secretary of the Navy Newberry, Rear Admiral Brownson, Chief of the Bureau of Navigation, and Rear Admiral Robley D. Evans, commander of the Atlantic Fleet, to decide some of the details in connection with the fleet's going to the Pacific. The fleet will consist of sixteen battleships and will start some time in December, going through the Straits of Magellan and up to San Francisco, and may also visit Puget Sound. The route for the return of the fleet has not yet been decided. The destroyer flotilla will leave for the Pacific about the same time as the fleet, but will not accompany it." *(NY Times*, August 24, 1907)

On August 24, 1907, it was reported that President Roosevelt had visited Secretary of State Root at a private hospital two weeks earlier.

> William Muldoon, at whose training farm and sanitarium, near White Plains, Secretary of State Elihu Root has spent the last three weeks, recuperating from overwork, said yesterday that Mr. Root is stronger to-day than he had been for many years...

...When Mr. Root reached Muldoon's place, however, both Mrs. Root and the President were alarmed over his condition, according to Mr. Muldoon. The Secretary was suffering from a general nervous breakdown, due to his exacting duties as Secretary of State...

...It will be news to a great many people that President Roosevelt visited Secretary Root at Muldoon's about two weeks ago and spent the greater part of an afternoon with him. The President made the journey from Oyster Bay in an automobile, and the fact that he was able to make the trip and get back to Sagamore Hill without attracting any public attention whatever, Mr. Muldoon declared, proved that the President was able when he had a mind to do so, to accomplish even the apparently impossible...*(NY Times,* August 24, 1907)

However, it was denied by Secretary Loeb that this visit ever occurred.

OYSTER BAY, L.I., Aug. 23 — Secretary Loeb, who keeps in almost constant touch with his chief, denied to-day that the President had visited Secretary Root at Muldoon's place. It was not possible to get any word direct from Sagamore Hill, but Secretary Loeb declared to-night that from his own knowledge he was prepared unqualifiedly to deny that President Roosevelt had been away from Oyster Bay this Summer, with the exception of his visit to Provincetown, Mass. *(NY Times,* August 24, 1907)

On August 27, 1907, Secretary Loeb met with Public Printer Charles A. Stillings. The visit was to allay Stillings's fears that he would be replaced.

OYSTER BAY, Aug. 27 — Charles A. Stillings, Public Printer, paid a visit to Oyster Bay in an automobile this afternoon, and returned to New York after having a conference with Secretary Loeb. He did not see the President. Mr. Stillings said he had been in New York to buy additional machinery for the Government Printing Office.

He received a telephone message from Washington this morning to the effect that the President was to displace him, but remarked after his conference with Secretary Loeb that nothing seemed to be known of the matter here.

Lawyer Frank B. Kellogg, who is to be the special counsel of the Government in the investigation of the Standard Oil Company of New Jersey, which will be begun in New York next Tuesday, called on President Roosevelt to-day. *(NY Times,* August 28, 1907)

Also on August 27, 1907, "Prince Wilhelm of Sweden arrived in New York...and after breakfast at the Hotel Astor started for Oyster Bay, where he lunched with President Roosevelt, when he delivered, it is said, a cordial message of friendship and good will to the President from his grandfather, the King of Sweden..." *(NY Times,* August 29, 1907)

On August 28, 1907, "As a first step toward mediation in order to obtain a lasting peace in Central America President Roosevelt and President Diaz *(of Mexico)* have sent a joint note to the five Central American republics suggesting that they hold a conference, or in some other way take action toward reaching an agreement." *(NY Times,* August 29, 1907)

On August 30, 1907, "Secretary of the Interior Garfield...took luncheon with the President...following his return from an extended trip to the West on which he visited Arizona, New Mexico, and Oklahoma, predicted that Oklahoma and Indian Territory will adopt their State Constitutions...By authority of the President, Mr. Garfield announced that no further effort will be made by the Administration toward bringing up again in Congress the question of the joint Statehood of Arizona and New Mexico. The verdict of the people recently expressed in these Territories will be accepted by the President as final, Mr. Garfield said." *(NY Times,* August 31, 1907)

On September 5, 1907, it was reported that the Atlantic fleet would not just visit the Pacific but would, in fact, circle the world. Furthermore, the Atlantic would be protected by nine new warships.

From a high authority THE TIMES received yesterday two important pieces of information bearing on the sending of Admiral Evan's battleship fleet to the Pacific.

In the first place, it is not the present intention of the Government to confine this armada's movements to our Pacific Coast. The President's plan...is to send the ships, after their visit to California ports, on to Hawaii and the Philippines. When orders are given for their return the route designated will be by way of the Suez Canal, completing the world tour.

In the meantime the Atlantic Coast will not be left unprotected. At the instance of President Roosevelt the Navy Department has already begun to formulate plans for the establishment of another Atlantic fleet, one that will replace the armada under Admiral Evans. *(NY Times,* September 5, 1907)

The President spent much of the remainder of the Summer of 1907 working on his annual message to Congress and on the text for a series of speeches he would make on his trip to the South and West.

Broadway Magazine (September 1907) contains a description of Moore's Building:

Secretary Loeb and his assistants do not look any too fresh when they resume their seats in the white automobile and are taken back to the executive offices in the village. These offices are located on a big floor in the principal office building in town — an ordinary two storey building, such as every American village boasts, along with a possible thousand or so inhabitants. The ground floor contains the largest grocery store in town, a dry goods shop, a barber shop, the plant and editorial rooms of the Oyster Bay Pilot and one or two other shops.

Secretary Loeb, however, was busy making official statements to the press corps.

OYSTER BAY, Sept. 6 — President Roosevelt will devote the remainder of his summer vacation to work on his annual message to Congress and the completion of the series of speeches he is to deliver on his trip through the West and South.

Secretary Loeb said to-day that visitors to Sagamore Hill would be decidedly scarce from now on. Throughout the Summer Friday has been the President's favorite day to bring together luncheon guests. No one was invited to-day, and Secretary Loeb exhibited a blank appointment list for the remaining three weeks of his stay at Sagamore Hill. *(NY Times*, September 7, 1907)

Also on September 6, 1907,

The presence in town this week of the Presidents of many of the large railroads, as is usual at this time of year, has been made the basis of rumors that the railroad men have been quietly conferring on questions arising from recent Federal enactments.

A story in circulation yesterday told of a meeting of railroad Presidents at the Waldorf-Astoria, which, it was said, resulted in conferences with President Roosevelt at Oyster Bay through the medium of Secretary Loeb. This gathering of railway magnates was said to have been chiefly concerned with the law regarding railroad accounting.

OYSTER BAY, N.Y., Sept. 6 — Secretary Loeb said to-night that the President had received no communication from the railroad Presidents. *(NY Times*, September 7, 1907)

Also on September 6, photographer Abbey G. Baker signed an agreement regarding photographs she would take in the White House in Washington.

> I hereby agree to submit to Mr. Wm. Loeb,
> Jr., Secretary to the President, proof of every
> photograph taken by me in the White House on
> *September 1907* to publish no such picture
> without first obtaining his approval; and to
> withhold the publication of any such picture
> until it is released by him.

Abby G. Baker

(TR Papers, Series 1, Reel 77)

Secretary Loeb then sent a memorandum to Mr. Forster in Washington informing him of Mrs. Baker.

WHITE HOUSE,
WASHINGTON.

Oyster Bay, N.Y.,
September 6, 1907.

Memorandum for Mr. Forster:

Please note the enclosed request from Mrs.
Baker. I have written her that if she will
call on you, you will arrange for the photograph-
ing she desires, including a picture of the
south front.

Wm Loeb Jr
Secretary.

(TR Papers, Series 1, Reel 77)

On September 7, Chief Wilkie of the Secret Service cabled Secretary Loeb with his assessment of information presented by the German Ambassador regarding specific people who might pose a danger to the President.

TELEGRAM.

White house,
Washington.

Hon. Wm. Loeb, Jr:

Was called upon by Mr. Adee about 10:30 this morning. He showed me the German Ambassadors letter. I know the source of his information and know his informant thoroly, also most of the people he mentions. Those who are characterized by the Ambassador's informant as the most dangerous, Navel and Klemenn are both working in New York, drinking a good of beer and doing a good deal of talking. Nothing however, with reference to the President. I will make further report to you by mail. Am thoroly satisfied that the Ambassador's informant is unworthy of belief, but nevertheless will look after the matter as if he were the most credible person in the world.

Wilkie.

September 7, 1907.

(TR Papers, Series 1, Reel 77)

On September 9, George Cortelyou, wrote to Secretary Loeb about the same matter.

TREASURY DEPARTMENT
OFFICE OF THE SECRETARY
WASHINGTON

Confidential.

Halesite, Long Island,
N.Y., September 9, 1907

My dear Mr. Loeb:

I have your letters of the 6th and 7th
instant, with inclosures concerning a supposed anarchistic plot. I had already written Wilkie about the President's trip to
Canton, before the receipt of your letters,
and directed him to see that every possible
precaution was taken; and I have of course
called his attention to these inclosures and
instructed him to have the matter thoroughly
looked into.

Very sincerely yours,

Geo. M. Cortelyou

Hon. Wm. Loeb, Jr.,
Secretary to the President
Oyster Bay, N.Y.

(TR Papers, Series 1, Reel 77)

Chief Wilkie wrote the detailed report for Secretary Loeb regarding the anarchists on
September 9.

TREASURY DEPARTMENT
OFFICE OF THE SECRETARY
WASHINGTON

September 9, 1907.

Hon. William Loeb, Jr.,
  Secretary to the President,
  Oyster Bay, N.Y.

Dear Mr. Loeb:

The letter from the German Ambassador to which your telegram referred, and about which I wired you Saturday, contained a lot of "information" which had been supplied probably through the German Consul at Chicago by a man named Dzubaniak, or, as he prefers to be known, Deihl, about whom I think I have spoken to you several times. Deihl was formerly employed as an informant on anarchist matters by the Austro-Hungarian Consul at Chicago; subsequently he took up the same line of work for the German Consul, by whom he is still regularly or occasionally employed. The information in his letter was:

First. "Anarchist Terrorist Havel" gave up his contemplated attendance on the anarchistic conference at Amsterdam with the intention of remaining at home and making an attempt on the President's life during the unveiling of the McKinley monument on September 29th, the President having been "condemned to death by the Terrorists" for his hostile position toward the working classes and especially on account of his hostility to the arrested leaders of the Western Federation of Miners."

Second. "An infernal machine with a clock concealed in a wreath, which was to be ostensibly the gift of the working men, is to be deposited on the McKinley monument. The clock to be set so that when the President should deliver his speech the explosion would occur."

Third. "Should the assassination of the President for the wrong done the working classes not succeed during his presidency it would be delayed until he retired into private life." Several Italians are named and the information volunteered that they are expert bomb makers.

Fourth. "The Terrorists of Chicago think they have found in Kleimann, who is afflicted with an incurable skin disease, and who is a pessimist, a man of action who would be, and who seems to be, willing to make an attempt on the President's life."

Fifth. "The Daily Socialist" a Chicago publication editorially warns the anarchists of the country against making any attempt on the President's life because of the harm it would do the socialistic interests in America. Thus conclusively showing (?) "that the Terroristic Anarchists" contemplate the assassination of the President.

If it had not been for more than seven years' experience with this informant I should possibly be inclined to accept his "information" as worthy of very serious consideration. I believe Deihl to be a man in sufficiently close touch with the labor organizations to know what they are doing, and possibly to know their temper, but in no single instance in the scores of statements that he has made to me directly, or through the Austrian Consul, or the German Consul, or the German Ambassador, or the State Department, or your office, or the office of the Superintendent of Police (to all of whom he has directed his communications in turn and sometimes simultaneously) have we been able to verify the existence of the alleged plot, or has anything ever happened to suggest that a plot ever existed. Not long ago it was reported, through the State Department, I believe, that there had been a meeting of the "Triangle" or "Inner Circle" of the anarchists at a given address in New York. Lots were drawn, and one man was selected to assassinate the President. A very careful investigation at New York disclosed the fact that names used in the report were the names of real persons, but that there was no such organization and the address where the organization was said to have held its fatal meeting was a vacant lot. The investigation was made by a man who was in close touch with the foreign anarchists in this country, and had such an organization existed as was described by Deihl, my informant would have been able to learn all of the facts about it.

Immediately after the assassination of Ex-Governor Steunenburg Deihl informed me that Steunenburg's assassination was plotted by the anarchists at Paterson, N.J., and that Steunenburg was the first of a list which included the Governors of every state where there had been any executive action which had met the disfavor of the radical branch of the labor unions. The President and all the members of his cabinet were on this same list and were to be exterminated. The subsequent developments in the Steunenburg case seem to have disposed of Mr. Deihl's version of the facts. I do not think there has been a public occasion in which the President has participated since 1900 that has not brought from Deihl "inside information" of plans for his assassination. He sent the picture of Havel to Washington to Major Sylvester

not long before the President went to Jamestown, with the
information that Havel was bent upon taking the President's
life and would probably do it at Jamestown. At that very
time Havel was living quietly in New York; living the life
of an ordinary laborer, and an agent of this service was in
close personal contact with him for weeks. He found Havel
to be an enthusiast in the matter of the social revolution
and intensely interested in the anarchistic propaganda
abroad, but was absolutely indifferent to conditions in
this country. Whatever Havel might have been abroad, and
however much of a "Terrorist" he might have been over there,
he differs little from the familiar type of saloon anarchist
known to the police of this country. He was at one time
an associate of Isaacs, Emma Goldman's notorious friend in
Chicago, and Deihl in his capacity as investigator for the
Austro-Hungarian Government was paying close attention to
Isaacs' daughter. He doubtless met Havel and may have learned
facts to warrant a statement about his being a "Terrorist" in
Europe, but I am convinced that his alleged information about
Havel's intentions in this country are absolute inventions.

Deihl has been a persistent and insistent applicant
for a place in our service, but owing to his thorough un-
reliability I considered him a dangerous man for this or
any other branch of the Government service. When you understand that he is employed by representatives of a foreign
government to discover anarchistic plots you can readily
understand that he has got to discover plots in order to
hold his job. If 1/10 of one percent of his alleged information as to plots and conspiracies had been true there
would have been an unending record of assassination of
administrative officials beside which the terroristic deeds
of Russia would pale into insignificance.

Pray do not understand me as taking the position that
Deihl's information should be ignored. I quite recognize
the possibility of the grain of truth in some one of his
statements and they will all be sifted carefully as far as
we are able to go. We know the man Kleman (not Kleimann)
to whom he refers, and have observed no tendency on his part
to sacrifice himself by an attempt on the President's life.

The thought has occurred to me that perhaps in self
protection it might be advisable to appoint this man in
our service where some sort of control could be exercised
over him, and where his methods of work could be subjected
to close scrutiny. I would not hesitate to do this were
I not satisfied that if he were able to pose as a Government officer he would speedily bring into disrepute not
only the branch of the service with which he was immediately connected, but would have greatly enlarged his field for

mischievous activity. Personally, I consider him, in a
way, in the same class with "The Young American Astrologer"
of Hoboken, who by predicting disaster to the President on
twelve or fifteen days of each month, hopes sometime something may happen which will justify him in claiming to have
"warned the authorities" of the impending disaster.

Respectfully,

John E. Wilkie
Chief.

(TR Papers, Series 1, Reel 77)

Also on September 9, 1907

OYSTER BAY, Sept. 9 — Secretary Loeb said to-day that the President, if he
spoke in Cleveland in the near future, would have nothing to say regarding
Congressman Burton's candidacy for Mayor of that city. *(NY Times*,
September 10, 1907)

On September 10, the President had, contrary to Mr. Loeb's earlier assertions, several
guests for luncheon.

OYSTER BAY, N.Y., Sept. 10 — Labor Commissioner Neill is no longer concerning himself with the telegraphers' strike, and his original effort to bring
about peace between the telegraph companies and their former employees represented all the part taken by the Administration in the controversy. Reports
to the contrary were denied by the Commissioner upon his leaving Sagamore
Hill, where he had luncheon with the President to-day.
    Others at the luncheon were Secretary Straus of the Department of
Commerce and Labor...Secretary Straus made a verbal report on his recent
Western trip to President Roosevelt and Commissioner Neill took up with the
President certain difficulties which have arisen in the attempted enforcement
of the eight-hour law. The telegraph strike was not considered. *(NY Times*,
September 11, 1907)

On September 17, Secretary Loeb issued the "Denial of the Cocktail."

OYSTER BAY, N.Y., Sept. 17 — Because of the widespread publicity given to
the statement of Bishop Berry of Detroit that either President Roosevelt or
Secretary Loeb, and not Mr. Fairbanks, was responsible for the cocktails
served at the luncheon tendered them by the Vice President at Indianapolis,
Secretary Loeb to-day issued the following formal statement in denial:
    "The statement is too absurd to be given any credence. Neither the President
nor his Secretary, either directly or indirectly, ordered anything of any kind at
the luncheon in question or at any other luncheon where they were guests."
(NY Times, September 18, 1907)

Also on September 17, 1907, General Luke E. Wright, the retiring Ambassador to Japan, visited Sagamore Hill. He gave the President his first hand accounting of the conditions in Japan and the attitude of the Japanese towards the United States. With the exception of the incident in San Francisco earlier in the summer, his report was quite optimistic. *(NY Times,* September 18, 1907)

On September 19, Secretary Loeb announced the details of President Roosevelt's upcoming camping trip to Louisiana.

> OYSTER BAY, L.I., Sept. 19 — President Roosevelt to-day perfected arrangements for his camping trip to Louisiana. The President will spend seventeen days in camp, and it will be the only absolute rest he has allowed himself this Summer. Though nominally on his vacation at Oyster Bay, there have been but few hours when he has not dealt with official business of some sort. President Roosevelt will pitch his camp in the northeastern corner of Louisiana on or about Oct. 5. The exact spot is yet to be determined.
>
> While the details of the trip have not been made public, the main features were announced by Secretary Loeb to-day... *(NY Times,* September 19, 1907)

On September 22, 1907 it was reported that "Tamemon Hitachiyama, the 220-pound champion wrestler of Japan, will probably visit President Roosevelt on Tuesday of this week, when he will present to the Chief Executive a handsome gold sword, with massive handle and scabbard, which was given to him by his townspeople of Mito, Japan, after he had carried off all the honors in Nippon for wrestling and had won the title of champion of champions. Hitachiyama hopes that he will have the honor of a few minutes on the mat with President, but he says that he has not received word as to whether the President will wrestle with him or not." *(NY Times,* September 22, 1907)

From Washington it was reported on September 22, 1907 that ex-Senator William E. Chandler had resigned from the Spanish Treaty Claims Commission. This resignation was expected since the Senator became involved in a "veracity controversy" with the President and since he had been nominated for membership in the Ananlas Club during the closing days of the fight over the Hepburn Rate bill. *(NY Times,* September 23, 1907)

> OYSTER BAY, N.Y., Sept. 22 — It was stated by Secretary Loeb to-night that ex-Senator William E. Chandler of New Hampshire had recently signified his wish to be relieved of his duties as Chairman of the Spanish Treaties Claims Commission. No date for his retirement has been set, it being understood that the resignation would take effect upon the appointment of his successor. No significance was attached to Mr. Chandler's request, the Secretary said, other than his personal wish to be relieved of the duties. *(NY Times,* September 23, 1907)

On September 23, *The New York Times* printed a brief summary of the President's activities during the Summer of 1907.

> OYSTER BAY, L.I., Sept. 22 — President Roosevelt's Summer vacation at his Sagamore Hill home will end at 10 o'clock Wednesday morning, when he, with Mrs. Roosevelt, members of the family, and the executive staff, will take a special train for Washington.

During the three and a half months the President has occupied the old homestead he has had the quietest, and at the same time the busiest, vacation since he became an occupant of the White House. The records show that since June 12 the President has received 125 persons. Some of the callers have been distinguished foreigners, and a few have made purely social calls, but the majority of them have been government officials on strictly government business.

His annual message to Congress is practically completed. The document needed only finishing touches. In addition to writing his annual message, the President prepared seven comprehensive speeches. One of these was delivered at Provincetown, Mass., recently, and the others will be made during the Western-Southern trip. *(NY Times,* September 23, 1907)

On September 24, 1907, it was reported that the President was preparing for his return to Washington.

OYSTER BAY, N.Y., Sept. 23 — Preparations for President Roosevelt's trip to Washington were in active progress here to-day. A special train of five cars will be required to effect the transfer of the belongings of the President and his party. Two express cars will be loaded by tomorrow with household belongings from Sagamore Hill, and the nine horses and carriages from the President's stable and that of Secretary Loeb...

...The work of dismantling the executive offices was begun to-day. Unless an emergency should arise, the President will receive no visitors in the two remaining days of his stay at Sagamore Hill. *(NY Times,* September 24, 1907)

On September 23, Stuyvesant Fish, former President of the Illinois Central Railway, delivered to Secretary Loeb a message for the President.

OYSTER BAY, Sept. 23 — Stuyvesant Fish came to Oyster Bay to-day, and, after being in conference with Secretary Loeb in the Executive offices for an hour, declined to be interviewed regarding the object of his visit. Mr. Fish said he was not going with the President on his Western trip, and that he should not see the President to-day. He left the Executive offices to make a call on Arthur Weeks, whom he said he had known for many years.

Secretary Loeb said Mr. Fish had given him a message to deliver to President Roosevelt, but he declined to divulge its contents. *(NY Times,* September 24, 1907)

On September 26, 1907, the President returned to Washington.

All Oyster Bay turned out to see the departure of President Roosevelt and his family, and he enjoyed the heartiest send-off from his neighbors. Accompanied by Mrs. Roosevelt, Miss Ethel and Quentin Roosevelt, he came down to the station from Sagamore Hill in a big white automobile. Secretary Loeb and his wife, Assistant Secretary Latta, the White House staff, and several Secret Service men made up the rest of the party. As soon as Mr. Roosevelt appeared the villagers swarmed around him. They wanted a parting handshake, and the President responded to their good wishes with right good will...*(NY Times,* September 27, 1907)

The Summer of 1908

Even before President Roosevelt left Washington in 1908 for his Summer in Oyster Bay, it was clear that the Summer would be full of domestic political activity. After all, the Presidential election was near, and Secretary Taft was the President's "hand-picked" successor. Furthermore, there was the Gubernatorial Campaign in New York and the President's "non-interference" was of great import here as well. The Executive Staff was also busy planning the President's upcoming hunting trip to Africa.

WASHINGTON, June 16 — Following the receipt of favorable dispatches from Chicago as to the way in which the convention was taking up its work, the President and Mrs. Roosevelt this morning decided to leave with their family for Oyster Bay next Saturday. It is possible that Secretary Taft will also get out of town this week...in readiness for the beginning of the campaign.

...The President and his family, accompanied by several Secret Service men, will make an early start from Washington next Saturday morning. Though the hour has not yet been definitely decided on, the Executive family expects to reach Oyster Bay about 5 o'clock that afternoon. A part of the White House retinue has already moved out to the Long Island country place, and everything will be in readiness...

...Ten picked Secret Service men have been detailed for the protection of the President at Sagamore Hill...(*NY Times*, June 17, 1908)

The President left for Oyster Bay on June 20, 1908 with Secretary and Mrs. Loeb and about thirty officials and employees of the White House. (*NY Times*, June 20, 1908)

President Roosevelt and his family moved from Washington to Oyster Bay for the Summer yesterday. Their special train reached Oyster Bay at 5:45 o'clock yesterday afternoon, and the President, amid the cheers of his neighbors who had assembled on the station platform to greet him, made his way through the throng to the carriages which had been sent from Sagamore Hill to take him and his family to their Summer home...

...Two important pieces of information in regard to President Roosevelt's future were disclosed by Secretary Loeb while the President's party was crossing from Jersey City to the Long Island station. One was that the President will break away from the old rule of accompanying the new President back to the White House after the inauguration of his successor next March. Instead, Mr. Loeb said, Mr. Roosevelt will take a carriage at the Capitol directly after the inaugural ceremony and drive to the railroad station on his way to Oyster

Bay. Mr. Loeb also said that the President would leave for his African hunting trip about April 1...

...On the Lancaster...Mr. Roosevelt was much interested in the infant son of his secretary, William Loeb, Jr.

"Who is going to be the next President, Willy?" his father asked.

"Billy Taft," lisped the little one, and all on board laughed heartily.

The trip to the Long Island Station was enlivened by the salutes given the tug — which was flying the President's flag — by the passing river craft. It was 3:25 o'clock when the Lancaster made fast to the Long Island Ferry slip, and the party at once made for the station...

...Twenty minutes were required to get the baggage on board the Long Island special, and at 3:45 o'clock, after the President had called good-bye to the crowd from the back of the last car, Mr. Loeb gave the signal to start...*(NY Times*, June 21, 1908)

The first Sunday in Oyster Bay, although quiet for the President, was busy for Mr. Loeb.

OYSTER BAY, L.I., June 21 — President Roosevelt attended services in Christ Church this morning...

...While the President was at church William Loeb, Jr., his secretary, went to the executive offices, over Moore's grocery store. The reporters called his attention to a report in a morning newspaper which said that Mr. Roosevelt might be called on to name the Chairman of the Republican National Committee because of the disagreement over a successor to Mr. New.

"I haven't heard of it," Mr. Loeb said.

"There is a rumor that you may be made the National Chairman," a reporter said.

"They seem to be doing all this in Washington," he retorted sarcastically. "We have heard nothing about the Chairmanship of the National Committee," he added. "There has been no word received here in that matter."

The Secret Service men guarding the President have had nothing of importance to do. The President's yacht Sylph has arrived in Oyster Bay Harbor and lies at anchor near Sagamore Hill...

...Secretary Loeb, who this year is making his home at the Seawanhaka Yacht Club on Centre Island, on the opposite side of the harbor from Sagamore Hill, to-day narrowly escaped becoming a hero. He was on his way to the Executive offices this morning when his attention was drawn to a man in the water calling for help. As he was about to jump in to aid the drowning man he saw a launch making for him...

...The attention of Secretary Loeb was called to-day to the dispatch from San Jose, Cal., containing the remarks of Representative E.A. Hayes before the Asiatic Exclusion League. Mr. Hayes was quoted as having said that he was the bearer of a personal message from the President of the United States to the people of California. The message, the Congressman said, was in explanation of the failure of exclusion legislation by Congress. The President was quoted as saying:

"I am still trying diplomacy. I am sending to Japan the sharpest correspondence that any nation has ever received. But tell your constituents that if I cannot get what I want by diplomacy I will get it by exclusion legislation."

Secretary Loeb said that he knew nothing of the remarks attributed to Congressman Hayes or of the reported message from the President. He had not seen the President to-day, he said, and so the matter had not been brought to the latter's notice. *(NY Times,* June 22, 1908)

In Washington, it was speculated that if Secretary of War Taft were to be elected President, he would appoint William Loeb, the President's secretary, as Secretary of the Navy.

WASHINGTON, June 21 — ...Mr. Loeb is regarded as in the lead for the naval portfolio, for he not only has the confidence and admiration of Mr. Taft, but he always has been interested in this especial department of the Government. Little credence is placed in the report current here that Mr. Loeb is under consideration for the Chairmanship of the Republican National Committee. His ambitions do not lie in that direction. It is generally conceded that Mr. Loeb could have had the management of the Taft campaign for the nomination had he desired it...*(NY Times,* June 22, 1908)

On June 23, 1908, it was reported that President Roosevelt intervened on behalf of two members of the Harvard crew who had been suspended for taking certain books from the Harvard Library. The President, a Harvard alumnus, intervened because his son, Theodore Roosevelt, Jr., urged him to do so. The younger Roosevelt felt that their suspension ruined Harvard's chances for beating Yale in an upcoming race. Consequently, the President wrote a letter to President Eliot of Harvard. This letter infuriated the President of Harvard who would not tolerate interference in the internal affairs of the university by anyone, including the President of the United States. The suspension of the two athletes was sustained by the Board of Overseers and President Roosevelt was informed of this by President Eliot.

OYSTER BAY, N.Y., June 22 — Secretary Loeb said to-day that President Roosevelt will have nothing to say concerning his correspondence with President Eliot of Harvard in behalf of Sidney Fish and Charles Morgan, Jr., the Harvard oarsmen who were suspended...*(NY Times,* June 23, 1908)

On June 24, 1908, Grover Cleveland, the only man to hold the office of President in two non-consecutive terms, died. President Roosevelt was one of the first to telegraph his condolences to Mrs. Cleveland.

OYSTER BAY, June 24 — News of the death of ex-President Cleveland was communicated to President Roosevelt at his Summer home here to-day, and caused radical changes in the President's plans for the immediate future. Mr. Roosevelt was deeply shocked at the tidings, and immediately telegraphed to Mrs. Cleveland at Princeton, tendering his sympathy and that of Mrs. Roosevelt, and asking to be notified at Mrs. Cleveland's earliest convenience of the time of the dead statesman's funeral. Afterward, announcement was made that President and Mrs. Roosevelt would attend the funeral services at Princeton on Friday.

The President's telegram of condolence to Mrs. Cleveland was as follows:

"Oyster Bay, June 24, 1908.
"Mrs. Grover Cleveland, Princeton, N.J.:
"Your telegram shocked me greatly. Mrs. Roosevelt joins in very deep and sincere sympathy. I have, of course, abandoned my intention of starting to-day for the New London boat races, so that if the funeral is either Thursday or Friday I can attend. I can also attend if it is Sunday, but if it is Saturday a number of men are coming here from various parts of the country on a business engagement which I cannot well break.
"Will you direct some one to wire me when the funeral is to be and where?
"THEODORE ROOSEVELT."

President and Mrs. Roosevelt, accompanied by Secretary Loeb, will leave Oyster Bay on a special train on Friday for Princeton to attend the funeral...*(NY Times*, June 25, 1908)

The conference which the President referred to in his telegram involved Secretary of War Taft, General Luke E. Wright, who would assume Mr. Taft's role as Secretary of War when the latter stepped down on July 1, and several members of the Republican National Committee. That the conference would continue as planned was also announced in *The New York Times*, June 25, 1908.

In a departure from his normal activities on behalf of the President, Secretary Loeb issued a statement on behalf of the President's son, Theodore Roosevelt, Jr.

OYSTER BAY, N.Y., June 24 — Secretary Loeb to-day issued this statement in reference to the published report that the President's son Theodore Roosevelt, Jr., intended to enter the employ of the United States Steel Corporation:
"The story as regards its implication is a pure falsehood. John Greenway, who was in the President's regiment, has told young Roosevelt that he will try him on a job simply as one of the ordinary miners and exactly as he tries hundreds of others every year and is trying hundreds this year.
"Young Roosevelt is at this moment off seeing if there is a chance at another job, where he was told he might get employment, having given up going on the Mayflower to the boat race for the purpose of looking at this particular place, which is in connection with a well-known manufacturing concern. He will probably not decide for two or three months which particular place he will try. Except for the publication in the newspapers neither the President nor young Roosevelt knows that the company for which Mr. Greenway is Superintendent has any connection either directly or indirectly with the Steel Corporation." *(NY Times*, June 25, 1908)

As planned, the conference between the President and Secretary Taft, Gen. Wright, and members of the Republican National Committee took place at Sagamore Hill on June 27, 1908.

Secretary Taft went back to Washington at 5 o'clock yesterday afternoon after another strenuous day, the greater part of which he devoted to a trip to Oyster Bay for a conference with President Roosevelt, Gen. Wright, the new Secretary of War, and National Committeemen Frank B. Kellogg of Minnesota and William L. Ward of New York.

It may be said that yesterday's conference resulted in some progress toward a settlement of the Chairmanship tangle. Despite his letter of self-elimination, Frank Hitchcock is by no means out of consideration for the place. Whatever the ultimate solution, it is practically certain that Mr. Taft will have the benefit of Mr. Hitchcock's extraordinary political genius during the campaign. If Hitchcock is not made Chairman of the National Committee, then some friend of his will be...*(NY Times*, June 28, 1908)

Upon his return to Washington, Secretary Taft announced that he had wanted Secretary Loeb for a high office.

WASHINGTON, June 28 — ...The nominee (*Secretary Taft*) and his brother (*Charles P.*) denied that the Chairmanship of the National Committee had been offered to the President's private secretary, William Loeb, Jr., and had been refused.

"I wish you would say," said Mr. Taft, "that the report that I offered the Chairmanship to Secretary Loeb is not quite accurate. What I did say to him was that I should be glad, in the event of my election, to have him identified in an important capacity with my Administration. I am fond of him and sincerely appreciate what he has done for me personally. He told me, however, that he expected to retire from politics at the conclusion of President Roosevelt's Administration to enter upon a business career, arrangements for which he has already made..." (*NY Times*, June 29, 1908)

On June 30, the President enjoyed a picnic with his family, thereby giving a break to the executive staff.

OYSTER BAY, L.I., June 30 — ...Congressman W.W. Cocks, who represents the President's district in Congress, drove over to Oyster Bay to-day from his home at Westbury. He arrived too late to see the President, but had a chat with Secretary Loeb. The Secretary afterward went to Seabright, N.J., where he remained for the night.

The Presidential picnic gave the employees of the executive offices a chance to take a holiday of their own. (*NY Times*, July 1, 1908)

On July 1, 1908, President Roosevelt met with S.S. McClure, representing the McClure publications , and Caspar Whitney, editor of Outing. Like many others, these men were eager to sign a contract with the President for the right to publish stories about his big game hunt in Africa at the close of his Administration. (*NY Times*, July 2, 1908)

On the same day, conferences were held in both Washington and Oyster Bay regarding the Chairmanship of the Republican National Committee. Although no official statement was made, it appeared at this time that Frank H. Hitchcock had been chosen.

OYSTER BAY, July 1 — National Committeeman Frank B. Kellogg of Minnesota, who is also the Special United States District Attorney appointed to prosecute sundry cases against the Standard Oil Company, called on President Roosevelt to-day, with National Committeeman William L. Ward of Westchester, N.Y. The greatest possible effort to keep secret this conference was made. Secretary Loeb issued denials until his collar wilted.

Messrs. Kellogg and Ward drove into Oyster Bay in an automobile runabout at 12:14 o'clock, and immediately made for Sagamore Hill. They remained three hours, lunching with the President. Mr. Loeb said, however:

"The gentlemen did not come here to see the President; they came to visit me."

And, after the three hour conference, Messrs. Kellogg and Ward did pay a visit of fifteen minutes to Mr. Loeb.

"What was the result of the conference?" Mr. Kellogg was asked.

"Ask Loeb," he replied.

The only information obtainable from him was that he expected to have the Standard Oil cases in such shape that he could go to Hot Springs, Va., next week, when the sub-committee of the National Committee meets on July 8 to name the Chairman who will direct the Taft campaign.

Mr. Loeb, when asked if there was any reason for making the visit to Mr. Roosevelt a matter of secrecy, did not answer.

It was a matter of discussion here to-night that the conference to-day meant nothing more nor less than a message from Mr. Roosevelt to the sub-committee appointed to name the Chairman of the National Committee for them, and ending the...dispute.

James T. Williams of the Publicity Bureau of the Republican National Committee was also at Sagamore Hill...*(NY Times*, July 2, 1908)

On July 2, 1908, *The New York Times* printed two denials made by Secretary Loeb on behalf of the President, Mrs. Roosevelt, and the President's daughter, Alice Roosevelt Longworth.

OYSTER BAY, July 2 — Two denials of newspaper stories were issued here to-day. One concerned the story that Mr. Roosevelt intended to buy the property of the Union Theological Seminary in New York and on the site would build a city mansion. The other denial concerned the story that Mrs. Roosevelt and Mrs. Longworth had been decorated by the Sultan of Turkey.

The denial of the first story was given out in typewritten form. It said:

> In reference to the report published this morning that the President proposes to purchase the Union Theological Seminary property, Secretary Loeb said that there were certain stories started that seemed to be even more remarkable for their insanity than for their sensationalism or mendacity. This particular story might just as well have been that the President intended to purchase the Parthenon and turn it into a private residence. The President has but one house, that at Oyster Bay, and has not the remotest intention of building another anywhere. Until the President's attention was called to this story in

the paper he not only had never heard it suggested, but he would not have believed that any human being would have put in type a statement so utterly insane.

The denial of the second story was caused by a protest of Greek citizens, made through Atlantis, the Greek newspaper in New York, and printed in to-day's TIMES.

"I have just received the protest," said Mr. Loeb, "but we have not been informed of any decorations from the Sultan. There has been none — save in the newspapers."

"Has the Turkish Government sent any communication to you or the President on this matter?" was asked.

"None," replied Mr. Loeb.

On July 3, 1908, President Roosevelt met with Thomas R. Shipp of Washington, Secretary of the National Conservation Commission. The Secretary gave to Mr. Roosevelt a verbal report from Chairman Gifford Pinchot on the organizational work performed by the commission. He also outlined the plans of the commission in obtaining statistics of the country's national resources.

OYSTER BAY, July 3 — ...At the request of Gifford Pinchot President Roosevelt dictated personal letters to all the various Governmental bureau chiefs, asking them to proceed as rapidly as possible in their co-operation with the conservation commission. The bureau chiefs will be asked to present statistics as to the present extent of the country's natural resources; how they have been utilized heretofore, and their present method of utilization; whether they have been wasted, and if so, how; and what method of conservation has been taken...

...Chairman Pinchot...will come to Oyster Bay next week to confer with the President...

On July 7, 1908 "President Roosevelt...sent a telegram to Rear Admiral Charles S. Sperry, Commander in Chief of the Atlantic Fleet, expressing his good wishes for the officers and men of the fleet on the eve of their departure for Australia, Japan, the Philippines, and New Zealand." (*NY Times*, July 8, 1908) That day the "Great White Fleet" of fifteen ships set sail for Honolulu from San Francisco. From Honolulu, the fleet proceeded to New Zealand, Australia, Japan, China, the Philippines, and through the Suez Canal. The fleet would arrive home just after the President's return to Washington at the end of his summer vacation.

In the morning of July 7, 1908, the President met with the new Public Printer, Robert Leech to discuss the situation in the Government Printing Office in Washington. He also met with Robert Bridges of Scribener's Magazine to discuss the publication of his stories resulting from his upcoming Africa trip. Rumors abounded that the President would receive one dollar per word. "The truth of this dollar-a-word story was emphatically denied at the executive offices...Mr. Loeb, the President's secretary, said that no contracts had been made with publishers, and that no such offers as rumored had been made to the President by the publishers." (*NY Times*, July 8, 1908)

Also on July 7, President Roosevelt boarded and inspected the *Roosevelt*, anchored off Sagamore Hill. This arctic exploration steamer would embark from Oyster Bay and later carry Robert Peary, on his journey to find the North Pole.

FIGURE 32: President Roosevelt meeting Robert Peary aboard the "Roosevelt" anchored in Oyster Bay.
Courtesy Theodore Roosevelt Collection, Harvard College Library

OYSTER BAY, L.I., July 7 — "Well, Peary, good-bye, and may you have the best of luck," said President Roosevelt as he left the arctic exploration steamer Roosevelt this afternoon, after the vessel had been brought to an anchorage off Sagamore Hill for his inspection.

The President remained on the Roosevelt nearly an hour, and during that time he inspected every part of the ship, shook hands with every man aboard, from Commander Peary to the stokers...

...Commander and Mrs. Peary arrived here from New York at noon and were driven in one of the Government automobiles to Sagamore Hill, where the explorer had a long conference with the President...Commander Peary sat on the veranda with the President before luncheon, and told him in detail his plans for the polar expedition...*(NY Times*, July 8, 1908)

WASHINGTON, July 7 — President Roosevelt has directed Civil Engineer Robert E. Peary, U.S.N., to make tidal observations along the Grant Land and Greenland shores of the Polar Sea for the Coast and Geodetic Survey during his dash for the north pole.

The President believes that such operations will throw light on the coast survey theory of the existence of a considerable land mass in the unknown sea of the arctic. *(NY Times*, July 8, 1908)

On July 8, 1908, Mr. Taft cabled Mr. Loeb with a proposed draft of a statement regarding the purchase of khaki cloth used to make army uniforms for soldiers in the Philippines. Although the English khaki available in Manila was cheaper and better suited for use in the tropics, the statement would make known that the prior purchase of English khaki was contrary to the the directions given by Congress. Furthermore, the President would direct that all future purchases be made from American manufacturers of khaki. It was clearly an election year statement to distance Mr. Taft from the mistaken purchase of English khaki instead of American khaki.

TELEGRAM.

The White House,

Washington.

1 HG B JM 413 Paid

HOT SPRINGS, Va., July 8, 1908.

Hon. William Loeb, Jr.,
    Secretary to the President,
        Oyster Bay, N.Y.

    Think that some statement ought to be made with reference to the charge that I have favored Chinese labor and English materials for the khaki uniforms of the Army. What would the President say to the following communication:

    "The contracts for the purchase of uniforms of Soldiers in the Army are made by the Quartermaster General with the approval and under the supervision of the Assistant Secretary of War. They are not brought to the attention of the Secretary of War except on appeal from the action of the Assistant Secretary. The Major General ~~Wood~~ *in command of the army in the Philippines* in a letter to the Department last Winter recommended that the khaki uniforms for the Army be bought in Manila because the English khaki which could there be had was more loosely woven, better suited to the tropics, and was cheaper, and the making was better and cheaper. Acting on this recommendation, and in Secretary Taft's absence and without consulting him, the assistant secretary, while acting as head of the Department made an order that contracts for the purchase and making of khaki uniforms for the army in the Philippines be made in Manila. Secretary Taft had no knowledge of this order and it was not brought to his attention until the day before he left office June 30th, when he received complaint of it from American manufacturers of khaki. In view of the imminent change of Secretaries, he concluded that it was an important matter of policy which should be submitted to the President for final action. Accordingly, one of his last official acts was to write to the President and state the facts, to point out that the order was contrary to the course prescribed by Congress in respect to the purchase of supplies for the construction of the Panama Canal, and to recommend to the President that the order made by the assistant secretary as *as to future purchases; it was too late to take action as to the purchases already made.* Acting Secretary be rescinded. He suggested that the only respect in which the order could be justified was in its application to the uniforms of the Philippine Scouts, a small and purely local organization whose bodily sizes and shapes were so different from American soldiers that it was difficult to fit them save by local manufacture. The President followed Secretary Taft's recommendation and directed the order to be rescinded as to all future purchases."

    I think either you might give it out or the War Department. Please let me know at once.

                        Wm. H. Taft.

(*TR Papers*, Series 1, Reel 83)

The same day, the statement was given out at the Executive Offices in Oyster Bay.

OYSTER BAY, July 8 — An official statement on the subject of khaki cloth in the Philippines was given out at the executive offices here to-day... *(NY Times,* July 9, 1908)

On July 9, 1908, Secretary Loeb issued an emphatic denial of the story that President Roosevelt said there exists a great possibility of war with Japan.

OYSTER BAY, L.I., July 9 — In reply to the passage in Congressman Hobson's speech at Denver in which Mr. Hobson said "not so very long ago the President of the United States said in my presence 'There exists the greatest possibility of war with Japan,' " this official statement was issued by Secretary Loeb after a long conference with Mr. Roosevelt to-night:

> In reference to the speech of Congressman Hobson, Secretary Loeb stated that the Congressman must, of course, have been misquoted. The President not only never made such a remark, but never made any remark even remotely resembling it. All that the President has ever said is that if there was a sufficient navy there would never be any possibility of this country getting into a foreign war.

Mr. Loeb said that the report that Mr. Roosevelt would take to the stump in Indiana for Mr. Taft was not worth submitting to the President.

Mr. Roosevelt spent the day camping at Lloyd's Neck...On his return to Sagamore Hill the President's day off was upset by Mr. Loeb's visit to tell about the Hobson speech. Mr. Loeb was held up at the hill for an hour past his usual time for departure. The result was the typewritten statement concerning Mr. Hobson's statement. *(NY Times,* July 10, 1908)

It was also announced on July 9, 1908 that the President had signed a contract with Scribners for the rights to publish the President's stories from his upcoming Africa trip.

OYSTER BAY, July 9 — President Roosevelt, through Secretary Loeb, to-day confirmed the story in *The New York Times* that he had signed a contract with the Scribners to write his hunting adventures in Africa for that firm. Mr. Loeb said that Mr. Roosevelt would write exclusively for Scribners, giving them serial and book rights. He declined to tell the monetary consideration, but it is understood, as was told yesterday, that Mr. Roosevelt will receive a large royalty. *(NY Times,* July 10, 1908)

On July 10, 1908, Secretary Loeb announced that a former Senator and Democrat wrote to him that he would vote for William Taft.

OYSTER BAY, L.I., July 10 — Secretary Loeb said he had received a letter from a former Democratic State Senator and member of Tammany Hall telling him that the ex-Senator would vote for Taft and had offered to bet "Tom"

Taggart $10,000 against $5,000 that Bryan would not be elected, and also $10,000 to $5,000 that Bryan would not carry New York State. *(NY Times, July 11, 1908)*

On July 11, 1908, President Roosevelt gave an address attacking Socialism at a dedication of a monument for Captain John Underhill, a prominent Long Islander.

> OYSTER BAY, N.Y., July 11 — To the memory of Capt. John Underhill, who became prominent in the government of the colonies as a statesman, and as a senior soldier achieved a high reputation in the Pequot war with the Indians, a monument was dedicated to-day before several hundred of his descendants at Matinecock, L.I. President Roosevelt attended the unveiling and made a short address...
>
> ...The President's address dealt with the duties of citizenship in this country as exemplified by the Underhill family. He denounced the doctrines of the Socialists, and gave his views as to the proper regulation of private and public business fortunes engaged in trade...*(NY Times, July 12, 1908)*

On July 11, Thomas Snowden, Commander of the "Mayflower" wrote to Secretary Loeb concerning preliminary plans for the President's trip to Newport, Rhode Island to speak at the Naval War College.

> U.S.S. Mayflower,
> Whitestone, N.Y.,
> July 11, 1908.

Dear Mr. Loeb,

       I beg to acknowledge the receipt of your letter of yesterday, informing me that the President will want to leave Oyster Bay on the Mayflower on Tuesday evening, July 21st, to visit the Naval War College, Newport, R.I., to arrive there the following morning, and to leave Newport that evening and reach Oyster Bay, Thursday morning, July 23rd, and that he wishes the Mayflower to remain at Oyster Bay until Monday, July 27th.

       The Mayflower will, therefore, unless otherwise directed, arrive at Oyster Bay on Tuesday, July 21st, prepared for the service outlined.

       At your convenience, will you kindly write me as to the number to be prepared for in the President's party.

> Very truly yours,
>
> *Thomas Snowden*,
> Commander, U.S.N.,
> Commanding.

Hon. Wm. Loeb, Jr.,
    Secretary to the President,
       Oyster Bay, N.Y.

(TR Papers, Series 1, Reel 83)

On July 12, 1908, an important conference was held at Sagamore Hill between the President, Secretary of State Root, and Assistant Secretary of State Bacon. The nature of the conference was not released to the press.

> OYSTER BAY, July 12 — President Roosevelt held a conference this after-noon with Secretary of State Elihu Root, and Assistant Secretary of State Robert Bacon. The three conferred at the President's home on Sagamore Hill for almost four hours. The exact nature of their deliberations could not be learned, but it is presumed that State affairs of an important nature were the subject of their discussion. It is thought likely that the foremost subject related to the strained situation at present existing between the United States and Venezuela, where diplomatic relations were severed by the United States as a result of numerous differences...
>
> ...Secretary Loeb was not present at the conference, having gone to visit Representative Cocks. The staff of the Executive office was on duty all after-noon awaiting some business of the President.
>
> When seen to-night the President's secretary said that the conference at Sagamore Hill to-day was connected with affairs in the State Department. He said that Secretary Root had been invited by the President to spend Sunday with him. The Secretary remains at Sagamore Hill to-night as the President's guest...*(NY Times*, July 13, 1908)

The following day, Assistant Secretary Bacon returned to Sagamore Hill. Again, there was no information released to the press on the nature of the conference.

> OYSTER BAY, L.I., July 13 — Assistant Secretary of State Robert Bacon reached Sagamore Hill before 10 o'clock this morning, having driven over from his home at Westbury, L.I., in his automobile. Mr. Root remained over night with the President after the extended conference of yesterday.
>
> Secretary Loeb said that there was no news to be given out regarding the visit of Mr. Root and the Assistant Secretary to the President. When asked if there was any information on the attitude of the United States in the Central American situation available here, he said there was nothing to be made pub-lic...*(NY Times*, July 14, 1908)

On July 15, Commander Snowden of the "Mayflower" wrote again to Secretary Loeb confirming the number of people sailing with the President to Newport, R.I.

U.S.S. Mayflower,
Whitestone Landing, N.Y.,
July 15, 1908.

Dear Mr. Loeb,

Many thanks for your letter regarding
the President's party to Newport.
I shall provide for eight people for two
days and can arrange for a few more or less.
The check for provisions used on the
New London trip was duly received.
With best wishes,
Sincerely yours,

Thomas Snowden.

(TR Papers, Series 1, Reel 83)

On July 16, Commander Snowden wrote to Secretary Loeb again regarding the President's trip.

U.S.S. Mayflower,
Whitestone, N.Y.,
July 16, 1908.

Dear Mr. Loeb:-

Replying to your letter of yesterday, just received, giving a list of the President's party for Newport, I would say that Oyster Bay to Newport is a ten hour trip and if agreeable to the President, it would be advisable to leave either place about sundown in the evening and reach the destination about 6 a.m. the following morning, or later as desired; but any arrangement suitable to the President can be carried out. Owing to the possibility of fog, it is advisable to allow sufficient time to meet any engagement the President may have made, but the above will do it.

The personnel of the party is noted and it is presumed that Mr. Netherland and Mr. McGrew will be quartered in the two vacant rooms in the Wardroom and mess with the Wardroom officers.

Upon reaching Oyster Bay, about noon the 21st,
I will report to Sagamore Hill to get details regarding
bringing on board passengers and baggage and whether dinner shall be provided on board for Tuesday evening.

Sincerely,

Thomas Snowden,

Commander, U.S.N.,
Commanding.

Hon. Wm. Loeb, Jr.,
    Secretary to the President,
    Oyster Bay, N.Y.

(TR Papers, Series 1, Reel 83)

On July 18, 1908, another important conference was held at Sagamore Hill. Among
other things discussed at the conference were the selection of a replacement for the
Assistant Attorney General and the neutrality laws with Mexico.

OYSTER BAY, July 18 — President Roosevelt to-day held a conference at
Sagamore Hill with United States Attorney General Bonaparte, Assistant
Secretary of State Robert S. Bacon, Don Enrique Creel, the Mexican
Ambassador in Washington, and W.I. Buchanan who through long experience
in the consular and diplomatic service of the United States and South and
Central American countries, has acquired a thorough knowledge of conditions
there.
    One of the principal things discussed by the President in his talk with
Attorney General Bonaparte was the selection of a successor to Milton B.
Purdy, ex-Assistant Attorney General and expert in anti-trust law administration...After the conference, Secretary Loeb announced that no decision had
been reached in the matter.
    With the two Government officials, Don Enrique and Mr. Buchanan, the
President discussed at length the present neutrality laws with Mexico. The
recent trouble in the neighboring republic and the part played in it by American
citizens living across the frontier has demonstrated to the satisfaction of
President Roosevelt and some members of his Cabinet that these laws need
strengthening if they are to be effectively enforced.
    A number of administrative matters now pending in the Attorney General's
office were discussed. One of these was the whiskey controversy growing out
of the pure food laws which the President desires to see rigidly enforced. *(NY
Times,* July 19, 1908)

On July 19, it was announced from Washington, that the President would meet with several naval officers at the Naval War College at Newport, R.I. All the chiefs of the naval

bureaus and several officers on the retired list were summoned to this meeting. The primary reason for going to this conference was the frequency of criticisms directed at the new fleet of warships, not least of all the report from Commander Key to the President, in which sweeping criticisms of the battleships North Dakota and Delaware were made. *(NY Times*, July 20, 1908)

On July 20, Commander Snowden of the Mayflower made final arrangements for the voyage to Newport with Secretary Loeb.

U.S.S. Mayflower,

Whitestone, N.Y.,

July 20, 1908.

Dear Mr. Loeb,

Your letter of the 18th instant, informing me that the President and Mrs. Roosevelt will dine at Sagamore Hill next Tuesday evening, and that Secret Service Agent Sloan will accompany the President on the trip to Newport, has been received.

There being only two available rooms in the wardroom, I will put Mr. Sloan in one of the after unused small rooms and he will mess with the wardroom mess.

I think this will be satisfactory.

All your wishes have been noted and will be carefully complied with.

With best wishes, I am,

Sincerely,

Thomas Snowden,

Commander, U.S.N.,

Commanding.

Hon. Wm. Loeb, Jr.,
        Secretary to the President,
            Oyster Bay, N.Y.

(TR Papers, Series 1, Reel 84)

Later that day, Commander Snowden wrote to Mr. Loeb again.

U.S.S. Mayflower,
Whitestone Landing, N.Y.,
July 20, 1908.

Dear Mr. Loeb,

Your letter regarding provision for Messrs.
Netherland and McGrew and requesting that the
launch be in at the railroad dock for them at
6.30 pm Tuesday has been received and the matters
will be attended to.

I am glad to know about providing dinner for
Tuesday evening.

Thanking you for your letter and with best wishes,

I am, sincerely yours,

Thomas Snowden.

(*TR Papers*, Series 1, Reel 84)

The President set sail from Oyster Bay on the Mayflower, the Presidential yacht, on July 21, 1908. Also on July 21, 1908, it was reported that William Taft would visit Sagamore Hill soon to go over with the President every part of his acceptance speech. Furthermore, "a direct telephone wire has been maintained between Sagamore Hill and Hot Springs for the last two weeks and consultations over this wire have been frequent..." between the President and Mr. Taft.

On July 22, the President spoke before the gathering at the Naval War College. This was the first time that the President had ever appeared before the college.

NEWPORT, R.I., July 22 — That President Roosevelt had two separate, two distinct, and two significant purposes in his extraordinary action in summoning the highest rank officers of the Navy to meet him at the Naval War College was made easily apparent to-day. One was to deliver through the college a message to the Nation, a message urging the necessity of adequate sea power as an effective guarantee of peace; the other was plainly to give countenance to the claims persistently advanced by so many of the navy that our present system of navy administration is inherently wrong...(*NY Times*, July 23, 1908)

The main points of Mr. Roosevelt's speech on naval policy were summarized by THE TIMES as follows:

No fight was ever won yet except by hitting, and the one unforgivable offense in any man is to hit soft.

When this Nation does have to go to war, such war will only be excusable if the Nation intends to hammer its opponent until that opponent quits fighting.

The Monroe Doctrine, unbacked by a navy, is an empty boast, and there exist but few more contemptible characters, individual or National, than the man or nation who boasts and when the boast is challenged fails to make good.

It is our undoubtful right to any what people, what persons, shall come to this country to live, to work, and to become citizens.

It is absolutely necessary that, if we claim for ourselves the right to choose who shall come here, we shall be in trim to uphold that right if any power challenges it.

The voyage of the sixteen battleships around South America, through the Strait of Magellan, from Hampton Roads to Puget Sound—that was the most instructive object lesson that had ever been afforded as to the reality of the Monroe Doctrine. *(NY Times, July 23, 1908)*

Upon returning to Oyster Bay the following day, the President announced that he would request the Attorney General to proceed with the prosecution of the Standard Oil case despite the decision handed down by the U.S. Circuit Court of Appeals, which reversed the fine imposed on the Standard Oil Company.

OYSTER BAY, N.Y., July 23 — President Roosevelt to-night announced in unmistakable terms the determination of the Administration to proceed with the prosecution of the Standard Oil case, despite the decision adverse to the Government handed down by the United States Circuit Court of Appeals yesterday.

This decision, the President thinks, in no way affects the merits of the case, and he makes known his decision to cause the action to be brought again before the courts in such shape, if possible, as to prevent technicalities interfering with a decision based upon the actual issues involved. The statement in the matter, made public to-night by Secretary Loeb, follows:

"The President has directed the Attorney General to immediately take steps for the retrial of the Standard Oil case. The reversal of the decision of the lower court does not in any shape or way touch the merits of the case, excepting so far as the size of the fine is concerned. There is absolutely no question of the guilt of the defendants or of the exceptionally grave character of the offense.

"The President would regard it as a gross miscarriage of justice if through any technicalities of any kind the defendant escaped the punishment which would have unquestionably been meted out to any weaker defendant who had been guilty of such offense. The President will do everything in his power to avert or prevent such miscarriage of justice. With this purpose in view, the President has directed the Attorney General to bring into consultation Mr. Frank B. Kellogg in the matter, and to do everything possible to bring the offenders to justice." *(NY Times, July 24, 1908)*

On July 23, 1908, the beginnings of a minor scandal were announced from the West Point Military Academy. On that day, eight cadets, two of whom were first classmen, were found guilty of hazing by a board of officers appointed by Col. Hugh L. Scott, Superintendent of the United States Military Academy, who also served on the board. The Military Board recommended to the Secretary of War that they be dismissed. The cadets would later, against direct orders, appeal their case to President Roosevelt. The President's vacillation on this issue caused much consternation among the officers in the army. *(NY Times,* July 24, 1908)

In Oyster Bay on July 23, the President met with the Republican nominee for President, William Taft and Secretary of State Root to discuss Mr. Taft's acceptance speech.

> William H. Taft, Republican nominee for President, arrived in this city (*New York City*) at 11 o'clock last night after an extended conference at Sagamore Hill with President Roosevelt and Secretary of State Elihu Root, in which the speech of acceptance which the former Secretary of War is to make at the notification ceremonies in Cincinnati to-morrow was discussed at length...
>
> ...The conference at Sagamore Hill occupied practically the entire afternoon. It was held in the President's library on the ground floor of his Summer home. Secretary Loeb was asked by the President to stay at Sagamore Hill while the conference was in progress...(*NY Times,* July 24, 1908)

On July 23, a comment made by the President in which he reiterated his anti-Standard Oil sentiments sent prices on the stock market down.

> The statement of President Roosevelt, commenting on the Appellate Court's reversal of the verdict in the Standard Oil rebate case, which was cabled to London before the opening of the New York Stock Exchange, and the apparent renewal of his attack on corporations sent heavy selling orders for execution into the London market...
>
> ...Before leaving town yesterday for an automobile tour of the Berkshires and White Mountains, Judge Peter Grosscup of the United States Court of Appeals made an emphatic reply to President Roosevelt's criticism of the reversal of the $29,240,000 Standard Oil fine by his court. Before leaving the Waldorf he dictated the following statement:
>
>> There is no more reason why I should take notice of the comment of Mr. Roosevelt than I would that of any private citizen, for the office that he fills and the office that the Judges of the Court of Appeals fill are entirely independent, though co-ordinate branches of Government.
>
> Judge Grosscup later said, in referring to the President's criticism:
>
>> Had any good all-around lawyer who had studied the case said that the opinion would have been different in the case of a weaker defendant, I might have been somewhat disturbed, but the comment of the President does not disturb me.

The President did not make any formal announcement regarding the Judge's comments.

OYSTER BAY, L.I., July 24 — President Roosevelt will make no comment on the statement of Judge Peter S. Grosscup of the Court of Appeals, made last night regarding the President's pronouncement on the decision of the United States Court of Appeals in reversing the fine of $29,240,000 imposed on the Standard Oil Company of Indiana.

Secretary Loeb made this announcement this morning.

On July 25, it was announced by Assistant Secretary of War Oliver in Washington, that the President had approved the recommendation that the eight cadets be discharged from West Point. The President's approval was given despite the cadet's personal appeal to Secretary of War Wright and other public men, an act of insubordination in and of itself. *(NY Times,* July 26, 1908)

Also on July 25, the situation in the New York Gubernatorial race changed dramatically when Governor Hughes announced that he would accept renomination as Governor of New York. With this announcement, President Roosevelt, directly and indirectly, became involved in the New York's Gubernatorial race.

OYSTER BAY, N.Y., July 25 — President Roosevelt was greatly interested to-day in the announcement from Gov. Hughes that he was willing to take a renomination for next Fall. The President got into communication with Timothy Woodruff, Chairman of the Republican State Committee, and Mr. Woodruff is expected here soon.

The President will make no statement or discuss the situation in any way until he has had a talk with Mr. Woodruff and other State leaders. The President is said to look with favor upon Gov. Hughes's candidacy, believing that it would add strength to the Taft ticket in New York State.

The President had a long conference to-day with George R. Sheldon, Treasurer of the Republican National Committee. Plans for levying political contributions were discussed, among them the Bryan plan of soliciting small contributions from farmers and wage earners. President Roosevelt is said to be in favor of this scheme. *(NY Times,* July 26, 1908)

On July 25 "President Roosevelt talked politics, finance, big game hunting, literature, and educational matters...to a number of callers who arrived at Sagamore Hill in response to his invitation...Altogether it was one of Mr. Roosevelt's busy days...Half a dozen callers were entertained at luncheon." Also, "the report that Mrs. Roosevelt had asked the Ben Greet players to give their initial performance of the Eastern tour at Oyster Bay was denied...by Secretary Loeb. He said that a request had been made by Mrs. Roosevelt to allow the performance at Sagamore Hill, but that the request had been refused." *(NY Times,* July 26, 1908)

On July 26, 1908, it was made public that "President Roosevelt accepted the honorary presidency of the Peace and Arbitration League, which is the outgrowth of the North Carolina Peace Congress, which has as its objective adequate armament and effective arbitration." *(NY Times,* July 27, 1908)

It was also announced on July 26, that Secretary Loeb would leave the following week for his Summer vacation.

> OYSTER BAY, L.I., July 26 — President Roosevelt's secretary, William Loeb, Jr., is furbishing up his rifles and other firearms and overhauling his fishing tackle preparatory to taking his Summer vacation and enjoying relaxation from the arduous duties of the important post which he occupies. He will leave next Friday for a month's recreation and sport in the woods...
> *(NY Times*, July 27, 1908)

On July 27, the President, through the Inter-State Commerce Commission, threatened to investigate the railroads of the country for violations of the anti-trust law if there was a general increase in freight rates. Although the statement was released in Washington, it was written in Oyster Bay.

> WASHINGTON, July 27 — President Roosevelt used the "big stick" to-day in an attempt to put an end to discussion of a general increase in freight rates by the railroads of the country. By his direction, the Inter-State Commerce Commission issued a statement that if a general increase was ordered by the railroads a thorough and searching investigation would be undertaken by the Government. The whole tenor of the statement is taken to mean that prosecutions under the anti-trust law will follow any concerted effort to raise tariffs...
> ...The President, it is believed, took this manner of replying to the shippers of Chicago and Cincinnati, who had memorialized him on the constantly reported intention of the railroads to advance rates. The manufacturers and merchants of the former city have organized what they term "a billion-dollar combination" to fight the advance, while the Cincinnati shippers also have come together to resist the increase...*(NY Times*, July 28, 1908)

It was also announced from Oyster Bay that Timothy Woodruff, Chairman of the New York State Republican Committee, asked for an appointment to see the President to discuss New York State politics in light of Gov. Hughes's announcement that he would accept renomination. *(NY Times*, July 27, 1908)

On July 28, Secretary Loeb announced that the President would not interfere in the Congressional and Gubernatorial races of the States. However, the President did not adhere strictly to this policy.

> OYSTER BAY, N.Y., July 28 — For the first time this Summer President Roosevelt's attitude with regard to the selection of candidates for Congressional and Gubernatorial offices was made known to-day.
> "The President will receive a number of political leaders during the Summer," said Secretary Loeb. "They will be both National and State men, but that does not mean that the President will interfere in any nomination. He will maintain an attitude of non-interference in the selection of all candidates, Congressional as well as Gubernatorial."
> Nevertheless, Timothy L. Woodruff, Chairman of the Republican State Committee, will visit President Roosevelt to-morrow and discuss with the

President the political situation in this State. Mr.Woodruff will arrive on the noon train and remain all afternoon. He will come alone, according to Secretary Loeb, but President Herbert Parsons of the Republican County Committee of New York is expected early next week.

The Times announced last Sunday that Mr. Woodruff was coming this week. Secretary Loeb emphatically denied on Monday that the State Chairman was coming at all. Last night, however, he admitted that Mr. Woodruff had asked the President if he might come down and discuss politics. To-day Mr. Loeb said that Mr. Woodruff would be here to-morrow at noon.

Despite the assertion of Mr. Loeb that Chairman Woodruff had requested an audience with the President, indications are plentiful that it was the other way about. The President, it was said to-day by one close to Mr. Loeb, considers Mr. Hughes the strongest man the Republicans could put up for Governor next Fall. More than that, it is asserted, Mr. Taft is of the same opinion. Consequently the President is not at all pleased with the attitude of Mr. Woodruff in tacitly opposing Gov. Hughes. The idea prevalent here is that the President has summoned the State Chairman to Sagamore Hill to give him a lecture on the A B C of politics.

Secretary Loeb told to-day of the President's deep interest in the election of Mr. Taft, and that he would consult with political leaders from both this State and other States during the Summer...*(NY Times*, July 29, 1908) (also reprinted in part in *Oyster Bay Guardian*, August 7, 1908)

Also on July 29, 1908, it was announced that Secretary of War Luke E. Wright would visit with President Roosevelt. The topic, it was speculated, would be the dismissal of eight cadets from West Point, which had been approved by the President earlier in the month.

OYSTER BAY, N.Y., July 28 — Secretary of War Luke E. Wright is expected at Sagamore Hill on Friday to spend the day with President Roosevelt. Secretary Loeb said to-day that Gen. Wright's engagement with the President was made some time ago, and that various state matters would be discussed.

Mr. Loeb denied that Gen. Wright had been summoned to Oyster Bay by the President for the purpose of conferring about the case of the eight West Point cadets who were dismissed from the Military Academy for hazing and whose dismissal the President strongly approved...*(NY Times*, July 29, 1908)

As promised, Timothy L. Woodruff, Chairman of the Republican State Committee, came to Oyster Bay on July 29, 1908. Rather than break his promise of non-interference, the President let Mr. Loeb do the talking at the conference.

OYSTER BAY, L.I., July 29 — President Roosevelt, on the visit here to-day of Timothy Woodruff of the Republican State Committee kept strictly within the bounds of his assertion that he would not meddle in local politics. Secretary Loeb did the meddling.

Mr. Woodruff came on the noon train, took luncheon with the President, sat all afternoon on the veranda of the President's home, at Sagamore Hill, absorbed in conversation with Secretary Loeb, and departed at 4 o'clock without disclosing the matters which they discussed beyond the general assertion that it was "politics." This much he cheerfully admitted, as Secretary Loeb did later. Mr. Woodruff, it is generally believed, came to Oyster Bay at the request of President Roosevelt, but he got his instructions, not from the President, but from Secretary Loeb. In other words, the President, it is asserted here, is using his accomplished Secretary to handle the political hot chestnuts.

When Mr. Woodruff arrived at noon he smilingly admitted that he had come to discuss politics with the President. He also said it was true that he and Benjamin B. Odell were on the Advisory Committee of the State Committee, as were nine others of his own selection, and that the names of the rest would be made public after the next meeting of the committee...

...The President met Mr. Woodruff on the veranda, shook his hand, and ushered him into the house, Mr. Loeb remaining in the background. After luncheon the President took Mr. Woodruff aside and talked to him earnestly for a few minutes. Then Mr. Woodruff and Mr. Loeb went out on the veranda, chose a shady corner, and began a confab that lasted until Mr. Woodruff had just time to catch the 4 o'clock train. Only once did the President interfere, and that was to bid Mr. Woodruff good-bye and to ask him to come again...

...It was stated here to-night on good authority that Secretary Loeb, speaking for the President, told Mr. Woodruff to go slow in the matter of the Hughes renomination, the situation requiring that the strongest possible Gubernatorial candidate should be selected, but that as Mr. Hughes was the strongest man now, nothing should be done to hurt his chances of getting the nomination.

While the State Chairman and Secretary Loeb were absorbed in political discussion on the veranda, President Roosevelt was not idle. In his library he held a long and animated conference with Francis B. Loomis, former United States Minister to Venezuela, and the present Minister to the Japan Exposition at Tokio, who came here to tell the President what he knew of the political situation in Ohio, his home State. He said later that he had brought very encouraging reports.

Secretary Loeb spent the entire afternoon at Sagamore Hill and did not return to the Executive office until long after Mr. Woodruff had gone. He would make no statement whatever about the afternoon's conference beyond saying that he had discussed politics with Mr. Woodruff.

It was said by one of the Executive force that Mr. Loeb would be the President's active agent in political affairs from now on, thus enabling the President to live up to his announcement that his attitude would be one of non-interference. Mr. Loeb is well posted on political matters, and he will be kept busy. (*The New York Times*, July 30, 1908)

On July 31, Gen. Luke E. Wright, the new Secretary of War visited Sagamore Hill to discuss with the President the matter of the dismissal of eight cadets from West Point. The Secretary of War felt that the dismissal was too severe a punishment while the President, who opposed hazing of any kind, continued to indorse the board's decision of dismissal. The Secretary of the Isthmian Canal Commission, Joseph Bishop, was also at Sagamore Hill and discussed with the President and the Secretary of War the conditions in the American Canal Zone. Gifford Pinchot also visited the President regarding the work of the National Forest Conservation Committee. In the afternoon, Secretary Loeb left for his Summer vacation. (*NY Times*, August 1, 1908)

On August 1, 1908 the President announced that he would reverse his decision regarding the dismissed cadets. This was in direct contradiction to a law passed by Congress and signed by President Roosevelt. Furthermore, it was the start of a controversy which would continue for several days.

According to army officers here, President Roosevelt brushed aside yesterday a mandatory law of the United States—an act passed by Congress and made into law by his own signature as President—when he reinstated as cadets of the United States Military Academy, at West Point, the eight young men who were found guilty of hazing in some of its worst forms ten days ago...

...The action of the President in sending the cadets back to West Point for reinstatement, followed a lengthy conference that he had at Oyster Bay with his new Secretary of War, Gen. Luke E. Wright, yesterday...

...The President has directed that these eight young men, several of whom pummeled their victims in the stomachs and jaws with their fists, shall be readmitted to the academy and punished according to the disciplinary methods of the academy. The disciplinary methods of the academy, so far as hazing is concerned, are fixed by Congress and the punishment that Congress fixed was duly approved by President Roosevelt.

The law provides not only for the dismissal of those who participated in the hazing, but even those who encouraged or countenanced it. Not a word about condonement for its offense is mentioned in the text of the law, and no officer of the Government from the President down is authorized to mitigate the punishment an iota...

"The only punishment under the law that the authorities of the United States Military Academy can impose upon these cadets," said one...officer, "is fixed by Congress, and that punishment is dismissal. Exactly how they can impose any lesser punishment is a little more than I can figure out..."

...That short statement explains the predicament in which the authorities at West Point find themselves, and there is reason to believe that when the eight cadets report for reinstatement, probably to-morrow, they will be allowed to resume their cadetships and suffer no punishment other than reduction to the ranks, while other cadets, guilty of infractions of minor regulations, will be walking tours of duty in the barracks triangle or suffering privations of recreation and privileges...

...When the President signed the order of the Military Board recommending the dismissal of the cadets, he did so before Secretary Wright had actually promulgated the order. Secretary Loeb said then that the President would put his foot down hard on hazing in the army and navy, and added that the matter was out of the President's hands, and the cadets could only be reinstated by an act of Congress.

The President, it is said, was reminded by the Secretary of War that he should at least have waited until the order was promulgated before signing it...The Secretary came here direct from Seagirt last night...

...Secretary Wright, it is said, talked plainly with the President about the cadets and informed him that, in his opinion, dismissal from the Academy was altogether too severe a punishment. He also pointed out that the President's action in signing the order was clearly illegal, and that the young men stood a good chance of being reinstated anyway. After considerable argument the President was brought around to Secretary Wright's way of thinking...

...At the Executive office in Oyster Bay Secretary Loeb said that the reason President Roosevelt had gone over Secretary Wright's head a few days ago and signed the order dismissing the cadets was because he wanted to frighten them, and that he had intended all along that they should be reinstated.

Those here who know the President, however, smile at the explanation and say it was merely another case of Mr. Roosevelt's impulsiveness and quote Secretary Loeb's remarks about his chief's abhorrence of hazing in all its forms and his declaration that it must be stamped out...*(NY Times*, August 2, 1908)

Also on August 1, 1908 Cuba's first election under America's supervision since the revolution of 1906 was held without significant disturbances. This was a clear victory for the President as well as for the Republican nominee, William Taft.

OYSTER BAY, N.Y., Aug. 1 — President Roosevelt, in reply to a cablegram, received to-night from Gov. Magoon, in which the latter told of the orderly election held in Cuba to-day, sent this message:

Oyster Bay, N.Y., Aug. 1.

Magoon, Havana:

I congratulate the people of Cuba on the orderly election that has been held and the vindication just shown of their capacity for self-government. I have no doubt that the next election will be as orderly and as fair, and I feel the greatest satisfaction at the serious and responsible way the Cuban people are preparing for the assumption of their full duties as an independent republic.

THEODORE ROOSEVELT

On August 2, 1908, a member of the Executive Staff in Washington joined the Staff in Oyster Bay.

OYSTER BAY, Aug. 2 — ...As the President was entering the church he espied, among those standing about, Warren S. Young, chief clerk of the Executive offices in Washington, who had just reached Oyster Bay to assist in the executive work here during the vacations of Secretary Loeb and other members of the staff. The President greeted Mr. Young warmly and invited him to sit with his family during the services...*(NY Times*, August 3, 1908)

On August 3, 1908, the President made a remarkable statement, that is, he said that he had taken no action regarding the dismissal of the cadets at West Point. This was in direct contradiction to the statements made by Secretary Loeb and Secretary of War Wright.

OYSTER BAY, L.I., Aug. 3 — President Roosevelt reversed himself again to-day in the matter of the dismissal of the eight West Point cadets. In a statement which is considered remarkable here, the President takes issue with both Secretary Loeb and Gen. Luke E. Wright, the Secretary of War, in saying he has taken no action in the case whatever, but is waiting on Secretary Wright to come to some decision. The statement was given out this afternoon by Assistant Secretary Forster, Secretary Loeb being away on his vacation. It is as follows:

> No action whatever has been taken by the President in the case of the cadets, the statements that they were originally ordered dismissed and that they had been ordered kept, being equally erroneous. An appeal was originally made to the President to interfere. He declined to take any action or to interfere in any way until the Secretary of War had expressed his opinion, the view of the department then being, seemingly, that the cadets should be turned out, but the Secretary not having come to any final decision.
>
> The Secretary then notified the President that instead of making any report he would like to discuss the matter with the President in person. He accordingly came on and the discussion was held, but no final decision was reached, the Secretary stating that he was not able to make a final and definite recommendation as to all the cases, and preferred to make none as regards any until he could do it as regards all.
>
> The President has not yet heard finally from the Secretary, and therefore, of course, has come to no final decision. This is the first announcement that the President has made in the matter at all, and he has never at any time come to any decision one way or the other, excepting to state that he would probably follow the views of the department.

The President's statement is in direct contradiction to the statements of both Secretary Loeb and Gen. Wright...

...The President's statement to-day came in the nature of a thunderbolt to the members of the executive force. The President's action in agreeing to the reinstatement of the cadets had been freely discussed, and those who knew his manner declared that he had simply acted impulsively, and that Secretary Wright, having shown him that he had gone the wrong way about it, did the best thing he could in making the announcement that the matter had been fixed up, and that the cadets were to be reinstated...

...The widespread criticism of the President's attitude, however, stirred him...Unfortunately Secretary Loeb had started on his vacation, and the President could not learn if what the Secretary was quoted as saying was true.

He hurriedly summoned Assistant Secretary Forster, however, and asked him what had taken place between Loeb and the correspondents. Mr. Forster was not present at the interview and could not enlighten the President. It was then that the President decided to deny that he had taken any action in the matter whatever. *(NY Times, August 4, 1908)*

On August 4, the President issued another statement regarding the dismissal of the cadets. However, this would not be the end of the scandal by any means because no face-saving compromise had yet to be agreed upon.

OYSTER BAY, L.I., Aug. 4 — President Roosevelt supplemented his remarkable statement of yesterday in regard to the dismissal from West Point of the eight cadets, wherein he flatly contradicted both the Secretary of War and Secretary Loeb, with another to-day, which makes the whole matter appear more involved than ever.

The President's intention in issuing the statement was apparently to mitigate the severity of his manifesto of yesterday and let Gen. Wright down a little easier...Here is the President's latest explanation, issued through Assistant Secretary Forster:

> Acting Secretary Forster again said that the President had not yet received the final decision of the War Department in the West Point hazing cases; that originally the department inclined to remove the cadets. When Secretary Wright was here he seemed inclined to think that they ought not to be removed, but he has evidently not yet come to any conclusion in the matter, and has notified the President that he wants the President to see Col. Scott, with whom he (Secretary Wright) has just been in consultation. The President, of course, will come to no final decision until he hears from Gen. Wright.

Col. Scott is expected here to-morrow, and his conference with the President may clear the situation, as it is well known that he is not in favor of leniency, but insists that the recommendation of the Military Board be carried out...It is predicted that Mr. Roosevelt will arrange a compromise and agree to allow several of the cadets to return...

...It is understood that the President has already been in communication with Secretary Loeb, and has asked for a full explanation of his part in the occurrence...*(NY Times*, August 5, 1908)

It was also reported on August 5 that "the Suffragettes will journey out to Oyster Bay to-night, where they will hold an open air meeting for the benefit of the President and such Taft men as may happen to be on hand for a round of advice...a meeting will be held in front of the Executive Offices at 7 o'clock." *(NY Times*, August 5, 1908) The meeting of the Suffragettes was not quite as successful as they had hoped.

> OYSTER BAY, N.Y., Aug. 5 — Four damp and dismal Suffragettes, headed by Mrs. Borrmann Wells of London, rode out to Sagamore Hill through a pelting rain this evening to try to convince the President that women should be allowed to vote. They returned to the village wetter still and more discouraged, for they had been stopped at the entrance to Mr. Roosevelt's grounds and were not allowed to peer inside...
>
> ...The three members of the National Progressive Woman's Suffrage Union who descended on the Summer capital with Mrs. Wells were Dr. Maud Glascow of New York, Mrs. Margaret E. Hunt, who is a real voter out in Colorado, and Miss Mary Coleman, who practices law in New York...
>
> "We are here to wake up the Summer capital of the United States," announced Mrs. Wells.
>
> It was suggested that they call up the executive office and arrange for an interview with the President.

"That has been attended to," said Mrs. Wells. "We communicated with the President several days ago and were informed that he was too busy to be seen. We are going out to Sagamore Hill, however, just the same and try and interest Mr. Roosevelt in our cause..."

The Secret Service men had been told that hundreds of women were coming. Six men were lined up in front of Moore's grocery store, under command of Assistant Chief Joe Murphy. Chief Sloan and Lawrence Richey were stationed at the entrance to Sagamore Hill, while another went to the station...When only four women alighted from the afternoon train a sigh of relief went up from the executive office...

...When the party returned from its fruitless trip to Sagamore Hill the women had dinner in the Octagon, and then Mrs. Wells and her co-workers sauntered down to Moore's grocery store, over which is located the executive offices, and where to-night's meeting was advertised to be held.

They waited in the rain for an hour, but not a woman showed up...*(NY Times,* August 6, 1908)

On August 7, 1908, Chairman Frank H. Hitchcock of the Republican National Committee visited President Roosevelt at Sagamore Hill. The conference was expected to determine whether or not Gov. Hughes of New York would be renominated to run for that post. *(NY Times,* August 7, 1908) The conclusions reached from this conference were reported the following day.

In their conference at Oyster Bay yesterday over the Gubernatorial situation in their State, the President and the National Chairman Frank H. Hitchcock are believed to have reached these conclusions:

That the situation in this State is extremely delicate; that while Gov. Hughes is exceedingly popular and has a large independent following, he has also antagonized a considerable number of voters who must be taken into consideration; finally, that a thorough canvass of the State with a view to ascertaining definitely the exact strength or weakness of the Governor is absolutely essential...*(NY Times,* August 8, 1908)

The President also met with Secretary of War Luke E. Wright and Col. Hugh L. Scott, Superintendent of the Military Academy at West Point on August 7, 1908. The conference was on the subject of the dismissal of the eight cadets from West Point but no statements were made regarding the conference or regarding the decisions made regarding the affair. "Assistant Secretary Forster, at the Executive Office, said he could throw no light on the conference at the present, but he thought that the President might later on make a statement." *(NY Times,* August 8, 1908)

The President also released a formal statement on August 7, 1908 which exonerated Mr. Taft from any censure for the dismissal of black soldiers at Brownsville.

OYSTER BAY, Aug. 7 — In a formal statement issued here to-night, President Roosevelt shoulders the entire responsibility for the dismissal of the negro troops after the Brownsville affair, thereby clearing the skirts of Candidate Taft of any possible censure which might be directed against him by the negro voters.

The statement was due to the publication in the afternoon newspapers of Gen. Corbin's declaration that Judge Taft was not responsible for the Brownsville order.

Assistant Secretary Forster, who is acting in the place of Secretary Loeb, made a night visit to Sagamore Hill after the departure of Gen. Wright, Col.Scott, and Chairman Hitchcock. Upon his return to the Executive Offices, Mr. Forster made this public:

"Gen. Corbin's statement is absolutely correct and it was entirely proper that he should make it. The substance of the message from the President, which he quotes, was made public long ago. In the Brownsville matter the entire responsibility for issuing the original order and for the planning to allow its suspension was the President's." *(NY Times*, August 8, 1908)

Many Blacks began to support Mr. Taft as a result of this statement Thus, the statement achieved the President's desired result.

Negroes of the city were discussing yesterday with much interest the exoneration of Mr. Taft by President Roosevelt from responsibility for the dismissal of the colored soldiers at Brownsville. At the time of their discharge without honor feeling among their race ran high, and it was openly declared that when the Republicans had again to appeal to the people they would find the negro vote had been alienated. The President's statement that Mr. Taft had interceded for the soldiers seems, however, to have put a different face on the matter. *(NY Times*, August 9, 1908)

In an effort to investigate and improve the social, sanitary, and economic conditions of farm life, the President announced on August 9, that he would appoint a special commission to look into such conditions throughout the country, and especially in the South.

OYSTER BAY, N.Y., Aug. 9 — With a view to bringing about better social, sanitary, and economic conditions on American farms, President Roosevelt has requested four experts on country life to make an investigation into the whole matter and to report to him with recommendations for improvements. The report and recommendations, with any additional recommendations which the President himself may desire to make, will be incorporated in a message which the President will send to Congress, probably early next year...*(NY Times*, August 10, 1908)

One of the most revealing looks inside the activities of the President's staff was given on August 12, 1908. Clearly, the staff was indispensable to the President.

OYSTER BAY, L.I., Aug. 12 — Despite the assertions that President Roosevelt would not meddle in politics this Summer, the President and his Executive staff of ten have been working day and night for the last two weeks as if their lives depended upon it. Instead of the daily trip to Sagamore Hill which Secretary Loeb has made for several Summers, Assistant Secretary Forster now makes two trips daily — sometimes three. The Executive force, in fact, has been so rushed with work that several of the staff have applied for sick leave and others say that they are on the verge of a breakdown. The daily routine has been changed entirely. Formerly the staff appeared for work at the Executive Office over Moore's grocery store at 8 A.M.; now they are on hand on some mornings as early as 7 o'clock.

Secretary Forster, carrying a huge bundle of official business, drives up to Sagamore Hill every morning an hour earlier than Secretary Loeb ever did. He returns with another enormous portfolio of business in the afternoon. That is scarcely out of the way before the hard-working assistant journeys to the Hill again, this time to remain until midnight or 1 o'clock the next morning.

On these night trips he always brings back as much official matter as he does in the day time, and an almost exhausted force of clerks has to wade in and get it all cleared up, ready for the following day's batch, before they can go home. Sometimes the gray dawn is breaking before the lights in the executive office are extinguished.

All this unwonted activity has stirred the greatest curiosity in the village, but the meaning of it all has been kept as secret as possible. It came out to-day, however, that it isn't the ordinary routine business that is swamping the President in his study until long after midnight, even on Sunday nights.

The President, it is said on good authority, is taking a leading, if silent, part in the direction of the Republican political machine, both State and National. An enormous amount of political matter comes to him daily, mostly in the shape of letters and telegrams. These bear directly on the political fortunes of Secretary Taft, and the President has thrown himself into the campaign work with his accustomed energy. Many of the letters and messages he answers in person with ample suggestions concerning the subject in hand.

It is said that Mr. Roosevelt has the whole National situation at his fingers' ends, and not a move is made without first consulting him and telling him all about it. And this is not all. It is reported that most of the matter sent out by the overworked clerks is in the form of political speeches or skeletons of speeches, for the use of the spellbinders in the campaign. Wherever a situation demands aggressive action the President sends to the Taft press bureau information or suggestions designed to smooth the way of the local leaders.

Chairman Hitchcock of the Republican National Committee keeps in daily touch with the President, and the local telegraph office, where two operators are on hand, has been requisitioned to help out the official operator at the Executive office.

Besides the heavy rush of political work, the President and his executive force have to keep pace with the ordinary Government business. To facilitate this, it is said, the two kinds of work have been separated, the latter being attended to in the mornings and the political business in the afternoons and at night.

On top of all this the President attends to his personal business, arranging the details of his coming trip to Africa, consulting with magazine writers about his stories, and a hundred and one things in which he is personally interested. Those close to him say it is astonishing how much work he accomplishes from day to day without the effort having any perceptible effect upon him...

...Secretary Loeb, who is fishing on the Minnesota lakes, departed just in time to escape the present inundation of work. *(NY Times*, August 12, 1908)

On August 12, 1908, President Roosevelt met with State Senator John Raines. The conference dealt with Gov. Hughes's renomination as Governor of New York. *(NY Times,* August 13, 1908)

On August 12 it was learned in Washington, that President Roosevelt was responsible for the delay in deciding the fate of the cadets dismissed from West Point. At the conference which took place on August 7, 1908 between the President, Secretary of War Wright and Col. Scott, Superintendent of the Military Academy, the President instructed Col. Scott "to investigate further the conditions surrounding the discharge of the young men by the Board of Inquiry...The result of Col. Scott's additional efforts are to be submitted to Secretary Wright, who will determine the extent and the form of punishment...It is altogether probable...that the order of the War Department will be submitted to Oyster Bay for approval..."(*NY Times,* August 13, 1908)

On August 13, the President met with certain State leaders, who were opposed to the renomination of Gov. Hughes, regarding their opinions on the renomination.

> OYSTER BAY, L.I., Aug. 13 — Important matters concerning the State political situation were discussed at length this afternoon by President Roosevelt, Congressman Herbert Parsons, Chairman of the Republican County Committee; William Barnes, and Francis Hendricks, all of whom, with ex-Gov. Odell and several others, were named Wednesday as an Advisory Committee to assist Chairman Woodruff in the campaign. It is generally believed here to-night that the question of whether or not Gov. Hughes is acceptable to the State machine was still unchanged at the end of the conference.
>
> A great deal of secrecy was thrown about the visit of the three politicians. It was given out at the Executive Office by Assistant Secretary Forster that they would come on the noon train. Instead they came from New York City by automobile...
>
> ...The party did not take the regular road through the village, but went by a circuitous route along lonely country roads until Sagamore Hill was reached...(*NY Times,* August 14, 1908)

The President also received on August 13, a telegram from Admiral Sperry, the Commander of the "Great White Fleet," which had just arrived at Auckland, New Zealand. The President sent a telegram in reply expressing his thanks to the Prime Minister of New Zealand and his congratulations to the fleet.
(NY Times, August 14, 1908)

On August 14, 1908, Congressman Andrew J. Barchfeld of Pittsburgh visited President Roosevelt to discuss conditions in Central America, having just returned from the region. *(NY Times,* August 15, 1908)

Also on August 14, an insane man, Moses S. Okun, was found by Secret Service men wandering about Sagamore Hill and was taken away under arrest. The President knew nothing about it until the next morning. The President was not at home at the time. *(NY Times,* August 15, 1908)

On August 17, another conference took place at Sagamore Hill regarding the renomination of Gov. Hughes of New York, this time with Congressman J. Sloat Fassett. The Congressman tried to convince the President that the Governor's renomination would be detrimental to the Republican Party.

> OYSTER BAY, L.I., Aug. 17 — President Roosevelt had a long conference this afternoon with J. Sloat Fassett, the Republican leader of Chemung, and, as has been the case at the many other conferences which the President has recently had with other State leaders, the State political situation was gone over thoroughly.
>
> Extraordinary efforts are being brought to bear to convince the President that the re-nomination of Gov. Hughes would be a blow to the Republican party. According to Representative Fassett, this pressure is not alone coming from the race track element and politicians but from the heads of railroad companies, labor organizations, business men and the public generally, who disapprove of Mr. Hughes for various reasons...
>
> ...The President will take no action regarding Mr. Hughes's renomination until he is more certain of the Governor's strength. He has given the word to the leaders who have journeyed here to see him that they must hustle around and find out something about the number of friends the Governor has...*(NY Times,* August 18, 1908)

On August 17, the President also met with the leader of the Nationalist Party in the Philippine Assembly. In this meeting he announced that he was in favor of Philippine independence, within twenty years.

> OYSTER BAY, L.I., Aug. 17 — President Roosevelt to-day told Senor Manuel Quezan, leader of the Nationalist Party in the Philippine Assembly, that he is in favor of granting independence to the Filipinos within the next twenty years. By that time, Mr. Roosevelt thought, the Filipinos would have advanced far enough to be able to work out their own destiny.
>
> Senor Quezan came to this country three months ago to ask the President to do something to stop the American invasion of the conquered lands, and he returns with the assurance that his countrymen will be protected as much as possible from the inroads of American business and political activity.
>
> It developed from Senor Quezan's visit to Oyster Bay to-day that the President has a direct wire running to Secretary Taft's headquarters at Hot Springs. The President had the special wire installed a few days ago, and there is scarcely a political move of any importance made by the Republican Presidential nominee that the President does not first know all about it. Senor Quezan's interview with the President to-day was arranged over this private wire by Mr. Taft, and it is of political significance as forecasting the attitude of the Taft administration toward the Philippines...*(NY Times,* August 18, 1908)

On August 18, 1908, Assistant Secretary Forster declared that President Roosevelt would not make campaign speeches for Mr. Taft.

OYSTER BAY, Aug. 18 — Assistant Secretary Forster put out a strong denial to-day of the statement that President Roosevelt was to take to the stump during the campaign for Taft.

"There is absolutely nothing to it," said Mr. Forster. "The President is not going to take the stump. The whole story is absurd."

Mr. Forster also denied the story that George Shiras of Washington, and formerly a lawyer of Pittsburgh, was going to accompany the President on his African hunting trip. *(NY Times*, August 19, 1908)

Also on August 18, the President urged Professor Bailey of Cornell University to reconsider his decision to decline the Chairmanship of the Rural Committee that the President had formed on August 9 to investigate the social, sanitary, and economic conditions of farm life.

OYSTER BAY, L.I., Aug. 18 — That President Roosevelt is much concerned over the action of Prof. Bailey of Cornell in declining to serve as Chairman of the Rural Committee which was formed by the President to uplift the farmers, was indicated to-day, when it is said he again urged the Professor to reconsider his withdrawal and to act as Chairman until after election, if he could not do so permanently.

The refusal of Prof. Bailey to accept the Chairmanship, according to indications here, was a severe setback for the President. When the professor sent his letter of refusal, it was said at the Executive office that it would be made public on the day following, but when Acting Secretary Forster was asked to give it out he refused, saying that the matter had not been finally adjusted. Since that time, it is said, the President has been in constant communication with Prof. Bailey, and has repeatedly urged him to reconsider his letter.

The belief here is that the appointment of the commission in the first place was simply a political move on the part of the President and a bid for the farmer vote for Secretary Taft...*(NY Times*, August 19, 1908)

On August 20, during a conference of National leaders at Sagamore Hill, it was finally agreed upon that Gov. Hughes would have the President's support for his renomination as Governor of New York State.

Gov. Hughes is to be renominated if President Roosevelt and the National leaders who met the President at Oyster Bay yesterday have their way. The voices of all were unanimous for the Governor. The President at the conference at Sagamore Hill issued an ultimatum to the effect that, as the Governor could undoubtedly poll the largest vote in the State, his name must head the State ticket...

...Those who took part in the conference besides the President were National Chairman Frank H. Hitchcock, Assistant Secretary of State Robert Bacon, George J. Smith, Treasurer of the State Committee, who was the only official representative of the State Republican machine present; James S. Sherman, candidate for Vice President; Representative W.S. Bennet of Manhattan, and Representative W.W. Cocks of Westbury, L.I.

No official announcement of the decision of the President was made either at Oyster Bay or in this city... (*New York City*)

...There will be no official announcement of the attitude of the National leaders on the Hughes question. The State organization is to be allowed to say that it has concluded that the people want Hughes, and that the organization always obeys the will of the people...

...The conference was brief, considering the importance of the subject under discussion. President Roosevelt listened to the reports of his visitors and then the dictum went forth that it was to be Hughes. Chairman Hitchcock went to Oyster Bay with his mind already made up on the subject, and he told the newspaper correspondents at Oyster Bay that he would have a statement to give out concerning Mr. Hughes after he returned from the conference at Sagamore Hill...he even went so far as to say that he would first go from the President's house to the Executive offices at Oyster Bay to give the statement out himself...After Mr. Hitchcock talked with the President, however, he changed his mind and telephoned down to the waiting newspaper men at the Executive office that there would be nothing to give out...(*NY Times*, August 21, 1908)

On August 21, 1908, the President received a telegram from the Governor General and Government of the Commonwealth of Australia upon the arrival of the Atlantic Fleet at Sydney, New South Wales. The President responded in kind.
(*NY Times*, August 22, 1908)

On August 22, 1908, an announcement was made from Washington which finally put to rest the scandal involving the dismissal of the eight cadets from the West Point Military Academy.

WASHINGTON, Aug. 22 — Announcement was made to-day by Secretary of War Wright that his recommendation for the punishment of the eight West Point Cadets suspended from the Military Academy for hazing had been approved by President Roosevelt.

Secretary Wright's announcement was made in the form of a formal statement...

...The order by Secretary Wright, based upon the President's approval, dismisses from the Academy the two first classmen under suspension...and the suspension without pay and allowances for one year of the six members of the third class...(*NY Times*, August 23, 1908)

On August 23, the President made public a report to him by the special commission appointed to investigate conditions in the Canal Zone.

OYSTER BAY, Aug. 23 — President Roosevelt to-day made public a report made to him on Aug. 6 by a special commission consisting of James B. Reynolds, Samuel B. Donelly, and Henry Beach Needham regarding conditions in Panama. The commission was appointed on April 25 last "to investigate conditions, especially as regards labor and accommodations, on the Isthmus of Panama."

That the President is pleased with the report is shown in a letter which he sent to each member of the commission on Friday. He expresses particular pleasure over the fact that the commission upholds the administration of Col. George W. Goethals, Chairman of the Isthmian Canal Commission. The President will submit the report to Congress with appropriate recommendations.

To a great extent the report is devoted to a statistical outline of the work that has been accomplished, the work that remains to be done, the physical possibilities with the equipment now in use, the number of men at present employed, and the railroad facilities for removing rock and dirt...*(NY Times,* August 24, 1908)

On August 25, 1908, it was announced from Washington that the President would return from Oyster Bay earlier than usual. It was assumed that the early return would facilitate his direction of the Taft campaign. Furthermore, it was speculated that Oyster Bay was "too isolated for campaign purposes and...Sagamore Hill is so situated as to make visits from politicians wishing to consult with him too conspicuous..." *(NY Times,* August 26, 1908)

On August 29, the President met with Baron Kogoro Takahira, the Japanese Ambassador to the United States. They had a long conference at Sagamore Hill and although they did not release the topic of the conference they did declare that it was neither the impending visit of the "Great White Fleet" to Japan nor a possible alliance between America and China. The President would explain the visit later in the same week. *(NY Times,* August 30, 1908)

On August 29, an unidentified visitor to the President revealed that the President was deeply disturbed by the fact that several Republican leaders in New York State, including Timothy Woodruff, were openly defying his order that Gov. Hughes be renominated. The visitor also announced that "although the President had announced that he wouldn't interfere with State politics, nevertheless he wasn't going to let young politicians who had selfish ends in view defeat the will of the people at the convention, even if he, the President, had to use stern measures." *(NY Times,* August 30, 1908)

On August 31, 1908, the President personally congratulated each member of the United States Olympic Team presented to him at Sagamore Hill after they had returned from the Olympic Games held in London.

On September 1, 1908, the President met with the recalcitrant State leaders who opposed the renomination of Gov. Hughes. The President declared that "It must be Hughes."

OYSTER BAY, L.I., Sept. 1 — President Roosevelt had it out with several of the Republican State leaders to-day, when he summoned them here and told them flatly that Gov. Hughes would have to be renominated. The leaders protested and tried to argue the President out of his position, but Mr. Roosevelt was firm, and when the conference was over the leaders crept away, crestfallen, as secretly as they came.

The name of only one of the leaders who came here to-day is known. He was William L. Ward of Westchester, a member of both the Republican National and State Committees. Two others are said to have been State Chairman Timothy L. Woodruff and President of the County Committee Herbert Parsons...

...No one at the Executive office would throw any light on the identity of the guests with Mr. Ward. When asked about it Mr. Forster replied that he did not know who they were...*(NY Times*, September 2, 1908)

On September 1, 1908 the reason for Baron Takahira's visit to Sagamore Hill earlier in the week was made public when a letter to Secretary of State Root from the President was released by Assistant Secretary Forster. According to the letter, the Ambassador's visit had to do with postponing the Tokio Exposition, the first international exposition held in Asia, from 1912, the year originally set, to the year 1917, so as to coincide with the fiftieth anniversary of the ascension of the Japanese Emperor. However, it was speculated that matters of greater importance were also discussed. *(NY Times*, September 2, 1908)

On September 2, 1908 for the first time in two years, the President attended a masonic lodge meeting at the Matinecock Lodge in Oyster Bay.

> OYSTER BAY, N.Y., Sept. 2 — President Roosevelt attended a Masonic lodge meeting in the village to-night for the first time in two years. The President, who is a third degree Mason, is a member of Matinecock Lodge, No. 806, which held the first meeting of the Fall tonight...
>
> ...Secretary Loeb, who has been on a month's vacation in the region of the Great Lakes, got back to Oyster Bay to-day.
>
> "I had the time of my life," said Mr. Loeb, "and I think I have some fish and hunting stories that will make even the President sit up and take notice..."*(NY Times*, September 3, 1908)

On September 6, a letter from the President was read at a celebration marking the new constitution of the Turkish Empire.

> Turks, Armenians, Syrians, Albanians, and even some former Greek subjects of the Sultan crowded into Carnegie Hall last night to help celebrate the granting of a constitution to the Turkish Empire. Mundji Bey, the Turkish Chargé d'Affaires at Washington...presided. Republican County Chairman Parsons spoke in English, and there were speeches in Armenian, Turkish, Arabic, Greek, and French...
>
> ...The occasion was especially indorsed from Washington via Oyster Bay, when James B. Reynolds read a letter from President Roosevelt...
>
> ...The letter follows:
>
> Oyster Bay, Sept. 4
>
> My Dear Mr. Reynolds: Through you may I present my regards to Munji Bey, the present Chargé of Turkey in this country, and express my great pleasure on the occasion which gives rise to the meeting next Sunday evening at Carnegie Hall?

All men all over the world who believe in liberty and order, who believe in a liberal Government, under which justice shall be done to every man without regard to his creed or race, must feel the keenest interest in and sympathy with the movement so full of hope for genuine progress which is now taking place in the Turkish Empire.

With heartiest good wishes for the success of your meeting, believe me, sincerely yours, THEODORE ROOSEVELT

(NY Times, September 7, 1908)

Also on September 6, 1908, George Smith, Treasurer of the Republican State Committee visited Oyster Bay. He met with Secretary Loeb until the President returned from church.

OYSTER BAY, L.I., Sept. 6 — For the first time this Summer a Sunday political visitor came here to discuss politics with the President. He was George J. Smith, Treasurer of the Republican State Committee. He reached here this morning...while the President was at church, but had a long conference with Secretary Loeb at the Executive office. Later Mr. Smith took Mr. Loeb for a sail on his yacht, and it is supposed that the two went to Sagamore Hill by way of the Emlen Roosevelt dock...*(NY Times,* September 7, 1908)

On September 8, 1908, it was reported that an armed crank shot at President Roosevelt earlier in the same week.

OYSTER BAY, Sept. 7 — For three days all the available Secret Service agents of the Government at Washington, headed by Chief John Wilkie himself, have been on a secret hunt for a man, who, they are satisfied, fired a shot from a revolver at President Roosevelt on Saturday last from ambush, while the President was out for a canter on his horse, accompanied by a person whose identity the detectives, for some unexplained reason, refuse to give.

The shot whizzed over the President's head, its "zip" being distinctly heard by him. Night and day since the occurrence the Secret Service men have hunted for the shooter.

To-day a crank, insane and armed with a revolver, fully loaded, walked into the grounds of the President's home on Sagamore Hill and demanded of the first Secret Service agent who held him up to see the President to lay before him an imaginary grievance. He was disarmed after a struggle, and is now in jail in Mineola.

The Government agents are convinced that the prisoner, who gave the name of John Coughlin and also said he was "St. Patrick," is the man who shot at the President last Saturday. They have not, however, questioned him on this point owing to his obviously demented condition...*(NY Times,* September 8, 1908)

The following day, it was denied by Secretary Loeb that anyone intentionally meant to shoot the President.

OYSTER BAY, Sept. 8 — Official denial was made to-day by Secretary Loeb of the rumors that the pistol shot fired near President Roosevelt last Saturday while the President was horseback riding, had been fired at the President from ambush. Others who were near the President when the incident occurred came forward with the statement that a shot had undoubtedly been fired, but whether at the President or not there was no means of knowing.

The companion with whom the President was riding when the shot was fired near him was Major W.A. Wadsworth...an intimate friend of the President...

...Secretary Loeb pooh-poohed any idea that any person would shoot at the President.

"That idea sounds ridiculous to me," said Mr. Loeb. "Why, people are shooting along the road there all the time for the game season is on. Besides, some one is shooting at targets along there all the time. You might just as well say that some one over on Centre Island, where I live, shot at me because they were out hunting."

Mr. Loeb is in error about the game season on Long Island being open, for it does not open until Nov. 1. When this was pointed out to him he said:

"Well, there is target practice going on there all the time."

The Secretary denied that Chief Wilkie of the Secret Service force had come on here from Washington to investigate the shooting or the arrest of the man Coughlin.

"Mr. Wilkie came here to confer with Secretary Cortelyou of the Treasury at Washington," said Mr. Loeb, "and not in relation to this matter."

Whatever Chief Wilkie's errand to Oyster Bay was, he made a trip to the Seawanhaka Yacht Club on Centre Island and had a long conference with Mr. Loeb before he left. *(NY Times*, September 9, 1908)

FIGURE 33: Seawanhaka Corinthian Yacht Club, Center Island, N.Y. Secretary Loeb occasionally used it as a temporary residence on Long Island.
Courtesy of Sagamore Hill

On September 8, it was reported that Secretary Loeb, on behalf of the President, denied that the President had interfered in any way in the recent Wisconsin primary election.

CHIPPEWA FALLS, Wis., Sept. 8 — Judge John J. Jenkins, Congressman from the Eleventh Wisconsin District, to-day received a letter from William Loeb, Jr., secretary to the President, in which Secretary Loeb says that statements made in a circular purporting to have been issued by Judge Smith of Superior on the eve of the Wisconsin primary election are false.

It is alleged by Judge Jenkins's friends that the circular in question brought about the defeat of Jenkins by Irvine L. Lenroot for the Republican Congressional nomination.

The letter is dated at Oyster Bay, Sept. 4, and reads as follows:

My Dear Judge Jenkins: I am in receipt of your letter of the 24 with inclosure. The statements which the circular says were made by the President, through his secretary, are absolutely false. Judge Smith called at the Executive Office and asked to see the President. He was told by Acting Secretary Forster that the President would not see him or any one else on a matter of a local political nature, and would not discuss it in any way.

Judge Smith then wrote a note to the President asking him to state whether or not the claim of Representative Jenkins that the President had written him a letter urging his renomination was true. Judge Smith was again told that the President refused to say anything whatever about the matter or discuss it in any way.

Mr. Forster told Judge Smith that a great many appeals to interfere with political protests were sent to the President, but that the President has invariably refused to take any part in any of them. Mr. Forster never made the statement that the President had been "persistently importuned by Mr. Jenkins and his friends to indorse Mr. Jenkins's candidacy."

There was no denial of any claims. There was simply refusal to say anything about the contest in any way.

I inclose a copy of a telegram which was sent in answer to a telegram concerning this matter. Yours very respectfully,

WILLIAM LOEB, Jr.,
Secretary to the President

The following is the telegram sent to some person in Superior, whose name is withheld:

Oyster Bay, N.Y., Aug. 27, 1908

The President has not interfered, and will not interfere, in any such matter. The President wrote Mr. Jenkins, as he has written various other Senators and Congressmen who have been assailed because of voting for the Currency bill and the bill for establishing mail lines, saying he is glad to say to any one that all the Congressmen who supported these measures judged those decrees as upholding the Administration and its policies.

The letter is signed by Rudolph Forster, acting secretary.

(*NY Times,* September 9, 1908)

On September 10, 1908, the President and Attorney General Bonaparte announced from Sagamore Hill that the Department of Justice would appeal to the U.S. Supreme Court the U.S. Circuit Court's decision that the commodities clause of the Hepburn Railroad Act is unconstitutional.

> OYSTER BAY, Sept. 10 — While Attorney General Bonaparte was in confer-
> ence with President Roosevelt at Sagamore Hill this afternoon the report of the
> decision given out to-day in Philadelphia by the United States Circuit Court of
> the Eastern District of Pennsylvania declaring that the commodities clause of
> the Hepburn Railroad Act is unconstitutional was conveyed to the President's
> home. The news was carried to the President and the Attorney General, and
> they immediately took up the matter. After the discussion they came to the
> conclusion that the Department of Justice should take an appeal from the deci-
> sion. *(NY Times,* September 11, 1908)

Also on September 10, the President met with Herbert Parsons and they discussed the potential candidates for the New York State Republican campaign ticket.

> OYSTER BAY, N.Y., Sept. 10 — Herbert Parsons, President of the New York
> Republican County Committee, came here to-day and had a long conference
> with President Roosevelt. Although Mr. Parsons would not go into details as to
> what it was all about, it is said here that his visit had to do almost solely with the
> making up of the State political slate, now that he has come boldly out in sup-
> port of Gov. Hughes, the President's choice. *(NY Times,* September 11, 1908)

On September 13, Assistant Secretary Forster again denied that the President would make campaign speeches on behalf of any of the candidates.

> OYSTER BAY, L.I., Sept. 13 — An official denial that the President is to take
> the stump in Mr. Taft's behalf was issued to-day.
> "For the twentieth time," said Mr. Forster, "the President wants to deny the
> statement that he is going to take an active part in the campaign this Fall. Mr.
> Roosevelt is extremely busy attending to the duties of his office, and he sees
> no occasion for taking the stump."
> Preparations for the departure of the President and his family for Washington
> on the 22nd are moving briskly forward. The President worked late to-night
> with his assistant secretary, Mr. Forster, and completed the draft of his next
> message to Congress...*(NY Times,* September 14, 1908)

As the New York State Republican Convention got under way on September 14, 1908, both the President and Secretary Loeb were actively lobbying for Governor Hughes's renomination.

> OYSTER BAY, N.Y., Sept. 14 — This has been the busiest day that Secretary
> Loeb has put in this Summer. Almost all day he sat at his desk in the Executive
> office, over Moore's grocery store, with a telephone receiver in his hand.
> Every few minutes he talked with the President over the special wire which
> runs to Sagamore Hill, and then called up Saratoga, and talked with either

Secretary Root, William L. Ward, National Committeeman, or Representative W.W. Cocks, who has been delegated to represent the President personally at the convention.

The President is said to be firmly convinced that Gov. Hughes's renomination is necessary for the success of the National Republican ticket.

Word came early this morning that the leaders of the opposition to Mr. Hughes were not satisfied with the President's avowal of his desire to have Mr. Hughes renominated, and that they would like to have him go more thoroughly on the record. The President, through Mr. Loeb, got into communication with Secretary Root at once, and said that, if necessary, he would issue a statement.

Secretary Root is said to have replied that such a statement would clear up matters considerably, and about 10 o'clock this morning Secretary Loeb gave out the following:

> The President has been in communication with Secretary Root and Congressman Cocks in reference to the Governorship situation, and has authorized them to state that, while he has no intention of dictating, yet to all his friends who have spoken to him on the matter he has said in the strongest possible terms that he favored the renomination of Gov. Hughes.

Many times during the morning either Mr. Root, Mr. Ward, or Mr. Cocks called up Secretary Loeb to ask for advice. In no instance did any of them talk with the President, as Mr. Roosevelt arranged it so that his secretary should do all his talking for him.

Mr. Loeb said in much more emphatic language than was contained in the statement given to the newspapers that the President would not stand for any dilly-dallying, but wanted the recalcitrants whipped in line.

It was not until noon that any really satisfactory news from the convention reached Mr. Loeb and then the President, apparently satisfied with the way things were going, called his boys about him and went for a row across Cold Spring Harbor to Lloyd's Neck. He returned early in the afternoon and once more directed his attention to Saratoga.

It is believed that Secretary Root and Committeeman Ward reported to Mr. Loeb that Timothy Woodruff, more than any one else, was to blame for the activity of the Hughes opposition. Several times Mr. Loeb tried to get Mr. Woodruff on the telephone for a personal talk, but he did not succeed.

Mr. Roosevelt received at 10 o'clock a very important message bearing on the situation. Although he had been in communication with Secretary Loeb all the evening at the Seawanhaka Yacht Club, the message had the effect of requiring Mr. Loeb's immediate presence at Sagamore Hill, whither he journeyed in his launch. Assistant Secretary Forster was already with the President. (*NY Times*, September 15, 1908)

On September 15, the following day, the news that Gov. Hughes had been renominated was received heartily at Sagamore Hill. It was the crowning victory for the President's long summer effort.

OYSTER BAY, L.I., Sept. 15 — President Roosevelt did not learn that Gov. Hughes had been renominated until late this evening. All morning he had remained at the telephone, receiving bulletins from Secretary Loeb, but when, shortly after noon, it looked as though Gov. Hughes could not be defeated, he...went for a picnic to Lloyd's Neck...

...Shortly after 4 o'clock the news of the nomination came to Secretary Loeb, and as the President had not returned, he jumped into an automobile and rode to Huntington to take dinner...While he was at dinner Mr. Loeb called up the President, who had returned in the meantime, and told him what happened.

"Bully," said the President. "Never for a moment did I have any idea that we would lose."

"It was a great victory for the President," said Mr. Loeb to-night. "In my opinion Mr. Hughes would never have been nominated if the President had not jumped in and taken hold of things.

"Late last night some of the opposition leaders called me up and asked me whom the President wanted for second place on the ticket. I told them that the President was not interested in who was to be Lieutenant Governor; that that matter could be adjusted among themselves, and that all the President wanted was to see Mr. Hughes renominated. I don't mind saying that Gov. Hughes won out by a mighty close margin, and the victory is due entirely to President Roosevelt..." *(NY Times*, September 16, 1908)

On September 16, 1908 it was announced that the President had invited everyone in Oyster Bay to come to Sagamore Hill so that he could greet them all before he returns to Washington.

OYSTER BAY, Sept. 16 — To-morrow will be Oyster Bay day at Sagamore Hill. The President and Mrs. Roosevelt have extended invitations to almost every person living within the town limits to come to Sagamore Hill and be greeted by the President and his wife before the former leaves here next Tuesday, not to return until after his African hunting trip, when he will be plain Mr. Roosevelt. Several years ago the President gave a similar reception, and more than 2,000 people thronged the grounds. To-morrow even more are expected, for Mr. Loeb has taken pains to see that practically every resident of the village received an invitation...

...A middle-aged woman with a three year-old baby walked out to Sagamore Hill this afternoon and made an effort to see the President. She was stopped by Chief Agent Sloan, who brought her back to the village in an automobile. To Secretary Loeb she gave her name as Mrs. Francis Caldwell and her residence as Canada. She said her husband was a physician, but she couldn't be induced to tell why she wished to see the President. Mr. Loeb warned her not to talk to reporters. *(NY Times*, September 17, 1908)

The following day, the President bid the populace of Oyster Bay good-bye.

OYSTER BAY, N.Y., Sept. 17 — President Roosevelt, at what he termed his farewell reception, shook hands with about 500 residents of this village at Sagamore Hill this afternoon. The President threw open his grounds to the neighbors, and mingling among them, met them all on a common footing...

...There was only one incident to mar the occasion. The Secret Service men roughly handled Charles Kursman, a leading business man of the town and a member of the President's lodge. The President was not aware of the disturbance at the time, although the matter was brought to his attention later...

...Kursman resented the attempt to force him out of line, and appealed to Chief Sloan of the Secret Service force. Agent Adams and several others crowded about the man. For a moment it looked as if there would be a struggle. Finally Secretary Loeb, who was standing near the President, was appealed to, and he sternly told the Secret Service men to allow Mr. Kursman to get into line...*(NY Times*, September 18, 1908)

On September 18, 1908 the President responded to an alleged letter sent by Congressman Joseph C. Sibley to John D. Archbold, Vice President of the Standard Oil Company. The Congressman denied ever sending such a letter.

OYSTER BAY, Sept. 18 — After being closeted with President Roosevelt for some time to-night at Sagamore Hill, Secretary Loeb gave out this statement regarding the alleged Sibley letter to John D. Archbold:

"When Secretary Loeb's attention was called to the alleged letter of ex-Congressman Sibley he stated that Mr. Sibley was one of several hundreds of people in the political and financial world who at different times appealed to the President not to prosecute the Standard Oil Company. To all of these people the President listened with politeness and consideration, but found himself unable to agree with any of them, however, and prosecutions were accordingly ordered continued, and are in progress at the present time." *(NY Times*, September 19, 1908)

On September 21, 1908, the President made public a letter written by Mr. Taft in which the latter declined a proposition offered to him. Mr. Taft was asked if he would object to the State Central Committee of Ohio passing a resolution indorsing Mr. Taft for President and Mr. Foraker for Senator in the interest of harmony. If Mr. Taft consented to this arrangement, all opposition to his nomination for President would be dropped on the part of Mr. Foraker and his influential friends in the Senate and elsewhere. By publishing this letter and by making the accompanying statement, the President gave the strongest endorsement he could to Mr. Taft and to Mr. Taft's integrity. The statement was, of course, released from Oyster Bay. *(NY Times*, September 22, 1908)

On September 22, 1908, the President left Oyster Bay for Washington. This was the end of Mr. Roosevelt's last Summer in Oyster Bay as President.

President Roosevelt ended his vacation at Oyster Bay yesterday morning, and, amid the cheers and good wishes of most of the inhabitants of the village, started for Washington...

...The train, with the President and his family, with Secretary Loeb and his family, and all the members of the Executive force, and several Secret Service men on board, reached Long Island City at 11:20 o'clock...*(NY Times*, September 23, 1908)

Index